The Challenge of Facework

SUNY Series in Human Communication Processes
Donald P. Cushman and Ted J. Smith, III. editors

The
Challenge
of
Facework

Cross-Cultural and Interpersonal Issues

edited by

Stella Ting-Toomey

STATE UNIVERSITY OF NEW YORK PRESS

Published by
State University of New York Press, Albany

© 1994 State University of New York

For information, address the State University of New York Press,
State University Plaza, Albany, NY 12246

Production by Bernadine Dawes
Marketing by Terry Abad Swierzowski

Library of Congress Cataloging-in-Publication Data

Ting-Toomey, Stella.
    The challenge of facework : cross-cultural and interpersonal
issues / Stella Ting-Toomey.
        p.   cm. — (SUNY series in human communication)
    Includes index.
    ISBN 0–7914–1633–X (alk. paper) : — ISBN 0–7914–1634–8
(pbk. : alk. paper)
    1. Facial expression.   2. Nonverbal communication (Psychology)
3. Facial expression—Cross-cultural studies.   4. Nonverbal
communication (Psychology)—Cross-cultural studies.   I. Title.
II. Series: SUNY series in human communication processes.
BF592.F33T56   1994
153.6′9—dc20   92–40892
                                                                              CIP

1 2 3 4 5 6 7 8 9 10

Contents

Preface

The goal of this book is to provide a forum for theorists and researchers to engage in an open dialogue concerning face and facework interaction. More specifically, the book serves a dual purpose: (1) to raise issues and to extend some of the current ideas in face and facework research in the cross-cultural and interpersonal settings, and (2) to illuminate some directions for future research in face and facework management process. The cultural and gender parameters of face and facework, the relational and situational features of the facework interaction process, and the discourse dynamics of the actual facework negotiation process are some of the questions being examined in this book.

Taken together, the conceptual and methodological questions that authors raise in their chapters hold tremendous research promises for individuals working in the areas of intercultural communication, interpersonal communication, language and social interaction, gender and communication, and communication theory. I believe this book contains many exciting and original ideas concerning face and facework. It has a well-spring of ideas for generating theoretical insights in face and facework negotiation process. As an area of inquiry, face and facework is a productive arena to raise questions about the theory construction process that cuts across cultural and interpersonal communication lines.

Many individuals contributed to the fruition of this book. First, I would like to extend my special appreciation to all the authors who donated their time and energy to this volume. Without their hard work and creative ideas, the book would not exist. Second, I would like to thank Donald Cushman who encouraged my undertaking of this book. His support and encouragement of the book, from inception to completion, is immeasurable. Third, I want to say a special "thank you" to Bill Gudykunst for his sustained support throughout each phase of the editing process, and for his generosity of response when

I needed a "reality" check. Fourth, I want to thank Beth Cocroft and Hiroshi Ota for their careful attention and help in serving as editorial assistants. Fifth, I want to thank the Faculty Development Office, California State University, Fullerton, for awarding me an affirmative action grant to complete this book project. I also want to thank my colleagues in the Department of Speech Communication for providing a supportive environment in which to conduct my scholarly work. In addition, I want to acknowledge the expert editorial support and help from Lois Patton and her staff, and also Bernadine Dawes at the State University of New York Press in making this book a reality.

Most importantly, I am deeply indebted to my two family members—Charles and Adrian—for their unending love and patience in waiting one more time for "one more book" to be completed. I thank them for their patience and unconditional love.

Finally, I want to dedicate this book to my parents. To my mother who teaches me about "face" or *mien-tzu*, and to my father, who teaches me to transcend and move beyond "face."

Stella Ting-Toomey
Fullerton, California

-1-
Face and Facework: An Introduction

STELLA TING-TOOMEY

Face entails the presentation of a civilized front to another individual within the webs of interconnected relationships in a particular culture. It is a metaphor that captivates the interests of scholars in diverse disciplines. Face is a claimed sense of self-respect in an interactive situation. It has been viewed, alternatively, as a symbolic resource, as social status, as a projected identity issue, and as a fundamental communication phenomenon. Facework involves the enactment of face strategies, verbal and nonverbal moves, self-presentation acts, and impression management interaction.

Face and facework have been researched in the areas of compliance-gaining and request/persuasive strategies (Applegate, 1982; Baxter, 1984; Craig, Tracy, & Spisak, 1986; Hale, 1986; Leichty & Applegate, 1991; Lim, 1990; O'Keefe & Shepherd, 1987, 1989; Tracy, Craig, Smith, & Spisak, 1984). They have been used as explanatory mechanisms in the study of politeness discourse (Brown & Levinson, 1978, 1987; Holmes, 1988, 1989; Holtgraves, 1992; Holtgraves & Yang, 1992; Katriel, 1986, 1991; Matsumoto, 1988; Scollon & Scollon, 1981, 1983; Shimanoff, 1985, 1987, 1988) and self-presentation behavior (Cupach & Metts, 1990; Edelmann, 1987, 1990; Goffman, 1955, 1956, 1959, 1967; Imahori & Cupach, 1991; Metts & Cupach, 1989; Schlenker, 1985).

Finally, face and facework have also been studied in connection with cross-cultural conflict styles (Ting-Toomey, 1988; Ting-Toomey, Gao, Trubisky, Yang, Kim, Lin, & Nishida, 1991; Trubisky, Ting-Toomey, & Lin, 1991), courtroom dramas (Penman, 1987, 1990, 1991), diplomatic negotiation (Brown, 1977; Cohen, 1991; Pharr, 1990; Ting-Toomey & Cole, 1990), management practice (Fairhurst, Green, & Snavely, 1984; Hiemstra, 1982; Hwang, 1987; Redding & Ng, 1983), and communication competence (Kim, 1993; Lim & Bowers, 1991). Indeed, the study of face and facework remains an enigmatic and enduring area of inquiry in relationship to a host of other research concepts.

The purpose of this book is twofold: (1) to review and extend some of the current ideas in face and facework research in the areas of cross-cultural and interpersonal communication, and (2) to illuminate specific theoretical and methodological challenges that surround the study of face and facework. While a systematic body of work has been accumulated in the area of face and facework, the inquiry of face and facework is still in its infancy. Many researchers have used the concept of "face" or "facework" in their studies loosely. In many of these studies, the conceptualizations, the linkages, and the operationalizations of face or facework in conjunction with other face-related concepts remain vague and fuzzy. How face is being conceptualized and evoked is not specified in some studies, and the corresponding relationships between face and facework process often are not articulated. Further, the cultural, relational, contextual, or communication parameters of face and face behavior have not been clearly identified.

The primary intent of this book is to begin wrestling with some of the issues raised here. Authors of the various chapters have proposed new ideas, propositions, or perspectives to account for the relationship between culture and face, and between interpersonal relationships and facework. They have also mapped out many fruitful directions and constructive ideas for future research into face and facework dynamics.

This essay serves as an introduction to some of these ideas. The chapter has a dual purpose: (1) to identify some of the underlying themes that run throughout the chapters of the book, and (2) to summarize the major ideas that are presented in each chapter.

Common Themes

Five common themes emerge from the chapters that follow: (1) face entails both cultural-universal and cultural-specific dimensions, (2) face is an identity-boundary phenomenon, (3) face carries both affective and social cognitive implications, (4) face and facework are located in the situated discourse process of interaction, and (5) face and facework operate across everyday situational contexts.

First, face has both cultural-universal and cultural-specific aspects. It appears that most authors in the book conceptualize face as a universal social phenomenon. Face involves the claimed sense of self-respect or self-dignity in an interactive situation. Facework involves the verbal and nonverbal negotiation aspects of face maintenance, face claim, and face expectation. Facework strategies can be used to diffuse, manage, enhance, or downgrade self and/or other's face. While the concept of face assumes universality concerning the claimed sense of self-respect or self-worthiness level, how one conceptualizes face and how one manages a facework episode is influenced by cultural variability (chapters 3, 4, 5, 8, and 9), gender variability (chapters 6 and 8), relational variability (chapters 7 and 10), and contextual variability (chapters 2 and 10).

Second, face is an identity-boundary issue. All authors touch upon the issues of face and identity implicitly or explicitly. While Penman (chapter 2) views face as self-identity through which communicators order their social world, Morisaki and Gudykunst (chapter 3) interpret the construal of self and face as two separate constructs. For them, it is the cultural variability in self-construals that affects our conceptualization of face, and hence, facework. For Chang and Holt (chapter 4) and Ho (chapter 9), face is a flexible, dynamic self/society metaphor in which personal, relational, and group boundaries are negotiated and redefined. While Chang and Holt emphasize the cultural-specific elements of face in Chinese culture, Ho emphasizes the basic sociometric dimensions and expectations of face claims and face congruence in reaching a balance point of a civilized, social life.

Scollon and Scollon (chapter 5), drawing from a sociocultural perspective, discuss the boundary conditions of self between Asian and Western cultures, and Shimanoff (chapter 6) reflects upon the role of identity expectation between females and males. For Scollon and Scollon, face is viewed as a sociocultural, normative identity question. For Shimanoff, face is viewed as a discourse functional question and a sociological identity question. On the facework strategy selection level, Edelmann (chapter 8) focuses on the strategy appropriateness dimension of identity-loss and identity-recovery in embarrassing situations, and Lim (chapter 6) focuses on the strategy effectiveness dimension of interpersonal identity-threatening situations.

Third, face involves both affective and social cognitive components. Face-related concepts such as pride, shame, embarrassment, blushing, respect, deference, justice, and honor involve both affective reactions and social cognitive judgments. These face-related affective reactions and social cognitive attributions have been discussed by various authors (e.g., by Penman, Morisaki and Gudykunst, Chang and Holt, Edelmann, Ho, Tracy and Baratz) in different chapters of the book. Facework, in essence, is viewed as an artful process of diffusing and managing self-focused emotions and other-focused emotions. Concurrently, facework involves attributions, calculations, and co-orientations. Facework moves, in essence, entail a high degree of affective creativity, cognitive creativity, and communication competence creativity.

Fourth, facework is located in the situated discourse. Penman (chapter 2) views the use of facework discourse as a process of re-creating the meanings of one's own and other's social lives. Tracy and Baratz (chapter 10) view face concerns and facework moves as located in the discourse setting and conjointly defined by the participants *in situ*. Scollon and Scollon (chapter 5) compare and contrast discourse logic between Asian and Western cultures. Shimanoff (chapter 6) reviews facework literature in connection with politeness discourse. According to Shimanoff, however, the concept of facework includes politeness, but politeness does not necessarily include all types of facework. Almost all authors in the book subscribe to a contextualized communication orientation in the study of face and facework. Terms like face-saving, face-threatening, face-compensating, face-losing, face-giving, and face-honoring are viewed as grounded in the verbal interchange process.

Some authors place a heavier emphasis on the normative values, roles, positional identities, statuses, and/or networks that surround the facework interaction process. Other authors focus their discussion on the relationship between discourse and context, and the transformational power of facework discourse itself. In summing up the different points of view, it appears that most authors believe that individuals have different degrees of choice in evoking, enacting, upholding, and/or violating self/other face concern issues via the discourse process.

The degree of choice, however, is affected by relational, socio-cultural, and competence variations.

Finally, face and facework are two ubiquitous concepts that are tied closely to everyday social and personal interactions. Face and facework permeate intercultural encounters, small group encounters, social network encounters, and interpersonal encounters. Face is, indeed, a network field concept with implications that extend beyond immediate dyadic or group boundaries, and across long-term spatio-temporal dimensions. The concepts of face and facework appear to be elastic in meanings and resilient in endurance. Lastly, authors in this volume present specific recommendations or challenges for researchers who are interested in grappling with the fundamental issues of studying face and facework across cultural, gender, interpersonal, and discourse lines.

The Chapters

This section summarizes the key ideas in each chapter. The first four chapters provide a broad context for the book. Chapters 2, 3, 4, and 5 address universal, moral, cross-cultural, cultural-specific, and communication issues in the study of face and facework. The next set of chapters, chapters 6, 7, 8, 9, and 10 focus more on specific theoretical and/or methodological ideas of face and facework research. More specifically, chapters 6 and 7 establish a backdrop to the study of interpersonal facework from a gender perspective and a relational intention perspective. Chapter 8 examines the effects of gender and culture on the use of interpersonal face-saving strategies in embarrassing situations. Chapters 9 and 10 take us through two different methodological journeys in the "doing" of facework research. Finally, the last chapter, chapter 11, is a distillation of ideas and reflections concerning the directions and challenges of theorizing about and doing facework research in cross-cultural and interpersonal contexts.

In chapter 2, Robyn Penman argues that facework is an enduring primary mechanism for regulating social life. Facework is posed as a central theme in which human beings come to develop a concept of self-identity, and through which they learn to morally order their social world. For Penman, the concept of face is a fundamental social condition of being human. While face, or self-identities are those "psychological ascriptions that we take on and negotiate in our interaction with others," facework refers to communication action in which social knowledge is generated conjointly between the interactants. She argues persuasively that both the enactment of facework and the study of facework itself carry a strong moral, evaluation dimension. Drawing evidence from her previous research concerning facework strategies in courtroom discourse, Penman proposes a hierarchical model that tracks the relationship between face game and moral orders. She juxtaposes the paradox of courtroom interaction as the interplay between the fact game and the face game, and concurrently, the interplay of two moral orders—those of justice and honor. Penman ends the chapter with the reflection that the moral dimension of facework can be used perhaps to evaluate our communication theories and research in practice.

In chapter 3, Seiichi Morisaki and William B. Gudykunst compare and contrast the conceptualization of face in Japan and the United States. The term for face in Japan, *kao*, refers to (1) the physical part of the body, (2) one's personal name or status, and (3) social face. Social face, in turn, can be subdivided to refer to the appearance one presents to others (*taimen*), or interdependent mutual face (*mentsu*). Drawing from the individualism-collectivism dimension (Triandis, 1990) and the independent and the interdependent construal of the self literature (Markus & Kitayama, 1989), they explicate the complexities of the relationship among cultural variability, self-construals, and face conceptualization.

They argue that while independent and interdependent construal of the self exist in both cultures, independent construal of the self tends to predominate in the United States and interdependent construal of the self tends to predominate in Japan. Extending this line of argument, they weave a comprehensive picture of the self-construal concept and face (*mentsu*) in Japan and the United States. Issues such as personal self-esteem and group self-esteem, emotions such as pride and shame, and identity dimensions such as desirable-undesirable and voluntary-involuntary are integrated with a detailed discussion of the cultural meaning of face. They conclude by identifying the difficulties and the challenges that face all cross-cultural researchers in the search for the conceptual equivalence of the meanings of face and facework.

Hui-Ching Chang and G. Richard Holt (chapter 4) present a Chinese perspective on face as a fundamental, interpersonal relationship issue. From the Chinese perspective, face is a dynamic, complex construct that is laden with both psychological and sociological meanings. Chang and Holt define face or *mien-tzu* as a quality claimed by the individual and accredited by society at large. Drawing from their ethnographic interview data, they examine the basic vocabularies, meanings, and functions of face and facework. They provide a lucid analysis of Chinese *mien-tzu* in the contexts of inter-relation (*kuan-hsi*) and human emotion (*ren-ching*). Based on the philosophical foundations of Confucianism, *mien-tzu* is viewed as both a burden and a lubricant of interpersonal relationship development. Chang and Holt build a fascinating case for the importance of studying face or *mien-tzu* from a cultural-specific perspective. They view face as a flexible symbolic resource that threads through the private versus the public domains, the ingroup versus the outgroup circles, and the personal versus the interpersonal goal orientations in Chinese culture. Chang and Holt end their chapter with the casting of face as a universal human communication phenomenon.

Drawing from the discourse literature, Ron Scollon and Suzie Wong Scollon (chapter 5) attempt to delineate the face parameters in Eastern and Western cultures. Based on their close examination of Asian and Western discourse patterns, they believe that marked discourse difference exists between the East and the West. They identify three default face parameters that closely affect East-West discourse pattern, namely: relationship, hierarchy, and ratification of face relationship. They argue that the differential assumptions between Asian and Western cultures concerning the relative emphasis on information and relationship, the hierarchical nature of interpersonal roles, and the contrast between negotiation and ratification of such roles pave the way to East-West discourse miscommunication. They conclude with a thoughtful discussion concerning the various boundary conditions of "self" in Asian and Western cultures and how these distinctive conceptualizations of "self" affect the moral basis of communication in Eastern and Western discourse.

Susan Shimanoff (chapter 6) examines facework through a detailed discussion of female and male differences in politeness discourse. She defines facework as "behaviors which establish, enhance, threaten, or diminish the images/identities of communicators." She reviews the previous research which has made explicit reference to politeness or facework and gender,

and compares and contrasts different approaches to the study
of facework and gender. With a conscientious, fine-tuned analysis of results of over 100 research studies, she finds that research on gender and politeness has not provided consistent
results concerning the relationship between gender and politeness. More importantly, most studies do not draw upon any
theoretical underpinnings for explaining the possible female
and male expectational differences on politeness. Based on a
face-needs theoretical model, Shimanoff reviews some of her
own work on emotional expressiveness and responsiveness.
She concludes that while females in her research tend to report
that they disclose more face-threatening emotions than males,
in actual conversations, females and males in these studies
communicate about emotions equally. Furthermore, both females and males have the same rank order for the relative face-
value of different types of emotional disclosures, even when
females actually self-reported that they engaged in more diverse emotional disclosures than males. By applying both functional (i.e., issues of approval, autonomy, and competence face)
and sociological (i.e., issues such as sex-role expectations,
status difference, and social distance) approaches as extensions to the face-needs' model, Shimanoff cogently persuades
us that the face-needs model may provide us with the key to un-
ravel the complexities of facework differences and similarities
across the gender divide.

Moving beyond the gender level of facework discussion,
Tae-Seop Lim (chapter 7) focuses on the interpersonal aspects
of facework strategy selection. Lim defines face as the positive
image that a person claims for him/herself. He observes that
face is a public, not a private phenomenon. Face also is concerned with one's projected image which may or may not be
concurrent with others' assessments of one's face identity. In
addition, face is cast in terms of claimed positive, rather than
negative, social values. Drawing from his previous research
(Lim and Bowers, 1991), Lim identifies the three basic types of
face: autonomy, fellowship, and competence. Facework is defined as the actions taken to deal with the face wants of one
and/or the other. While autonomy face is addressed by *tact* facework, fellowship face is supported by *solidarity* strategy type,
and competence face is addressed by *approbation* strategy
type. Using the dimensions of face-giving, face-withdrawing,
face-moderation, and face-disregarding, specific verbal tactics
that reflect tact, solidarity, and approbation facework types are

explained. Ten theoretical propositions are formulated based on a discussion of the essential determinants of the concept of face-threat legitimacy (status difference, relational intimacy, and role right). He concludes the chapter by appealing to the importance of studying the role of intention in the effective management of interpersonal facework relationships.

Moving beyond the social cognitive realm of facework strategies, Robert J. Edelmann (chapter 8) discusses embarrassment and face-saving strategies in social interaction. Embarrassment is viewed as a state in which a person has failed to maintain an appropriate identity and has, in short, lost face. Face-saving, in this context, refers to all those "social actions both verbal and nonverbal taken by both the actor and observer to overcome feelings of embarrassment in an attempt to regain social composure and the smooth flow of interaction." Embarrassment can be elicited by external cues (e.g., a faux pas, impropriety, and social transgression) or internal cues (e.g., bodily, facial cues and associated cognitions). In a detailed review of the classification schemes of embarrassing events, Edelmann is able to distill four major categories to classify embarrassing events: (1) individual behavior, actor or actress responsible, (2) interactive behavior, shared responsibility, (3) audience provocation, observer responsible, and (4) audience behavior, observer responsible. In carefully sifting through the face-saving strategy literature, five main categories of face-saving are identified: apologies (including remediation), accounts (including excuses and justifications), avoidance (including escape), humor (including laughter) and aggression. The relationship between embarrassing event type and mediating factors (such as gender, status, culture, and propensity to blush) on face-saving strategy used is examined. In closing his chapter, Edelmann directs our attention to several fruitful areas of research that can enrich our understanding of embarrassing events, facework strategies, and interactant/observer reactions.

From conceptualization to operationalization, David Yau-Fai Ho (chapter 9) attempts to bridge the conceptualization of facework to address the measurement issues of face dynamics. In fact, he sees the word "facework" as such a static term that he (personal communication) proposes henceforth we should use the concept "face dynamics" to replace "facework". Drawing from his cross-cultural psychology background, he calls forth a radical repositioning of the study of face and facework from a

methodological relationalism perspective. In his relational conception of face dynamics, face is a field concept and a sociometric concept. Face, as a field concept, includes the following
domains: (1) actions by the individuals, either self-initiated or
in response to those of others, (2) actions by others closely
associated with the individual, (3) actions directed at the individual by people whom the individual is interacting with,
(4) actions directed at the individual by people closely associated with those with whom the individual is interacting, and
(5) actions directed at people closely associated with the individual by those with whom the individual is interacting
directly or indirectly. Face, in these embedded relational contexts, is viewed as a dynamic field wherein relational forces
and counterforces shape and unfold the "multiple faces" of
the actors in the social arena. Ho conceptualizes face as a universal phenomenon. He argues that any individual who does
not wish to renounce the social nature of her/his existence
must show a fundamental regard for face. However, the criteria by which a person's face is judged are rooted in specific
cultural values, and hence, are culture-relative. On the operationalization level, Ho recommends ten classes of attributes to
be collected in the study of face dynamics. While his recommendations are not measurement-specific (i.e., specific interview or survey items), they spark some stimulating directions
for future research in the inquiry of face and facework within
and across cultural lines.

In Chapter 10, Karen Tracy and Sheryl Baratz argue for the
advantages of studying face and facework using a case study
approach. After a careful review of Brown and Levinson's
(1978, 1987) politeness theory, they critique the theory on
grounds that the theory "forces researchers a priori to impose
face concerns on interactants" and the model "decontextualizes individual utterances and facework strategies, and promotes the assumption that the relationship between discourse
strategies and face concerns is universally fixed and unproblematic." In using a case study as an exemplar to their approach to the study of facework, they illustrate how through
the systematic analysis of interview transcripts, they are able
to locate specific face concerns of the participants in the setting. In addition, according to Tracy and Baratz, the case study
approach resists the temptation to oversimplify the complexity
of facework with predetermined theoretical lens. Finally, they
convincingly argue that through in-depth open-ended inter-

views and participant observation methods, they are able to unpack the identity attribution process and the situational factors that impinge upon the facework setting. They conclude that the extension of the scope of the basic facework case study and the reconsideration of a broader facework process pose as two challenging directions for future communication scholars.

The book concludes with chapter 11, in which Ting-Toomey and Cocroft invite researchers who are interested in face and facework research to engage in an open dialogue across boundaries. In addition, by drawing upon the ideas from various chapters in the book, several conceptual and methodological directions and challenges for future theorizing and researching in face and facework are mapped out and proffered.

References

Applegate, J. (1982). The impact of construct system development on communication and impression formation in persuasive contexts. *Communication Monographs, 49,* 277–289.

Baxter, L. (1984). An investigation of compliance-gaining as politeness. *Human Communication Research, 10,* 427–457.

Brown, B. (1977). Face-saving and face-restoration in negotiation. In D. Druckman (Ed.), *Negotiations: Social-psychological perspectives.* Beverly Hills, CA: Sage.

Brown, P., and Levinson, S. (1978). Universals in language usage: Politeness phenomenon. In E. Goody (Ed.), *Questions and politeness: Strategies in social interaction.* Cambridge: Cambridge University Press.

———. (1987). *Politeness: Some universals in language usage.* Cambridge: Cambridge University Press.

Cohen, R. (1991). *Negotiating across cultures: Communication obstacles in international diplomacy.* Washington, D.C.: United States Institute of Peace Press.

Craig, R., Tracy, K., and Spisak, F. (1986). The discourse of requests: Assessment of a politeness approach. *Human Communication Research, 12,* 437–468.

Cupach, W., and Metts, S. (1990). Remedial processes in embarrassing predicaments. In J. Anderson (Ed.), *Communication yearbook 13.* Newbury Park, CA: Sage.

Edelmann, R. (1987). *The psychology of embarrassment.* Chichester, UK: John Wiley and Sons.

———. (1990). Coping with embarrassment and blushing. In J.Anderson (Ed.), *Communication yearbook 13.* Newbury Park, CA: Sage.

Fairhurst, G., Green, S., and Snavely, B. (1984). Face support in controlling poor performance. *Human Communication Research, 11,* 272–295.

Goffman, E. (1955). On face-work: An analysis of ritual elements in social interaction. *Psychiatry: Journal for the Study of International Processes, 18,* 213–231.

———. (1956). Embarrassment and social organization. *American Journal of Sociology, 62,* 264–271.

———. (1959). *The presentation of self in everyday life.* New York: Doubleday.

———. (1967). *Interaction ritual: Essays on face-to-face interaction.* Garden City, NY: Doubleday

Hale, C. (1986). Impact of cognitive complexity on message structure in a face-threatening context. *Journal of Language and Social Psychology, 5,* 135–143.

Heimstra, G. (1982). Teleconferencing, concern for face, and organizational culture. In M. Burgoon (Ed.), *Communication yearbook 6.* Beverly Hills, CA: Sage.

Holtgraves, T. (1992). The linguistic realization of face management: Implications for language production and comprehension, person perception, and cross-cultural communication. *Social Psychology quarterly, 55,* 141–159.

Holtgraves, T., and Yang, J.-N. (1992). Interpersonal underpinnings of request strategies: General principles and differences due to culture and gender. *Journal of Personality and Social Psychology, 62,* 246–256.

Holmes, J. (1988). Paying compliments: A sex-preferential politeness strategy. *Journal of Pragmatics, 12,* 445–465.

———. (1989). Sex differences and apologies: One aspect of communicative competence. *Applied Linguistics, 10,* 194–213.

Hwang, K. (1987). Face and favor: The Chinese power game. *American Journal of Sociology, 92,* 944–974.

Imahori, T., and Cupach, W. (1991). A cross-cultural comparison of the interpretation and management of face: American and Japanese responses to embarrassing predicaments. Paper presented at the Conference on Communication in Japan and the United States, California State University, Fullerton, CA.

Katriel, T. (1986). *Talking straight: Dugri speech in Israeli Sabra culture.* Cambridge: Cambridge University Press.

———. (1991). *Communal webs: Communication and culture in contemporary Israel.* Albany, NY: State University of New York Press.

Kim, M. S. (1993). Culture-based interactive constraints in explaining intercultural strategic competence. In R. Wiseman and J. Koester (Eds.), *Intercultural communication competence*. Newbury Park, CA: Sage.

Leichty, G., and Applegate, J. (1991). Social-cognitive and situational influences on the use of face-saving persuasive strategies. *Human Communication Research, 17*, 451–484.

Lim, T. S. (1990). Politeness behavior in social influence situations. In J. Dillard (Ed.), *Seeking compliance: The production of interpersonal influence messages*. Dubuque, IA: Gorsuch-Scarisbrick Publishers.

Lim, T. S., and Bowers, J. (1991). Face-work: Solidarity, approbation, and tact. *Human Communication Research, 17*, 415–450.

Matsumoto, Y. (1988). Re-examination of the universality of face: Politeness phenomena in Japanese. *Journal of Pragmatics, 12*, 403–426.

Metts, S., and Cupach, W. (1989). Situational influence on the use of remedial strategies in embarrassing predicaments. *Communication Monographs, 56*, 151–162.

O'Keefe, B., and Shepherd, G. (1987). The pursuit of multiple objectives in face-to-face persuasive interaction: Effects of construct differentiation on message organization. *Communication Monographs, 54*, 396–419.

———. (1989). The communication identity during face-to-face persuasive interactions. *Communication Research, 16*, 375–404.

Penman, R. (1987). Discourse in courts: Co-operation, coercion and coherence. *Discourse Processes, 10*, 210–218.

———. (1990). Facework and politeness: Multiple goals in courtroom discourse. *Journal of Language and Social Psychology, 9*, 15–38.

———. (1991). Goals, games and moral orders: A paradoxical case in court. In K. Tracy (Ed.), *Understanding face-to-face interaction: Issues linking goals and discourse*. Hillsdale, NJ: Lawrence Erlbaum.

Pharr, S. (1990). *Losing face: Status politics in Japan*. Berkeley, CA: University of California Press.

Redding, S., and Ng, M. (1983). The role of "face" in the organizational perceptions of Chinese managers. *International Studies of Management and Organization, 13*, 92–123.

Schlenker, B. (Ed.) (1985). *The self and social life*. New York: McGraw-Hill.

Scollon, R., and Scollon, S. (1981). *Narrative, literacy and face in interethnic communication*. Norwood, NJ: Ablex.

————. (1983). Face in interethnic communication. In J. Richards and R. Schmidt (Eds.), *Language and communication*. London: Longman.

Shimanoff, S. (1985). Rules governing the verbal expression of emotions between married couples. *Western Journal of Speech Communication, 49,* 147–165.

————. (1987). Types of emotional disclosure and request compliance between spouses. *Communication Monographs, 54,* 85–100.

————. (1988). Degree of emotional expressiveness as a function of face-needs, gender and interpersonal relationship. *Communication Reports, 1,* 43–53.

Ting-Toomey, S. (1988). Intercultural conflict styles: A face-negotiation theory. In Y. Kim and W. Gudykunst (Eds.), *Theories in intercultural communication*. Newbury Park, CA: Sage.

Ting-Toomey, S., and Cole, M. (1990). Intergroup diplomatic communication: A face-negotiation perspective. In F. Korzenny and S. Ting-Toomey (Eds.), *Communicating for peace: Diplomacy and negotiation*. Newbury Park, CA: Sage.

Ting-Toomey, S., Gao, G., Trubisky, P., Yang, Z., Kim, H. S., Lin, S., and Nishida, T. (1991). Culture, face maintenance, and styles of handling interpersonal conflict: A study in five cultures. *The International Journal of Conflict Management, 2,* 275–296.

Tracy, K., Craig, R., Smith, M., and Spisak, F. (1984). The discourse of requests: Assessment of a compliance-gaining approach. *Human Communication Research, 10,* 513–538.

Trubisky, P., Ting-Toomey, S., and Lin, S. (1991). The influence of individualism-collectivism and self-monitoring on conflict styles. *International Journal of Intercultural Relations, 15,* 65–84.

-2-
Facework in Communication: Conceptual and Moral Challenges

ROBYN PENMAN

The concept of face, and the work we do to present it, is fascinating. The more I read on the concept and the area of interpersonal communication generally, the more it seems that the concepts face and facework capture something basic and enduring about our communication practices. The word "face" was used in an everyday sense as far back as the fourth century B.C. in China (Ho, 1975). And we can hear people in our contemporary Western world still using the concept in much the same way to generally refer to a persons' social identity, character, or reputation. That it has endured as a concept in the everyday sense for so many centuries is striking.

Research into face and facework is much more recent, but what the concept lacks in research history it makes up for in boundary crossing. The starting point for most of this recent research can be traced directly to Goffman's pioneering work on social interaction (e.g., 1959, 1971, 1972). For Goffman, face is "the positive social value a person effectively claims for himself [or herself] . . . in terms of approved social attributes" and facework is "the actions taken by a person to make whatever he [or she] is doing consistent with face" (Goffman, 1972, 5). Tracy's (1990) paper on "The Many Faces of Facework" offers an excellent review of the many areas of inquiry that have built on Goffman's seminal work. She identifies two major traditions: (1) social psychology-based research, and (2) the sociolinguistics-based politeness theory.

Tracy (1990) identifies three distinct areas of inquiry in the social psychology-based tradition: those directly based on Goff-

15

man's work, self-presentation studies, and bargaining and conflict research. While each of these areas have different concerns, they all offer a notion of how an actor's concerns with self-image or identity feature in communication and how these concerns can produce actions that may affect others' identity concerns as well.

The sociolinguistics tradition which is based on the politeness theory of Brown and Levinson (1978, 1987) has perhaps had the most direct impact on face research. One of their important, although sometimes troublesome, contributions is the distinction they make between negative and positive face. According to Brown and Levinson (1978), positive face is concerned with the desire to have a positive and consistent self-image appreciated by at least some others, and positive facework is oriented towards negotiating the desired self-identity. Negative face is concerned with the desire for freedom of action and freedom from imposition by others, and negative facework is orientated towards establishing and maintaining the desired distance and interpersonal constraints between self and other. While this theory has been subject to much criticism, including that of the originators (e.g., Brown and Levinson, 1987; Coupland, Grainger, and Coupland, 1988; Craig, Tracy, and Spisak, 1986), it still makes important contributions that can be drawn upon to elaborate the dynamics of facework.

But there is more to the research story than these traditions. In the interpersonal communication literature there are many lines of inquiry that seem to point to the same mechanism that the concept of facework has been used to label. While the nomenclature has varied over time, the work of the constructivists (e.g., Clark and Delia, 1979), that of the dramaturgical approach (e.g., Goffman, 1959), and the Palo Alto group (e.g., Watzlawick, Beavin, and Jackson, 1967) all make a distinction between informational and relational levels of communication. Regardless of the school, the descriptions of the relational function are compatible with other descriptions of facework—the relational function is concerned with how we negotiate the relationship between ourselves and others in the interaction. But perhaps it is Clark and Delia's (1979) more elaborate distinctions that show the parallels. They argued that it is both the individual's identity and the relationship definition that is being negotiated at the relational level of communication. The concepts of negotiating individual identity and relationship definition are remarkably similar to those of positive and negative face, respectively.

Although this brief overview is by no means exhaustive, I hope it is sufficient to indicate the pervasiveness of the general concepts of face and facework. While the labels can change, the features to which the concepts point remain remarkably consistent: they are features that concern identity and relationships. I also want to suggest we need a more complex understanding of these features if we are to progress in our understanding of face and facework. Craig and colleagues, (1986) and Tracy (1990) have also suggested the need for a more complex understanding of social life in which to locate the concepts of face and facework. For them and for me, the basis for this more complex understanding lies in locating facework as part of a communication process: facework is something we do in communication.

In this chapter I write about communication and facework from a particular point of view based on new developments in ways of thinking about social practices. These new ways of thinking have been labelled by some as representing a paradigm shift from "modern" to "postmodern" science (e.g., Bernstein, 1983; Toulmin, 1982). Whether this is actually so, only time will tell. But, at the least, these new developments all reflect, and stem from, a rejection of the old paradigm that falls under the specific rubric of "empiricism" or the more general one of "foundationalism" (e.g., Rorty, 1980). This chapter takes on board all the arguments against those positions and explores what a radically different one may mean for understanding facework in communication.

A More Complex Understanding

Basic Assumptions

Central to this new point of view is the proposition that the meaning of something does not reside in any outside, objective, or independent reality; rather, meanings are created out of our communicative practices (e.g., Gergen, 1982, 1985; Penman, 1988). Being created out of our communication, meanings are a function of the joint action between people, not of any one person per se.

This basic proposition negates the foundationalist belief that we understand our world through our direct experience of it. Instead, it is claimed that there is no isomorphic relationship between our experience and our understanding of the world. What we take to be our experience of the world does not, in itself, dictate the terms by which it is understood. This claim invites us to challenge the objective basis of conventional knowledge and to accept that there is no objective basis at all. As such, the conventional objective-subjective dichotomy has no role to play. If there is no objectivity, the distinction becomes meaningless.

What we understand about our world is a function of, and limited by, the language we use. Wittgenstein's contributions in this regard are important. His lengthy explorations in *Tractatus* of the relationship between language and the world led him to conclude that such a relationship was ineffable because of the very nature of language (Janik and Toulmin, 1973). Later, in *Philosophical Investigations*, Wittgenstein approached the problem in a different way, with the use of the concept of a "language game." This concept "is meant to bring into prominence the fact that the *speaking* of language is part of an activity or form of life" (Wittgenstein, 1958, p. 11). It is via language, in communication, that we bring about the world as we know it.

Language is, as Potter and Linton (1985) have put it, constitutive of what it represents. Our words act to represent things in our worlds, albeit not directly, and in that representing actually bring the "things" about. Because language is not directly anchored to objective experience, but has instead this dual constitutive and representative role, our communicative activities and the meaning generated have an inherent uncertainty. In principle, the meanings implicated in joint communicative action are always indeterminate. But, in practice, this is not always wholly so. We seem to have an amazing capacity for creating order out of the potential chaos of communicative indeterminacy. In a rather curious way, this order is brought about *out of* uncertainty. While the basis of language is uncertain, its main function is to create social orders and sustain them (Mills, 1940).

Within this understanding of our social world, communication takes on a very different guise than that conventionally given. In the conventional world, communication is most often talked about as if it were a transmission process, with information/messages being sent from one place/person to another (see Reddy, 1979). In that transmission view the message is independent of the senders and receivers. In contrast, this new view takes communication as being "ontologically formative" (Shotter, 1989). All our understandings are dependent on and formed in the communication process.

Face and facework are one of the many concepts formed in our communication process. Face and facework do not exist as phenomena independent of ourselves in our communicative activities, rather, they are phenomena that we bring about *in* those activities. And we do so in two ways: in our communicative activities we generate the labels of face and facework, and we continue to engage in the actions to which we fit the labels.

Identity and Relationship

When communication is seen as ontologically formative, our understanding of social life by necessity becomes more complex. We must grasp what it is to both generate and maintain social understandings that have no objective foundation. We must also come to terms with what it is to both generate and maintain our own self-identity in a world that is not independent of ourselves.

Traditional understandings of the concept of 'self' are grounded in a cognitive-psychological framework. In that framework, the self is treated as a solid core of 'inner' knowing that is developed from experiences with an external reality. In contemporary Western culture this inner knowing is related to such things as emotions, ideas, plans and memories that, while residing in the mind, have various assumed relations with the real world. But there is a circular character to the propositions relating mental events to the outside world, and virtually all that can be known about the mind lies implicit in the definitional structure of language itself (Gergen, 1989).

More recent writings in the new framework, argue eloquently against the need to postulate an 'inner' mental world to account for self. Instead we must, as Harré puts it, conceive of selfhood without "the myth of 'self' as a diaphanous homunculus hidden within" (Harré, 1989, p. 22). The key to an alternative conception of self is the recognition that it is as communicatively generated and maintained as are all other concepts (e.g., Gergen, 1989; Shotter, 1989).

But self-concepts are linguistically generated in a particular way. The difference is contained in Wittgenstein's (1958) important distinction between avowals—first-person uses of psychological terms which must be criterionless—and

ascriptions—second- and third-person uses based on induc-
tive evidence (Harré, 1989). We cannot directly point to an inner feeling and assign meaning to it (avowal) in the same way
we can point to say a dog and call it "dog." When I point to a dog
and call it by that name, you can say yes, I agree, it is a dog, see
it has four legs, barks, and does other doggy things. But we
cannot do this with our inner feelings because we have no common basis between ourselves to agree that the criterion for the
concept is met. We cannot say as we do with a dog, yes I agree
that you have a pain because I can see this, this, and this.

The important point about this distinction between avowals and ascriptions is that they are acquired differently. First-
person avowals can only be learnt after we have understood
second-person ascriptions. In other words, we acquire our self-
concept out of the ascriptions that others give to us. We are
given the psychological labels for our concept of self in our interactions with others.

This view of the development of a self-identity is in contrast
to traditional ones, such as those in Piagetian theory. In those
more traditional views, the infant is assumed to be born into
the world as an empty vessel—a *tabula rasa*—and becomes a
social being by a process of socialization or learning. The infant is assumed to *internalize* the norms of their society in a
progressive, sequential order, adding bit by bit the skills
needed to be a social being. But research into mother-infant interaction suggests the mother does not so much *pour* skills
and knowledge into the infant as she *completes* the infant
(e.g., see Richards, 1974). And she does so by the attribution of
intent (e.g., Snow, 1977).

In the early months the parents act *as if* the infant is feeling, doing, thinking certain things and constantly assign the
label for their inference ("Oh, you're trying to get that" or "You
poor thing, you're hungry aren't you?"). They later attribute
more complex labels to action that take on features of self-
ascription (e.g., "Oh, what a clever girl you are" or "You're a
good boy"). Without this attribution on the part of others, we
would not know what it was to be clever, good, hungry, or goal-
directed. It is through being given these labels, or ascriptions,
as the second person in a dialogue that we can later take them
on in the first person and avow that that is what we are.

But not even in our first person role of avowing ourselves,
can we genuinely say that we possess our self-characteristics
inside ourselves. We might, as contemporary culture would

have it, *believe* that this is so but that does not make it really so. The point is we have no way, other than through language and our interactions with others using it, to gain and maintain a self-description.

The nature of our self-identity and the constancy of it are a function of the communicative practices in which we are situated. If, for example, our practices are constant, then so too will the self-identity we avow. And if our practices are varied and complex then so too will be our self-identity. Gergen (1989) specifically argues that our understanding of our self arises from our mastery of discourse—if one is inarticulate or linguistically undifferentiated, one will have only limited self-understanding. But I would suggest that we can extend this argument beyond lingusitic skills to all manner of communicative skills.

What is also important about this social view of self-identity is that it is integrally related to the concept of relationship. In order to have a view of myself I must gain it in a relationship, in dialogue with others. But I cannot just do what I please in this relationship. The relationship, as Shotter (1989) puts it, is "ours." In acting in the relationship I do so with the expectation that you will intervene in some way if I do something considered to be wrong. Thus my self-identity is constantly subject to affirmations and negations in the negotiating of a relationship.

I hope by now I have been able to draw a picture of how we form and maintain our self-identity that suggests striking parallels with the concepts of face and facework. Face, or self-identity, are those psychological ascriptions that we take on and negotiate in our interaction with others. But the picture I have developed should suggest more. It also suggests the mechanisms by which this happens and its centrality to our human, social condition.

Facework is not something that we do some of the time, it is something that we unavoidably do all the time—it is the core of our social selves. That it is called face and facework is curious but not critical here. What is critical is that the mechanism the label stands seems to be as enduring as human social existence. In the very act of communicating with others we are inevitably commenting on the other and our relationship with them. And in that commenting we are maintaining or changing the identity of the other in relationship to us.

The Moral Dimension

The concept of face, though, has to do with more than just self-identity. It also includes an implicit concept of judgment. In the traditional Chinese sense, there were actually two understandings of face. The second understanding of face was directly in terms of a person's moral worth or good character. In more recent research, this moral element is not brought to the fore but is nevertheless still there. I have also implied this is my account of how identity is generated, maintained, and changed. In that account, I made reference to the expectation that other people in the dialogue would intervene if I did something *wrong*. The idea of right and wrong communicative action is central to the concept of facework and to the generation of our own face.

The notion that morality is connected to communication is also central to many of the theoretical traditions contributing to the new framework, and these theoretical traditions are not necessarily new. For example, Dewey in 1922, wrote an essay critical of the then current moral philosophy. For Dewey, (1981), "the facts upon which it [morality] depends are those which arise out of active connections of human beings with one another, the consequences of their mutually entwined activities" (1981, p. 722). Habermas (1975) makes an analogous argument (e.g., see McCarthy, 1984). For Habermas, interaction is the dialectic of the moral life; claims to right and wrong are implicit in all modes of communication.

The new framework within which I am writing here allows further development on this moral dimension to our communicative activity. All of the underlying assumptions of this new framework point to the centrality of morality to our communicative practices (Penman, 1992). Of particular import to the argument here are the assumptions that communicative action has a voluntary base, that knowledge is socially constituted, and that it is based on values.

In engaging in communicative action, and facework is a feature of that action, human beings are assumed to act in a more or less voluntary manner. In putting forward this proposition, we are also assuming that humans are, more or less, agents of their own lives (e.g., see Harré, 1979). But we are not necessarily assuming a total lack of environmental constraints, or total free will in the classic philosophic sense. We are simply saying that human beings have some capacity to act voluntarily. And in exercising that capacity they must concomitantly be assumed to be responsible for their actions. Notions of voluntary action and responsibility go hand in hand with notions of morality.

In engaging in communicative action it is also assumed that we are creating our social knowledge. The basis for this argument was discussed at length earlier. But the further implication is important: if our social knowledge is an outcome of our joint actions and not of a direct relation with reality, then the basis for that knowledge is valuational not objective. The language we use and the knowledge generated in communicative action is not based on fact per se, but on our beliefs and values about what reality might be. And these values, by their very nature, incorporate what it is we believe to be good and desirable.

In generating our social knowledge in a voluntary manner based on values, we should not be able to avoid the moral dimension of our actions. Unfortunately, much communication and other social research has done just that—avoided the moral dimension. This dimension has been avoided because the assumptions of the mainstream paradigm obscure it. In the mainstream paradigm, the major concern is with identifying communicative phenomenon that can be said to be objectively real or true. In that paradigm the search is for truth; whereas here truth is set aside in favor of morality (see Penman, 1992, for further arguments).

But, as always, with the new framework, there are two sides to this moral dimension. On the one hand, it is argued that all communicative action has a moral dimension because all communication and the knowledge generated within it is based on value. On the other hand, our study of that communicative action also has a moral dimension; as researchers we are not exempt from engaging in the generation of knowledge based on values. This latter aspect will be developed further in the last section of this chapter.

For the moment, though, we need to look at the first aspect and its implications for facework. Basically, I am arguing that whether we are aware of it or not, we are always making moral judgments in our communicative action. We are always approving and disapproving, confirming and negating—the dialogue of the participants on the basis of their communicative actions. As Cronen (1986, p. 6) has put it: "There is no society we know of that does not operate by some set of obligations, prohibitions and legitimations." In the very act of negotiating meaning in joint action, we rely on a set of beliefs about what is right and what is wrong. This is why the concept of facework is so important. It is a concept that captures this important moral dimension to communicative action, albeit not a dimension typically referred to in facework research.

A Primary Concept?

There has been increasing interest with the concept of facework in recent years—and this book illustrates that interest. I would like to suggest that this interest comes out of increasing awareness of the importance of understanding communication per se and of understanding the dynamics of that process that go beyond the exchange of simple messages. For many of us working in this area, the notion of facework has provided a focus for looking at communication dynamics. But I believe that the notion can do more than it has to date, especially if we take the notion into the new framework I have sketched above.

Within this new way of thinking, facework can act as a central theme for furthering our understanding of how we develop a concept of a self-identify and how we morally order our social world. In acting as this central theme, the concept also helps to highlight the critical role of communication in generating and maintaining our social world. But, curiously, at the same time it forces us to seriously consider what we mean by knowledge being socially constituted.

Central to my argument is the assumption that knowledge does not have an objective, immutable base in the 'real' world and is not out there waiting to be found or discovered. This applies as much to our knowledge about facework as it does to any other ways of making sense of communication and our social world. So, how can it be that the concept has been so enduring? Surely that means it is real?

The simple answer to the second question is yes and no. It is real to the extent that we believe it to be real and it is not real to the extent that it is not independent of our communication. But the more important question concerns why it seems to have been such an enduring concept. While we do not need to say that face and facework exist in some independent reality to account for the endurance of the concept, we must accept that there are certain phenomenan that are regenerated time after time—not because they are real outside of our interactions, but because the common constraints engendered out of our interactions brings them about time and time again. While our human understanding is inherently uncertain, the organized settings for our activities bring about a certain consistency and constraint on the possibilities (Shotter, 1986).

I am arguing here that facework is one of the consistencies brought about by the organized setting of humans relating to others in a social existence. That it has endured, despite the exigencies of the human social condition, suggests the basicness of the mechanism. By basicness I am not suggesting it is unsophisticated, rather it is primary in that it provides a shared basis for a social order. We could not have a social order without something like the mechanism that I am labelling as facework. It is in this mechanism of facework that we bring about a stability to our joint actions. Facework acts to regulate joint action and stop it from entering the realm of the chaotic.

A Cautionary Research Note

We need to be careful about these arguments and suggestions. To reiterate, I am not saying that face and facework are empirical facts that we need to further discover. The assumptions of this new framework argue against empirical research in the traditional sense, that is, in the empiricist sense. In particular, the assumption that social knowledge is created in the communicative realm, without an objective immutable base in the 'real' world, means it is not possible to adopt an objective position for studying our social world. Research data are not waiting out there in the external world to be found or discovered; it is created inside the intersubjective realm. In generating accounts of, or even describing communicative action, we are creating a story to make sense of our world (e.g., Rorty, 1980; Shotter, 1987).

The stories that we create implicate a different form of knowledge than that conventionally called scientific. Again, this radically different form of knowledge is not new, and it has not just been created out of this new framework. There is an extraordinarily long philosophical tradition that argues for what has been called practical knowledge. From Aristotle's *Nichomachean Ethics* (e.g., Sensat, 1979) to the work of critical social theorists such as Habermas (e.g., 1975), a recurrent distinction has been made between knowing about things in the world and knowing of the world. Knowing *of* the world and understanding the problems of the human condition requires practical knowledge, not scientific.

The assumption of the new framework provides a good grounding for bringing about practical knowledge. But it is not easy, especially because we, as a community of scholars and researchers, are well-imbued ·with the modern mainstream philosophic tradition that values scientific knowledge as para-mount. Even if we as individuals do not adopt this stance, the majority of the scholarly community and the broader cultural one still do. In the remainder of this chapter I describe re-search that endeavors to reach for practical knowledge of the dynamics of facework in communication. But it does not al-ways succeed as well as it could, and I shall discuss this prob-lem as it arises.

The research is a series of related studies that uses the con-cept of facework as a central theme to understand the dynam-ics of communication in courts; particularly, the dynamics of the interaction between barristers and witnesses in examina-tion and cross-examination episodes. It is useful to point out, however, that the concept of facework was not the starting point for this research. Rather, the initial concern was how to account for what goes on communicatively in courts and how this account could be used to critique concepts of procedural justice. But as I groped for ways of making sense, of ordering and categorizing the discourse patterns, the idea of face and facework developed to play the key role. Many other concepts could have been used. Yet, somehow, the notion of facework captured something that seemed vital. It remains to be seen, however, where it can lead us in other contexts and whether it opens up new possibilities and new options for action.

Meanings and Facework

When we try to make sense of communicative phenomena, we are fundamentally engaged in a meaning-creation process. We are not explorers seeking to discover what is out there; we are brave, and sometimes foolish, re-creators of the meanings of others' social lives. In re-creating the meanings using the concept of facework we are faced with a range of challenging problems.

The Challenges

The first challenge is one of position. This concept of position is an important one to the new framework when it is accepted that there is no objective observer position to be taken. Two

quite different authors have proposed the basis for understanding the concept of position (Shotter, 1984; Sless, 1986).
We can give accounts from different positions in the communication process, and what we see will vary depending on the
position: "As the position he [or she] occupies changes so does
the scene, and as certain views become visible, others disap-
pear" (Sless, 1986, p. 31). And, as importantly, no one position
is better than another.

As researchers, we must choose what position we will take.
But, as researchers, some positions are excluded. We cannot
give accounts from the direct participatory positions of first
person reader and author, to use Sless' (1986) words, or from
the position of I (first person) or you (second person), to use
Shotter's (1984) words. We are always removed from those positions and can only give accounts from the position of author/
reader at least twice removed or from the position of the third
person. When we adopt the (nonobjective) observer's position,
we are in the third-person role. This is the role I took with the
facework studies.

The second challenge arises from the possibility of multiple
descriptions of any given communicative actions. There can be
as many different labels as there are positions for labelling.
And from each position, we can choose to assign more than
one label to the one action. In other words, we may act with
more than one intent and/or we can construe another's actions
as being multiply intended. Recognizing the possibility of multiple intents or goals is not new. In fact, for some it is taken as
a 'commonplace' (e.g., Farrell, 1983, p. 263). However, the
other basis of multiplicity is less frequently accepted: that different people can apply different act descriptions to the same
action. These 'sources' of multiplicity create problems for actors and researchers alike.

The third challenge arises from the need to see the description of any given action as subject to infinite revision (Gergen,
1982). Any action, communicative or otherwise, takes place
within broader temporal and structural contexts. The labelling of a given communicative action at a particular point in
time and in a given structural context is subject to constant
revision as the retrospective and emergent contexts change
with the process. In other words, the labelling of a given communicative act is a function of context and this context is continually changing. As the context changes, new descriptions
emerge.

The important point of these challenges is that the basis for any particular description of communicative acts is not fundamentally empirical; it relies instead on a weaving of interdependent and continuously modifiable interpretations. Given that the action itself has no independent ontic status (e.g., Anscombe, 1957; Winch, 1958), our concern needs to be with the manner of description per se, that is, with the manner of the story we develop. Taking the propositions given above, we need to develop a manner of description that allows for the possibility of multiple interpretations occurring within a constraining and changing context.

One Way of Assigning Meaning

From our removed, or third-person position, we must ask what features are we going to draw upon to label an act as facework and of what sort. Research suggest that facework is neither a simple or a straightforward act to label. In an earlier paper (Penman, 1990), I raised a number of problems associated with this meaning assignment process. These problems are indicated both in the research literature and in the new way of understanding, and I will briefly review them here for you.

At the very beginning I indicated that we can conceive of facework in terms of facework done to and for the self as well as facework done to and for the other. This draws on the politeness theory of Brown and Levinson (1978, 1987). We can also make a further distinction between positive (self-image) and negative (interpersonal distance) facework in line with Brown and Levinson (1978, 1987). Just with these distinctions we have four types of facework categories: self-directed positive and negative facework, and, other-directed positive and negative facework. Further complexities are introduced by recognizing that communicative acts of actors may be multifunctional (e.g., Baxter, 1984; Craig et al., 1986) and that these multifunctions may be served sequentially or simultaneously. Moreover, the multifunctions may be expressed in either a direct or indirect way (Brown & Levinson, 1978; Haverkate, 1986).

Considering this range of possibilities, I proposed that we can differentiate between at least sixteen different facework strategies—at least conceptually—and that these sixteen different strategies were not mutually exclusive. This is a rather complex conception that is further confounded by trying to label facework acts in practice.

When we engage in communication as participants we know full well that much of what is said and done is ambiguous—did he or she really mean that or did I take it the wrong way? This ambiguity is an inherent feature of communication. But not only is communication inherently ambiguous, participants can also be intentionally misleading. Craig and colleagues (1986) point directly to this problem in their own study on facework: "We need a scheme of interpretation that shows how the hearer or observer can recognize the intention to use a strategy. The extent to which such a scheme could be constructed in principle is limited, however, by the (unknown) extent to which discourse is genuinely ambiguous" (Craig et al., 1986, p. 453).

This problem is one faced by all studies attempting to classify, or assign meaning to, discourse. However, it is not one that is always recognized as such. Traditional approaches to coding communicative behavior have assumed that inconsistencies in the classification arise from poorly conceived coding and training procedures—not from the inherent ambiguity of the phenomena being coded. When we start from the position that all discourse is inherently indeterminate, different problems arise and different solutions are required.

At the heart of a different solution is the attempt to use features of the discourse that, as a participant, I would also use. If we, as researchers, are to attempt the foolhardy task of meaning-assignment then we can only do so in the same general way that we do as participants—albeit from a different position with a different view. For example, what type of communicative act would lead me to say that he or she is threatening my positive face while enhancing his own? As a first step to answering this, I would say, well it depends—it depends on who he or she is, in what context, what has gone before, and so on. In other words, I would draw on a range of information to help my inference process.

Drawing on this sort of participant experience and other research work, various inference strategies can be suggested. In my previous paper (Penman, 1990), I identified three specific strategies—(1) episode location, (2) distinctions between positive and negative face, and (3) connections between linguistic output and function—that assisted with the courtroom discourse.

The notion of an episode is a familiar, although not an uncontroversial one in the communication literature. It is based

on the observation that members of society typically are able to
see particular segments of conversations as distinct wholes
(Gumperz, 1972). A number of theorists (e.g, Pearce & Cronen,
1980) have argued that episode identification is important in
understanding the meaning assigned to any particular act. In
order to recognize what facework strategy could be in opera-
tion, it is first necessary to know in what episode it is taking
place. In addition, the goal that appears to be achieved at the
end of any particular episode is an important retrospective clue
to the nature of the facework that has occurred.

Distinguishing between positive and negative facework is
partly a function of the context in which the interaction occurs
and the goals of the interaction. In the context of the courts,
the linkage between the speaking and acting role complicates
the distinction. The barrister is always asking questions and
thus always, at least according to Brown and Levinson (1978,
1987), constraining the freedom of action (negative face) of the
witness. In this sense, every question on the part of the barrister can be taken as other-directed negative facework. Yet it is
quite frequently the case that their questions do more than
this. It proved important in the courtroom analysis to make a
distinction between questions and answers regarding 'facts'
and those regarding rationality of and motivation for actions.
This distinction between facts and motivations and rationality
aided in making distinctions between negative and positive
facework. Questioning or defending the rationality of actions
has direct implications for the person's positive face—a rational person being more credible than an irrational one. Questioning and explaining about concrete facts, on the other
hand, is more likely to be only directed towards negative face.

This distinction, however, cannot be a firm one. There will
be instances where a direct, factual question can also have
demeanor implications. For example, the question, "Did you
drink the entire bottle of scotch?" is not only imposing on the
other's negative face by asking for factual information, but also
the other's positive face by suggesting alcohol indulgence. We
must also recognize that this distinction between facts and
motivations and rationality may not be generally applicable in
other contexts. But its relevance to the courtroom is clear. In
courtroom parlance, information on what happened is concerned with establishing the 'facts of the matter', while information on the reasons and rationality of the witnesses is
concerned with demeanor, or self-presentation of the witness.

And it is both 'facts' and demeanor that play a role in judicial decision-making.

The final procedural issue concerns the link between linguistic output and function. As Craig and colleagues (1986) argue, a specification of this link is important in reliably identifying and coding strategies. This is, in fact, the greatest problem of any scheme of classification of conversational data. How exactly, for example, is the mitigation of the positive face of the other achieved in practice? What words and work structures bring about the assigning of this label? The ambiguities and uncertainties of language use means this relationship between function and syntax will always be problematic. In fact, it has been argued (e.g., Austin, 1962) that there is *no* characteristic linguistic form for any function; there is no direct link between syntax and pragmatics. Nevertheless, we, as participants, do seem to draw on some linkages, however uncertain and changing. And, in developing the conceptual schema and testing it on instances of courtroom discourse data, some crude guidelines emerged—at least for the context.

Three different types of utterances could be identified according to *some* linguistic criterion and these bore *some* relation to different types of facework—but not necessarily a consistent or precise one. The linguistic criterion that seemed to distinguish between the types of utterances was that of direct-indirectness. Kearsley (1976), in his review of taxonomies of questions, identifies the direct-indirect dimension as the major distinguishing feature of all questions. According to Kearsley, indirect questions are declaratives which contain an embedded, partial interrogative; while direct questions are sentences with a clear interrogative character. Goffman (1976) and Robinson and Rackstraw (1972) show that this direct-indirect dimension is equally applicable to answers. Basically, a direct reply is one which has lexical continuity with the question, is relevant to the question, is nontautological, is not obviously false, and is informative to the questioner. These are analogous to the characteristics that Grice (1975) uses for defining maximally efficient utterances.

With the aid of these inference devices, a classification schema that can be used in practice was developed (see Penman, 1990). The scheme along with the inference procedures captures all but one of Craig and colleagues' (1986) requirements. The scheme, while typological in form, does not meet the joint criteria of being mutually exclusive and exhaustive.

The scheme is exhaustive in its superstrategy categories, however these strategies are not construed as mutually exclusive; they cannot be if we are to capture the possibility of multiple goals. It is recognized that this creates problems for some statistical analyses but does not exclude quantification altogether—if that is wanted. The choice was between simplifying the model for particular quantitative needs and attempting to capture the real multifunctionality of utterances. Here the decision was for the latter. This approach to labelling facework also relies on a more complex means of understanding social life. Rather than following a traditional methodology that assumes certainty and singularity of meaning, I have commenced with the assumption that meaning is inherently problematic and manifold. The end result is an interpretative approach that, in its very application, is a crude model of how participants in the discourse process just might enact and infer their own and other's facework maneuvers.

Questions and Consequences

The development of the conceptual schema and the detailed inference procedures was a complex process in itself. The application of the process to over sixteen hours of courtroom discourse was even more so. During this stage of the research, I was continually plagued by two questions: (1) Have I really escaped the empiricist's web? and (2) How do I know this view of the discourse is any 'good'?

My concern about the solution to assigning facework-meaning to discourse arises because the classification schema developed comes close to conventional coding schemas used in other research traditions. Should the generation of practical knowledge be this complex? Is it necessary to be as conceptually and methodologically rigorous as I was? The answer may be "no" to all these questions. There must be other ways to arrive at understandings about facework, and ways that do not require such complex meaning assignment processes. But this does not mean that the consequences are bad or wrong.

In the end, the story that is generated—albeit out of a perhaps unnecessarily complex analysis process—can only be judged in terms of what it may allow us to do with understanding conversations and what options for actions it creates for us. The conceptual schema was used, along with other procedures to be discussed later, to try to make sense of courtroom discourse. The outcomes of this analysis has been presented in an earlier paper (Penman, 1990), but let me summarize the key points here to show the consequences of this approach.

In the courtroom discourse data, one of the more obvious features was the number of what could be called conversational difficulties. The discourse often simply did not "flow"—there were numerous requests for clarification, resayings, repeatings, and expressions of misunderstandings (Penman, 1987). Using the facework interpretative schema on a number of court cases, it was obvious that facework maneuvers could account for a wide range of the identified conversational difficulties. In other words, difficulties were arising because both the witnesses and barristers were dealing with goals other than purely informational, or fact, ones. It also seemed obvious that the official court procedures and the rules of discourse employed to maintain them, placed the witness at a disadvantage in this facework context. Witnesses' facework was almost always directed towards their own face, and usually protecting it, while barristers' facework was most commonly directed towards the witness, and usually threatening it. Moreover, it also seemed that witnesses appeared to have many more multifunctional utterances than barristers, especially when being cross-examined. In all, it appeared as if witnesses' facework was on the whole far more complex than barristers. This makes sense when we consider the nature of the adversary process in courts: it is a process in which the barrister holds the power position and the witness is relatively powerless, and it is a process that includes episodes of cross-examination with the aim of discrediting witness's accounts (and often the witnesses themselves).

To confirm whether or not the facework discourse analysis was completely misdirected, we interviewed six witnesses and nine barristers after their court cases had finished. These interviews were open-ended and aimed at a general exploration of what the participants thought was happening in the court communication process. All the barristers and witnesses expressed beliefs that indicated an awareness of the mechanism of facework, although, of course, none used that particular label. For example, one barrister summed it up as "it's a fairly insulting way of carrying on a dialogue"; while another added "what you're often doing there is not purely setting out on an information-gathering expedition but you're trying to color the material so the court will make a value judgment about what's reliable and what's not as a result of the demeanor and general style of the witness." And witnesses said things like "I find it a bit awkward because it's sort of degrading . . . and that's what the whole game is about really."

Interestingly, witnesses and barristers also seemed to draw on the distinction between positive and negative face, again not in those words. Instead, they made reference to the way they as barristers tried to limit what the witness said or as witnesses how the barristers constrained their responses (impingement of negative face). They also made reference to what they as barristers were trying to do to the self-presentation of the witness or what they as witnesses were trying to do in maintaining—often with little success—their own self-image (threats to positive face).

These interview data offer some support to the usefulness of the concept of facework in making sense of what goes on in courts. And the discourse analysis of the facework maneuvers compellingly supports research reports of what it is like to stand in the witness box in court. The essence of these reports, from our own research and others (e.g., see Danet, 1980) is that courtroom interaction is an extremely degrading experience. The complex story of facework created in the studies summarized here, can well account for why the experience is so degrading: people are not allowed to engage in, or are constrained in, a fundamental part of their social life—facework.

I would like to suggest, then, that the procedures have been of value because they allowed me to create a story that articulates *why* people feel as bad as they do when they stand in the witness box in court and *why* courtroom discourse appears so problematic for all concerned. But we can tell a more elaborate story than that with the notion of facework when we use it to explore the moral dimension.

The Moral Challenge and Facework

In the first section of this chapter I proposed that all of our communicative practices contain a moral dimension; we are always approving and disapproving, confirming and negating our dialogue partners. I also proposed that the concept of facework captures this critical moral dimension in our communication. The question now remains as to how the concept can be used to develop a moral story. Again I shall draw on the courtroom studies to illustrate my approach to this question, with specific reference to Penman (1991).

Considerations

The concept of a moral order has been used by those contemporary communication theorists concerned with the moral dimension of communicative life (e.g., Cronen, 1986; Harré, 1984; Pearce, 1989), where a moral order includes a set of practices and resources that promote morality. Harré (1984, p. 245) specifies four features of a moral order:

1. Rituals exist for the public marking of respect and contempt.
2. Actions are treated as displays of character, not just as instrumental ways of achieving purposes.
3. Moral commentaries are given that describe, prescribe and evaluate conduct.
4. There is an asymmetrical distribution of the rights to perform the practices listed above.

Clearly all of these features can be expressed in our communicative practices. Equally, it would seem that facework must be involved in that expression. So we need a way to take the facework analysis described earlier and use it to build a story of moral orders. To do this I drew on three related concepts: rules, games, and hierarchies of meanings.

In the first instance, I propose that moral orders are indicated by sets of rules that guide communicative practices in different contexts. But we cannot treat this proposal simply. While rules are undeniable a feature of morality, morality cannot merely consist in the adherence to those rules (Larmore, 1987). It could well be the case that adherence to one particular moral order leads a person to the breaking of rules in another moral order incommensurate with their own. It could also be the case that there is more than one moral order being enacted in any communicative context (Pearce, 1989).

The possible complexities of communication practices related to moral orders can be captured in Wittgenstein's (1958) notion of a language game. He gives, however, no precise definition of a language game. This would, in fact, be contrary to his arguments. These games can loosely be characterized as consisting of sets of moves that appear to be employed according to some rules or conventions. We do not have to propose a strict definition of a game or of the rules on which it may be based. For Wittgenstein and this argument, it is sufficient that rules *appear* to be guiding the sequence of action.

The assumptions of a language game are quite pertinent to discourse in courts. It is highly likely that witnesses will not know (in the sense of being able to articulate) the rules in court and yet they will have to follow them. The force of law, if nothing else, will make them appear to be following rules. And they will appear to be doing so when recurrent conversational patterns occur. These recurrent patterns can be taken as indicative of adherence to, or deviation from, a language game. According to Wittgenstein (1958), this is no more or less than how we identify a game of tennis or poker and how we distinguish one type of game from another.

But we must also allow for the possibility of more than one game. In order to do this we also need to use a conceptual device that will allow us to distinguish between, and explore the relations between various games. The concept of hierarchical levels of meaning can do this; it is a common approach, at least in logic, to handling the problem of multiple meanings. Various authors have proposed and used a model of hierarchical levels of meaning (e.g., Frentz & Farrell, 1976; Pearce & Cronen, 1980; Watzlawick, Beavin, & Jackson, 1967). Pearce and Cronen's model was found the most useful because of the multiplicity of levels and the potential variability in the relationship between them. To show how these concepts are useful it is best to look at the consequences of their application.

Consequences
The courtroom discourse data were systematically analyzed for recurrent patterns of communicative behavior that could be taken to be indicative of games being played. Two games were inferred: a fact game and a face game. The fact game is the one officially played in court. It is concerned with obtaining relevant factual information in the most efficient manner. But the difficulty that all participants, barristers, and witnesses had in playing that game indicated that more than one game was being played. The other, unofficial game appeared to be about facework. The relationships between these games and the moral orders they seem to indicate can be shown with the aid of the hierarchical model in figure 1 (from Penman, 1991).

The facts game is located at the content level of meaning; it is concerned strictly with information, with the facts of the case. The face game, however, is enacted at the speech-act or relational level of meaning and, in doing so, acts as a framework within which the content level of meaning is interpreted,

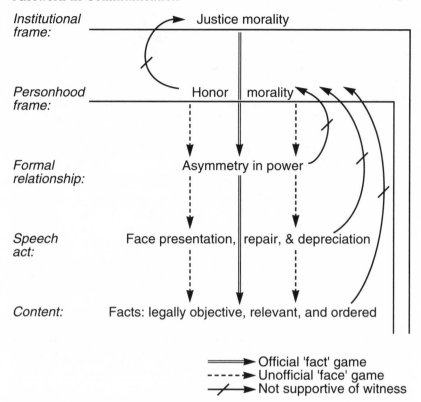

Fig. 1. A Model of the Goals, Games, and Moral Orders in Court-rooms.

however implicitly. Superordinate to these two levels is that of a formal relationship. On courts this formal relationship is an asymmetrical power relationship in which the representatives of the law are superordinate to those who stand in the witness box. Both the fact and the face game are played out in the context of this formal, asymmetrical power relationship.

But it is the higher levels of meaning that indicate the moral orders of courtroom discourse. As indicated in figure 1, the superordinate meaning-frame for all courtroom discourse is the institutional frame. This is equivalent to Pearce and Cronen's (1980) level of cultural pattern; the institution of law being a major element in any cultural pattern. The official fact game and the fundamental premises of the legal institution lead to the claim that the moral order expressed in the institutional frame is one of a justice morality. This justice morality condones the use of impartiality and clear reason in making a just determination from the legally defined 'facts of the case'. Within this justice morality only the official fact game can be explicitly acknowledged. This game requires the formal set of relationships between barrister/judge and witness—that relationship in which the court and its representatives are formally empowered to use the witness to arrive at the 'facts of the matter' in the most efficient and expeditious manner.

However, in playing this official game, a number of meaning contexts are denied—most importantly, that at the speech-act level. It is via this context that another equally important, but unofficial game is played—the face game. The moves that appear in this game strongly suggest it stems from another moral order—an honor morality. Harré (1984) has identified certain features of honor moralities that well fit the situation in court. In the first instance, honor moralities are typified by asymmetrical relations of respect and condescension—as is clearly the case in court, not only at the formal relationship level but in the very playing of the face game itself. Dueling and the use of champions are also characteristic of honor moralities and, again, this would seem to apply directly to courts. In this situation, we have the barrister acting as champion for one party, engaging in a verbal duel against the other.

I want to suggest then that both the witness and the barrister are unofficially operating within an honor morality. And, despite the lack of formal rules, the unofficial game and its honor morality is still seen to count and, in important ways, for both the judge and the jury. Work by Backman (1976) suggests that juries use an honor morality to make decisions regarding guilt and innocence. My own analyses of judges' instructions to juries show the frequent use of the instruction to "consider the witnesses' demeanor," that is, how they presented themselves as persons. And the interview data I described earlier also indicate that the witnesses and the barristers are equally aware of the importance of demeanor.

This analysis of moral orders brings to the forefront a set of dynamics that is not yet recognized within the legal institutional frame. Within that frame, communication is seen simply as a tool for legal ends and so are the people in the process. Yet despite the court 'forcing' communication into a simple, instrumental role, it is unable to contain it as such. The end product is a paradoxical situation in which two games—the fact game and the face game—and two moral orders—those of justice and honor—are incommensurate.

Recognition of this situation provides the basis for a critical reconsideration of the judicial process based on an adversary system. In general, the analyses and arguments lead to the conclusion that the process of justice as enacted in the adversary system neither facilitates the establishment of the facts of the case nor ensures a just hearing in the best possible manner. The facts which are established are severely distorted because the court ignores or denies the critical role of context and the process whereby the so-called facts are established. Moreover, the court's formal rules of discourse and the adversary process combined, act to treat all witnesses as worthy of contempt; while at the same time demanding that it and its representatives are treated with respect. The court treats all witnesses as worthy of contempt by not explicitly recognizing the importance of the face game in the witness examination and cross-examination procedure.

With this moral order analysis and critical reconsideration of the adversary system of procedural justice, I have brought the research program back to my original concern—how to make sense of the dynamics in courts in such a way that procedural justice could be critiqued. The concepts of face and facework played a critical role in the sense-making process in this research. These concepts also led me to a story that not only suggests why witnesses, in particular, are disadvantaged in courts but also ways in which it could be better. Clearly, it would be best to openly acknowledge face concerns and openly allow for facework validation.

Future Challenges

The new framework within which these studies of facework are couched offers many further challenges to us. The basic assumptions of the framework imply that it is only up to us—all of us—to create and confront them. In the writing of this chapter I have aimed to show how the concept of facework can be developed within this new framework. In doing so, I have been able to weave in a number of interesting threads from many research areas. That I have been able to do this indicates the potential of the concept of facework and has opened up further possibilities. For me, three particularly exciting possibilities have been opened and I offer them to you as further challenges.

The Endurance of Facework

In the first section of this chapter I noted that the concept of facework, or at least the mechanisms that the label stands for, has surfaced time and again in our everyday and research understandings. Given that you accept the propositions of the new framework, this is superficially, a startling phenomenon. Yet even within this new framework, with its emphasis on continual creation and uncertainty of meaning, the endurance of the concept is not necessarily contradictory.

There are limits to what we as humans can co-create in our social lives. The very organization of the settings in which we live bring about certain consistencies and constrain other possibilities. The writings of Shotter (e.g., 1986), drawing on the much earlier writings of Vico, expand on the way in which organized settings can bring about certain consistencies in our social lives. But I think there is further work to be done in this new framework to develop a more elaborate understanding of this process; especially as it relates to facework. Indeed, it is likely that the concept of facework can continue to play an important role in helping to develop a more complex understanding of the relationship between communication practice and social life.

I am also tempted to suggest that other traditions and ways of thinking could well make a contribution to understanding why such a feature as facework is so enduring. One such possible tradition is that of Gibson's (1979) ecological theory of perception. In his account of how we perceive the world, he relies heavily on a concept of 'affordances'—the things that an animal perceives other things can be used for. For him, physical entities in the world are such that they afford the observer to see properties in terms of their uses. This, he argues, also holds true for behavior: "behavior affords behavior" (Gibson, 1979, p. 135). Now, could it be that the affordances in our behavior are such that facework is a primary one?

Developmental Issues

In exploring the central themes of identity and relationship in the first section, I drew your attention to some important research in the area of early infant development and mother-infant interaction. That research provides a coherent base for the concept of identity I used in this chapter, but it also raises further challenges about the concept of identify and its relationship with other facework research.

In my own reading of the facework research literature, drawing on the three different groups mentioned at the start of the chapter, it seems that the concept of identity is too often taken as given, as nonproblematic. More needs to done on what it means to facework and other communication dynamics when the concept of self is seen as integrally interdependent on our communicative practices. And more especially could be done on developmental aspects of facework. Undertaking facework research on young children could well help further in understanding the intricacies of the concept and could well help in creating other options for understanding and action. Taking a developmental viewpoint to facework could also help in elaborating the story as to why it is so enduring.

Moral Judgments

The final challenge that really cannot be neglected, especially by those operating within the new framework used in this chapter, is that of judging the worth of studies on facework. The work I have described here is not exempt from having to come to terms with the second aspect of the moral issue that I raised in the first section—the moral dimension of research and theory. If all theory and research is invention and not neutral discovery, then all research is also value-based. If all research is intervention, then it is in some way or another intervention into a moral order. We may wish to ignore the moral problems implied by these arguments, especially if we believe that our inquiry should be objective and value-free. Unfortunately, that will not make the problem go away.

To confront this problem requires us to accept that there are some communicative practices that are better than others, and that, similarly, there are some communication theories that are better than others. In a recent paper I suggested a means by which theories and research into communication can be judged (Penman, 1992). Here I want to suggest something a little different, but not incompatible with the previous suggestions. Could it be that we could use the same notion of face to make judgments about theories of and research into communication and the same notion of facework to negotiate those judgments?

References

Anscombe, G. (1957). *Intention.* Oxford: Blackwell.

Austin, J. (1962). *How to do things with words.* Oxford: Clarendon Press.

Backman, C. (1976). Explorations in psycho-ethics: The warranting of judgments. In R. Harré (Ed.), *Life sentences.* New York: Wiley.

Bateson, G. (1973). *Steps to an ecology of mind.* London: Paladin.

Baxter, L. A. (1984). An investigation of compliance-gaining as politeness. *Human communication research, 10,* 427–456.

Bernstein, R. (1983). *Beyond objectivism and relativism.* Oxford: Blackwell.

Brown, P., and Levinson, S. (1978). Universals in language usage: Politeness phenomena. In E. Goody (Ed.), *Questions and politeness: Strategies in social interaction.* Cambridge: Cambridge University Press.

————. (1987). *Politeness: Some universals in language usage.* Cambridge: Cambridge University Press.

Clark, R., and Delia, J. (1979). Topoi and rhetorical competence. *Quarterly Journal of Speech, 65,* 187–206.

Coupland, N., Grainger, K., and Coupland, J. (1988). Politeness in context: Intergenerational issues. *Language in Society, 17,* 253–262.

Craig, R. T., Tracy, K., and Spisak, F. (1986). The discourse of requests: Assessment of a politeness approach. *Human Communication Research, 12,* 437–468.

Cronen, V. (1986). The individual in a systemic perspective. Paper presented at the 15th Anniversary of Interaktie Akademie, Antwerp, Belgium.

Danet, B. (1980). Language in the legal process. *Law and Society Review, 14,* 445–564.

Dewey, J. (1981). *The philosophy of John Dewey.* (Ed. J. McDermot). Chicago: University of Chicago Press.

Farrell, T. B. (1983). Aspects of coherence in conversation and rhetoric. In R. Craig and K. Tracy (Eds.), *Conversational coherence.* Beverly Hills, CA.: Sage.

Frentz, T., and Farrell, T. (1976). Language-action: A paradigm for communication. *Quarterly Journal of Speech, 62,* 333–349.

Gergen, K. (1982). *Towards transformation in social knowledge.* New York: Springer-Verlag.

————. (1985). The social constructionist movement in modern psychology. *American Psychologist, 40,* 266–275.

———. (1989). Warranting voice and the elaboration. In J. Shotter and K. Gergen (Eds.), *Texts of Identity*. London: Sage.

Gibson, J. (1979). *The ecological approach to visual perception*. Boston: Houghton Mifflin.

Goffman, E. (1959). *The presentation of self in everyday life.*Garden City, NY: Doubleday.

———. (1971). *Relations in public*. New York: Harper and Row.

———. (1972). *Interaction ritual: Essays on face-to-face behavior.* Harmondsworth, UK: Penguin.

———. (1976). Replies and responses. *Language and Society, 5,* 273–313.

Grice, J. (1975). Logic and conversations. In P. Cole and J. Morgan (Eds.), *Syntax and semantics*. Vol. 3, *Speech acts*. New York: Academic Press.

Gumperz, J. (1972). Introduction. In J. Gumperz and D. Hymes (Eds.), *Directions in sociolinguistics*. New York: Hold, Rinehart and Winston.

Habermas, J. (1975). *Legitimation crisis*. (T. McCarthy, trans.). Boston: Beacon Press.

Harré, R. (1979). *Social being*. Oxford: Blackwell.

———. (1984). *Personal being*. Cambridge, MA: Harvard University Press.

———. (1989). Language games and the texts of identity. In J. Shotter and K. Gergen (Eds.), *Texts of identity*. London: Sage.

Haverkate, H. (1986). A model for analyzing politeness strategies in verbal interaction. Paper presented at the XIth World Congress of Sociology, New Delhi, India.

Ho, D. Y. (1975). On the concept of face. *American Journal of Sociology, 81,* 867–884.

Janik, A., and Toulmin, S. (1973). *Wittgenstein's Vienna*. New York: Simon and Schuster.

Kearsley, G. P. (1976). Questions and question asking in verbal discourse: A cross-disciplinary review. *Journal of Psycholinguistic Research, 5,* 355–375.

Larmore, C. E. (1987). *Patterns of moral complexity*. London: Cambridge University Press.

McCarthy, T. (1984). *The critical theory of Jürgen Habermas*. Cambridge: Polity Press.

Mills, C. W. (1940). Situated actions and vocabularies of motive. *American Sociological Review, 5,* 904–913.

Pearce, W. B. (1989). *Communication and the human condition*. Carbondale: Southern Illinois University Press.

Pearce, W. B., and Cronen, V. (1980). *Communication, action and meaning.* New York: Praeger.

Penman, R. (1987) Discourse in courts: Co-operation, coercion and coherence. *Discourse processes, 10,* 201–218.

———. (1988). Communication reconstructed. *Journal for the Theory of Social Behavior, 18,* 301–310.

———. (1990). Facework and politeness: Multiple goals in courtroom discourse. *Journal of Language and Social Psychology, 9,* 15–38.

———. (1991). Goals, games and moral orders: A paradoxical case in court? In K. Tracy (Ed.), *Understanding face-to-face interaction: Issues linking goals and discourse.* Hilsdale, N.J.: Lawrence Erlbaum.

———. (1992). Good theory and good practice: An argument in progress. *Communication Theory, 1,* 234–250.

Potter, J. and Linton, I. (1985). Some problems underlying the theory of social representations. *British Journal of Social Psychology, 24,* 81–90.

Reddy, M. (1979). The conduit metaphor. In A. Ortony (Ed.), *Metaphor and thought.* London: Cambridge University Press.

Richards, M. (Ed.) (1974). *The integration of a child into a social world.* London: Cambridge University Press.

Robinson, W. P., and Rackstraw S. J. (1972). *A question of answers,* Vol. 1. London: Routledge and Kegan Paul.

Rorty, R. (1980). *Philosophy and the mirror of nature.* Oxford: Blackwell.

Sensat, J. (1979). *Habermas and Marxism.* London: Sage.

Shotter, J. (1984). *Social accountability and selfhood.* Oxford: Blackwell.

———. (1986) A sense of place: Vico and the social production of social identities. *British Journal of Social Psychology, 25,* 199–211.

———. (1987). The social construction of an 'us': Problems in accountability and narratology. In R. Burnett, P. McGee and D. Clarke (Eds.), *Accounting for personal relationships: Social representations of interpersonal links.* London: Methuen.

———. (1989). Social accountability and the social construction of 'you'. In J. Shotter and K. Gergen (Eds.), *Texts of identity.* London: Sage.

Sless, D. (1986). *In search of semiotics.* Totowa, N.J.: Barnes and Noble.

Snow, C. E. (1977). The development of conversations between mothers and babies. *Journal of Child Language, 4,* 1–22.

Toulmin, S. (1982). The construal of reality: Criticism in modern and postmodern science. *Critical Inquiry, 9*, 93–111.

Tracy, K. (1990). The many faces of facework. In H. Giles and P. Robinson (Eds.), *The handbook of language and social psychology.* Chichester, UK: John Wiley and Sons.

Watzlawick, P., Beavin, J., and Jackson, D. (1967). *Pragmatics of human communication.* New York: Norton.

Winch, P. (1958). *The idea of a social science.* London: Routledge and Kegan Paul.

Wittgenstein, L. (1958). *Philosophical investigations.* (G. E. M. Anscombe, trans.). Oxford: Blackwell.

-3-
Face in Japan and the United States

SEIICHI MORISAKI
and
WILLIAM B. GUDYKUNST

In all cultures, face and facework are ubiquitous concepts (Ho, 1976; Ting-Toomey, 1988). Face is inherently an ambiguous concept and the ambiguity is due in part to its inconsistent use by researchers (Cole, 1989). The conceptualization of face is affected by cultural values and communication styles, and cultural variables affect the strategies of facework individuals use (Ting-Toomey, 1988; Tracy, 1990).

The purpose of this chapter is to examine cultural differences in the concept of face in Japan and the United States. In the United States, face currently is used to explain diverse communicative behaviors. Face, for example, is used to explain conflict, embarrassment, compliance-gaining tactics, social status, and/or linguistic politeness strategies (i.e., why people apologize when they make a request, why they compliment people's haircuts or acquisition of a new pair of glasses, why they threaten others and call them names, why they joke when they spill a glass of milk, and why they change topics of conversation; Tracy, 1990, p. 209).

Face also appears to be an important concept in Japan. The concept has been used by a few authors (e.g., Hill, Ide, Ikuta, Kawasaki, & Ogino, 1986; Ide, Kawasaki, Ikuta, & Haga, 1986; Matsumoto, 1988) in discussing politeness strategies, and in discussions of various aspects of Japanese society (e.g., Hendry, 1987; Masatsugu, 1982; Pharr, 1990). Face, however, is not emphasized in major analyses of Japanese social relations (e.g., Doi, 1973, 1986; Hamaguchi, 1977, 1983; Miyanaga, 1991; Nakane, 1970, 1972) or recent reviews of Japanese communication (e.g., Midooka, 1990; Wierzbica, 1991). We believe that there is at least one plausible explanation for the lack of emphasis on face in explaining Japanese communication. Many Japanese who write on Japanese society and communication tend to look for "unique" aspects of Japanese culture. This line of work often is referred to as *nihonjinron* (literally discussions of the Japanese).[1] Since the origin of the concept of social face (*mien-tzu* in Chinese, *mentsu* in Japanese) is Chinese (Ho, 1976; Hu, 1944), writers looking for unique aspects of Japanese culture would not focus on face. The lack of emphasis on face in discussions of Japanese society, nevertheless, does not mean that the concept is unimportant in understanding Japanese communication.

The Japanese term *kao* literally translates as face. It has at least three uses: (1) to refer to the physical part of the body, (2) to refer to a person's name, status, or "famousness," and (3) to refer to social face. There are, however, at least two ways social face has been used. One is based on the Chinese concept of *mien-tzu* (discussed below), or *mentsu* (*menmoku* is a synonym). The second use of social face refers to the appearance one presents to others (a use of "face" similar to Goffman's usage; see below). To differentiate the two uses, we refer to this meaning using the Japanese term *taimen*.[2] Most writers using social face in their analysis of Japanese social relations use the *taimen* meaning of social face (e.g., Hendry, 1987; Lebra, 1976).

There are numerous phrases in Japan involving *kao*, some of which involve *mentsu*, some of which do not. Phrases which involve *mentsu* include *kao-o tsubushita* (he/she crushed my face), *kao-ni doro-o nutta* (she/he flung mud in my face), *kao-ni kakawaru* (it will damage my reputation), *kao-ni menjite* (for the sake of my face). Phrases which do **not** involve **mentsu** include **kao-ga hiroi** (a broad face), *kao-pasu* (face pass), *okina kao-o suruna* (don't make a big face—a person with a big face is "pushy"), *kao-o uru* (to sell oneself).[3] We demonstrate in this chapter that the *mentsu* meaning of *kao* can be used to link several concepts used by *nihonjinron* writers.

In order to lay the groundwork for the discussion of face in Japan and the United States, a brief historical overview of the work on face is provided. Next, cross-cultural work on face and facework is reviewed. Differences in cultural values, communication styles, and conceptualizations of the self in Japan and the United States are isolated in the final section.

Historical Overview of the
Concept of Face

One of the earliest definitions of face is given by Hu (1944). Hu argues that there are two types of face in Chinese culture: *lien* and *mien-tzu*. *Lien* "refers to the confidence of society in the moral character of ego" (p. 61). *Mien-tzu* refers to the social prestige which involves a "reputation achieved through getting on in life, through success and ostentation" (p. 45). Loss of *lien* puts "ego outside the society of decent human beings and security" (p. 61). Loss of *lien* "entails not only the condemnation of society, but the loss of its confidence in the integrity of ego's characters." "As the confidence of society is essential to the functioning of the ego, the 'loss of *lien*' has come to constitute a real dread affecting the nervous system ego more strongly than physical fear" (p. 50; emphasis in original). In Chinese culture, "ego almost always belongs to a closely integrated group on which is reflected some of his [her] glory or shame. His [her] family, the wider community of friends, and his [her] superiors, all have an interest in his [her] advancement or set-backs. So a person does not simply 'lose his [her] own face' " (p. 50). In Hu's conceptualization, therefore, face is an interdependent phenomenon.[4]

Goffman's (1955) definition of Euro-American face was influenced by the Chinese concept of face (e.g., Hu, 1944; Macgowan, 1912; Smith, 1894; Yang, 1945). He conceptualizes face as "the positive social value a person effectively claims for himself [herself] by the line others assume he [she] has taken during a particular contact. Face is an image of self delineated in terms of approved social attributes" (p. 213). For Goffman, a "line" is "a pattern of verbal and non-verbal acts by which he [she] expresses his [her] evaluation of the participants, especially himself [herself]" (p. 213).

Goffman (1955) argues that face can be lost, saved, and/or given. To lose face means "to be in wrong face, to be out of face, or to be shamefaced" (p. 215). Individuals are in wrong face when they fail to present proper identities or take a proper "line" in a situation. To save face means "the process by which the person sustains an impression for others that he [she] has not lost face" (p. 215). To give face means "to arrange for another to take a better line than he [she] might otherwise have been able to take" (p. 215).

Goffman (1967) further suggests two foci of face: self-face (one's own face) and other-face (other's face). One not only defends self-face but also protects other-face during interactions. When one fails to present one's image of self competently, one takes counteractions to face-threatening incidents, called face-work (Goffman, 1955, 1967). He goes on to point out that "the person's face clearly is something that is not lodged in or on his [her] body, but rather something that is diffusely located in the flow of events in the encounter and becomes manifest only when these events are read and interpreted for the appraisals expressed in them" (Goffman, 1955, p. 214). To study facework "is to study the traffic rules of social interaction" (Goffman, 1955, p. 216). Goffman develops his concept of face with a theatrical metaphor. In his role theory, Goffman (1959, 1974) analyzes human communication as action on a metaphorical stage playing out roles in interaction with others. In Goffman's conception, "face is put on as the participants alternate the roles of performer and observer in the due course of interaction" (Choi & Choi, 1990, p. 8). Facework is manifested through communication by presenting and projecting various aspects of one's self. One person's face, for example, is negotiated socially, but it is not interlinked with other's face. Face, therefore, is an "independent" phenomenon in Goffman's conceptualization.

Following Hu (1944), Goffman (1955, 1956, 1959, 1967) and others (e.g., Lin, 1935; Stover, 1962), Ho (1976) conceptualizes face similar to Hu's concept of face in Chinese culture. Ho defines face as

> the respectability and/or deference which a person can claim for himself [herself] from others, by virtue of the relative position he [she] occupies in his [her] social network and the degree to which he [she] is judged to have functioned adequately in that position as acceptably in his [her] general conduct; the face extended to a person by others is a function of the degree of congruence between judgements of his [her] total condition in life, including his [her] actions as well as those of people closely associated with him [her], and the social expectations that others have placed upon him [her]. In terms of two interacting parties, face is the reciprocated compliance, respect, and/or deference that each party expects from and extends to, the other party. (p. 883)

Ho also points out that when it is "defined at a high level of generality, the concept of face is a universal" (p. 882).

In Ho's (1976) view, face "is never a purely individual thing. It does not make sense to speak of the face of an individual as something lodged within his [her] person; it is meaningful only when his [her] face is considered in relation to that of others in the social network" (p. 882). Face and facework, therefore, do not arise when a person is independent of others, but only when a person is interdependent with others. Ho treats face "as a sociological, rather than psychological, construct" (p. 876).

Following Ho (1976), several scholars extended Goffman's (1955, 1956, 1959, 1967) concept of face and facework. Most of this work focuses on linguistic face redress strategies or politeness in interpersonal communication. The most influential study in this line of work is Brown and Levinson's (1978) politeness theory. Brown and Levinson define face as "the public self-image that every member wants to claim for himself [herself]" (p. 66). They propose two kinds of face: positive and negative face. Positive face is "the positive consistent self-image or 'personality' (crucially including the desire that this self-image be appreciated and approved of) claimed by interactions" (p. 66). Negative face is "the basic claim to territories, personal preserves, rights to non-distraction—i.e., to freedom of action and freedom from imposition" (p. 66). Brown and Levinson list the three situational factors which affect determination of one's use of politeness: social distance, relative power, and the absolute ranking of the impositions in the particular culture. When communicators are not in an intimate relationship, when they differ in power, and/or when they make high face-threat request, they perceive a serious face-threat and lose face. Brown and Levinson argue that depending on the characteristic amount of concern for the other-face communicators will use one of five different superstrategies: (1) to perform without redress action, boldly; (2) to perform the action with positive politeness; (3) to perform a redressive action with negative politeness; (4) to perform the action indirectly (i.e., off record); and (5) "don't do the FTA [face-threatening act]" (p. 77).

Brown and Levinson's (1978) politeness theory has been used in numerous communication studies by researchers who examine or extend Brown and Levinson's original politeness theory. The specifics of these studies are not of concern here, but it is important to point out that like Brown and Levinson's (1978) original theory, the researchers treat face as an independent phenomenon.

There are several criticisms of Brown and Levinson's (1978) politeness theory (e.g., Baxter, 1984; Lim & Bowers, 1991; Penman, 1990). Based on earlier criticisms, Brown and Levinson (1987; summarized by Tracy, 1990, p. 213) isolate five major criticisms of their theory:

> (1) basing their theory on speech acts had problems; (2) the politeness ranking of their strategies will not always hold; (3) there are probably more factors that affect the perceived face-threat of an act than power, distance, and rank; (4) politeness as conceived in the theory may be culturally biased; (5) positive and negative politeness may be different in kind, rather than higher and lower amount of global politeness.

To summarize, the results of this historical overview suggest that there are different conceptualizations of face and facework which researchers and theorists have used. Goffman (1955, 1956, 1959, 1967), Brown and Levinson (1978, 1987), and other Western scholars conceptualize face as an independent phenomenon. The Western conceptualizations, however, is different from Hu's (1944) and Ho's (1976) conceptualizations. It is important to recognize that "the particular aspects of face that are valued and pursued are highly influenced by culture" (Tracy, 1990, p. 219). Unlike the Western approach, Hu and Ho, both Chinese, conceptualize face as interdependent phenomenon (i.e., face is only an issue when individuals are members of social groups and the individuals' linkages to others is involved). It, therefore, appears that there are cross-cultural differences in the use of the concept face. In the next section we review an important line of research based on Ting-Toomey's (1988) theory that begins to isolate cross-cultural differences in face-negotiation.

Cross-Cultural Comparisons of Face in Japan and the United States

Ting-Toomey (1988) developed a theory designed to explain how people in individualistic and collectivistic cultures negotiate face and deal with conflict. She assumes that: (1) people in all cultures try to maintain and negotiate face in all communication situations; (2) the concept of face is especially problematic in uncertainty situations when the situated identities of the interactants are called into question; (3) conflict, as a class of uncertainty situations, demands active facework management: self-face concern and mutual-face concern, and negative-face maintenance (control need), and positive-face maintenance (affiliative-inclusion need); and (5) the cultural variability dimension of individualism-collectivism will influence members' selection of one set of conflict styles (e.g., avoidance and obliging styles) over others (e.g., confrontational and solution-oriented styles).

In her theory, Ting-Toomey (1988) isolates two concerns in face-negotiation: concern regarding the loci of face being negotiated (self-face, other-face, and mutual-face), and the face-need concern (negative face and positive face). Negative facework (e.g., speech acts such as apology for an imposition, prerequest ritual, compliance-resistance act, and command act) focuses on the negotiation process between two interdependent parties concerning the degree of threat or respect each give to one another's sense of freedom and individual autonomy. Positive facework (e.g., speech acts such as self-disclosure, compliment, and promise) entails the degree of threat or respect each give to one another's need for inclusion and approval.

Based on the two dimensions, Ting-Toomey (1988) isolates four types of facework: self-positive face maintenance, other-positive face maintenance, self-negative face maintenance, and other-negative face maintenance. Self-positive face maintenance involves the use of certain communication strategies to defend and protect one's need for inclusion and association. Other-positive face maintenance involves the use of certain communication strategies to defend and to support the other person's need for inclusion and association. Self-negative face maintenance involves the use of certain interaction strategies to give one's self freedom and space, and to protect self from other's infringement on one's autonomy. Finally, other-negative face maintenance involves the use of certain interaction strategies to signal respect for the other person's need for freedom, space, and disassociation.

As indicated earlier, Ting-Toomey (1988) uses individualism-collectivism as a way to explain cultural differences in face-negotiation and the management of conflict. Given the importance of this dimension of cultural variability to Ting-Toomey's theory (and our conceptualization presented below), we discuss individualism-collectivism in some detail before summarizing her theory.

Individualism-collectivism is the major dimension of cultural variability isolated by theorists across disciplines (e.g., Hofstede, 1980; Ito, 1989b; Kluckhohn & Strodtbeck, 1961; Marsella, DeVos, & Hsu, 1985; Triandis, 1988, 1990). Individualistic cultures emphasize the goals of the individual over group goals, while collectivistic cultures stress group goals over individual goals. In individualistic cultures, individuals assume responsibility for themselves and their immediate family. In collectivistic cultures, individuals belong to collectivities or ingroups which look after them in exchange for the individuals' loyalty (Hofstede, 1980). Following Triandis (1988), ingroups are "groups of people about whose welfare one is concerned, with whom one is willing to cooperate without demanding equitable returns, and separation from whom leads to discomfort or even pain" (p. 75).

Triandis (1988) contends that ingroups are more important in collectivistic than individualistic cultures. Lebra (1976), for example, points out that collectivism "involves cooperation and solidarity, and the sentimental desire for the warm feeling of *ittaikan* ("feeling of oneness") with fellow members of one's group" (p. 25) and that this feeling is shared widely in Japan.[5] Triandis argues that the larger the number of ingroups, the narrower the influence and the less the depth of influence. Since individualistic cultures have many specific ingroups, ingroups in individualistic cultures exert less influence on individuals' behavior than ingroups do in collectivistic cultures where there are a few general ingroups. Triandis' conceptualization also suggests that members of collectivistic cultures draw sharper distinctions between members of ingroups and outgroups, and perceive ingroup relationships to be more intimate than members of individualistic cultures.

Most scholars agree that the United States is an individualistic culture and Japan is a collectivistic culture.[6] While these terms are not heavily value laden in the United States, the translations of both terms are value laden in Japan. Ito (1989b), for example, points out that Japanese scholars do not use the translation of the term collectivism, *zentaishugi*, because it often is used to refer to dictatorial political systems. Rather, they use terms like group oriented (*shudanshugi*; Nakane, 1970, among others), relationalism (*aidagarashugi*; Kumon, 1982), contextualism (*kanjinshugi*; Hamaguchi, 1982), or inter-individualism (*saijinshugi*; Ito, 1989a). Ito

(1989b) also points out that the term used for individualism in Japanese, *kojinshugi*, also has negative connotations (e.g., selfishness).[7]

Given this overview of individualism-collectivism, we can now summarize the face aspects of Ting-Toomey's (1988) theory. Ting-Toomey contends that members of individualistic cultures like the United States express more self-face maintenance than members of collectivistic cultures like Japan. Members of collectivistic cultures, in contrast, express greater mutual-face and other-face maintenance than members of individualistic cultures. Ting-Toomey also argues that members of individualistic cultures use autonomy-preserving strategies (i.e., negative-face needs) when managing conflicts more than members of collectivistic cultures. Members of collectivistic cultures, on the other hand, use approval-seeking strategies (i.e., positive-face needs) more than members of individualistic cultures when managing conflict. She also contends that members of individualistic cultures tend to use direct face-negotiation strategies more than members of collectivistic cultures, while members of collectivistic cultures tend to use indirect face-negotiation strategies more than members of individualistic cultures.

Ting-Toomey, Gao, and colleagues (1991) tested part of the face portion of Ting-Toomey's (1988) theory.[8] The measure of face used in this study was developed by Baxter (1984) in the United States. Factor analysis of the items yielded two dimensions that they labelled self-face and other-face.[9] The results for Japan and the United States were inconsistent with the theoretical predictions for both self-face and other-face.[10] The Japanese respondents were more concerned with self-face than the respondents in the United States, while the respondents in the United States were more concerned with other-face than respondents in Japan. The results of this study are, in part, an artifact of the facework measurement used. The scale did not tap mutual-face (i.e., the interactive component of face), or the interdependent aspects of face isolated by Hu (1944) and Ho (1976). We believe that the study may have tapped the *taimen* reading of *kao*, but not the *mentsu* reading.

Two additional studies (Cole, 1989; Ting-Toomey, Trubisky et al., 1991) have examined aspects of face and face-negotiation in Japan and the United States. Cole (1989) interviewed Japanese students studying in the United States and North Americans regarding their conceptualizations of face. The interviews were conducted in English. Japanese definitions included honor, pride, claimed self-image, trustworthiness, individual standing or rank, politeness, respect extended by others, considerateness, and dignity. North American definitions included credibility, individual reputation, self-respect, ego, claimed position in interaction, appearance of strength, recognized positive worth, pride, status, lack of embarrassment, and self-defense. Japanese perceived they lost face when they were not able to maintain ingroup harmony (e.g., when they shamed or disgraced a friend or coworker). North Americans, in contrast, perceived they lost face when they personally failed (e.g., lost an argument).

Cole (1989) also found that Japanese perceive insults/criticisms and rude/inconsiderate behavior from others as face threats, while North Americans perceive threats to their credibility and/or self-image as face threats. Both groups, however, agreed that a face threat requires some self-protective action. Japanese saw allowing others to look good or take a prestigious position as giving face. The North Americans interviewed, in comparison, did not associate any particular behaviors with giving face. There were also differences in the situations individuals thought maintaining self-face was important. Japanese wanted to preserve self-face in private, informal, and intimate situations. North Americans, in contrast, wanted to maintain self-face in public, formal, and nonintimate settings.

As indicated earlier, Cole's (1989) study was conducted in English. Japanese and North American responses, therefore, must be considered as tapping aspects of face that emerge when communicating in English. The use of English in the interviews, however, influenced the way Japanese responded. Using English, for example, does not allow the interdependent nuances of face in the Japanese language to be manifested (see Wetzel, 1985, for a discussion of ingroup-outgroup issues in the Japanese language). Cole's study might have tapped aspects of the *taimen* reading of *kao*, but not the *mentsu* reading.

Ting-Toomey, Trubisky, and colleagues (1991) developed a facework typology using data from Japan and the United States. They asked students in the two countries how they would get a group member who had failed to perform adequately on a group project to redo his or her work. After giving the situation, Ting-Toomey, Trubisky and co-workers asked the respondents to describe the most polite and most impolite strategies they could use to gain compliance with their request, any why the strategies were polite or impolite. They then isolated facework themes in the respondents' answers to these questions. Four themes emerged: individual versus group orientation, directness and tone, face constituent (e.g., the way the face was affronted), and locus of concern.

Ting-Toomey, Trubisky, and colleagues' (1991) study suggests that there are some common facework themes in Japan and the United States. This study, however, may not have isolated interdependent aspects of face in Japan. The incident used to elicit responses, for example, involved members of an important ingroup in Japan (i.e., the members were all students at the same university), but the questions did not tap "mutual" aspects of face among the group members (i.e., how the face of a person making a request is interdependent with the person of whom the request is made and interdependent with the other group members).

To summarize, the concepts of face and facework appear to be affected by the individualism-collectivism dimension of cultural variability. The work Ting-Toomey, Gao, and colleagues (1991), Ting-Toomey, Trubisky, and colleagues (1991), and Cole (1989) provide initial data on how facework strategies are influenced by individualism-collectivism. While this line of work is important in understanding cultural differences in face and face work, the scales used and the questions asked do not appear to tap interdependent aspects of face.

Independent and Interdependent Face in Japan and the United States

In Western cultures, face is viewed as being "put on as the participants alternate the roles of performer and observer in the due course of interaction" (Choi & Choi, 1990, p. 8). In other words, Westerners have "independent face" (i.e., a person's face is independent of any other person's face). Face and facework arise in intrapersonal (private) or interpersonal (person-to-person) communication. Face negotiation (e.g., face-losing and face-saving) occurs in interpersonal situations (e.g., a person who threatens the face of another person and a person whose face is threatened). Westerners can engage in face-negotiation when only two people are involved in the interaction.

The Western concept of face lacks universal applicability because the concept of independent face is not relevant in non-Western cultures (e.g., those in Asia, South America). Matsumoto (1988), for example, contends that Brown and Levinson's (1978, 1987) positive/negative constituents of face is not relevant in Japan.[11] She argues that the Western notion of face consists "of the desire for the approval of wants and the desire for the preservation of one's territory [i.e., negative face want]" (p. 405). Mastsumoto goes on to point out that "Japanese do not have their own territory" (p. 405).[12] In Japanese culture, the importance of the position in relation to the others in one's group is emphasized more than the individual territory. The Japanese notion of face involves an "acknowledgement and maintenance of the relative position of others" (p. 405). Consistent with Hu (1944) and Ho (1976), Matsumoto, therefore, sees face in Japan as an interdependent phenomenon.

To further illustrate, Hwang (1987) contends that Chinese society and other similar societies such as Japan have different rules of social interaction from those of West. "In such societies, norms of reciprocity (*bao*) are intense, but these norms are heavily shaped by the hierarchically structured network of social relations (*guanxi*)" (p. 944). Reciprocity and social relations are negotiated through facework.

Choi and Choi (1990) suggest that the interpersonal character of Western face (e.g., Brown & Levinson, 1978, 1987; Goffman, 1955, 1957) is derived from the interaction between a participant who takes into account the performance and an another "independent" individual. Korean social face, *chemyon*, in contrast, is "based on somewhat *fixed* symbolic value systems of the society . . . a socially perceived, or expected quality of an individual in association with his/her particular social position or status" (Choi & Choi, 1990, p. 8; emphasis in original). "While the Western face performance is 'person-wise' social, the Korean *Che-Myon* activity is 'context-wise' social" (p. 18). In other words, Choi and Choi argue that a Korean's face is not independent of others, but rather it is interdependent with others (i.e., one person's face is interdependent with the face of others in his/her group). Face-negotiation occurs only when a person is interdependent with others (e.g., a person who threatens another's face, a person whose face is threatened, and a person who shares an interdependent self with the victim) when three or more persons are involved in Asian cultures (not all three have to be physically present).[13]

The diverse conceptualizations of face used in Western and Asian cultures are based on inconsistent metatheoretical approaches (e.g., rule, dramatism, or strategic approach), as well as different conceptualization of the self and the aim of communication in Western and Asian cultures. While cultural differences in individualism-collectivism are important, they cannot fully explain the conceptual differences of face across cultures alone. To accomplish this, it is necessary to incorporate cultural differences of self-conceptualizations (Kashima, 1989) into our conceptualization of individualism-collectivism. Markus and Kitayama's (1991) theoretical framework which isolates "the difference between a construal of the self as independent and a construal of the self as interdependent" (p. 224) provides a framework on the self that is consistent with Triandis' (1988, 1989) conceptualization of individualism-collectivism.

Markus and Kitayama (1991) contend that people in different cultures use different construals of the self: the independent and the interdependent construal of the self. While Markus and Kitayama draw on work in which the authors discuss individualism-collectivism (e.g., Hofstede, 1980; Schwartz & Bilsky, 1990), they do not link independent and interdependent construals of the self directly to individualism-collectivism. We believe, however, that there is a direct relationship: the independent construal of self *predominates* in individualistic cultures and the interdependent construal of self *predominates* in collectivistic cultures.

People in most Western (individualistic in our view) cultures use an independent construal of the self. The independent construal of self involves the view that an individual's self is a unique, independent entity. Geertz (1975), for example, illustrates this view when he describes the Western self "as a bounded, unique, more or less integrated motivational and cognitive universe, a dynamic center of awareness, emotion, judgment, and action organized into a distinctive whole and set contrastively both against other such wholes and against a social and natural background" (p. 48; see Johnson, 1985; Sampson, 1988; Waterman, 1981; for more detailed discussions).

Markus and Kitayama's (1991) view is schematically presented in figure 1. As can be seen in this figure, in the independent view of self, the self is separated from others. The self-representations (as indicated by the "x"s in figure 1) "usually

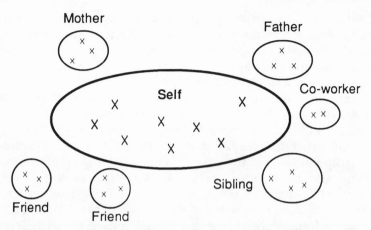

Fig. 1. Independent Self-Construal in the United States. Adapted from Markus and Kitayama (1991, p. 226).

have as their referent the individual desire, preference, attribute, or ability" (p. 226); that is, core conceptions, salient identities, self-schemata, personal identity, or personal self-esteem. Westerner's cultural "goal of independence requires construing oneself as an individual whose behavior is organized and made meaningful primarily by reference to one's own internal repertoire of thoughts, feelings, and action, rather than by reference to the thoughts, feelings, and actions of others" (p. 226). Johnson (1985), for example, defines the Western concept of self:

> as a *unitary phenomenon;* it is used to refer to a particular, individual person (or person-system) and not to a "personality" or to an aggregate of factors which "add up" to a person. The concept of self is typically separated into a nominative ("I") *self-as-subject,* and an accusative ("me") *self-as-object. Self-as-object* includes both the idea of *self as a social object to others and that of the self as a social (and psychological) object unto itself.* (p. 93; emphasis in original)

The important tasks of a person with an independent self-construal are to be unique, strive for her or his own goals, express self, and be direct (e.g., "say what your mean"; Markus and Kitayama, 1991). An individual's self-esteem is based in his or her ability to express him- or herself, and in her or his ability to validate her or his internal attributes (Markus & Kitayama, 1991).

Markus and Kitayama (1991) contend that people in many non-Western cultures such as Asian, African, Latin-American, and southern European cultures (collectivistic cultures in our view) use an interdependent construal of the self. "Experiencing interdependence entails seeing oneself as part of an encompassing social relationship and recognizing that one's behavior is determined, contingent on, and, to a large extent organized by what the actor perceives to be the thoughts, feelings, and actions of *others* in the relationship" (p. 227).[14] Hsu (1985) illustrates the importance of relations to others when he discusses why he uses the Chinese concept of *jen* instead of the Western concept of personality.

> I suggest the term *jen* advisedly because the Chinese conception of [hu]man (also shared by Japanese who pronounce the same Chinese word *jin*) is based on the *individual's transactions with his [her] fellow human beings.* When the Chinese say so-and-so "*ta pu shih jen*" (he [she] is not a *jen*), they do not mean this person is not a human animal; instead they mean that his [her] behavior in relation to other human beings is not acceptable. Consequently terms like "*hao jen*" (good *jen*), "*huai jen*" (bad *jen*), etc., follow the same meaning. (pp. 32–33)

The interdependent construal of self is presented in figure 2. As can be seen in this figure, the self intersects with others. The self-in-relation (as indicated by "x"s in figure 2) exists in the intersections of overlapping selves. The relationship between the self and others is not stable. The self-in-relation to specific others guides behavior in the specific social situation.[15] Depending on the situation, different aspects of the interdependent self will guide a person's behavior. If the behavior is taking place at home, the family aspects of the interdependent self will guide behavior; if the behavior is taking place on the job, the co-worker interdependent self will guide behavior. The other self-representations (as indicated by "x"s in figure 2) are less important than the self-in-relation in regulating observable behavior.

The important tasks of a person with an interdependent self-construal are to "fit-in" with the group, act in an appropriate fashion, promote other's goals, "occupy one's proper place," to be indirect, and "read other's mind" (Markus & Kitayama, 1991). The importance of fitting-in is illustrated by White and

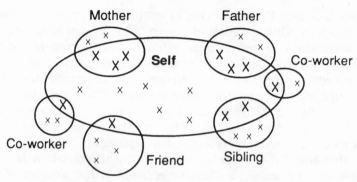

Fig. 2. Interdependent Self-Construal in Japan. Adapted from Markus and Kitayama (1991, p. 226).

LeVine's (1986) discussion of *sunao*, the characteristics Japanese parents value in children:

> A child that is *sunao* has not yielded his or her personal autonomy for the sake of cooperation; cooperation does not suggest giving up the self, as it may in the West; it implies that working with others is the appropriate way of expressing and enhancing the self. Engagement and harmony with others is, then, a positively valued goal and the bridge—to open hearted cooperation, as in *sunao*—is through sensitivity. (p. 58)

Markus and Kitayama (1991) also point out that "giving is not a sign of weakness, rather it reflects tolerance, self-control, flexibility, and maturity" (p. 229).

Self-esteem is based on one's ability to adjust to others, and one's ability to maintain harmony in the social context when an interdependent self-construal predominates (Markus & Kitayama, 1991). Miyanaga's (1991) description of interaction rituals in Japan illustrates this pattern. She points out that communicators'

> body movements, tone of voice, degree of avoidance of eye contact, laughter, smiles, serious expressions, and even the degree of body tension are, to a certain extent, carefully controlled to constitute cues.
>
> At the same time, a person tries as much as possible to catch the cues given by others. If a person keeps missing the given cues, he [she] will be judged "blunt" or "dull" (because he [she] is unreceptive), "impolite" (when it is judged that he

[she] is deliberately choosing to miss cues), or *gaijin mitai* (like a foreigner). High receptivity is admired. The Japanese word generally used to indicate such receptivity is *sasshi,* which literally means "to guess." It implies that one guesses the real intention of others in spite of their surface disguise. (p. 85)

Miyanaga goes on to point out that when ingroup member-ships are shared (i.e., there are interdependent self-construals), each partner understands when the other will follow behavioral norms and when the other will violate the be-havioral norms.

Hamaguchi's (1983) summary of the ways individuals view themselves in Japan and the United States is consistent with Markus and Kitayama's (1991) conceptualization of indepen-dent and interdependent self-construals.[16] In the United States,

an "individual" . . . holds a conviction that he [she] is a firmly established substance which is solely independent, and, therefore, cannot be invalidated by others. Also, he [she] is convinced that he [she] is the master of himself [herself], but at the same time he [she] is liable for his [her] own deeds. The individual objectifies such an assertion (that he [she] is un-doubtedly himself [herself]) and the sense of autonomy. (pp. 140–41)

Japanese, in contrast, view themselves contextually:

For the Japanese, "self" means the portion which is distrib-uted to him [her], according to the situation he [she] is in, from the living space shared between himself [herself] and the other person with whom he [she] had developed a mutually dependent relationship.

A reason why this self-consciousness of the Japanese is formed this way is probably that self and others are in a sym-biotic relationship, and that they believe that their beings de-pend largely on other being. . . . This relativistic "self" can easily be mistaken for being unindependent. . . . However, here, selves are "mutually dependent," and their spontaneous fulfillment of the needs are intentionally controlled. (p. 142)

While Hamaguchi does not use the terms, his descriptions of how individuals view themselves also is compatible with cultural differences in individualism-collectivism in Japan and the United States.

There is extensive evidence to support Markus and Kitayama's (1991) claim that the independent self-construal predominates in the United States and the interdependent construal predominates in Japan (e.g., Hess et al., 1986; Shikanai, 1978; Takata, 1987; Yoshida, Kojo, & Kaku, 1982). While we cannot summarize all of the research here, we highlight some of the research to lay the foundation for our discussion of face.[17] One important issue is that of conformity. Given Markus and Kitayama's conceptualization, greater conformity would be expected in Japan when the interdependent self-construal is activated than when it is not activated, and greater conformity would be expected in Japan when the interdependent self is activated than in the United States when the independent self is activated. The research supports this speculation. Williams and Sogon (1984) discovered that when confederates are members of Japanese respondents' ingroups, conformity is much higher than in Asch's (1956) original study. Frager (1970) also found that when the confederates are strangers to Japanese respondents (i.e., a situation that should not activate the interdependent self-construal), conformity is lower than in Asch's study.

Markus and Kitayama's (1991) conceptualization also suggests that Japanese should be more concerned with engaging in socially appropriate behavior and modifying their behavior based on their relationships to others than North Americans. A recent study (Gudykunst et al., in press) designed to develop a measure of self-monitoring appropriate in Japan supports this speculation. Gudykunst and his colleagues found that when monitoring their behavior, people in the United States focus on how they can change their behavior to meet generalized expectations of others in the situation (i.e., how a prototypic person would behave). Japanese, in contrast, focus on how they can behave appropriately given their relationship to specific people in the situation.

The nature of the self-construal also should influence the way individuals manage topics and take turns in conversations. Yamada (1990), for example, found that Japanese "take short turns, distribute their turns relatively evenly, and continue to distribute their turns evenly regardless of who initiates a topic" (p. 291). Yamada also discovered that Japanese organize topics in conversations interdependently, while North American organize their topics independently.

Before discussing independent and interdependent face in Japan and the United States, it is necessary to return to a point we made earlier. At the beginning of this section, we pointed that independent construals of the self *predominate* in individualistic cultures and interdependent construals of the self *predominate* in collectivistic cultures. It is important to recognize, however, that everyone has both an independent and interdependent construal of the self.[18] Further, people with predominately interdependent construals of the self exist in individualistic cultures like the United States and people with predominately independent construals of the self exist in collectivistic cultures like Japan. We believe that the critical issue is which self-construal individuals use in guiding their behavior in a particular situation. There are two rationales to support this argument—one based on individualistic and collectivistic values, and the other based on the components of the self-concept.

Schwartz (1990) argues that the individualistic and collectivistic values do not necessarily conflict. With respects to individualistic values, he points out that

> hedonism (enjoyment), achievement, self-direction, social power, and stimulation values all serve self interests of the individual, but not necessarily at the expense of any collectivity. . . . These same values might be promoted by leaders or members of collectivities as goals for their group. (p. 143)

With respect to collectivistic values, Schwartz indicates that

> prosocial, restrictive conformity, security, and tradition all focus on promoting the interests of others. It is other people, constituting a collective, who benefit from the actor's concern for them, self-restraint, care for their security, and respect shared traditions. This does not necessarily occur at the expense of the actor. (p. 143)

Individuals, therefore, can hold both individualistic and collectivistic values, but one set of values tends to predominate. Similarly, cultures are simultaneously individualistic and collective, but one form tends to predominate.

The components of the self-concept also suggest that everyone has both independent and interdependent construals of the self. The self-concept involves "the set of cognitive representations of the self available to a person" (Turner et al., 1987, p. 44). Turner and his associates argue that everyone uses three basic self-categorizations to define him- or herself: human identity, social identity, and personal identity. Our human identity involves those features that we share with all other humans (in contrast to other forms of life). Social identity is based on our ingroup-outgroup categorizations and includes those self-representations we share with members of our ingroups. More formally, Tajfel (1981) defines social identity as "that aspect of the individuals' self-concept which derives from their knowledge of their membership in a social group (or groups) together with the value and emotional significance attached to that membership" (p. 255). Our personal identity involves those aspects of the self that define us as unique individuals. We believe that personal identity is comparable to an independent construal of the self, while social identity is comparable to an interdependent construal of the self.[19] Trafimow, Triandis, and Goto's (1991) research suggests that everyone has private self and collective self cognitions and that these cognitions are stored in different locations in memory.

In individualistic cultures like the United States, an independent construal of the self and personal identity predominate to influence behavior.[20] In intergroup situations, however, behavior is based mainly on social identity and individuals' interdependent construal of the self guides their behavior. The interdependent construal of the self also is a theme in some religious groups (e.g., Quakers), in small towns, and in rural areas (Bellah et al., 1985). Further, Gilligan (1982) argues that women in the United States are socialized to be interdependent, while men are socialized to be independent. In addition, there appears to be a trend in social science to view the self in relational terms (e.g., Curtis, 1991; Elias, 1991).

The interdependent construal of self in individualistic cultures is diagrammed in figure 3. In comparing figures 2 and 3, it should be noted that the amount of overlap in the self-construals differ with the overlap being larger in collectivistic cultures (i.e., figure 2) than in individualistic cultures (i.e., figure 3).

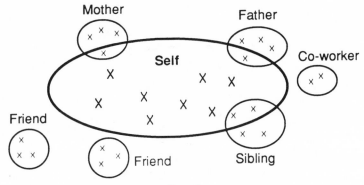

Fig. 3.
Interdependent Self-Construal in the United States.

In collectivistic cultures like Japan, an interdependent
construal of self and social identity predominate to influence
behavior.[22] In some situations, however, behavior can be based
on personal identity and individuals' independent construal of
self will guide their behavior. To illustrate, Befu (1977, 1980a,
1980b, 1989), one of the major critiques of the group model in
Japan, argues that there is a strong sense of "personhood"
in Japan:

> A reexamination of empirical cases of the so-called "group ori-
> entation" in Japan would probably reveal that group orienta-
> tion is more apparent than real, and that behind the
> appearance of group solidarity one will find each member be-
> ing motivated more by personal ambition than by his [her]
> blind loyalty to the group. Put another way, in many cases
> Japanese are [or anyone else is, for that matter] loyal to their
> groups because it pays to be loyal. (1977, p. 87)

Mouer and Sugimoto (1986) also argue that there are numerous ways that the autonomous individual (i.e., independent
self-construal) is manifested in Japanese society. They also
point out that there is a gravitation toward individual activity
during leisure time.[23]

Cousins' (1989) research suggests that Japanese independent self may be highly contexualized. When asked to describe
themselves without a context, Japanese used more social role
descriptors than North Americans, and the North Americans
used more psychological attributes than the Japanese. When

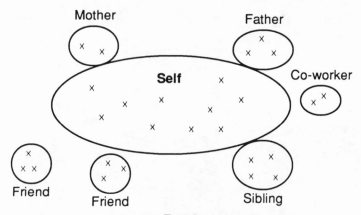

Fig. 4.
Independent Self-Construal in Japan.

asked to describe themselves in a specific context (i.e., at home), however, the Japanese used more unique psychological attributes than the North Americans.

The independent construal of self in collectivistic cultures is diagrammed in figure 4. In comparing figures 1 and 4, it should be noted that the "independence" differs. In figure 1, others are totally independent of the self (note space between ellipses). In figure 4, others are not as "independent" of self as in figure 1 (note the ellipses are touching). We believe that the independent self-construal will guide behavior in Japan when individuals are dealing with outgroup members with whom they do not have ongoing relationships (e.g., strangers).

While an independent construal of self exists in Japan, the interdependent construal predominates.[24] Similarly, the interdependent construal exists in the United States, but the independent construal predominates. Table 1 contains a summary of the implications of independent and interdependent self-construals.

Before proceeding, it is important to make an additional point about independent and interdependent self-construals (read personal and social identity). Deaux (1991) argues that identities vary along at least two dimensions: desirable-undesirable and voluntary-involuntary. Voluntary identities require "more effort to maintain" (p. 79) than involuntary ones. Also Deaux suggests that the desirability dimension "influences the degree to which that identity will be proclaimed or hidden—will serve as a source of self-esteem or be a cause of shame" (p. 79). Deaux points out that some people have a "master" identity with other identities subsumed under it, while others may give equal importance to their identities. We believe that members of collectivistic cultures in general, and Japanese in particular, are likely to treat their social identity associated with their major ingroup as a master identity that is desirable and involuntary.

When the independent self-construal predominates, individuals base their personal self-esteem on their ability to express themselves and in the validation of their internal attributes (Markus & Kitayama, 1991). When the interdependent self construal predominates, individuals base their collective self-esteem on their ability to adjust and maintain harmony with others (Markus & Kitayama, 1991). Self-esteem can be derived from both personal and social identities (Crocker & Luhtanen, 1990). It, therefore, is plausible to talk about personal and collective self-esteem. It is important to recognize, however, that an individual's self-esteem is a combination of both personal and collective self-esteem. As Josephs (1991) points out:

> On the one hand, self-esteem is based on fitting in, being accepted, pleasing others, and gaining approval for meeting the expectations of others. On the other hand, self-esteem is based upon realizing one's unique potentialities; being an individual in one's own right; and having others recognize, respect, affirm, support, and encourage one's personal talents and individual uniqueness. (pp. 8–9)

He goes on to point out that if self-esteem is based only on fitting in, it can lead to "mindless conformity"; if it is based only on uniqueness, it can lead to "social alienation." "A balance must be achieved between fitting in and being an individual in one's own right" (p. 9). The balance, however, will be different in individualistic and collectivistic cultures.

While the predominate locus of self-esteem differs in Japan and the United States, the general process of managing threats to self-esteem appears to be similar. When individuals perceive a threat to their self-esteem, they respond emotionally by feeling shame or some emotion associated with shame (e.g., embarrassment, humiliation; Scheff, 1990). Scheff argues that the feelings of pride and shame are the fundamental emotions, and they "signal" the state of our social bonds. Feeling pride

Table 1. INDEPENDENT AND INTERDEPENDENT
SELF-CONSTRUALS AND FACE IN JAPAN AND THE
UNITED STATES

Self or Face Issue	Euro American Independent Self and Face in the United States	Interdependent Self and Face in Japan
Definition of Self	Separate from others in the social context; focus on personal identity	Connected with others in context; social identity predominates
Structure of Self-Construal	Unitary, relatively stable	Flexible, social identity changes with context
Important Features of Self-Construals	Internal, private (based on abilities, thoughts, and feelings)	External, public (based on roles, relationships)
Interaction Tasks	Be unique	Belong, fit in
	Self-actualize, express personal identity	Engage in appropriate behavior; occupy one's proper place
	Work toward personal goals	Work toward group goals
	Self-evaluation; social comparison	Self-definition; relationships define self
Basis of Self-Esteem	Ability to express self; validation of internal abilities (personal)	Ability to adjust to and maintain harmony with others (collective)
Speech Acts	Direct speech acts ("say what you mean")	Indirect speech acts ("read other's mind")
Expression of Emotions	Direct expression of emotions	Indirect expression of emotions
Nonverbal Behavior	Unique explicit	Group implicit
Boundary Regulation	Individual-based	Group-based
Emotional Response to Self-Esteem Threat	Shame	Shame
Face Concern	Independent self-face, independent other-face, independent mutual-face	Interdependent mutual self-face, interdependent mutual other-face, interdependent mutual group-face

Table 1. (continued)

Self or Face Issue	Euro American Independent Self and Face in the United States	Interdependent Self and Face in Japan
Face Need	Autonomy, boundary	Inclusion, approval
Moves in Facework	Face-maintaining, face-defending, face-saving	Face-maintaining, face-protecting, face-saving

Source: Portions of the table are adapted from Markus and Kitayama (1991) and Ting-Toomey (1988).

indicates an intact, secure social bond. Feeling shame, in contrast, indicates a severed or threatened social bond.[25] While the general process of managing threats to self-esteem is similar, the conditions under which Japanese and North Americans experience threats to their self-esteem differ. In the United States, shame is felt most frequently when there is a threat to personal self-esteem. In Japan, shame is felt most frequently when there is a threat to collective self-esteem.

We contend that, in addition to the predominate self-construal and locus of threat to self-esteem, the locus of face also differs in Japan and the United States. For Euro Americans in the United States, face is located in the independent self. As figure 5 suggests, when two people communicate they must deal with each others' independent face during their interaction. Maintaining *independent self-face,* therefore, is an issue that must be addressed in all interactions since all interactions involve the independent self-construal (i.e., personal identity). In interactions in the United States, individuals also are concerned with the other person's *independent other-face,* and *independent mutual-face* issues. While other-face and mutual-face are the issues, the major face need that individuals are addressing is that of autonomy or establishing boundaries. Individuals try to maintain, defend, and save their independent self-face.[26]

In individualistic cultures like the United States we would expect slightly different patterns of face-negotiation in intragroup (i.e., involving ingroup members) and intergroup (i.e., ingroup-outgroup) situations. In intragroup situations, we expect Euro Americans to be more concerned with independent self-face than with independent other-face, although they will still be concerned with independent other-face. In intergroup

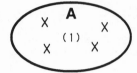 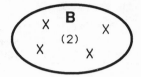

Fig. 5. Independent Face-Construal in Interpersonal Situations in the United States. With "A" as the referent: (1) = Independent self-face; (2) = Independent other-face.

situations where there is an ongoing relationship (i.e., it is expected that they will interact in the future) between the individuals involved, we expect Euro Americans to be relatively equally concerned with independent self- and other-face. In intergroup situations where there is *not* an ongoing relationship between the individuals involved (i.e., the participants do not expect to interact in the future), we expect that Euro Americans will be concerned more with independent self-face than with independent other-face.

In Japan, face (*mentsu*) is located at the intersection of interdependent selves. Figure 6 illustrates the "typical" face situation when two people from different groups are interacting. Person A is a member of one group (e.g., organization, university) and he or she shares part of his or her self with members of his or her group. Person B is a member of a different group and she or he shares part of her or his self with other members of her or his group. The parts that are shared are illustrated by the large "x"s in the diagram (small "x"s indicate parts of the selves not shared). Since face is an interdependent phenomenon, it is not possible to talk about *independent* self-face. The face that is at stake for person A is his or her *interdependent mutual self-face.* Person A, however, would also be concerned about the face that person B shares with other members of her or his group, what we call *interdependent mutual other-face.* There also is an area where all group members self construals overlap that we label interdependent self-group-face and interdependent other-group-face (see figure 7 for illustration). The major face need being addressed is one of inclusion or approval.

In intergroup situations where there is an ongoing relationships between the groups involved, we expect that Japanese will be concerned relatively equally with interdependent mutual self-face, interdependent self-group-face, as well as

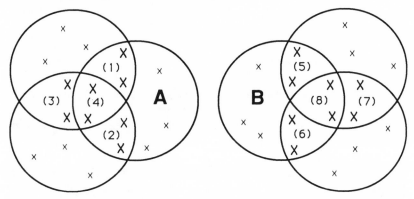

Fig. 6. Interdependent Face-Construal in Intergroup Situations in Japan. With "A" as the referent: (1), (2) = Interdependent mutual-self-face; (3), (5), (6), (7) = Interdependent mutual-other-face; (4) = Interdependent self-group-face; (8) = Interdependent other-group-face.

interdependent mutual-other-face and interdependent other-group-face. In intergroup situations where there is not an on-going relationship between the individuals involved, we expect that Japanese will be concerned more with interdependent mutual self-face and interdependent self-group-face than with interdependent mutual-other-face and interdependent other-group-face.

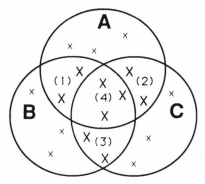

Fig. 7. Interdependent Face-Construal in Intragroup Situations in Japan. With "A" as the referent: (1), (2) = Interdependent mutual-self-face; (3) = Interdependent mutual-other-face; (4) = Interdependent self-group-face.

It is important to note here that the other members of the group do *not* have to be physically present in the situation for interdependent mutual self- or other-face to be threatened. It is only necessary that the other members may find out what happened that the person involved in the interaction behaved inappropriately. As Matsumoto (1988) points out, "loss of face is associated with the perception by others that one has not comprehended and acknowledged the structure and hierarchy of the group" (p. 405).

While the "typical" interaction in Japan where face issues arise is intergroup in nature, face issues also can arise in intragroup situations. Figure 7 illustrates a three person group with each members self overlapping the other members selves. Note that there are four areas of overlap. In the diagram, we can isolate A's interdependent mutual self-face with B (area 1; note that this is also B's mutual interdependent self-face with A), A's interdependent mutual self-face with person C (area 3), B's interdependent mutual self-face with C (area 4), and interdependent self-group-face (area 2). We believe, however, that the interdependent self-group-face can be threatened only in an intergroup situation, and, therefore, it is not an issue in intragroup situations. In intragroup situations, we expect that Japanese will be concerned equally with interdependent mutual-other-face and interdependent mutual-self-face.

There is one additional situation in Japan that needs to be addressed; that is, the situation when individuals are interacting based predominately on their independent self construals. This situation is diagrammed in figure 8. Situations where individuals would interact based mainly on their independent self-construals include, but are not necessarily limited to, interaction in a situation where no one else is known and no other members of an ingroup are present (e.g., traveling in another culture). In these types of situations the other members of the group are not physically present (and, therefore, are not drawn as intersecting circles, but rather as touching circles), and they would not necessarily become aware of anything that happens during the interaction unless the person involved chooses to tell them. One Japanese proverb illustrates the processes involved here: *Tabi no haji wa kakisute* (literally "the traveler easily discards his/her sense of shame"). The proverb illustrates that outside their social networks, Japanese do not need to worry about shame, because the shame involved does not lead to a loss of face (*mentsu*). When the independent self-

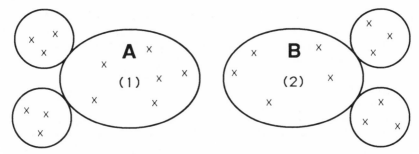

Fig. 8. Face When Independent Self-Construal Predominates in Japan. With "A" as the referent: (1) = Independent self-self; (2) = Independent other-self.

construal predominates, only the "appearance one presents to others" reading of *kao* is applicable (*taimen*).

There is one additional issue with respect to face that needs to be discussed, the time framework within which face is negotiated. In individualistic cultures like the United States, relationships do not necessarily last throughout one's life (see Gudykunst & Ting-Toomey, 1988, for a discussion of different orientations toward relationships). Individuals, therefore, are concerned with negotiating face in the immediate situation in which an encounter is taking place. In collectivistic cultures, in contrast, ingroup relationships tend to be maintained throughout one's life. The negotiation of face, then, is not limited to the immediate situation, but rather it is a long-term concern for the life of the relationship and the social networks in which individuals are embedded.

As suggested earlier, the concept of face allows several concepts used in *nihonjinron* analyses to be linked in explaining Japanese communication. To begin, the major face need for Japanese is inclusion and approval of the ingroup. Inclusion and approval are insured, in part, by following the rules of the situation (see Edgerton, 1985, for a discussion of the importance of rules in Japanese society) and/or engaging in ritualistic behavior. Lebra (1976), for example, argues that ritualized behavior allows a person to maintain his or her face, as well as the face of the person with whom he or she is interacting.[27] She goes on to point out that

> face is most vulnerable in unpredictable situations. The most common means of keeping it safe, then, is to minimize the

> options and uncertainties that might arise in a situation. Rit-
> ualism is the answer. Ritualism refers to rigid, meticulous
> control of interaction behavior in a predetermined way so as
> to prevent embarrassing surprises. (p. 125)

Engaging in ritualistic behavior allows one to occupy one's
"proper place."

The importance of occupying one's proper place in Japanese culture is emphasized by Lebra (1976) when she argues
that "by proper place occupancy I mean one's awareness of the
place assigned to one in a social group, institution, or society
as a whole; one's capacity and willingness to fill all social obligations attached to that place; and one's claim to recognition of
that place by others" (p. 67). Lebra uses the concept of *bun*
(meaning "portion," "share," or part") to describe Japanese interdependence. She isolates three implications of *bun:*

> First, the individual is conceived as a fraction. To the extent
> that he [she] derives his [her] self-identity from his [her] *bun*
> he [she] does not count as an integer but only as a part or frac-
> tion of the whole.
>   Second, *bun*-holders are interdependent. The individual
> as a *bun*-holder, cannot be self-reliant but must be dependent
> on other *bun*-holders. The awareness of one's self-sufficiency
> and interdependence with others is an essential concomitant
> of the *bun* concept. Third, every member of society is sup-
> posed to be a *bun*-holder. While an individual counts only as
> a fraction and depends on other individuals, every individual
> is provided with such a fraction, which makes his [her] life
> meaningful. (pp. 67–68)

Matsumoto (1988) argues that concern for others and one's relationship to them is a sign of maturity in Japan. She also contends that Brown and Levinson's (1978) negative face (i.e.,
being unimpeded in one's action) is not applicable because of
the importance of fitting in and maintaining harmony in
Japan.

Hendry (1987) argues that "it is in choosing the appropriate 'face' for a particular occasion that one is able to successfully fulfil one's social role in the world" (p. 42).[28] In Japan, if a
person maintains his or her *bun*, he or she cannot loose face
within the ingroup or threaten the face of another ingroup
member. If a person exceeds her or his *bun*, however, she or he
can loose face and/or threaten other member's interdependent
mutual face.

To allow Japanese to fit in and maintain harmony with their group, indirect speech acts and taciturnity are used in doing facework. Hamaguchi (1977) argues that Japanese taciturnity implies that "people fear that self assertion may possibly open up cracks in a friendly relationship with those people who form the very basis of one's own subsistence" (pp. 127–8). Japanese make several distinctions that are relevant to maintaining harmony in their relations with others: *koteki* (public) versus *shiteki* (private), *soto* (outside) versus *uchi* (inside), *omote* (front) versus *ura* (behind), *tatemae* (overt principle) versus *honne* (real intent), *giri* (obligation) versus *ninjo* (human feeling).[29] Doi (1986), for example, suggests that *tatemae* "refers to conventions created by people on the basis of consensus. . . . [It] always implies the existence of a group of people in its background who assent to it" (p. 36). He goes on to point out that *honne* refers to the "fact" that while members of the group may consent to the *tatemae*, "each have their own motives and opinions that are distinct from it, and that they hold these in the background" (p. 37).

Maintaining face requires that *tatemae*, not *honne*, be expressed in public. Hendry (1987), for example, argues that in Japan a person must

> either be co-operative or be left out, either be happy or laughed at as "strange" and "peculiar." But this co-operative individual is not losing its *individuality* or individual identity by participating in group activities. It is merely demonstrating one of the "faces" it learns to have for different situations. This "face" is part of the *tatemae* or "public" behavior appropriate in this particular context, and an individual will have several such "faces" for different situations. These different "faces" are reflected in different speech forms used on different occasions, and none of them negates the existence of a complete self using them all. (p. 50, emphasis in original)

Hendry goes on to point out that if Japanese fail to fulfil their duties (e.g., not meet obligations based on *giri*), they will lose face. A Japanese who points out that another person has not met his or her obligations, however, would also lose face.

To summarize, the conceptualization of face is different in Japan and the United States. In the United States individuals focus on meeting their need for autonomy and establishing boundaries by maintaining their independent self- and other-face, as well as mutual-face when they communicate. In Japan individuals focus on meeting their need for inclusion and approval by maintaining their interdependent mutual self- and other-face when they communicate. Face is more of a concern in uncertain situations in Japan than in the United States. In the United States individuals are concerned with maintaining face in the immediate situation more than over the course of a relationship. In Japan individuals are concerned with maintaining face over the course of a relationship more than in the immediate situation.

Table 2 contains a summary of our argument in the form of propositions. Given that there has been virtually no research on face (*mentsu*) in Japan or the United States that has taken into consideration the issues raised here, the propositions should be considered hypotheses for future research. The propositions proposed here generally are compatible with Ting-Toomey's (1988) theory. The present propositions, however, differ in several respects. First, the propositions involve drawing a distinction between independent and interdependent face. Second, the propositions are based on the assumption that there is no conceptual equivalence between independent face in individualistic cultures and interdependent face in collectivistic cultures. Third, given the lack of conceptual equivalence, the propositions proposed here suggest that researchers must make comparisons within cultures rather than cross-cultural comparisons in studying face.

The propositions proffered here also are compatible with those proposed by Kim (1993). While she does not differentiate independent from interdependent face, Kim isolates interactive constraints on facework in individualistic and collectivistic cultures. She argues that in comparison to members of individualistic cultures, members of collectivistic cultures (1) are concerned more with "the perceived importance of face support in the pursuit of primary goals," (2) have higher thresholds "for 'acceptable' levels of face support," and (3) use more strategies that "involve maximizing the face support constraint" (pp. 144–145). We would argue, however, that Kim's propositions require slight reformulation to be totally consistent with those proposed here. Minimally, each of her propositions must be limited to those relationships in collectivistic cultures in which individuals share an interdependent self construal. The propositions, for example, would not be appli-

Table 2. SUMMARY OF PROPOSITIONS ON FACE IN JAPAN AND THE UNITED STATES

1: The independent self-construal serves as the major generative mechanism for behavior in individualistic cultures; the interdependent self-construal serves as the major generative mechanism for behavior in collectivistic cultures.

1a: The independent self-construal serves as a generative mechanism for behavior more than the interdependent self-construal for Euro Americans in the United States, however, the interdependent self-construal does serve as a generative mechanism for behavior but to a lesser degree.

1b: The interdependent self-construal serves as a generative mechanism for behavior more than the independent self-construal in Japan, however, the independent self-construal does serve as a generative mechanism for behavior but to a lesser degree.

2: Personal self-esteem is important in influencing behavior in individualistic cultures; collective self-esteem is important in influencing behavior in collectivistic cultures.

2a: Personal self-esteem is more important in influencing behavior for Euro Americans in the United States than collective self-esteem.

2b: Collective self-esteem is more important in influencing behavior in Japan than personal self-esteem.

3: Shame (and shame related emotions such as humiliation, embarrassment) is the predominant emotional response to threats to personal or collective self-esteem.

3a: Euro Americans in the United States experience shame when their personal self-esteem is threatened more than when their collective self-esteem is threatened.

3b: Japanese experience shame when their collective self-esteem is threatened more than when their personal self-esteem is threatened.

4: The need for autonomy and boundaries is the major face need in individualistic cultures; the need for inclusion and approval is the major face need in collectivistic cultures.

4a: The need for autonomy and establishing boundaries is more important in facework for Euro Americans in the United States than the need for inclusion and approval, however, the need for inclusion and approval must still be met.

4b: The need for inclusion and approval is more important in facework in Japan than the need for autonomy and establishing boundaries, however, the need for autonomy and establishing boundaries must still be met.

5: Independent face is important in individualistic cultures; interdependent face is important in collectivistic cultures.

5a: In intragroup situations in the United States, Euro Americans will be concerned with independent self-face more than with independent other-face or independent mutual-face.

Table 2. (*continued*)

5b: In intragroup situations, Japanese will be concerned equally with interdependent mutual-other-face and interdependent mutual-self-face.

5c: In intergroup situations where there is an ongoing relationship between
the individuals involved, Euro Americans in the United States will be
concerned equally with independent self-face, independent other-face,
and independent mutual-face.

5d: In intergroup situations where there is *not* an ongoing relationship between the individuals involved, Euro Americans in the United States will
be concerned with independent self-face more than with independent
other-face or independent mutual-face.

5e: In intergroup situations where there is an ongoing relationship between
the groups, Japanese will be concerned equally with interdependent mutual self-face, interdependent mutual other-face, and interdependent mutual group-face.

5f: In intergroup situations where there is *not* an ongoing relationship between the groups, Japanese will be concerned with interdependent mutual self-face and interdependent mutual group-face more than with
interdependent mutual other-face.

6: In individualistic cultures, individuals are concerned with negotiating
independent self- and other-face in certain (i.e., where others' behavior is
relatively predictable) and uncertain (i.e., where others' behavior is relatively
unpredictable) situations; in collectivistic cultures, individuals are
concerned with interdependent mutual self-face in uncertain situations.

6a: Euro Americans in the United States are concerned with negotiating independent self-face in uncertain and certain situations equally.

6b: Japanese are concerned with negotiating interdependent mutual self-
face in uncertain situations more than in certain situations.

6c: Japanese are concerned with negotiating interdependent mutual other-
face in certain and uncertain situations equally.

7. In individualistic cultures, individuals are concerned with negotiating
face in the immediate situation; in collectivistic cultures individuals are concerned with negotiating face in the relationship over the life of the relationship.

7a: Euro Americans in the United States are concerned with negotiating independent self-face in the immediate situation more than with their face
over the life of the relationship.

7b: Japanese are concerned with negotiating interdependent mutual self-
and other-face over the life of a relationship more than in the immediate
situation.

cable when the independent self construal predominates (e.g., with outgroup members with whom individuals do not have an ongoing relationship, with close friends). It also is necessary to recognize that in collectivistic cultures individuals do not have to do all of their facework in the immediate encounter, but rather they have to maintain face over the life of the relationship.

Conclusion

As indicated earlier, the term for face in Japan, *kao*, has at least three different usages: (1) to refer to the physical part of the body, (2) to refer to one's personal name or status, and (3) to refer to social face. The social face meaning can be further subdivided to refer to the appearance one presents to others (*taimen*, a usage similar to Goffman's); and *mentsu*, interdependent face (a usage similar to Ho's and Hu's). Research to date has not examined *mentsu* in Japan. Future research is necessary to determine if *mentsu* operates only when the interdependent self-construal is affecting behavior or if it operates when the independent self-construal is affecting behavior in Japan. It appears that *mentsu* is an issue only when the interdependent self-construal is the generative mechanism for behavior. The appearance one presents to others (*taimen*) aspects of *kao*, in contrast, should be an issue when the independent self-construal is a generative mechanism for behavior.

Similarly, research is needed to determine if face is an issue when the independent self-construal *and* the interdependent self-construal are generative mechanisms for behavior in the United States. It appears that the face associated with the independent self-construal in the United States is different from the face associated with the interdependent self-construal (e.g., in the same ways that personal and collective self-esteem differ). There are several related issues that need to be investigated. One involves looking at face associated with particular identities—does face (or face maintenance strategies) differ depending on the identity guiding behavior? Based on Deaux's (1991) work, it could be speculated that the strategies individuals use to negotiate face will differ depending on whether the identity is perceived as desirable or undesirable, as well as whether it is perceived as voluntary or involuntary. Further, the strategies individuals use to maintain face should differ if they have a "master" identity or if they weigh their identities relatively equally.

Studying these issues across cultures is not easy. First, there are not clear terminological equivalences for the various "types" of face isolated here in English and Japanese (e.g., there is not an English equivalent of *mentsu;* face as used in English is closer to the *taimen* meaning of *kao*). Further, we believe that *mentsu* is not the same as the face that would operate in when the interdependent self-construal is a generative mechanism for behavior in the United States. In this situation in the United States, individuals may share a social identity, but they are not necessarily interdependent.

Another issue that has to be addressed in future research is that there are individuals in Japan whose independent self-construal is the primary generative mechanism for behavior, and there are people in the United States for whom the interdependent self-construal is the predominant generative mechanism for behavior. To illustrate, our discussion of the independent self-construal in the United States has been limited to Euro Americans. Members of other ethnic groups (e.g., Asian Americans, Native Americans) may use an interdependent self-construal more than an independent self construal. Similarly, as Gilligan's (1982) research suggests, women may use an interdependent self construal more than men in the United States. The generalizations for Japan may apply to those individuals in the United States whose behavior is based on an interdependent self-construal. It may not apply to artists, entrepreneurs, and other individualists in Japan (Miyanaga, 1991).

To complicate matters further, the self-construal serving as a generative mechanism for behavior can change within an encounter. To illustrate, an encounter between two individuals may begin as intergroup in nature (i.e., interdependent self-construals would predominate in both Japan and the United States), but change to interpersonal during the conversation. When the encounter becomes interpersonal, the independent self-construal would probably continue to operate in Japan. The independent self-construal would tend to predominant in Japan in close friendships or in situations where the person is totally unknown.

To conclude, there are several major challenges for future researchers in Japan and the United States. Researchers in both cultures must isolate situations in which the independent and interdependent self-construals predominate. Once these situations are isolated, it is necessary to determine the nature of face and facework that are manifested in these situations. It is important that researchers examine how participants' identities influence their facework in specific situations. Only when this groundwork is completed will we be in a position to discuss conceptual equivalence of face and facework in Japan and the United States.

Notes

General note: We want to thank Stella Ting-Toomey for her comments on an earlier version of the paper. We also want to thank Hiroshi Ota for his comments during discussions of the paper.

1. See Dale (1986) and Mouer and Sugimoto (1986) for critiques of this approach.

2. The characters for the terms we are using are as follows:

kao: 顔	*mentsu:* 面子
menmoku: 面目	*taimen:* 対面

3. Masatsugu (1982) does not differentiate the different meanings of *kao* in his discussion of "face," but his conclusion is compatible with the argument we present below: " 'Face' in the emotionally charged Japanese language contains the notion of self directed toward others" (p. 51). Hendry (1987) and Lebra (1976) uses the term face, but their usage tends to fit the appearance one presents to others (*taimen*) meaning of social face. Some of their conclusions, however, are applicable to *mentsu*. Tasker (1987) incorrectly equates face with *tatemae* (a Japanese concept we discuss in the last section).

4. We discuss independent and interdependent face in detail in the final section. It is necessary, however, to use these terms as "markers" of the differences in approaches to the study of face prior to our detailed discussion.

5. Lebra's (1976) contention that *ittaikan* is shared widely in Japan should not be taken to imply that Japan is a homogeneous culture. Miyanaga (1991) argues that there is

antagonism between those from the eastern and western regions of Japan; those from the west often complain that they never feel accepted in Tokyo, located in the east. In western Japan, people from the east are referred to as *bando mono,* literally "a person from the east," which carries a derogatory connotation of "uncivilized." In the same way that ethnic background carries associative connotations in [North] Amer-

ica, regional (prefectural) backgrounds are socially significant to the Japanese. (p. 12)

Miyanaga goes on to point out that all Japanese speak two "kinds" of
Japanese: standardized and their own dialect or accent. Standard
Japanese is spoken in social situations, but individuals use their own
dialect or accent with members of their ingroups.

6. Triandis, Bontempo, Villareal, Asai, and Lucci (1988) tested
several of the predictions regarding ingroups in Japan and the United
States. They discovered that Japanese students only report that they
would pay attention to the views of their co-workers more than students in the United States. They conclude that "the Japanese feel honored when their ingroups are honored and pay attention to the views
of some, but not all, ingroups; they subordinate their goals to the
goals of some ingroups, but they do not conform much" (p. 333). One
partial explanation for Triandis and colleagues' finding is that they
did not take into consideration the degree to which the respondents
identified with their culture. Gudykunst, Nishida, Chung, and Sudweeks (1992) found that strength of cultural identity and perceived
typicality influence the individualistic and collectivistic values students in Japan and the United States hold. Yamaguchi (1990) found
that collectivism among Japanese is associated positively with sensitivity to rejection, affiliative tendency, and self-monitoring, while it is
associated negatively with need for uniqueness and internal locus of
control.

7. Critiques of the group model of Japanese society (e.g., Befu,
1980a, 1980b) suggest that acceptance of this model with its emphasis on harmony and *giri* (voluntary feelings of obligation) leads scholars to overlook Japanese "personhood" (e.g., concepts such as *seishin*
or *jinkaku*; see also Hamaguchi's 1977 discussion of interpersonal-
ness). Befu, for example, argues that *seishin* deals with "individuals
qua individuals." "*Seishin* has to do with one's spiritual disposition,
one's inner strength, which results from character building and self-
discipline" (Befu, 1980b, 180–81; see Rohlen, 1973, for a discussion
of this concept). It also should be noted that focusing only on the individualistic tendencies in the United States leads scholars to overlook
collectivistic aspects of the culture (for a recent discussion see Bellah,
Madsen, Sullivan, Swidler, and Tipton, 1985, 1991; Wuthnow, 1991).
Recent work (e.g., Gudykunst, Nishida, Chung, and Sudweeks, 1992;
Miyanaga, 1991) suggests that individualism-collectivism is a dialectic. With respect to individualism, this implies that both orientations
co-exist in Japan and the United States (and other cultures as well)
and that the two orientations influence different aspects of behavior.
See Elias (1991) for a discussion of how individuals attempt to balance their "I" and "we" identities.

8. Ting-Toomey, Gao and colleagues (1991) also tested the conflict portion of the theory and an extension linking face to conflict styles. These aspects of the theory are not directly applicable here and, therefore, are omitted.

9. We argue below that these measures do not directly tap these constructs. The rationale depends on the conceptualization of face we present.

10. The results for other-face for South Korea, China, and Taiwan, however, were consistent with Ting-Toomey's (1988) theory.

11. There are, however, at least two studies that have used Brown and Levinson's theory to discuss politeness in Japan (i.e., Hill et al., 1986; Ide et al., 1986).

12. In reviewing an earlier draft of this chapter, Ting-Toomey suggested that if "negative-face" is viewed as a boundary-oriented construct, the difference might be that it is individual-based in the United States and group-based in Japan.

13. It is not the physical presence of others that matters. Face is a social cognitive phenomena—it depends on how individuals think of their relations to others.

14. Yamaguchi (1991) concurs that Markus and Kitayama's (1991) conceptualization applies in Japan.

15. Plath (1989) suggests that self-construals differ across the life span. He discusses different "schedules" for selfhood in Japan.

16. The following translations of Hamaguchi's writing were presented by Miyanaga (1991, 18–19).

17. Markus and Kitayama present some supporting evidence based on Japan–United States comparisons. We focus here on studies not reported in their paper that address issues of interest to face.

18. Triandis (personal communication) has argued that everyone has both individualistic and collectivistic thoughts. This position also is supported by recent writings on the United States (e.g., Bellah et al., 1985; Wuthnow, 1991) and Japan (e.g., Miyanaga, 1991). Japanese writers of the *nihonjinron* (literally discussions of the Japanese) tradition (e.g., Hamaguchi), however, would argue that Japanese are unique in their self-conceptions and that they only have an interdependent self-construal. While we agree that the interdependent (contextual) predominates, we believe there also is an independent construal as discussed below. For a critique of the *nihonjinron* approach, see Dale (1986).

19. It should be noted that, following Gudykunst and Lim (1986), we believe that the personal and social identity operate in every encounter, but one tends to predominate at any given moment.

20. There also are individuals whose interdependent construal of self predominates (see Bellah et al., 1985; Wuthnow, 1991).

21. Brewer (1991) argues that people try to maximize their assimilation (e.g., fitting into a group) and their uniqueness in defining

their social identities. We believe that her argument applies in individualistic cultures, but not in collectivistic cultures.

22. There are, of course, specific individuals whose independent construal of self predominates (see Miyanaga, 1991; Valentine, 1990).

23. Mouer and Sugimoto also given several examples of proverbs that reflect an independent self-construal; e.g., *seishin itto nanigotoka narazaran* ("where there is a will, there is a way"), *jigo jitoku* ("one must pay the consequences for one's misdeeds"). They also point out that "the phrase *karasu no katte desho* (literally 'as the crow pleases') which can indicate that one can have one's own reason for doing things" (p. 195) has come into use in recent years.

24. Roland (1988, 1991) dismisses the independent self-construal in Japan focusing exclusively on the "familial-group" self using an interdependent conceptualization.

25. Much of Scheff's argument vis-à-vis shame is based on Lewis (1976). Lewis draws a distinction between acknowledged and unacknowledged shame that cannot be addressed here. Scheff also argues that in the United States individuals are socialized to repress feelings of pride and shame. He also contends that individualism is a myth that is a defense against the loss of secure social bonds.

26. Goffman would argue that individuals in the United States also try to "give" face to others. Ting-Toomey (personal communication), however, concludes, based on unpublished data, that people in the United States have a difficult time conceptualizing giving face to another person.

27. Lebra (1976, 121–29) isolates strategies for "defending" and "displaying" face. The strategies she isolates appear to deal with the *taimen* meaning of *kao* rather than the *mentsu* meaning. We, therefore, do not discuss them here.

28. As indicated earlier, we believe that Hendry is using the *taimen* meaning of *kao*, not the *mentsu* meaning.

29. For a critique of these distinctions, see Dale (1986).

References

Asch, S. (1956). Studies of independence and conformity. *Psychological Monographs*, 70, no. 9 (whole no. 416).

Baxter, L. A. (1984). An investigation of compliance-gaining as politeness. *Human Communication Research*, 10, 427–456.

Befu, H. (1977). Power in the great white tower. In R. Fogelson and R. Adams (Eds.), *The anthropology of power*. New York: Academic Press.

———. (1980a). A critique of the group model of Japanese society. *Social Analysis*, 5/6, 29–43.

Befu, H. (1980b). The group model of Japanese society and an alternative. *Rice University Studies, 66,* 169–187.

Befu, H. (1989). A theory of social exchange as applied to Japan. In Y. Sugimoto and R. Mouer (Eds.), *Constructs for understanding Japan.* London: Kegan Paul.

Bellah, R., Madsen, R., Sullivan, W., Swidler, A., and Tipton, S. (1985). *Habits of the heart: Individualism and commitment in American life.* New York: Harper Row.

———. (1991). *The good society.* New York: Knopf.

Brewer, M. B. (1991). The social self: On being the same and different at the same time. *Personality and Social Psychology Bulletin, 17,* 475–482.

Brown, P., and Levinson, S. (1978). Universals in language usage: Politeness phenomenon. In E. Goody (Ed.), *Questions and politeness: Strategies in social interaction.* Cambridge: Cambridge University Press.

———. (1987). *Politeness: Some universals in language usage.* Cambridge: Cambridge University Press.

Caudill, W., and Scarr, H. (1961). Japanese value orientations and culture change. *Ethnology, 1,* 53–91.

Choi, S. C., and Choi, S. H. (1990). Che-Myon: Koreans' social face. Unpublished paper, Chung-Ang University, Seoul, South Korea.

Cole, M. (1989). A cross-cultural inquiry into the meaning of face in the Japanese and United States Culture. Paper presented at the Convention of the Speech Communication Association, San Francisco.

Cousins, S. D. (1989). Culture and self-perception in Japan and the United States. *Journal of Personality and Social Psychology, 56,* 124–131.

Crocker, J., and Luhtanen, R. (1990). Collective self-esteem and in-group bias. *Journal of Personality and Social Psychology, 58,* 60–67.

Curtis, R. C. (Ed.). (1991). *The relational self.* New York: Guilford.

Dale, P. N. (1986). *The myth of Japanese uniqueness.* New York: St. Martin's.

Deaux, K. (1991). Social identities: Thoughts on structure and change. In R. Curtis (Ed.), *The relational self.* New York: Guilford.

Doi, T. (1973). *The anatomy of dependence* (J. Bester, trans.). Tokyo: Kodansha.

———. (1986). *The anatomy of self* (M. Harbison, trans.). Tokyo: Kodansha.

Edgerton, R. B. (1985). *Rules, exceptions, and social order.* Berkeley: University of California Press.

Elias, N. (1991). *The society of individuals.* (E. Jephcott, trans.). London: Blackwell.

Frager, R. (1970). Conformity and anticonformity in Japan. *Journal of Personality and Social Psychology, 15,* 203–210.

Geertz, C. (1975). On the nature of anthropological understanding. *American Scientist, 63,* 47–53.

Gilligan, C. (1985). *In a different voice: Psychological theory and women's development.* Cambridge, MA: Harvard University Press.

Goffman, E. (1955). On face-work: An analysis of ritual elements in social interaction. *Psychiatry, 18,* 213–231.

――――. (1956). Embarrassment and social organization. *American Journal of Sociology, 62,* 264–271.

――――. (1959). *The presentation of self in everyday life.* New York: Doubleday.

――――. (1967). *Interaction ritual: Essays on face-to-face interaction.* Garden City, NY: Doubleday.

――――. (1974). *Frame analysis: An essay on the organization of experience.* Cambridge, MA: Harvard University Press.

Gudykunst, W. B., Gao, G., Nishida, T., Nadamitsu, Y., and Sakai, J. (in press). Self-monitoring in Japan and the United States. In S. Iwaki, Y. Kashima, and K. Leung (Eds.), *Innovations in cross-cultural psychology.* Lisse, Netherlands: Swets and Zeitlinger.

Gudykunst, W. B., and Lim, T. S. (1986). A perspective for the study of intergroup communication. In W. B. Gudykunst (Ed.), *Intergroup communication.* London: Edward Arnold.

Gudykunst, W. B., Nishida, T., Chung, L., and Sudweeks, S. (1992). The influence of strength of cultural identity and perceived typicality on individualistic and collectivistic values in Japan and the United States. Paper presented at the Asian Regional Congress of the International Association for Cross-Cultural Psychology, Kathmandu, Nepal.

Gudykunst, W. B., and Ting-Toomey, S. (1988). *Culture and interpersonal communication.* Newbury Park, CA: Sage.

Hamaguchi, E. (1977). "Nihon rashisa" no saihakken (The rediscovery of "Japaneseness"). Tokyo: Nihon Keizai Simbunsha.

――――. (1982). Nihonteki shudanshugi towa nanika (What is Japanese groupism). In E. Hamaguchi and S. Kumon (Ed.), *Nihonteki shudanshugi* (Japanese groupism). Tokyo: Yuhikaku (Sensho).

――――. (1983). Kanjin-shugi no shakai Nihon (Japan, society of contextual men). Tokyo: Touyou Keizai.

――――. (1985). A contextual model of the Japanese. *Journal of Japanese Studies, 11,* 289–321.

Hendry, J. (1987). *Understanding Japanese society.* London: Croom Helm.

Hess, R., Azuma, H., Kashiwagi, K., Dickson, W., Nagano, S., Hollo-way, S., Miyake, K., Price, G., Hatano, G., and McDevitt, T. (1986). Family influences on school readiness in Japan and the United States. In H. Stevenson, H. Azuma, and K. Hakuta (Eds.), *Child development and education in Japan.* New York: Freedman.

Hill, B., Ide, S., Ikuta, S., Kawasaki, A., Ogino, T. (1986). Universals of linguistic politeness. *Journal of Pragmatics, 10*, 347–371.

Ho, D. (1976). On the concept of face. *American Journal of Sociology, 81*, 867–884.

Hofstede, G. (1980). *Culture's consequences.* Beverly Hills, CA: Sage.

Hsu, F. L. K. (1985). The self in cross-cultural perspective. In A. Marsella, G. DeVos, and F. Hsu (Eds.), *Culture and self.* London: Tavistock.

Hu, H. C. (1944). The Chinese concept of "face." *American Anthropologist, 46*, 45–64.

Hwang, K. (1987). Face and favor: The Chinese power game. *American Journal of Sociology, 92*, 944–974.

Ide, S., Hori, M., Kawasaki, A., Ikuta, S., and Haga, H. (1986). Sex differences in politeness in Japan. *International Journal of the Sociology of Language, 58*, 25–36.

Ito, Y. (1989a). A nonwestern view of the paradigm dialogues. In B. Dervin, L. Grossberg, and E. Wartella (Eds.), *Rethinking communication.* Newbury Park, CA: Sage.

———. (1989b). Socio-cultural backgrounds of Japanese interpersonal communication style. *Civilisations, 39*, 101–137.

Johnson, F. (1985). The western concept of self. In A. Marsella, G. DeVos, and F. Hsu (Eds.), *Culture and self.* London: Tavistock.

Josephs, L. (1991). Character, structure, self-esteem, regulation, and the principle of identity maintenance. In R. Curtis (Ed.), *The relational self.* New York: Guilford.

Kashima, Y. (1989). Conceptions of person: Implications in individualism/collectivism research. In C. Kagitcibasi (Ed.), *Growth and progress in cross-cultural psychology.* Lisse, The Netherlands: Swets and Zeitlinger.

Kim, M. S. (1993). Culture-based interactive constraints in explaining intercultural strategic competence. In R. Wiseman and J. Koester (Eds.), *Intercultural communication competence.* Newbury Park, CA: Sage.

Kluckhohn, F., and Strodtbeck, F. (1961). *Variations in value orientations.* New York: Row, Peterson.

Kumon, S. (1982). Soshiki no Nihongata moderu to obeigata moderu (Japanese and American models of organizations). In E. Hamaguchi and S. Kumon (Eds.), *Nihonteki shudanshugi* (Japanese groupism). Tokyo: Yuhikaku (Sensho).

Lebra, T. S. (1976). *Japanese patterns of behavior.* Honolulu: University of Hawaii Press.

Lewis, H. (1976). *Psychic war in men and women.* New York: New York University Press.

Miyanaga, K. (1991). *The creative edge: Individualism in Japan.* New Brunswick, NJ: Transaction.

Lim, T. S., and Bowers, J. W. (1991). Facework: Solidarity, approbation, and tact. *Human Communication Research, 17,* 415–450.

Lin, Y. T. (1962). *My country and my people.* New York: Hitchcock.

Markus, H. R., and Kitayama, S. (1991). Culture and the self: Implications for cognition, emotion, and motivation. *Psychological Review, 98,* 224–253.

Masatsugu, M. (1982). *The modern samurai society.* New York: AMACOM.

Matsumoto, Y. (1988). Reexamination of the university of face: Politeness phenomena in Japanese. *Journal of Pragmatics, 12,* 403–426.

Macgowan, J. (1912). *Men and manners of modern China.* London: Unwin.

Midooka, K. (1990). Characteristics of Japanese-style communication. *Media, Culture, and Society, 12,* 477–489.

Mouer, R., and Sugimoto, Y. (1986). *Images of Japanese society.* London: Kegan Paul.

Nakane, C. (1970). *Japanese society.* Berkeley, CA: University of California Press.

———. (1972). *Tekio no joken* (Conditions of adjustment). Tokyo: Kodansya.

Nishida, H. (1981). Value orientations and value changes in Japan and the U.S.A. In T. Nishida and W. Gudykunst (Eds.), *Readings in intercultural communication.* Tokyo: Geirinshobo.

Penman, R. (1990). Facework and Politeness: Multiple goals in courtroom discourse. *Journal of Language and Social Psychology, 9,* 15–38.

Pharr, S. (1990) *Losing face: Status politics in Japan.* Berkeley: University of California Press.

Plath, D. (1989). Arc, circle, and sphere: Schedules for selfhood. In Y. Sugimoto and R. Mouer (Eds.), *Constructs for understanding Japan.* London: Kegan Paul.

Rohlen, T. (1973). Spiritual education in a Japanese bank. *American Anthropologist, 75,* 1542–1562.

Roland, A. (1988). *In search of self in India and Japan.* Princeton: Princeton University Press.

———. (1991). The self in cross-civilizational perspective: An Indian-Japanese-American comparison. In R. Curtis (Ed.), *The relational self*. New York: Guilford.

Sampson, E. E. (1988). The debate on individualism. *American Psychologist, 43,* 15–22.

Scheff, T. J. (1990). *Microsociology: Discourse, emotion, and social structure*. Chicago: University of Chicago Press.

Schwartz, S. (1990). Individualism-collectivism. *Journal of Cross-Cultural Psychology, 21,* 139–157.

Schwartz, S., and Bilsky, W. (1990). Toward a theory of the universal content and structure of values. *Journal of Personality and Social Psychology, 58,* 878–891.

Shikanai, K. (1978). Effects of self-esteem on attributions for success and failure. *Japanese Journal of Experimental Social Psychology, 18,* 47–55.

Smith, A. (1894). *Chinese characteristics*. New York: Revell.

Stover, L. (1962). *"Face" and verbal analogues of interaction in Chinese culture*. Unpublished doctoral dissertation, Columbia University.

Tajfel, H. (1981). *Human groups and social categories: Studies in social psychology*. Cambridge: Cambridge University Press.

———. (1982). Social psychology of intergroup relations. *Annual Review of Psychology, 33,* 1–39.

Tajfel, H., and Turner, J. C. (1979). An integrative theory of intergroup conflict. In W. G. Austin and S. Worchel (Eds.), *The social psychology of intergroup relations*. Monterey, CA: Brook/Cole.

Takata, T. (1987). Self-depreciative tendencies in self-evaluation through social comparison. *Japanese Journal of Experimental Social Psychology, 27,* 27–36.

Tasker, P. (1987). *Inside Japan*. London: Sidgwick and Jackson.

Ting-Toomey, S. (1985). Toward a theory of conflict and culture. In W. Gudykunst, L. Stewart, and S. Ting-Toomey (Eds.), *Communication, culture, and organizational processes*. Beverly Hills, CA: Sage.

———. (1988). Intercultural conflict styles. In Y. Y. Kim and W. B. Gudykunst (Eds.), *Theories in intercultural communication*. Beverly Hills, CA: Sage.

Ting-Toomey, S., Gao, G., Trubisky, P., Yang, Z., Kim, H. S., Lin, S., and Nishida, T. (1991). Culture, face maintenance, and styles of handling interpersonal conflict: A study in five cultures. *The International Journal of Conflict Management, 2,* 275–296.

Ting-Toomey, S., Trubisky, P., Bruschke, J., Nadamitsu, Y., Sakai, J., Nishida, T., and Baker, J. (1991). Face and culture: Toward the development of a facework taxonomy. Paper presented at the Western States Communication Association, Phoenix, AZ.

Tracy, K. (1990). The many faces of facework. In H. Giles and W. Robinson (Eds.), Handbook of language and social psychology. Chichester, UK: John Wiley.

Trafimow, D. M., Triandis, H. C., and Goto, S. G. (1991). Some tests of the distinction between the private self and the collective self. Journal of Personality and Social Psychology, 60, 649–655.

Triandis, H. C. (1988). Collectivism vs. individualism: A reconceptualization of a basic concept in cross-cultural psychology. In G. Verma and C. Bagley (Eds.), Cross-cultural studies of personality, attitudes and cognition. London: MacMillan.

———. (1989). The self and social behavior in differing cultural contexts. Psychological Review, 96, 506–517.

———. (1990). Cross-cultural studies of individualism-collectivism. In J. Berman (Ed.), Nebraska Symposium on Motivation (vol. 37). Lincoln: University of Nebraska Press.

Triandis, H. C., Bontempo, R., Villareal, M., Asai, M., and Lucca, N. (1988). Individualism-collectivism: Cross-cultural perspectives on self-ingroup relationships. Journal of Personality and Social Psychology, 54, 323–338.

Turner, J. C., Hogg, M., Oakes, P., Reicher, S., and Wetherell, M. (1987). Rediscovering the social group: A self-categorization theory. Oxford: Blackwell.

Valentine, J. (1990). On the borderlines: The significance of marginality in Japanese society. In E. Ben-Ari, B. Moeran, and J. Valentine (Eds.), Unwrapping Japan. Manchester, UK: Manchester University Press.

Waterman, A. S. (1981). Individualism and interdependence. American Psychologist, 36, 762–773.

Wetzel, P. (1985). Ingroup/outgroup dexis. In J. Forgas (Ed.), Language and social situations. New York: Springer-Verlag.

White, M., and LeVine, R. (1986). What is an Ii ko (good child)? In H. Stevenson, H. Azuma, and K. Hakuta (Eds.), Child development and education in Japan. New York: Freeman.

Wierzbica, A. (1991). Japanese key words and core cultural values. Language in Society, 20, 333–385.

Williams, T., and Sogon, S. (1984). Nihonjin daigakusei ni okeru shudankeisei to tekio kodo (Group composition and conforming behavior in Japanese students). Nihon Shinrigaku Kenkyu (Japanese Psychological Research), 126, 231–234.

Wuthnow, R. (1991). Acts of compassion: Caring for others and helping ourselves. Princeton: Princeton University Press.

Yamada, H. (1990). Topic management and turn distributions in business meetings: American versus Japanese strategies. *Text, 10,* 271–295.

Yamaguchi, S. (1990). Empirical evidence on collectivism among the Japanese. Paper presented at the Conference on Individualism-Collectivism, Seoul, Korea.

————. (1991). "Jiko" no shitenkara no shudan oyobi bunkasa eno aprochi (Approaches to group processes and cultural differences from the perspective of the self). *Shakaishinrigaku Kenkyu* (Research in Social Psychology), *6,* 138–147.

Yang, M. (1945). *A Chinese village.* New York: Columbia University Press.

Yoneyama, T. (1973). Basic notions in Japanese social relations. In J. Bailey (Ed.), *Listening to Japan.* New York: Praeger.

Yoshida, T., Kojo, K., and Kaku, H. (1982). A study on the development of self-presentations in children. *Japanese Journal of Educational Psychology, 30,* 30–37.

-4-
A Chinese Perspective on Face as Inter-Relational Concern

HUI-CHING CHANG
and
G. RICHARD HOLT

Facework has served as an important construct to provoke social scientific dialogue about human interaction. Goffman
(1959, 1967), who laid the groundwork for this line of research
with his dramaturgical analysis, describes "face" as a means of
impression management for social actors' interaction with others on the stage of life. The centrality of the concept of face in
analyzing human interaction has long been acknowledged. Ho
(1976), for example, elaborates the importance of the concept of
face in any social system:

> Face is the respectability and/or deference which a person can
> claim for himself from others, by virtue of the relative position
> he occupies in his social network and the degree to which he
> is judged to have functioned adequately in that position as
> well as acceptably in his general conduct; the face extended to
> a person by others is a function of the degree of congruence
> between judgments of his total condition in life, including his
> actions as well as those of people closely associated with him,
> and the social expectations the others have placed upon him.
> (p. 883)

If social interaction is unavoidable, then so is mutual concern for face. Taking a sociolinguistic approach, Brown and
Levinson (1987) relied on the concept of face in discussing politeness strategies, offering positive and negative face-wants as
the underlying mechanism regulating directness and indirectness in linguistic expression. Indeed, Brown and Levinson ar-

gue that the desire for face is a universal phenomenon, underlying the constitution of linguistic expressions in a wide variety of different languages and cultures.

In the field of communication, many scholars have utilized the concept of face as a construct to analyze communicative strategies and performances, addressing issues in such areas as compliance gaining (Baxter, 1984; Tracy, Craig, Smith, & Spisak, 1984; Craig, Tracy, & Spisak, 1986), emotional disclosure (Shimanoff, 1985, 1987), conflict styles (Ting-Toomey, 1988; Ting-Toomey, Gao, Trubiski, Yang, Kim, Lin, & Nishida, 1991), managerial communication (Fairhurst, Green, & Snavely, 1984), and diplomatic communication (Ting-Toomey & Cole, 1990).

Nevertheless, we feel that communication studies have given insufficient attention to the phenomenon of face considered from a cultural perspective. Human interaction assumes different forms and meanings depending on the cultural environment. The concept of face, as a form of respect which interactants assume toward each other in the course of their interaction, also varies in its contents in different cultural environments. Precisely because of this variation, face needs to be explored in situ within its "home" system of cultural meanings in order to assess how members of a given culture choose to regulate their interpersonal lives. Employing a cultural approach to the concept of face, we can achieve three goals simultaneously. First, we can acquire an in-depth understanding of the concept within a cultural system, through investigating the role face plays in influencing human interaction among members of the culture. Second, we can assess the importance of face in analyzing human interaction, through acquiring new understanding of the meanings of human interaction with reference to the concept of face, Third, we can assess the validity, or at least the usefulness, of the claim for face as a universal organizing theme of human interaction, given its diverse expression in various cultures. This kind of in-depth, emic, understanding in probing the meaning of face in one particular cultural environment is a vital first step in evaluating the appropriateness of the concept of face as a universal, etic, construct.

The Chinese concept of face (or *mien-tzu*) is complex and dynamic. While there are many facets to the long-developed set of Chinese cultural practices relating to face, as we delineate the intersection between face and relationships, we will argue that the complexity of Chinese interpersonal relationships has paved the way for face to be actively utilized to facilitate (or, alternatively, to hinder) interpersonal activities, and even to solve (or, alternatively, to prevent solution of) interpersonal problems. To substantiate our theoretical perspective, we will present interviewees' accounts from our earlier studies[1] to illustrate the variety of ways in which face can be employed in the conduct of interpersonal relationship. We will present our findings by addressing the following four issues: (1) the cultural dimension of the concept of *mien-tzu;* (2) the significance and meaning of interpersonal relationship, *mien-tzu,* and human emotion, to the Chinese; (3) the social significance of *mien-tzu* as it impacts interpersonal relating; and finally, (4) the implications of the analysis and challenges posed to the current research on facework.

The Concept of *Mien-tzu*

The concept of face, known to Chinese as *mien-tzu*[2] is central to Chinese construal of their social life. The impact of *mien-tzu* on Chinese cultural life has been noted by many people for a significant portion of China's history. Early missionaries and travellers wrote of their astonishment at the pervasiveness of the concept of *mien-tzu* among Chinese (Bard, 1905; Danton, 1938; Smith, 1895). Lin (1939), a Chinese scholar well-known in the West, referred to face, fate, and favor as the "three sisters" who control Chinese life. Commenting negatively on the influence of these three factors upon the Chinese, Lin argued that their impact lies in a gentle but penetrating power which Chinese find difficult to resist: "their voices are soft, their ways are gentle, their feet tread noiselessly over the law courts, and their fingers move silently, expertly, putting the machinery of justice out of order while they caress the judge's cheeks" (pp. 195–96). LaBarre (1946a, 1946b) addresses the phenomenon of *mien-tzu* as it is revealed through various linguistic expressions. In a systematic and scholarly analysis of *mien-tzu,* Hu (1944) elaborated in detail the significance of the concept of *mien-tzu* and a related concept, *lien,* to Chinese culture. Finally, Yang (1945), in his study of a village in Shantung province on the mainland, explained how *mien-tzu* can be a cause for conflict and how it can be utilized as a means of solving conflict through outside intervention.

While the above anecdotal observations and systematic analyses are based upon life in mainland China, many modern

Chinese scholars share a similar viewpoint about *mien-tzu* in regard to present-day Taiwan.[3] Several studies have utilized the concept of *mien-tzu* to explain interpersonal interaction and relationships (Ch'en, 1989; Chu, 1989; Hwang, 1987, 1988, 1989; King, 1989a, 1989b). These and other studies share the common perception that *mien-tzu* helps Chinese orchestrate their daily lives, influencing the way they interact with one another, bringing the delicate philosophical nuances to face into the realm of daily existence. Given the importance of *mien-tzu* to the Chinese, a closer examination of its various meanings is in order.

Mien-tzu: Its Meanings

Literally speaking, *mien-tzu* refers to human physiognomy ("the face").[4] However, the Chinese concept of *mien-tzu* is heavily laden with psychological and sociological meanings. It is different from the concept of "face" as commonly understood in the work of Western social scientists, such as Goffman (1959, 1967). As Yang (1945) explains,

> "Face" is a literal translation of the Chinese character of *lien* or *mien*. Although *lien* or *mien* means just what the English word face does, the Chinese expression *tiou lien* (losing face) or *yao mien-tzu* (wanting a face) has nothing to do with face in our usual understanding of the term. It does not mean a certain expression on, or the physical appearance of, the face, such as implied by "a funny face" or "a sad face." When we say in Chinese that one loses face, we mean that he [or she] loses prestige, he has [or she] been insulted or has been made to feel embarrassment before a group. When we say that a man wants a face, we mean that he wants to be given honor, prestige, praise, flattery, or concession, whether or not these are merited. Face is really a personal psychological satisfaction, a social esteem accorded by others. (p. 167)

Several scholars echo Yang's analysis. Hu (1944) defines *mien-tzu* as "a reputation achieved through getting on in life through success and ostentation" (p. 45). Hwang (1989) contends that *mien-tzu* is a "social status or prestige acquired by one's accomplishment in the society; whereas '*mien-tzu* work' is a behavior of impression management, performed purposefully in order to create certain images of oneself in front of others" (p. 305). Since social recognition and social status are major sources of *mien-tzu*, Hsiang (1974) argues that the term *mien-tzu* is now synonymous with the term "honor" (p. 52). However, Lin (1939) argues that "to confuse face with the Western 'honor' is to make a grievous error" (p. 200; see also Ho, 1976). This disagreement arises, perhaps, because of the distinction between honor as shared (as in Chinese societies) and honor as individually owned (as in Western societies).

The difficulty in arriving at a common definition for *mien-tzu* is due primarily to the complex socio-psychological implications of the concept itself. As Lin (1939) explains,

> [F]ace is psychological and not physiological. Interesting as the Chinese physiological face is, the psychological face makes a still more fascinating study. It is not a face that can be washed or shaved, but a face that can be "granted" and "lost" and "fought for" and "presented as a gift." . . . Abstract and intangible, it is yet the most delicate standard by which Chinese social intercourse is regulated. . . . Face cannot be translated or defined. It is like honor and is not honor. It cannot be purchased with money, and gives a man or a woman a material pride. It is hollow and yet is what men fight for and what many women die for. It is invisible and yet by definition exists by being shown to the public. It exists in the ether and yet cannot be heard, and sounds eminently respectable and solid. It is amenable, not to reason but to social convention. (pp. 199–200)

While most scholars see *mien-tzu* as grounded in external social acknowledgment, for King (1989b), it also has its moral element which impels a person to work hard and to achieve higher moral standards.[5] In spite of scholars' diverse opinions, all these definitions seem to support the general idea that *mien-tzu* reflects one's reputation achieved and maintained through the scrutiny of others, with the standard of acknowledgment reflecting not only social values, but moral values as well. To put is simply, *mien-tzu* can be seen as a measure of the recognition accorded by society. As we will elaborate, it is this social dimension inherent in the conception of *mien-tzu*, together with its somewhat obligatory character, that leads to consideration of *mien-tzu* as inter-rational concern.

Mien-tzu: Its Dynamism and Complexity

The richness and complexity of *mien-tzu* can be demonstrated by analyzing its various expressions in the Chinese language.[6] In examining these linguistic expressions, we begin by exploring how *mien-tzu* can be seen as a quality claimed by the individual and accredited by society at large, and then move to an examination of the role *mien-tzu* plays in interpersonal activities. The personal and interpersonal facets of *mien-tzu* are two sides of the same coin: the individual claims *mien-tzu* from the society, and eventually places his/her *mien-tzu* under the scrutiny of others in the process of relating.

The personal perspective: mien-tzu *as claimed by the individual.* Although *mien-tzu* is not like a personality trait possessed by an individual (Ho, 1976), observing *mien-tzu* from the personal perspective reveals an individual's concern about the extent to which she/he is to be recognized by society. Several linguistic expressions suggest that *mien-tzu* can be a quality claimed by the individual, so that individuals may vary in their attitudes toward their own *mien-tzu*. Expressions such as "(someone) loves [their] *mien-tzu* very much" (meaning that one is overly concerned about *mien-tzu*), and "(someone) is particular about *mien-tzu*" (meaning that ones pays particular attention to issues of *mien-tzu*) are two important expressions used by Chinese. Moreover, regarding the extent to which the individual wants to claim *mien-tzu* for him-/herself, *mien-tzu* can be said to have an almost quantitative dimension. Individuals are frequently described as differing in their degree of "face-lovingness": a person who is more interested in having *mien-tzu* may be described as a person who cares more about social values and social judgments. On the other hand, when one has done something dishonorable, it is said that one's "face cannot be hung," meaning that one cannot face others because one's self-respect has been challenged.

The concept of *mien-tzu* is also associated with social values, governed by the principle that the amount of *mien-tzu* one can enjoy is proportionate to the social and relational status one possesses. The amount of *mien-tzu* one can claim in front of others is determined by the recognition accorded by others. Since *mien-tzu* is a quality claimed for oneself, it becomes a front, a mask that one uses to augment and signify personal social prestige. Consequently, one's success in achieving increased social status may be described as a process of gaining more *mien-tzu*. Many linguistic expressions describe face-augmentation: "having much *mien-tzu*," "having *mien-tzu*," "having less *mien-tzu*," and "having very much less *mien-tzu*." These linguistic expressions denote differing degrees to which one is or is not honored through one's *mien-tzu*, as this status is reflected in the eyes of others. Because the possibility for one to move upward in the social ladder always exists, *mien-tzu* can be said to be "worth fighting for."

This connection between *mien-tzu* and social values shows both flexibility and inflexibility. On one hand, one's social prestige may constrain the extent to which one can claim *mien-tzu* in front of others; on the other hand, external formality based on varying degrees of *mien-tzu* can frequently be adjusted in accordance with social circumstances. *Mien-tzu* may be exaggerated, added to, or decreased, depending upon how one chooses to present oneself in front of others. One may do something to enhance *mien-tzu*, that is, "add to *mien-tzu*," or compete with someone to gain more *mien-tzu* ("struggle for *mien-tzu*"). For example, one may augment *mien-tzu* by inviting a person to dinner at an outstanding or expensive restaurant, or by inviting important people to be guests at a dinner. In both cases, one's public image has been enhanced through manipulation of *mien-tzu.*

Mien-tzu can be claimed not only by individuals, but can also be shared by members of the ingroup, or by people in specific social situations. More often than not, members of the family of an individual who has *mien-tzu* may share pride in that individual's achievements (Lin, 1939). This sharing also implies that one is expected to protect the *mien-tzu* of the whole family or the ingroup.

The interpersonal perspective: mien-tzu *as defined in interaction.* A second significant aspect of *mien-tzu* is that, as suggested by several linguistic expressions, it is defined in the process of interaction, in the give-and-take of daily social life. Social others, whether specific individuals or the society at large, have a stake in the individual's maintenance or protection of *mien-tzu. Mien-tzu* is said to be distributed among all interactants in a situation, as reflected in the common phrase, "everybody gets *mien-tzu*," meaning that matters are handled in such a way that everyone shares the honor of "looking good."[7] When matters are not handled properly, it is said that "everybody has no *mien-tzu*." Interactants are expected to know how to respect the *mien-tzu* of others in order to ensure smooth social interaction.

Precisely because of the involvement of others, it is possible for social actors to maneuver *mien-tzu* in interpersonal encounters. Since issues of *mien-tzu* cannot be avoided, they must be negotiated between interactants themselves. Several examples of the coupling of indicators of action with *mien-tzu* reveal its dynamic utilization. When practical needs arise, one may choose to "do *mien-tzu*" (meaning to manipulate *mien-tzu* in order to provide a future resource). When someone requests a favor, the other may decide to "give (or not give) a *mien-tzu*" (meaning to honor someone's *mien-tzu*), or to "take care of one's *mien-tzu*" (meaning to do something special for someone because of his or her *mien-tzu*). Whatever one has to do, one must not forget to "leave *mien-tzu* for someone" (meaning to avoid doing something to harm another's *mien-tzu*). When one does not want to grant the other a *mien-tzu*, at least one should "pad (someone's) *mien-tzu*" (meaning to show insincere deference in order to avoid offending the other's *mien-tzu*). As these and many other expressions show, the Chinese have developed a detailed set of social techniques for interacting with others in ways that permit protection of each actor's *mien-tzu* (King, 1989a).

Summary. These different Chinese expressions demonstrate the flexibility, dynamism, and utility of *mien-tzu; mien-tzu* is simultaneously a quality claimed by the individual through social recognition, and a quality to be actively engaged in the process of interpersonal relating. *Mien-tzu* is flexible, because it is not a fixed image one portrays for oneself on the stage of life, but an image which can be "added to" or "decreased" in the process of interaction. *Mien-tzu* is utilizable, because it is concerned not only with present conditions, but serves as a resource that can be stored and invested for future use. *Mien-tzu* is dynamic, because it is not only an image or identity one can claim for oneself to enhance social status, but is something which can be used as a means to renegotiate relational obligations. The functioning of *mien-tzu* in interpersonal relations can be understood only if one is able to appreciate the complexity of Chinese relations. To elaborate how the concept must be situated within a system of cultural meanings, we now turn to a fuller explanation of the intricate connection among relations, human emotion, and *mien-tzu*.

Relationship as Focus of Attention: *Mien-tzu*, Relations, and Human Emotion

The functioning of *mien-tzu* needs to be understood by reference to Chinese relations (*kuan-hsi*) and human emotion (*ren-*

ching). Indeed, some analysts (Hsiang, 1974; Hwang, 1989) have argued that *mien-tzu*, human emotion, and interpersonal relations must be understood as a whole.

The Chinese emphasis upon human interaction as the fundamental groundwork of its philosophical systems has been well documented (Chan, 1963, 1967; Fung, 1983). These fundamental assumptions have influenced the way Chinese conduct their lives, resulting in endless connected chains of interpersonal relationships. Particularly significant is the Confucian ideal of different orders of relationships as reflecting varying degrees of human emotion (*ren-ching*). By observing different degrees of relationships and human emotion, the Chinese express, or at least try to appear to express, emotional concern toward each other by showing respect for the relational partner's *mien-tzu*. *Mien-tzu* must be understood within this system of inter-relational positioning. Noting the effect of differing orders of relationships on the Chinese, Hsiang (1974) observes, "there is no way to talk about 'human emotion' between strangers. To work for our acquaintances or friends, to give them *mien-tzu*, and to make them happy, is so-called 'human emotion' " (p. 56). To put it simply, if one does not have a good or important relationship, it will be difficult for one to claim sufficient *mien-tzu* in the presence of another because there is so little "human emotion" involved.

We argue that the central character of Chinese relationship lies in its emphasis upon human emotion (*ren-ching*),[8] the standard against which the quality of *mien-tzu* is measured. To understand the interconnection among human emotion, *mien-tzu*, and relations, we must first understand the role relationships play in Chinese social life. To explicate this thesis, we build a link between the philosophical realm (as reflected in the Confucian school and other streams of philosophical thought) and the cultural realm (as reflected in the folk concepts of relation) (*kuan-hsi*). Let us consider, first, the philosophical ideal of Chinese relationship, and second, the practical social expression of the ideal.

The Philosophical Ideal

Confucius taught that human morality is based on five basic relationships as the proper place where one learns humanity. According to Confucian philosophy, society is possible and stable only when the five basic relationships are appropriately maintained: (1) father-son (the relation of *closeness*); (2) emperor-subject (the relation of *righteousness*); (3) husband-wife (the relation of *distinction*); (4) elder-younger (the relation of *order*); and (5) friend-friend (the relation of *faithfulness*). Depending upon whether the relationship is close or distant, different ways of interacting should be employed (Fung, 1983).

As Geng (1982) has noted, three out of these five bases of relationship occur within the family (father-son, husband-wife, and elder-younger). Since the family serves as the basis of the society, one relates to the outside world much in the same way as one relates to members of the family. The regulating factors in family relationships are said to be extendable to the whole town, the whole society, and consequently, to the whole country. Even if there is no blood connection or marriage relation, Chinese are still able to apply the rules of ordering between interactants; it is possible to do this, for example, based upon the comparative *ages* of interactants.

To learn to regulate one's proper relations with others, Confucius maintained that one must learn to practice the rules of *li* (propriety) (Chan, 1963; Graham, 1989). While the complex behaviors governed by *li* are often read as the imposition upon individuals of the values of a "collective" society, Confucian philosophy is less a system of *rules* than a means of self-examination and self-development. *Li*, as a set of norms appropriate to one's natural moral development, are not simply prescriptive rules imposed from without.

"Human emotion," the common emotional responses shared by human beings, can be seen as the guiding spirit of Chinese cultural life (Liang, 1964; Hsiang, 1974; King, 1989a). Behavior considered appropriate to a person occupying a particular position is to be understood from the human being's natural emotional responses toward relational partners. It is human emotion (or human feeling) which enables one to make clear distinctions among different orders of relationships. According to the classic *Li-Yun*, human emotion includes "enjoyment, anger, sorrowfulness, happiness, love, disgust, and desire . . . these seven we human beings are capable of without learning them" (Legge, 1967, p. 50). One naturally has more concern for those with whom one is more intimate, and less concern for those in more distant relation. In this way, rules of order (*li*) serve to refine human nature. An example is the relationship between a loving father and a pious son: their interaction is less dictated by external behavioral codes than a product of the natural emotion flowing from their hearts. To learn to appreciate the difference between different orders of relationships, the *individual* must develop ethically and morally.

The emphasis on relationships in Confucianism can be understood from its central virtue, *ren*, which denotes "all those moral qualities which should govern one man in his relations with another. . . . Briefly defined, it is the manifestation of the genuine nature, acting in accordance with propriety (*li*) and based upon sympathy for others" (Fung, 1983, p. 69). In the ideal Confucian society, to hold one's own position appropriately is to show respect and emotional concern for the other through elevating one's spiritual understanding to encompass the universe as whole. Hence, individuals must learn not only to harmonize with their fellows but also with the universe (Graham, 1989). As Tu (1985) notes, according to Confucian philosophy, one's ability to achieve a harmonious relationship with others is the greatest *spiritual* accomplishment of one's life. For Confucianism, the task of formulating the appropriate behavior will lead to an inwardly elevated life experience.

Compared with the Western philosophical focus on "reason" as a guiding spirit of civilization, Chinese philosophies focus upon "emotion," are humanistically oriented, and are heavily laden with ethical concerns. According to the Confucian ideal, human emotion is not simply a private, selfish emotional response, but part of nature endowed by heaven, corresponding to the cosmos and actualized in human life. The concern for human emotion also leads to the hierarchical ordering of relational position. The permeation of various degrees of human emotion into differing orders of relationship provides the context in which *mien-tzu* is to be played out according to (1) the varying degree of relationship, and (2) the hierarchical system of social ordering. The ordering of relationships provides the first impetus for the individual to be concerned about *mien-tzu*. Unavoidably, individuals are placed into a system of hierarchical positioning relative to each other; one's *mien-tzu* can thus be said to correspond to one's positions in the relational hierarchy.

Practical Social Expression of the Ideal

While the ideals of Confucianism are undoubtedly influential in Chinese society, these ideals have nevertheless been practically transformed to fit broader Chinese cultural patterns. To elaborate this important instantiation of the Confucian ideal,

we turn now to a discussion of the Chinese conception of relation (*kuan-hsi*) and human emotion (*ren-ching*).

As noted above, Confucian philosophy assumes that different relationships imply different norms of interaction. This
principle of behaving "according to the relationship" is one key
element in Chinese society, described by Fei (1947) as "manners of different orders." Fei compares the evolution of Chinese
interpersonal relationships to a stone cast into the water, generating ripples moving outward from the center: the innermost
ripples represent those closest to the social actor, with different
degrees of the ripple effect representing different degrees of intimacy and obligation. Contrary to the accepted classification
of Chinese society as "collectivist" (Hofstede, 1980), Fei's analogy implies that the individual is the *self*-created center of an
ever-expanding set of relationship "circles."

From a practical point of view, being part of an integrated
network of interpersonal relationships is of surpassing importance in Chinese society. This practical concern is revealed
through the concept of "relations," or what the Chinese call
"*kuan-hsi.*" Literally, *kuan-hsi* can be translated as "relations."
At a deeper and more subtle level, however, *kuan-hsi* refers to
the manner in which Chinese strategically employ relations as
a social resource. *Kuan-hsi* implies a close connection between
people, an interlinkage which brings along with it interactants'
special rights and obligations. It is this latter, deeper, more
subtle level of meaning which paves the way for *mien-tzu* to
function in solving interpersonal problems. Put simply, to
grant *mien-tzu* is to acknowledge the importance or validity of
the *kuan-hsi* of the interactants. *Kuan-hsi* is the token which
permits *mien-tzu* to work.

The importance and usefulness of interpersonal relationship can be seen in the Chinese tendency to utilize an intermediary to solve a variety of interpersonal problems (see, for
example, Fried, 1953; Jacobs, 1978). Fried noted many instances in which an intermediary, because of his/her connection with the target person, is asked to aid someone else.
Similarly, in the realm of politics, Jacobs (1978), in his study of
a Taiwanese rural township, concludes that interpersonal relationship lies behind the formation of political factions; one
will very seldom ask for a favor from a stranger, but rather will
seek out interpersonal connections which will enable one to
get the job done (p. 265). The person sought out as intermediary is able to use his/her relationship to get the target person to

agree to help; the intermediary's help is sought because s/he can "claim *mien-tzu* in front of others."

Use of intermediaries in this fashion works because of the necessity to acknowledge *mien-tzu*. This necessity is both a blessing and a burden. The existence of a complex network of interpersonal relationships provides many Chinese with social and emotional support, but on the other hand, it can also impose upon them a heavy responsibility toward people with whom they have close relationships. Mutual social responsibility implies that certain occurrences of *mien-tzu* must be acknowledged, depending on the degree of relationship between interactants.

So pronounced is the Chinese emphasis upon interpersonal relationships that a cursory examination might lead one to conclude that Chinese practice a form of nepotism which disproportionately emphasizes "particularistic ties" (or, *kuan-hsi*) among interactants. Nevertheless, despite the seeming pragmatism of the Chinese system, one must remember that the Confucian ideal of interpersonal relationship (built upon "human emotion") is in fact derived from the *differing* degrees of emotion one interactant has for the other. Expression of emotional concern for the other is in effect to acknowledge the *mien-tzu* of the other.

To understand how *mien-tzu* is built upon the emotional concern one has for another, we need to explore the role emotion plays in Chinese relationships. Here we see how the original philosophical attitude toward "human emotion" has been actualized in Chinese interaction. Indeed, the emphasis on emotion as a major component of relationship is observable even in more instrumental Chinese relationships. Although there may appear to be no obvious natural emotional concern between instrumental partners (and hence no claim of *mien-tzu*), there occurs nonetheless, through contact and interaction, a building up of concern so that, at some future date, the relationship may be utilized to protect one's own interests.

An example will serve to illustrate how difficult it can be to separate the "emotional" from the "pragmatic." In an early community study, Fried (1953) noted that among the Ch'uhsien of the mainland, there are two contrasting types of relationships: the first, friendship, is characterized as mutual concern and brings with it equal status, whereas the second, *kan-ch'ing* (*which can also* be translated as "emotion"[9]) "not only recognised exploitation but is a technique of ameliorating it" (p.

224). Fried concludes that the latter kind of relationship has less warmth than the former; thus *kan-ch'ing* often serves to bridge gaps between people of different social status in the absence of kin ties (pp. 226–227). When there is no close relationship upon which one can rely, one needs to cultivate *kan-ch'ing* so as to function well in the society.

It is interesting to note that, although the *kan-ch'ing*-type relationship accents utility, it is nevertheless performed under the name of "emotion." There is no contradiction here: *kan-ch'ing* is built through contact and by constant interaction with others. As Fried (1953) puts it, "even *kan-ch'ing*, however, requires more fertile social soil" (p. 224), and involves a great deal of individual effort and care. Fried (1953) offers the example of a seemingly instrumental relationship between a merchant and a customer:

> Under the old, pre-inflation, credit system of buying there was a frequent development of something approaching friendship between a merchant and a steady customer. This relationship was an advantage to both parties in its encouragement of the growth of *kan-ch'ing*. It made possible a number of deepening contacts which preceded the simple ties of trade and which now might become permanent, thus extending the mutual exchange of help in the placement and security of related individuals or friends and the exchange of credit or other facilities. During the period of inflation, when supplies were reduced and a black market arose in consumer's goods, well established relationships of this type became a prime medium, in the general absence of effective bonds of kin, of protection from the adverse effects of a collapsing economy. (p. 190)

Ironically, the emotional element here prevents the relation between the merchant and a customer from being purely economic. Because this emotional component exists within the relationship, the relationship is viewed as being somewhat particularistic, or at least is distinguishable from other common, nonintimate relationships. This sense of particularity, the specialness of relationship, implies distinctive relational obligations. Within the confines of these mutual obligations, it becomes possible for *mien-tzu* to be employed as a relational resource.

Commenting on Fried's research, Jacobs (1978) further explains the difficulty of distinguishing the emotional from the pragmatic:

> Without exception, each informant confirmed Fried's analy-
> sis by saying *kan-ch'ing* is "utilized." The explanation be-
> comes simple if we remember *kan-ch'ing* occurs when people
> work together and co-operate. With the existence of *kan-
> ch'ing*, there are no disputes or fights. But *kan-ch'ing*, ac-
> cording to Matsu informants, is necessary for more than just
> peace; it is essential for successfully carrying out any activ-
> ity. . . . Without *kan-ch'ing* one cannot do things. Without
> *kan-ch'ing* lots of problems and possibly arguments occur. In
> other words, the concept of "utilization" (*li-yung*) implies the
> existence of *kan-ch'ing*. As one younger leader explained, "Of
> course one can use *kan-ch'ing*. If *kan-ch'ing* cannot be used
> it isn't *kan-ch'ing*. (p. 263)

Since relationship is what gets the job done, one must cultivate a somewhat close tie before further transactions can be
conducted. Regardless of whether such strategically built interpersonal ties imply some degree of exploitation, such "exploitation" is made possible only when there is a true or assumed
emotional concern; thus, even "functional" relationships are
not devoid of emotion (Jacobs, 1978).[10] The fact that it is still
a "contact" makes it a "*kan-ch'ing*," and since "*kan-ch'ing*" is
shared, it is a "relationship."

The emotional component not only serves as the basis
upon which a good relationship can be built, it is also an active
process through which relationships can be maintained. As
King (1989a) puts it, "Human emotion . . . does not exist ab-
stractly; it is closely related with concrete, particular social cultural systems" (p. 86). According to Hsiang (1974), the act of
acknowledging a relationship means that one shows one's "human emotion" toward relational partners. To show one's emotional concern for the other is to respect the other's *mien-tzu*.
The interconnection between human emotion and *mien-tzu* is
well explained by Hsiang (1974): "Giving people *mien-tzu*
makes it easy to gain for oneself 'human emotion,' whereas
hurting other's *mien-tzu* results in hurting one's 'human emotion' " (p. 57).

Through the process of "giving" and "claiming" *mien-tzu*,
relational partners reaffirm the bond between them by offering
each other emotional support. Hu (1944) illustrates: "if A has
mien-tzu with B, he can be certain that B will render him
friendship services on occasion, and also that B will increase
A's *mien-tzu* in front of other people in every possible way. This
bond ensures reciprocity, so that the greater the circle of those

with whom 'one has *mien-tzu*,' the better one can counter adversity" (p. 59).

In other words, to show an appropriate amount of "human emotion," and to give *mien-tzu* to each other, is to give life to the relationship. Judgments about what constitutes an appropriate amount of human emotion, as well as the extent to which *mien-tzu* is to be granted, is based upon the depth/closeness, or the importance, of a given relationship. In Chinese society, one must flexibly be attuned to fluctuations in human emotion. Failing to do this, King (1989a) notes, can result in social approbation:

> When we say this person "does not know human emotion," in fact we are saying, "this person has no idea of the relations between people." This is a relatively negative comment. On the other hand, when we say this person "well-understands human emotion" or "understands emotion and is reasonable," we are referring to the fact that such a person is good at dealing with people, good at arriving at the best place between people. This is a form of praise. (p. 79)

Interactions lacking in human emotion may, to a greater or lesser extent, be publicly criticized. Accordingly, it is important for one to know what people like and dislike and how they should behave, so that one may avoid being seen as lacking in "human emotion" (Wen, 1988). This concern for human emotion grants Chinese access to a number of unique cultural resources, such as *mien-tzu*, to help them function smoothly in the interpersonal realm. It is within the web of interpersonal relationships (*kuan-hsi*), with its emphasis upon human emotion as the primary good, that the claiming and granting of *mien-tzu* between interactants is made possible.

Summary
We have elaborated the concept of *mien-tzu* by situating it within the larger Chinese sociocultural system. *Mien-tzu* is closely tied to the Confucian ideal of social ordering, in which people of different relational status can be said to possess different kinds and amounts of *mien-tzu*, with the further requirement that such *mien-tzu* must be respected among interactants. Moreover, due to the Chinese perspective upon human emotion as the guiding principle of interpersonal interaction, *mien-tzu* becomes a means through which relational

partners express their emotional concern toward each other according to the depth of the relationship involved. This analysis corresponds to our earlier discussion on the concept of *mien-tzu:* it can be a quality claimed by the individual according to his/her social position, and can also be applied flexibly in interpersonal relating. We will now discuss how Chinese interpersonal interaction is organized under the concern for *mien-tzu,* and will demonstrate the necessity for maintaining a proper balance between insisting upon one's own *mien-tzu* and giving acknowledgment of the other's *mien-tzu.*

Mien-tzu and Interpersonal Relating

Mien-tzu and interpersonal relating cannot be separated from each other, and it is this fact that holds two contradictory facets of Chinese social life together in uneasy tension: on the one hand, *mien-tzu* may become a barrier to interpersonal relating, while on the other hand, *mien-tzu* provides a facilitating mechanism to improve interpersonal effectiveness. For the Chinese, a balance must be reached, between de-emphasizing *mien-tzu* so as not to worsen an already difficult situation, and emphasizing *mien-tzu* enough to maintain smooth social interactions. The delicate balance requires each actor's understanding of the Chinese conception of *mien-tzu,* encompassing both constructive and destructive elements for interpersonal relationships.

Mien-tzu as a Barrier: A Source for
Interpersonal Difficulties

Mien-tzu as a guiding principle for social interaction commands mutual respect. If the *mien-tzu* of the interactants is not appropriately handled, their relationship may be damaged. As Ho (1976) notes, the opportunities for misstep are extensive indeed:

> Since social expectations are reciprocal in nature, potential conflicts arise when there is a discrepancy between what a person expects or claims from others and what others extend to him. The possibility of losing face can arise not only from the individual's failure to meet his obligations but also from the failure to act in accordance with his expectations of them—that is, not only from the individual's own actions, but also from how he is treated by others. (p. 873)

The need for smooth interaction underscores the importance of knowing *how* to communicate in order to save each
other's *mien-tzu*. For Chinese, this understanding is not simply an issue of social technique; it is also a measure of one's
wisdom in dealing with the world (King, 1989b). Protecting
each other's *mien-tzu* implies that interactants take their relational responsibilities seriously, and is a sign of respect both
for oneself and for the other. Since damaging the other's *mien-
tzu* may mean the end of a given relationship, it is incumbent
on each social actor to protect each other's *mien-tzu* by all
available means (King, 1989b, 332).

Although flexibility and warmth are part of Chinese relationship, there are times when Chinese relationships can become very cold and rigid, due to excessive concern for *mien-
tzu*, which often leads to interpersonal difficulty and prevents
an immediate and expeditious solution of interpersonal problems. A particularly important concern is the image of oneself
in the eyes of one's relational partner. In a given relationship,
for example, the existence of *mien-tzu* gives rise to a certain
status consciousness, governing which of the conflicting parties will be expected to "lower his [or her] head" (i.e., admit
wrongdoing) first. One male middle manager we interviewed
pointed out the importance of yielding: "There must be one
party who can first admit, 'You are right and I am wrong.' If
there is such a fact, and one party is willing to recede, then
they should be able to get along with each other again."

Unfortunately, when the interactants care too much about
their *mien-tzu*, they may refuse to "lower their head" first, even
though they may really want to compromise, and indeed may
cease to interact for long periods of time, even years. Hsiang
(1974) explains that, because Chinese are extremely sensitive,
mien-tzu becomes particularly important to them. Especially
problematic is the situation in which one party assumes a
higher relational position than the other party. A story was told
to us by a forty-year-old female employee regarding a minister's
wife, who was accused by her aunt of being a thief. Because
neither was willing to "lower their head" first, they remained
separated for several decades:

> She has not talked to her aunt, [and has not] visited her for
> more than thirty years. Why? Because when she was a teen-
> ager, she went to her aunt's home. Someone stole a cucumber,
> and her aunt accused her and [slapped] her face. After she

left, she carried her hate from that time on. She no longer [spends time] with her aunt . . . in fact, if one party is [more] mature, then it will not be like that.

One day while learning about internal consciousness, she thought about [the incident] and went to call her aunt immediately. When her aunt received this phone call, on the other side of the phone line, she heard her aunt cry right at that moment. She told her aunt, "Years ago, I did not steal your cucumber." Her aunt said, "I know. Because I found out who really stole the cucumber."

Now [if] we think about that, it is very childish. Had her aunt phoned her and said, "I am too quick [to accuse you] during the time," it would be okay. But her aunt holds back and [does not want to say]. The other side does not want to say [anything] either, because she feels that she was hurt. The result is this [estrangement] for so many years.

The interviewee suggests that if the aunt had been willing to sacrifice her *mien-tzu* in front of her niece by talking things out, she would not have had to live with her guilt for more than thirty years:

Orientals are always like that, when they commit an error, they do not want to apologize for it. In fact, you don't even need to be [that clear]. You probably can just say, "In fact, I . . . already knew what happened." You state the event, and she will know that she will not be accused because the truth has come out. . . . [The aunt] already knows that it is not her [niece], but she [the aunt] cannot "hold down her *mien-tzu* to say, "I already know it was not you. It was a mistake at that time." Perhaps inside her heart she does feel guilty. Therefore, when the minister's wife called her, she cried immediately after so many years. You can see that she must feel very guilty. Why do you need to have this guilt for so many years and hurt both of you?

A second example shows how the concern for *mien-tzu* is related to the Chinese hierarchical social structure. When asked whether she thinks Chinese are too "fond of *mien-tzu*," the interviewee replied with a story of father-and-son,

Among Chinese, the father is the older generation. If today he has some conflict with his child, and there is a third party involved in the situation, even if the son is correct, the father would not apologize to his son. He will think, "I am the father, how could I apologize to you?" This is a common occurrence. If he is older, that is, if he belongs to the older generation, or has higher status, then he cannot "pull down *lien*." He loves his *mien-tzu* to death and thinks, "my status is higher than yours, how can I apologize?" It is his fault but he wants the other to "remedy the situation." This is much too common in Taiwan. This is not reasonable.

Respect for the elderly is well established in Chinese traditions inherited from Confucius. The elderly, being important members of the society, request more respect from younger people, and consequently need more *mien-tzu* from them. The extent to which one can claim *mien-tzu* depends upon who one interacts with, since the relative social positioning is defined within and between interactants. Particularly in the relationship between father and son (one of the five basic Confucian relationships), the father can claim his *mien-tzu* as a father. It is in front of the son that the father's "*mien-tzu* cannot be held," that is, he cannot lose his self-respect in front of his own child.

This example shows the impact of ordering in Chinese interpersonal transactions. When people are placed into different statuses and orders of relationships, the issue of *mien-tzu* becomes more problematic. If *mien-tzu* is an attribute predominantly associated with one's social and relational position, it is not surprising to find that the relative importance of social position has conditioned the extent to which *mien-tzu* can be acknowledged: anyone who occupies the relatively higher position in a given relationship has more to say about his or her *mien-tzu*.

Another of our interviewees, a twenty-seven-year-old female clerk, describes this excessive concern for *mien-tzu* as "taking things too seriously," that (as the folk saying has it) "they won't cry without seeing the coffin": "I think Chinese sometimes take [things] too seriously. . . . Not until they have destroyed the whole situation and the event becomes very serious will they realize they have done something wrong and regret what they have done. They have made the event too big and cannot find a way to remedy it."

Because of the concern for one's *mien-tzu*, interactions which take place in public often imply greater risk than those occurring in private. One middle manager explains that the public situation is different because, "everyone wants to insist that he is right . . . because there are so many people in that situation." By insisting on their own opinions in an attempt to protect their own *mien-tzu*, ironically, such individuals may end up sacrificing the relationship without dealing with the problem.

Therefore, an effective communicator must know enough not to push the issue too far: in other words, one must act in ways which will protect the other's *mien-tzu*. Typically, such communication is somewhat more circumscribed; to protect the other's self-image and feelings, he or she is not confronted directly. One female interviewee suggests a gentle touch in dealing with conflicts:

> If it is her fault and she knows that, but because she "loves her *mien-tzu*," she cannot apologize in front of you, you can still forgive her. If she already knows her fault, there is no reason to force her to say, "I am sorry." You can see that event as already having passed away. There is no need to force her and embarrass her. This is not good for you, either.

Under the mechanism of *mien-tzu*, it is possible for the relationship to return to its normal state in the absence of reference to substantive issues. This indirect way of handling interpersonal problems is highly valued in Chinese society; it addresses the concern and warmth one has for the other, as Hu (1944) explains:

> The motive is to avoid any action or words that might make the other fellow feel insignificant; rather is it believed that by elevating his self-esteem his good performance will be assured. . . . Individuals of good standing in society, whose words carry weight with their fellows, are particularly expected to "leave other people some *mien-tzu*," an attitude also described as "great in capacity," as opposed to narrowness in dealing with others. (pp. 58–59)

One who can graciously "leave someone a *mien-tzu*" is said to be "great in capacity," meaning that one is generous and kind toward the other. As one of our interviewees put it, one must allow "stairs for people to leave the stage" (that is, a face-saving means of exit from the conflict). Failure to provide "stairs" can itself be taken as a form of offense. Parties deprived of a means of graceful exit from conflict may not only passively resist by refusing to cooperate, but may actively seek revenge

(Hsiang, 1974; Yang, 1945). This is due to the fact that refusal to grant *mien-tzu* constitutes a denial of "human emotion," which in turn implies a refusal to acknowledge the relationship. Hwang (1989) explains how *mien-tzu* operates upon the Chinese norm of reciprocity to ensure revenge:

> When one meets great difficulty and begs "human emotion" from resource controllers, if they do not "give him *mien-tzu*" and refuse him, he will feel his self-esteem is damaged, and experience the feeling of "no *mien-tzu*." Under the social norm of "mercy for mercy, and revenge for revenge," if he has an opportunity in the future, it is very possible that he will let them "look not good on their [own] *mien-tzu*," and finally end up with "everyone has no *mien-tzu*." Therefore, in such situations, it is best for the resource controller to "save human emotion so that people can see each other in the future," that is, "do human emotion" to him [one who requests something under the name of *mien-tzu*]. (p. 307)

Because of the serious consequences which may result from damage to one's *mien-tzu*, social actors prefer to protect each other's *mien-tzu* in interaction. Moreover, such attention is not limited to public, formal relationships. Even between father and son, of niece and aunt, it is equally necessary to engage in mutual protection of *mien-tzu*. This constraining power of *mien-tzu*, however, at the same time enables Chinese interactants to fashion smoother and more harmonious relationships. In the following section, we will see how *mien-tzu* (face), human emotion (*ren-ching*), and relations (*kuan-hsi*) are interwoven to facilitate smooth interpersonal interaction.

Mien-tzu as a Lubricant: A Source for Interpersonal Effectiveness

As a dynamic social resource available to Chinese relational partners, *mien-tzu* is often activated by a request. Because most Chinese treat mutual acknowledgement of *mien-tzu* as obligatory, they generally expect that a request under the name of *mien-tzu* will be successful. Indeed, given the intimate connection between *mien-tzu* and the depth or closeness of a relationship, *mien-tzu* is frequently used as a metaphor for renegotiating mutual rights and obligations. With a close relational partner, one can always "ask for *mien-tzu*" to get things done.[11] Hence, it is natural for Chinese, when they need help from someone with whom they are not familiar, to find an appropriate person (an intermediary who has a closer tie, or who is considered to be important, to the target person), to approach the target for them. The close tie between the intermediary and the target ensures the success of the petitioner's request. The target is willing to grant the request under the aegis of his/her relationship in order to show emotional concern for the *intermediary*, rather than for the person who makes the request. In other words, The intermediary is the one whose *mien-tzu* will be acknowledged. By utilizing appropriate interpersonal connections (*kuan-hsi*) and through application of the participants' *mien-tzu*, one is more likely to secure needed services and assistance.

Moreover, given the importance of allowing conflicting parties a means of graceful exit, the intermediary also provides "stairs" for the disputants to leave the stage of conflict. Metaphorically, when a third party is engaged in the process of conflict resolution, the *mien-tzu* of the conflicting parties can be protected "under the cover" of the intermediary's *mien-tzu*. Hu (1944) provides an example of how a mediator of good standing—that is, one who has sufficient *mien-tzu*—can solve a seemingly intractable conflict:

> As soon as two people lose control of themselves in a quarrel, a mediator, usually an older person, will appear at once, separate the two and argue with them till they stop. To give his words effect he asks each person to stop "out of regard for my *mien-tzu*." Such an appeal by an individual of some standing . . . must not be disregarded. (Hu, 1944, 60)

Since each party *must display* concern for the mediator, and must honor the mediator's *mien-tzu*, there is really no reason to continue fighting. Fighting results from preoccupation with one's own selfish interests; upon the intermediary's involvement, the focus changes to the intermediary's interests.

Another factor regulating the degree to which an intermediary's *mien-tzu* will be acknowledged is awareness of relational hierarchy. This awareness can function in two ways. First, the higher the relational position the intermediary occupies in a particular relationship, the more likely it is that she/he can claim *mien-tzu* in the presence of the disputants. In a given relationship, *mien-tzu* implies hierarchical order. For example, if one's parents serve as an "inter-relational mediator" to solve a conflict between oneself and a friend, the parents' *mien-tzu* is not to be taken lightly, in accordance with the Chinese interpersonal norm that older people should receive respect from younger. Second, in general, the higher the social status one achieves, the more desirable one becomes as a target for other to build up relationships with, and hence the more power one's *mien-tzu* assumes.[12] Since the person of high status can claim more influence in negotiating mutual rights and obligations, his/her intervention makes successful resolution of a conflict much more likely.

These seemingly abstract cultural norms are played out in concrete social interaction, as shown in an example provided by a male manager. In his account, notice the delicate interweaving of relations, face, and human emotion used to "smooth the ruffled feathers" of his dissatisfied client.

> For example, if I need to solve problems for my subordinates. Suppose some clients are not satisfied with my subordinates. How can I not "go out the door" to help my subordinates solve the problem? When I need to solve the problem I must go visit [the dissatisfied client], or he may already have called to express his anger. First I need to know, who is he? Where is he? Who is his father? Who is his wife? What does he like? Who are his friends? What is his hobby? If I must face him, I at least can "climb" this *kuan-hsi* to cultivate with him a sense of sameness, let him feel close about me. He may be dissatisfied about our company, about my subordinates, or about my superiors.
>
> When you go to visit him, of course you still need to be very polite. At least you need to invite him to drink some tea. Bring some good tea with you and say, "I know that you like to drink tea, why don't you try this?" Half of his anger will go away. If you are acquainted with his wife, or his friend is your friend, just tell your friend, "Please tell him that I am going to visit him. Please say some good words for me."

One can note in this incident two levels of *mien-tzu*. First, the manager *himself* volunteers to serve as an intermediary to utilize his own *mien-tzu* to mediate the conflict between his subordinates and clients. Second, he actively engages in the process of finding *other* intermediaries ("Who is his father?", "Who is his wife?", "Who are his friends?"), whose *mien-tzu* may be connected to the client, to mediate for him. In this incident, conflict is recast and to some extent lessened by appeal to the *mien-tzu* and human emotion characteristic of the various "inter-relations" of the people who are involved, or come to be involved, in the conflict. Let us further explore the specific normative mechanisms which enable the participants to use *mien-tzu*.

First, one sees the effect of the cultural norm that the higher the relative position one occupies, the better one's ability to claim face and thus solve the conflict. The manager's *mien-tzu* and his relationship with the client is more powerful than the relationship between his subordinates and the client because he has a higher position than his subordinates, and in the society as a whole, a manager is considered to have high social status. Hence, it is the manager's *mien-tzu* that is more likely to be acknowledged by the dissatisfied client.

Second, however, in his attempt to involve the dissatisfied client's father, wife, and friends, the interviewee seeks relationships that are close and important to the dissatisfied client, and thereby to lessen the intensity of the conflict. Especially for Chinese, who place a great deal of emphasis upon family relationships, a conflict which is partially mediated by a family member is less serious than it might be otherwise. This also is true of good friends, whose words will carry more weight than will a stranger's. In other words, the *mien-tzu* of the target's father, mother, wife, husband, or siblings, being more important to the target, is much more likely to be acknowledged than the *mien-tzu* of the manager himself.

On the one hand, the manager's *mien-tzu* and human emotion must be acknowledged by his subordinates and his client, while on the other hand, the *mien-tzu* and human emotion of the second-level intermediaries must also be acknowledged both by the manager and the client. These two sets of relationships function in different ways and yet tend toward the same goal: the solution of the conflict through a concern for *mien-tzu*. By employing various interpersonal relationships, the manager was able to solve the conflict and at the same time enhance the reputation of his company by protecting the *mien-tzu* of his employees.

It is worth reemphasizing, however, that the functioning of *mien-tzu* in conflict resolution cannot be divorced from Chinese ideals on different orders or relationships. As Gallin (1966) notes, "The effectiveness of mediation that was directed toward the preservation of local autonomy and harmony was possible, in large part, because of the society's acceptance of

the hierarchical relationship system, in which all relationships—except, perhaps, personal friendships—are based on
the positions individuals hold relative to each other" (p. 268).
The effect of hierarchical positioning on conflict resolution is
also discussed in Yang's (1945) analysis of governance in a traditional mainland Chinese village:

> When two leading families, or two village dignitaries, or two
> clans, come into conflict, the case will not be ignored but
> must be mediated by the village leaders. . . . Usually this is
> done through the good offices of the village leaders, but when
> the gentry or the chief clans are involved, the ordinary village
> leaders do not have sufficient prestige to intervene. In these
> cases, leaders from other villages are called in. These may
> be no more capable than the local leaders, but because they
> are from a different village their presence means more to the
> conflicting parties, and therefore, they have a greater "mien-
> tzu." Many disputes are thus settled by outside intervention.
> (p. 165)

Some conflict can be solved *only* through certain individuals whose *mien-tzu* will be acknowledged in recognition of
their social standing. In his analysis of a Taiwanese village,
Gallin (1966) states, "local conflict was resolved on the local
level by respected individuals whose 'words could be heard' and
respected." (p. 268). Such influential people are often considered good candidates for the role of mediator, based primarily
on the amount of *mien-tzu* they may claim. Conflicting parties
will "see the *mien-tzu*" of the intermediary and be willing to
compromise; it is either that, or else risk damaging the *mien-
tzu* of the intermediary (by refusing to acknowledge the relational prestige of the intermediary), with the subsequent social
criticism this may entail.

The traditional emphasis upon hierarchical relational position and the impact of *mien-tzu* is observable in today's Taiwan. Unfortunately, although feelings and human emotion
must be taken into account in solving conflicts, one sometimes
encounters a situation in which the intermediary's *mien-tzu*
and human emotion carry such weight that the less powerful
conflicting party finds it difficult to resist any proposed compromise. This is generally seen as an exploitation of the cultural norm that the person with higher social position receives
more *mien-tzu*-consideration: relationship is utilized to solve

the conflict, not out of any concern for the intermediary on the part of the disputants, but because the intermediary's power, *in and of itself*, commands disputants to acknowledge his or her *mien-tzu*. This represents the fullest expression of the practical and utilitarian aspects of *kuan-hsi*, and hence more involves the observance of ritualistic rules than an acquiescence to "real" human emotion. There is more emphasis on form than content.

An example of *mien-tzu* manipulation is provided in the account of a forty-year-old lawyer, who describes how a person can gain advantage in a labor negotiation by invoking *mien-tzu* to coerce compliance:

> When laborers have disputes with their boss, usually the boss has more channels to talk about "human emotion." If you ask the boss to give some "human emotion" to the laborers, usually it has no effect. The boss will say "I cannot recede," neither does he feel any burden of "human emotion." Although laborers and those who want to help them have relatively greater power, the boss has even greater "interpersonal relations." He can ask laborers to consider "human emotion" for him, according to their respective [difference in] power. The boss possesses a greater [degree of] "interpersonal relations," and is able to use "human emotion" more than the laborers.
>
> If the laborers ask for ten dollars, for example, the boss will go through a lot of "*kuan-hsi*" [relations] to tell the laborers, "*You should give [your] boss some 'mien-tzu.' Five dollars are [sic] enough.*" Normally the laborers need to back away, because they have a "burden of human emotion." . . . These lawyers or the labor union [who represent laborers] cannot insist against the boss any longer; they will accept some compromise by telling the laborers that "The boss has sincerity. You don't need to ask for ten dollars. Five dollars are [sic] okay." [Emphasis added]

In this example, several interesting facts deserve mention. First, both the boss and the laborers both have their own spokespersons. The lawyer serves as an intermediary between the laborers and their boss, and a third party of considerable status serves as an intermediary between the lawyer representing the laborers and the boss. Second, the bargain between the boss and the laborers is made under the name of "giving someone more *mien-tzu*." The *mien-tzu* to be acknowledged is that of the boss, not the laborers. Third, although the boss has higher social economic status than the laborers, the request for *mien-tzu* is not made directly by the boss, but by another who is powerful enough to secure the boss' *mien-tzu* in the eyes of the laborers. Finally, the compromise is made possible because the laborers owe "human emotion" both to their boss and the influential person who speaks for the boss.

This example serves to illustrate the involved and complicated nature of power networks in Chinese society. By appealing to more important and significant people, one can have more power in negotiating. While the boss already has higher position than laborers, the powerful third party is used to further augment the boss' *mien-tzu*. Clearly, the boss is also in a better position to utilize more powerful relationships. The *mien-tzu* of both the powerful intermediary and the boss are to be acknowledged by both parties, even though the results of the compromise favor one conflicting party over the other. It is instructive to follow the layers of interrelation in this example to reveal how *mien-tzu* functions as a resource in Chinese life.

The effectiveness of *mien-tzu* in interpersonal functioning leads Hwang (1987) to refer to the utilization of *mien-tzu* as "the Chinese game of power" (p. 944). Chinese, according to Hwang, "use many different means to enforce [their] own image and power in the other's mind, so as to influence the other, and acquire the life resources one wants" (p. 298). As discussed earlier, the higher the social position one occupies, the more "developed" one's *mien-tzu* will become. In this regard, *mien-tzu* has reward value, like a form of currency with which one may "buy" social resources. As King (1989b) puts it, "the social aspect of *mien-tzu*...is like the credit card. Having *mien-tzu* is like having good credit, so that [one] has a lot of purchasing power" (p. 330). *Mien-tzu* can be acquired by the individual him- or herself, and can be utilized as a token to obtain social resources when necessary.

Work on one's *mien-tzu*, therefore, involves attempts to manipulate degrees of relationship so as to augment one's social resources. As Chu (1989) comments, "in a Chinese society which emphasizes moral relationships, and viewing harmony as the core of their cultural value, 'speaking human emotion,' 'pull *kuan-hsi*,' and 'requesting *mien-tzu*,' become the guiding principles of behavior in interpersonal interaction" (p. 40). These observations echo the point made by Hu (1944), who contended: "The value that the society attaches to *mien-tzu* is ambivalent. On the one hand, it refers to well-earned popularity . . . 'reputation' in its best sense; on the other hand, it implies a desire for self-aggrandizement" (p. 61).

Of course, one should note that not every aspect of *mien-tzu* concerns resource allocation. Indeed, the concept of *mien-tzu* is not only utilized by the important people in manipulating social resources, but it is also manifested through any aspects of Chinese interpersonal interaction, confirming its importance as a guiding principle reflecting respect for the other's self-esteem.

Conclusion

A full understanding of *mien-tzu* as a specifically Chinese cultural concept necessitates considering the complex connections among relations (*kuan-hsi*), human emotion (*ren-ching*), and face (*mien-tzu*). If the interactants' *mien-tzu* is not properly taken care of, the relationship may be damaged even if there is no conflict over substantive issues. One might conclude that, given the importance of *mien-tzu* for the Chinese, showing respect for each other's *mien-tzu* in any interactional situation constitutes, in itself, a "substantive" issue. On the other hand, *mien-tzu* also contributes to effective interpersonal relating, given the fact that it encompasses both emotional and pragmatic elements. One may have sincere emotional concern for the other, and consequently show respect for the other's *mien-tzu;* conversely, respect for another's *mien-tzu*, as one part of the interactants' relational responsibilities, can be utilized to help one to function within Chinese society. One sees the mutual permeation of the emotional and the utilitarian in personal, business, and political interactions, all conducted under the name of *mien-tzu*.

Challenges and Reflections

If we simply attempt to describe *mien-tzu* by itself, without reference to other cultural concepts, we run the risk of losing the essence of *mien-tzu*'s cultural meaning, leading in turn to the misjudgment that Chinese tend to overemphasize external formality at the expense of personal autonomy. Indeed, equating *mien-tzu* with formality utterly fails to capture the richness and delicacy of Chinese interactional episodes which manifest subtle awareness of other parties' *mien-tzu*. By taking a cultural perspective, we can acquire a good understanding of the meanings of face to the Chinese. Conversely, the discussion of

the concept of *mien-tzu* also provides an in-depth understanding of Chinese cultural life, demonstrating the importance of
face in helping us reexamine some commonly held beliefs
about Chinese. Based on what we have learned, we can further
extend the concept of face as an organizing construct to social
scientific inquiries on human communication across cultural
boundaries.

Connections between the Private and the Public

Mien-tzu, the Chinese concern for face, is one important
mechanism which bridges private and public interactional
concerns. It is misleading to assume that *mien-tzu*, with its elements of external formality, diverges from private, personal
concerns. Given the flexibility and complexity of *mien-tzu* in
Chinese relationships, the lines between the public and the
private, the social and the personal, are never clearly drawn.
Although the concept of *mien-tzu* itself suggests recognition
credited by the society at large, recognition and its application
in interpersonal activities cannot be detached from the Confucian ideal of hierarchical relational positioning and its associated degrees of human emotion.

Earlier, we noted that the extent to which *mien-tzu* is to be
recognized depends both upon the social position one occupies, as well as the depth of a given relationship. While the
former condition suggests commonly agreed-upon value judgments, the latter condition suggests that the *mien-tzu* one can
claim in front of another is based upon personal and private
concerns. In essence, then, *mien-tzu* is composed of essentially private concerns functioning in public; *mien-tzu* brings
Chinese personal life to the public arena. For Chinese, the
more private, emotional concern which ingroup members ex-
hibit for each other, through the medium of interpersonal connections, can be extended to more distant social others. From
emotional concern to acquiring social resources, Chinese are
flexible in their utilization of various kinds of relationships. As
we have shown, to utilize *mien-tzu* effectively in any interpersonal encounter requires flexibility in searching for the most
appropriate and available interconnection, whether a more intimate personal contact, or a relationship which is built primarily upon practical considerations. Within this complex of
interrelationships, one *mien-tzu* can be related to another,
linking the private to the public.

Reexamining Chinese Cultural Life as Collectivism

As we have elaborated *mien-tzu* serves as a metaphor for recognition of relationships, and may be flexibly attuned to various situations through connecting one *mien-tzu* with another. From our analysis of how *mien-tzu* facilitates Chinese interpersonal effectiveness, the characteristics of collectivism, often thought to be related to the Chinese, can be reexamined.

The individualism-collectivism continuum is one of the most important constructs in cross-cultural studies; among many dimensions which differentiate these two extremes, one of the most important dimensions is the role of ingroups (Hofstede, 1980; Triandis, 1988; Triandis et al., 1988). According to Triandis, ingroups in a collective society are more stable, fewer, impose greater responsibilities, and exert greater control over their members, compared with those in individualistic societies. Collectivist societies tend to draw a clearer line between ingroups and outgroups than individualistic societies: "people [of collective societies] are trained to cooperate with members of a few ingroups and compete with everyone else" (Triandis, 1988, p. 60). Moreover, in collectivist societies, group goals, as defined by ingroups, are considered to be more important than individual goals: "An essential attribute of collectivist cultures is that individuals may be induced to subordinate their personal goals to the goals of some collective, which is usually a stable ingroup (e.g., family, band, tribe)" (Triandis et al., 1988, p. 324). Hence, the emphasis in collectivism is said to place upon social orientation, which "represents a tendency for a person to act in accordance with external expectations or social norms, rather than internal wishes or personal integrity, so that he would be able to protect his social self and function as an integral part of the social network. Here solidarity and social consciousness are more decisive as determinants of behavior than individuality and self-assertion" (Yang, 1981, pp. 159–60).

As we examine Chinese cultural life from the perspective of *mien-tzu* as inter-relational concern, several issues deserve attention. First, the assumed stability and fewer numbers of ingroups in collectivist societies can be misleading. Though their in-groups are fewer and more stable than those of individualist cultures, in Chinese culture at least, due to the role of *mien-tzu*, the line between in- and out-groups can often be made flexible. Indeed, the mechanism of *mien-tzu* provides an effective means through which new, but temporary ingroups may be established via the concern for human emotion. In everyday activity, Chinese ingroup connections can always be extended, since the *mien-tzu* will be acknowledged when appropriate connections are established. Second, although group goals are important to the Chinese it is precisely this importance that allows *mien-tzu* to function flexibly to fulfill personal goals. The emphasis upon mutual *mien-tzu*-giving not only regulates a person's behavior within a given relationship, it also provides Chinese with a way to approach their goals through interpersonal connections. By observing how *mien-tzu* functions in the presence of human emotion, we can understand how the collectivity is defined with reference to the particular ties one possesses; these particular ties provide the foundation upon which collectivity or community may be built. Unfortunately, the active aspect of Chinese relationships is seldom recognized; scholars typically tend to examine only one side of the issue, concluding that Chinese are controlled externally and that they exercised little personal individual autonomy.

The Concept of Mien-tzu in Other Cultural Systems

In our discussion of the Chinese concept of face, we have shown how Chinese interaction is conducted within a delicate balance, between not stressing *mien-tzu* too much, and at the same time protecting each other's *mien-tzu*. Our cultural perspective provides one example of the importance of issues of face in interpersonal relating. Similar to Ho's (1976) suggestion that the criterion against which face is evaluated reveals the magnitude of social change, we contend that an understanding of the intersection between face and interpersonal relationships provides a vantage point to judge the functioning of interpersonal relating in various cultural settings. Although cultures vary in their emphasis and orientation toward face, the fundamental issues of how to present oneself in the eyes of others, nevertheless, remain to be solved by all of humankind, regardless of whether one's cultural groups is labeled "collectivist" or "individualist" (Ho, 1976).

Just as *mien-tzu* is a unique construct formulated by Chinese, the Western cultural conceptions of face (as in Goffman's work) also derive their contents from the cultures in which they are situated. Western understanding of facework is very much influenced by the idea of impression management, reflecting the dominant individualistic value characteristics of

Western cultures. This can be contrasted with the Chinese conception of *mien-tzu* which places more emphasis on the nature of the *relationship*. *Mien-tzu* suggests a further, very important, question to be raised: considering the semantic implications of "face" and "*mien-tzu*," in applying the concept of "face" to analyze human interaction across cultures, have we paid insufficient attention to the issue of culture in analyzing face as an emic construct?

It is interesting to ask to what extent a cultural concept, particularly as it is revealed through linguistic labels, marks its idiosyncratic cultural practices. Fortunately, if it is language that makes cultural resources available to us, the *lack* of a set of linguistic terms does not necessarily negate the existence of a cultural resource. While the richness and complexity of *mien-tzu* as relational concern remains specific to Chinese, other cultures, without access to the extensive Chinese set of cultural vocabularies, may nevertheless share a universal human problem: the fundamental issue of how to present oneself in front of others. We believe that such fundamental concerns can be more fully addressed through the investigation of different manifestations and solutions to the problems of self-presentation within different cultural boundaries. Through examining the role culture plays in shaping the contents of face, we are able to extend the analysis of the concept of face into different cultural settings. It is for this reason that the study of face and facework is a fruitful area for scholars to engage in dialogue, an area where the relationship between culture and communication can be best understood.

Notes

1. In this paper, interviewees' accounts from our earlier studies are presented to illustrate how the concept of *mien-tzu* is actualized in modern Taiwan. These studies are part of a research project which focuses upon the overall patterning of Chinese interpersonal relationships and communication, in which Chinese in Taiwan talk about four organizing metaphors (*mien-tzu, pao, yuan,* and *kuan-hsi*) in their conceptualization of relationships. In all, fifty-five in-depth interviews were conducted in Mandarin Chinese and Taiwanese in Taiwan, during May and June of 1990. Interviewees vary in their educational background: more than 80 percent of the interviewees have received a college education, and almost 95 percent of inter-

viewees reside in Taipei, the capital city of Taiwan. While interviewees very in their occupations, most work in commercial companies. About 80 percent of the interviewees are aged between 30 and 40 years. For this chapter, only several selected interview accounts which relate to issues of *mien-tzu* and which are important to our discussion are presented to facilitate a conceptual understanding of the Chinese concept of face, or *mien-tzu*. We do not intend to make any claim for generalizability of the interviewee accounts before thorough and detailed analysis of these interview contents is conducted.

2. In this paper, all romanizations are based upon Wade-Gile system (Choy, 1980).

3. One must note that there are some clear distinctions between earlier and modern scholars: (1) differences in time; and (2) differences in location. The earlier scholars made their observations in China at the turn of nineteenth century, whereas the modern scholars quoted in this article made their observations in Taiwan at the turn of the twentieth century.

4. Two Chinese terms correspond to the English term "face": *mien-tzu* and *lien*. Hu (1944) marked the distinction between the two: while *mien-tzu* refers to external social recognition, *lien* has internal moral connotations. Although the distinction is not insignificant, as King (1989a; 1989b) and Ho (1976) have pointed out, such standards are often interchangable according to place and time. In this chapter, we have chosen to focus upon *mien-tzu* to avoid unnecessary confusion with various and interchangeable linguistic terms.

5. King contends that there is a close connection between the concept of shame, as described in the Confucian classics, and the concept of *mien-tzu*. Drawing upon the Confucian moral teachings on propriety, or *li*, King argues that, in interacting with others, it is likely that these norms may fall prey to external formality, thus accounting for the social character of *mien-tzu*. Nevertheless, the self-sanctioned, introspective moral reasoning required of each individual in interacting with others also allows for *mien-tzu* to become important: one may be shamed by one's inability to achieve certain moral standards. Under such conditions, *mien-tzu* needs no audience. To put is simply, with its strong social character, the concept of *mien-tzu* also encompasses a strong element of morality; one not only wants to be acknowledged by others, one also wants to be acknowledged by oneself.

6. These linguistic expressions are derived from the observations of the scholars we quote, particularly Hu (1944), Huang (1989), and King (1989), as against the primary author's judgment about how these terms are used in contemporary Taiwanese society. The latter judgment is based upon the data collected in the study.

7. An amusing but revealing example of how this is achieved occurs in one popular Chinese television program aired in Taiwan. The program, roughly similar to the American program, "The Love Con-

nection," allows a contestant to choose among five potential dating partners. However, in the Chinese version, the four contestants who are not chosen are matched with dating partners from the audience at the conclusion of the program! Since each of the pairs of contestants is given a chance to express appreciation for their "date," everyone's *mien-tzu* is protected.

8. For a more extensive discussion of the utilization of Chinese relationship, see Chang and Holt (1991).

9. There are two similar but different Chinese terms which relate to emotion. In this article, we translate the Chinese *ren-ching* as "human emotion," since *ren* refers to "human beings," whereas "ching" refers to emotion. *Ren-ching*, in a philosophical sense, denotes human beings' common emotional response, although it also implies an obligatory affective component which serves to define the responsibility one has toward the other. Another Chinese term, *kan-ch'ing*, is translated as "emotion": *kan* refers to "sense or feeling," and *ching* to "emotion." *Kan-ch'ing* at the cultural level reflects a unique kind of relationship, frequently referring to the "emotional" basis for a more instrumental relationship which has no blood connection. While the distinction can be extensively discussed, in this chapter, we have focused attention on how emotional concern serves as a major regulating factor in the establishment and maintenance of Chinese relationships as a foundation upon which *mien-tzu* can be engaged.

10. Although Jacobs (1978) does not agree with Fried's assessment that *kan-ch'ing* implies a "recognized degree of exploitation," he contends instead that "*kan-ch'ing* has a truly emotional aspect" (p. 262).

11. An overheard conversation between Chinese illustrates this idea: "Good morning, Mr. Huang. How are you? I am Mr. Wang in the Institute. I have a friend who has come from another state and is interested in buying some books from your store. . . . I wonder if it is possible for you to grant me a *mien-tzu* and give her a special discount?" As one might expect, the *mien-tzu* requested was happily granted, and the person interested in buying books was given a fifteen percent discount through the good offices of Wang's *mien-tzu*, as manifested in the relationship between Wang and the bookstore owner.

12. It might be argued that the centrality of "social status" as a factor influencing conflict resolution indicates that Chinese society is "class-conscious." However, we must note that so-called high social status refers to more than simply social, economic, or political standing. To Chinese, a well-educated person, a virtuous person, or a well-respected person, even if lacking in social or political power, can also be considered a "high status" individual.

References

Bard, E. (1905). *Chinese life in town and country.* New York: The Knickerbocker Press.

Baxter, L. A. (1984). An investigation of compliance-gaining as politeness. *Human Communication Research, 10,* 427–456.

Brown, P., and Levinson, S. C. (1987). *Politeness: Some universals in language usage.* New York: Cambridge University Press.

Chan, W. T. (1963). *A sourcebook in Chinese philosophy.* Princeton, NJ: Princeton University Press.

———. (1967). Chinese theory and practice, with special reference to humanism. in C. A. Moore (Ed.), *The Chinese mind.* Honolulu: University of Hawaii Press.

Chang, H. C. and Holt, G. R. (1991). More than relatoinship: Chinese and the principle of kuan-hsi. *Communication Quarterly, 39,* 251–271.

Ch'en, C. C. (1989). A theoretical analysis and empirical research on the psychology of *mien-tzu.* In K. S. Yang (Ed.), *The psychology of the Chinese.* Taipei: Kui-Kuan Books [In Chinese]

Choy, R. (1981). *Read and write Chinese: A simplified guide to the Chinese characters* (4th ed.). San Francisco: China West Books.

Chu, J. I. (1989). Chinese social interaction: the issue of *mien-tzu.* In K. S. Yang (Ed.), *The psychology of the Chinese.* Taipei: Kui-Kuan Books. [In Chinese]

Craig, R., Tracy, K., and Spisak, F. (1986). The discourse of requests: Assesment of a politeness approach. *Human Communication Research, 12,* 437–468.

Danton, G. H. (1938). *The Chinese people.* Boston: Marshall Jones Company.

Fairhurst, G. T., Green, S. G., and Snavely, B. K. (1984). Face support in controlling poor performance. *Human Communication Research, 11,* 272–295.

Fei, H. T. (1947). *Country China.* Shang-hai: Observatory Publishing Co. [In Chinese]

Fried, M. H. (1953). *Fabric of Chinese society: A study of the social life of a Chinese county seat.* New York: Octagon Books.

Fung, Y. I. (1983). *A history of Chinese philosophy,* vol. 1 (D. Bodde, Trans.). Princeton, NJ: Princeton University Press.

Gallin, B. (1966). Conflict resolution in changing Chinese society: A Taiwanese study. In M. J. Swartz, V. W. Turner, and A. Tuden (Eds.), *Political anthropology.* Chicago: Aldine.

Geng, L. C. (1982). Li, order, and blood relatoins: The order of human relationships in traditional Chinese culture. In G. F. Lan and

T. G. Liou (Eds.), *New essays in Cinese culture: religion and ritual.* Taipei: United Publishing Company. [In Chinese]

Goffman, E. (1959). *The presentation of self in everyday life.* Garden City, NY: Doubleday.

———. (1967). Interaction ritual. Garden City, NY: Doubleday Anchor.

Graham, A. C. (1989). *Disputers of the Tao.* LaSalle, IL: Open Court Publishing Company.

Ho, D Y. F. (1976). On the concept of face. *Amercian Journal of Sociology, 81,* 867–884.

Hofstede, G. (1980). *Culture's consequences: International differences in work-related values* (abridged edition). Beverly Hills, CA: Sage.

Hsiang, T. C. (1974). *Research on Chinese characteristics.* Taipei: Shang-wu Publishing Comany. [In Chinese]

Hu, H. C. (1944). The Chinese concepts of "face." *American Anthropologist, 46,* 45–64.

Hwang, K. (1987). Face and favor: The Chinese power game. *American Journal of Sociology, 92,* 944–974.

———. (1988). The human emotion of the Chinese. In K. S. Yang (Ed.), *The thinking and behaviors of Chinese.* Taipei: Yuan-liou Publishing Company. [In Chinese]

———. (1989). Human emotion and *mien-tzu:* The Chinese power game. In: K. S. Yang (Ed.), *The psychology of the Chinese.* Taipei: Kui-Kuan Books, Inc. [In Chinese]

Jacobs, J. B. (1978). A preliminary model of particularistic ties in Chinese political alliances: *Kan-ch'ing* and *kuan-hsi* in a rural Taiwanese township. *China Quarterly,* June, 237–273.

King, Y. C. (1989a). An analysis of "humna emotion" in interpersonal relations. In K. S. Yang (Ed.), *The psychology of the Chinese.* Taipei: Kui-Kuan Books. [In Chinese]

———. (1989b). "*Mien,*" "shame" and the analysis of Chinese behavior. In K. S. Yang (Ed.), *The psychology of the Chinese.* Taipei: Kui-Kuan Books. [In Chinese]

La Barre, W. (1946a). Some observations on character structure in the Orient, II. The Chinese, part one. *Psychiatry, 9,* 215–238.

———. (1946b). Some observations on character structure in the Orient, II. The Chinese, part two. *Psychiatry, 9,* 375–396.

Legge, J. (Trans.). (1967). *Li chi, book of rites,* vol. 1. New Hyde Park, NY: University Books.

Liang, S. M. (1964). *The essence of Chinese culture.* Hong Kong: Chi-ch'eng Books. [In Chinese]

Lin, Y. T. (1939). *My country and my people.* New York: The John Day Company.

Shimanoff, S. B. (1985). Rules for governing the verbal expression of emotions between married couples. *Western Journal of Speech Communication, 49,* 147–165.

————. (1987). Types of emotional disclosures and request compliance between spouses. *Communication Monographs, 54,* 85–100.

Smith, A. H. (1895). *Chinese characteristics.* New York: Fleming H. Revell Company.

Ting-Toomey, S., Gao, G., Trubisky, P., Yang, Z., Kim, H. S., Lin, S. L., and Nishida, T. (1991). Culture, face maintenance, and styles of handling interpersonal conflict: A study in five cultures. *International Journal of Conflict Management, 2,* 275–296.

Ting-Toomey, S., (1988). Intercultural conflict styles; A face-negotiation theory. In Y. Kim and W. Gudykunst (Eds.), *Theories in intercultural communication.* Newbury Park, CA: Sage.

Ting-Toomey, S. and Cole, M. (1990). Intergroup diplomatic communication: A face-negotiation perspective. In F. Korzenny and S. Ting-Toomey (Eds.), *Communicating for peace: Diplomacy and negotiation.* Newbury Park, CA: Sage.

Tracy, K., Craig, R., Smith, M., & Spisak, F. (1984). The discourse o f requests: Assessment of a compliance-gaining approach. *Human Communication Research, 10,* 513–538.

Triandis, H. (1988). Collectivism vs. individualism: A reconceptualisation of a basic concept in cross-cultural social psychology. In G. K. Verma and C. Bagley (Eds.), *Cross-cultural studies of personality, attitudes and cognition.* New York: Macmillan Press.

Triandis, H., Bontempo, R., Villareal, M. J., Asai, M., and Lucca, N. (1988). Individualism and collectivism: Cross-cultural perspectives on self-ingroup relationships. *Journal of Personality and Social Psychology, 54,* 323–338.

Tu, W. M. (1985). Selfhood and otherness in Confucian thought. In A. J. Marsella, G. DeVos, and F. L. K. Hsu (Eds.), *Culture and self: Asian and Western perspectives.* New York: Tavistock Publications.

Wen, C. I. (1988). The kuan-hsi of the Chinese. In K. S. Yang (Ed.), *The thinking and behaviors of Chinese.* Taipei: Yuan-liou Publishing Company. [In Chinese]

Yang, K. S. (1981). Social orientation and individual modernity among Chinese students in Taiwan. *The Journal of Social Psychology, 113,* 159–170.

Yang, M. C. (1945). *A Chinese village.* New York: Columbia University Press.

-5-
Face Parameters in East-West Discourse

RON SCOLLON
AND
SUZIE WONG SCOLLON

Communication between Asians and Westerners, particularly Northern Americans, is often confusing for both parties.[1] Significant differences in patterns for the introduction of topics (Scollon & Scollon, 1991), in rhetorical structures (Kaplan, 1966; R. Scollon, 1991a), and in face (S. Scollon, 1989) give rise to the stereotypes of the "inscrutable Asian" and the "frank" or "rude" Westerner (Scollon & Scollon, in press; Young 1982). For example, the tendency for Westerners to introduce the main topic (or thesis or premise) early in a conversation or an essay contrasts with the Asian tendency to delay the introduction of such topics until considerably later. This difference in expectations causes confusion between people who hold opposite expectations.

These observations parallel those made for a number of culturally, ethnically, or subculturally different groups when members of those groups communicate with each other. Gumperz (1982) led the way in showing how processes of conversational inference can lead to such negative interpersonal reactions. Our own research has shown the development of negative stereotypes in communication between mainstream English-speaking Americans and Athabaskan people in Northern Canada and Alaska (Scollon & Scollon, 1981). Certainly the most widely known and perhaps most immediately recognized stereotypical reactions to discourse differences are the work of Tannen (1986, 1989, 1990) who has written about discourse between men and women in North American society.

133

What has not been so widely discussed in the literature, though it has certainly been widely known by researchers who have studied comparative discourse or rhetoric, is that these attempts to research processes of stereotyping have themselves frequently been accused of fostering the same sort of negative stereotypes.[2] Kaplan (1966), for example, found that his insightful contrastive study of rhetorical patterns in Chinese students' English compositions met with considerable criticism from Chinese scholars (Chen, 1986; Chou, 1989; Lin, 1987).

There may be one of two problems here: It is possible that our descriptions are simply wrong; of course, we hope not. It is also possible that while such descriptions are adequate in some objective, analytical way, they are failing to take into account some other aspect of the participants' understanding of the situation, and it is that other aspect to which they are reacting. If the latter is the case, then it is likely that it will be useful to broaden our analytical goals to encompass this other aspect. We will argue that the factor which Asians are taking into consideration is face; that they have an understanding of why communication normally takes place that is significantly different from that of Westerners, and that, further, the Asian understanding of face relations between the researcher and his or her subjects will help us to understand our own goals as researchers. Finally, we will suggest that the most fruitful future direction for study which will enrich our concepts of face and of facework will be the comparative cross-cultural analysis of the concept of the person.

Face Parameters: Initial 'Default' Parameters

Twenty or thirty years of the analysis of face-to-face spontaneous discourse[3] have shown quite conclusively that patterns of contingent exchange of speaking turns are rather limited in scope. While it can be clearly shown that there are pairs, triplets, or quadruplets of rather fixed sequences, to our knowledge it has not been demonstrated that conversants are ever constrained beyond, perhaps, a maximum of four consecutive turns. In other words, while it was shown quite early on by Schegloff (1972) that the initiation of an exchange granted the right to the introduction of topics to the initiator, we have argued elsewhere that Chinese, for example, delay the introduction of the topic (S. Scollon, 1989; Scollon & Scollon, in press).

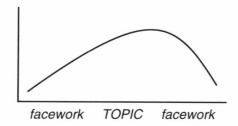

Fig. 1.
Asian Conversational Pattern

Normally, conversational responses are typically to the last thing said. In this sense, it is the nature of conversation to be contingent, not planned.

We would like to claim, nevertheless, that Asian conversations show a general pattern, a kind of macrostructure, which is quite different from the pattern one sees in a Western conversation. We have argued that Asian conversations show a pattern which can be described as a parabolic arch, beginning with incidental topics and minor points. The main topic is introduced somewhat later. Except for the fact that conversations take place in real time, one might call this pattern centrist, because it is quite customary after the introduction of the main topic for this to be followed again by a final period of 'small talk' (see fig. 1 for a diagram of such a pattern).

The Western pattern, by contrast, begins with an early introduction of the initiator's main point. This is followed by a line of supporting developments or just small talk, but then there is often a conclusion with a reiteration of the main or concluding point (see fig. 2).We believe these differing patterns lie at the heart of a great deal of confusion in East-West discourse since each side expects different positions of main and subsidiary topics.

While these descriptions are uncannily like the prototypical patterns for such written genres as the essay and drama (R. Scollon, 1991b, 1991c), we hesitate to conclude that the conversational pattern is in some way patterned after such literate genres. After all, most people who show these patterns in their day-to-day conversations are quite unaware of the literary patterns. In this we hold with the general focus in Western linguistic analysis on speech as the primary source of such discourse

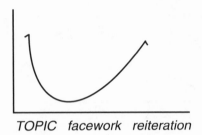

TOPIC   facework   reiteration

Fig. 2.
Western Conversational Pattern

phenomena. We further believe there is no need to have re-course to such cross-influences between speaking and writing, because a more direct explanation can be found in the inter-play between the universal characteristics of conversational in-ference and the several initial assumptions the participants make about face.

Different Initial Face Parameters: East and West

It is certainly not the case that Asians speak only of relation-ships and Westerners speak only of information. We maintain that any communication must inherently program both of these functions. Nevertheless, when East meets West in an or-dinary conversation, there will be a relative difference in the initial assumptions made about what the relationships be-tween the participants will be and also a relative difference in their assumptions about the first task to be dealt with in their exchange.

Westerners who travel in Asia are amazed or amused by the insistent exchanges of business cards as well as the intent study made of them by the recipients. For example, one sees two men bow as they exchange cards. Until the cards have been read the bow cannot be concluded because the senior or higher member of the two must rise up first. In any exchange be-tween an Asian and a Westerner it is a fair bet that the Asian will be relatively more concerned with establishing their rela-tionship and with establishing their hierarchical positioning in that relationship than the more (apparently[4]) egalitarian North American. The consequence of this is, unfortunately, straightforward. The Asian will want to take relatively more time with these matters than his or her Western counterpart will feel is productive. The Westerner, on the other hand, will be impatient to get the main topic on the table so that it can be determined whether it is worth all of this posturing. After all, if there is no chance of concluding a contract, why get to know anybody at all?

Thus the Asian concern with establishing and ratifying their relationships and positions is likely to be taken by the Westerner as obfuscation or even evasiveness. On the other hand, the Westerner's concern for getting topics onto the table so that they will be in a position to discuss issues will seem to the Asian rude or aggressive, or, perhaps, these early issues brought up by the Westerner will be understood as incidental— part of the ratification of relationships, not issues to be seriously discussed.

Is this an East-West difference?
We believe that the marked difference between the typical Asian pattern in a discourse and the typical Western pattern is the outcome of this relative difference in their assumptions about what is the fundamental purpose of communicating. The macro-discourse patterns we have observed arise out of the fact that the assumptions about face and the role of communication in ratifying face are so widely held throughout Asia and, in contrast, the assumptions about the ultimate negotiability of relationships and the informational function of communication are so widely held in the West. The test of this is in the exceptions we have observed in both Asia and in the West.

The pattern of topic delay which we have mentioned here actually is only practiced in a set of relationships which we have called "inside" relationships (Scollon & Scollon, 1991, in press). One sees quite a different pattern in Asia when one observes "outside" or service relationships. These are the situations in which the participants are and remain strangers to each other, such as in taxis, train ticket sales, and banks. In "outside" (or nonrelational encounters) one sees a pattern which if anything is more directly informational than what one sees in the West. In fact, Westerners often are struck with the contrast they see between the highly polite and deferential Asians they meet in their business, educational, and governmental contacts and the rude, pushy, and aggressive Asians they meet on the subways of Asia's major cities.

By way of contrast in the West we only have to imagine a situation in which a person's topic is that he or she wants to borrow a large amount of money from someone else. He or she is then likely to be as deferential as a mandarin, putting off bringing up the topic of the financial touch until the ground-work has been very carefully laid.

In other words, we believe that we are talking about dis-course universals here governing topic, face relationships, and the initial assumptions made by participants when an ex-change is begun. East or West, we believe that in any case where a participant believes that the establishment or ratifica-tion of relationship is relatively more important than the exchange of information, we will see a centrist (Asian) macro-pattern. Wherever we see the relative ascendancy of informa-tion, we will see the Aristotelian (Western) pattern. Tannen's (1989, 1990) analysis of this same polarity in talk between men and women at the subcultural level is a case in point. Whether we are talking about Asians and Westerners or men and women within Western society, what is crucial is difference in percep-tions, not absolute, preset patterns.

Three Default Face Parameters: Relationship, Hierarchy, and Ratification

"To save face" is a phrase which came into English from Chi-nese (Oxford Universal Dictionary). As a term for discourse analysis, "to save face" came into currency through the work first of Goffman (1967) and later Brown and Levinson (1978). It is no wonder, then, that face should be a central concept we will want to invoke to understand East-West discourse. Stover (1974) reiterates what virtually all Sinologists have said for Chinese, though Stover puts it somewhat more strongly: "Face is no mere cosmetic feature of poise of self-expression. Face stands for what is most important in the only human relation-ships that really count, those between persons of unequal sta-tus—and *everyone* is unequal" (pp. 247–48). In this comment are embedded two of the three default Asian face parameters, relationship and hierarchy: (1) Everyone is related to everyone else—the concept of nonrelation or ambiguous relation is not allowed; and (2) All relationships are hierarchical, however mi-nutely. For example, identical boy twins are still arrayed as 'older brother'/'younger brother.'

These concepts are deeply embedded in the Asian concept of face, however unpalatable they might be to more (apparently) egalitarian Western understandings of ideal human relationships. One who forgets this in thinking of Asian communication does so at the risk of major misunderstanding. And because face is so crucial an aspect of any Asian concept of the self, the third default Asian face parameter, the ratification of face relationships, stands at the center of an Asian concept of the purposes of communication. This third default face parameter will require some further explanation.

The Ratification of Face Relationships

Since Ferdinand de Saussure's *Course in Linguistics,* linguists as well as most other Western scholars whose subject is language have shared the assumption that language is primarily speech. This position of de Saussure has been taken up in a context which extends back at least to the dictum of the Royal Society that its proceedings should take place in plain, unelaborated language (both spoken and written) which is, ideally, modelled on plain, natural speech.

In addition to (or perhaps as a consequence of) this tendency to emphasize plain speech in our thinking about language, there is another tendency to emphasize the informational or ideational function of language. Of course, nearly every scholar who takes up the subject of the functions of language insists that language has multiple and simultaneous functions. The two broadest categories generally center on the communication of information on the one hand and the establishment of relationship on the other. We all know of the informational emptiness of many greetings: How are you? Good morning. Have a nice day! and the rest. But those who go to the exteme of asserting that some large percentage of language is only for the communication of relationship or affect are quickly reminded that this affect is carried on a channel that at least looks like an informational channel.

For our purposes we do not really care what the deepest, fundamental function of language is. That seems like a question that in the long run could never be made empirical anyway. Our concern is with what the ordinary person believes the nature of language to be. Whatever its underlying functions may be, the belief structure of a language's users will have major consequences in their use of the language, and this is what we are interested in discussing here.

Even though scholars generally insist on the multiple functions of language, in the West there is a lingering sense that somehow the communication of information is the primary function. Other functions, though mentioned, tend to get short shrift in their arguments. Within Western contexts, the model of language that drives other theorizing, at least up until very recently, is that of communication being information exchange, hypothesis testing, argumentation, and the verification of reference and truth. This is so much the case that the word "communication" itself has come to take on the burden of this model. A cursory glance through the many books available on "communicative" methods of language instruction, for example, shows a central focus on information as the functional core of language use. Furthermore, the bias for spoken communication over written communication is so strong that writing is often either ignored or even specifically avoided in such methodologies.

Chinese do not see the world this way. For the Chinese, language is writing,[5] and not just any writing; language is writing in what Westerners call Chinese characters (R. Scollon, 1991a, 1991b). This perception of language is so old and so deep for Chinese that trying to establish any other perception of language is an exercise in futility. Those who have taught linguistics in both Western and in Chinese universities will attest to the ease with which the disciplinary bias against writing on behalf of spoken language, parole, can be taught in the West and conversely how opaque the Chinese literate screen is when one tries to teach such elementary linguistic subjects as phonetics.

This Chinese love of, one might almost say obsession with, writing is as old as China and forms a contrast with the Western love of speech which even before the great outdoor orations and debates we find in the poems of Homer was probably the norm. Tsien Tsuen-Hsuin (1962), in his study of the beginnings of Chinese books and inscriptions makes the telling point that the Chinese put all of their prayers into writing in contrast to the Western practice of oral prayers. In recent times, the noted Chinese philosopher and statesman, Hu Shih (1986), said the following without the slightest sense of irony: "A man [or woman] who can think freely is able to express his [or her] thought in written language. That is freedom of speech" (pp 87–88).

The archaeologist Chang Kwang-Chih (1983) contrasts the earliest uses of writing in China with the earliest uses of writing elsewhere in the world. The earliest Western antecedents emphasized economic transactions. If Jack Goody (1977) is right in his analysis, writing was used for perhaps a millennium and a half in the Near East before anything but accounting records were kept. In contrast to this economic use of writing in what became the West, writing in China from the first tortoise shell inscriptions functioned to ratify membership among the clans and lineages of the ancient Chinese villages. And here it is important to point out that that membership included generations both living and deceased. Writing was, in fact, for the Shang people the primary means of communication with the deceased ancestors to whom they ascribed the knowledge and power to direct the lives and fortunes of living descendants. Many Chinese scholars as well as Sinologists believe that this oracular use of writing to remain the central concept of language for Chinese people. Whereas Westerners believe we communicate primarily to exchange information and in that information exchange to negotiate our interpersonal relationships, Chinese believe we communicate first to ratify[6] our inherited social relationships, and within those relationships to transmit the knowledge of preceding generations.

In spite of the Chinese idea that language is writing, virtually all Chinese do a great deal more speaking than writing. This is true now even with relatively high literacy rates in such places as Taiwan. The farther back into the past we look, of course, the lower the general literacy rates and therefore the more reliant most Chinese are upon spoken language. It would take us rather far afield to try to account for all uses of language by Chinese even if such an endeavor were possible. One contrast between China and the West, though, merits our attention. Earlier we said that language use was associated more with ratification of social position in China and with negotiation in the West. Even the most superficial comparisons of China and the West note the relative differences placed on group identity and individuality. Without getting bogged down for the moment in the difficulties of such terms as "individuality,"[7] we would like to note that where ratification of the existing order (social or intellectual) is felt to be primary, one will find that writing or highly formulaic uses of spoken language will be preferred.[8] Where negotiation of intersubjective reality or information exchange are thought to be primary, one will find that argumentative or conversational spoken language will be preferred. The Socratic dialogue remains the iconic image of Western language, while the calligraphed poem is that of Chinese.

The difference that we would like to highlight between Western and Chinese concepts of language, then, is not so much a distinction between information and relationship as it is a difference in how information and relationships are conceived. The Western concept of information seems to resonate with the scientific model in which information is thought to be new, acquired within an experimental paradigm, and transmitted through a complex set of constantly renegotiated social relationships. The traditional Chinese concept of information focuses on the accumulated wisdom of the ancestors (or perhaps party officials) transmitted within a matrix of established social relationships. For Westerners, the paradigmatic communication mirrors scientific exploration; for Chinese, the paradigm comes closer to the rituals of communication with ancestors

Stereotyping in Intercultural or Intergroup Research

We want to return now to the problem with which we started: Why are descriptions of culturally differing patterns of communication often responded to by those described as negative stereotypes? It may be possible to understand at least part of this picture by looking at Levinson's (1990) argument about the nature of conversational inference. Levinson recently summarized two decades of the linguistic study of conversation with the felicitous phrase: "We are a species adjusted to adjusting to each other" (p. 18). He characterizes the thinking which underlies ordinary conversation as "interactive intelligence." Quite apart from conversation, humans show, he argues, a quite general capacity to make significant inferences about what other people are thinking. This interactive intelligence shows a number of properties, four of which Levinson believes are central. Humans behave as if

1. Patterns cannot be random. Any perceived pattern is taken to be meaningful or intentional.
2. Examples are taken as prototypical. Because an example is salient enough to come to mind, it is immediately assumed that it carries the essential characteristics of the general phenomenon one is thinking about.

3. Samples are representative. Because each example is taken as prototypical, any sample of examples is thought to be enough to represent the whole.
4. Conclusions are determinate. We do not draw probabilistic conclusions.

While Levinson's (1990) paper is preliminary, it is highly suggestive of a productive arena of further study. It is based on a number of properties which have been quite solidly established about conversational inference. Research has shown that conversational inferences are

1. Rapid. Estimates vary, of course, but most researchers would agree with Levinson that a time period of one second or less is approximately the period in which such inferences are drawn. Such inferences may come at the rate of one per second in ordinary conversation.
2. Nonunique. The same premises lead to different inferences which depend on the context as perceived by the participants.
3. Ampliative. The inferences drawn go beyond the information given. One "reads" in an enormous amount of interpretive context.
4. Overdeterminative. Inferences tend to be clear, unambiguous, and, because they go beyond the information given, therefore stereotypical.

In this analysis, all conversation is inherently stereotypical. It is part of the essential aspect of "adjusting to others" that we make every attempt to "read between the lines," and to reach the conclusions we believe they are trying to reach. When the people who are talking to each other are reasonably alike or well known to each other, this process works relatively well. Indeed, Levinson (1990) argues that communication is not logically possible without some such jumping to conclusions.

The problem to which we have given a certain amount of attention in our own work arises when the people in communication with each other do not share fundamental contextual bases and therefore jump to widely differing conclusions. At a conversational rate of speed, it does not take many false inferences in sequence to create highly divergent assessments of "what is going on." While we have concentrated on cases where differences are likely to be maximal, such as between urban, educated, mainstream English-speaking Americans and Northern Athabaskan hunters, Tannen (1990) has repeatedly reminded us that the same processes are at work in the highly problematical communications between men and women of virtually identical cultural, educational, professional, and age groups. In other words, stereotyping is quite likely an inherent aspect of human communication, and at the same time it is also a perennial problem.

In an earlier and very important work, Brown and Levinson (1978) put forward a set of communicative universals of face. They described the inherent bipolarity in all communications between the need to show and grant to others involvement at the same time as showing and granting to others independence. At that time they used the terms positive politeness (to show involvement) and negative politeness (to show independence). In our own work we preferred to use the words "solidarity" (for involvement) and "deference" (for independence) (Scollon & Scollon, 1981). In order to establish terms which would be descriptively neutral Tannen (1986) suggested that "involvement" and "independence" are preferable.

Levinson's (1990) summary of the "nature of conversational inference" is well established in the literature of discourse and conversational analysis. But if one takes a somewhat longer look, we believe that this work repeatedly emphasizes the Western assumptions about the nature of language which bedevil East-West discourse. In a sense one could say that the principal feature of communication—that we are a "species adjusted to adjusting to each other"—is a gloss for saying that we are a species which prefers involvement to independence, solidarity politeness to deference politeness, the positive strategies of getting into the mind of one's conversants to the negative strategies of patiently hearing the other out while making (or showing) no assumptions about what he or she thinks.

Certainly, a history of Asian conversational analysis shows up a somewhat different view. For example, we find in the Li Chi, dating from before Confucius, the following recommendations:

> In going to take counsel with an elder, one must carry a stool and a staff with him (for the elder's use). When the elder asks a question, to reply without acknowledging one's incompe-

tency and (trying to) decline answering, is contrary to propriety. (Legge 1967, p. 67)

When he sees an intimate friend of his father, not to presume to go forward to him without being told to do so; nor to retire without being told; nor to address him without being questioned—this is the conduct of a filial son. (p. 68)

When he is following his teacher, he should not quit the road to speak with another person. When he meets his teacher on the road, he should hasten forward to him, and stand with his hands joined across his breast. If the teacher speaks to him, he will answer; if he does not, he will retire with hasty steps.(Legge 1967, p. 70)

If the host have not put some question, the visitor should not begin the conversation. (p. 74)

If there be any subject on which the elder has not touched, let him not introduce it irregularly. (p. 75)

When sitting by his side, and the teacher puts a question, (the learner) should not reply till (the other) has finished. (p. 75)

When one, in attendance on a superior man, replies to a question without looking round to see (if any other is going to answer), this is contrary to rule. (p. 101)

While Levinson (1990) argues for an "interactional intelligence" which shows highly involving strategies of adjusting to others, it may be well to remember that it is also in the nature of conversation to limit the extent to which one jumps to conclusions, to let others differ from oneself (and to assume that they will want to do so), and not to conclude what you think the other is trying to conclude. We would hope that a somewhat fuller accounting of this "interactional intelligence" would look to the ways in which humans do, in fact, go beyond the limits of stereotypical reactions. In other words, we feel that Levinson's (1990) own work argues strongly for taking into consideration the other side of the involvement/independence polarity in the nature of conversational inference.

Brown and Levinson's (1978) work on politeness strategies of communication gives a clear indication of what goes wrong when two (or more) parties to a communication make differing assumptions about the appropriateness of involvement or independence. We have argued, based on their work, that if two parties disagree on whether independence or involvement is appropriate, the use of involvement tends to communicate a power disparity between the parties (Scollon & Scollon, 1983). If I believe it is best to show you deference, but you show me solidarity, my reaction will be to assume that you intend to exercise power over me. We call our children or students by their first names (involvement) but expect them to use the more deferential (or independent) titles or last names.

We think this set of relationships and perceptions can be applied to researchers and their subject populations as well, whether those subjects are called collaborators (an "involvement" term) or not. In fact, the naming switch from "subjects" to "collaborators" in recent years indicates a considerable interest in exercising, or at least displaying, involvement patterns of the relationship between researchers and those they study and describe.

This argues that where it is perceived that distance, deference, and independence is required or expected because, for example, the researcher and subject are of different cultural groups, and involvement is given or displayed, then a power difference is accentuated. There may be no more powerful display of involvement than a quite penetrating analysis of behavior; it may feel to those described as a kind of personal exposure. In other words, a good cultural analysis by someone outside the group may well be felt (because of face universals) like an exercise of power. When involvement is displayed but independence is desired or expected, power is the perception.

When subject populations object to cultural analyses as stereotypical, we believe it is the perception of power which is causing the problem, not the accuracy of the description. Since Asians virtually always assume relationships are hierarchical, the only question regarding the relationship with the researcher is whether he or she is asserting (or ratifying) a superior or accepting (and ratifying) an inferior position to those studied. Universals of face in asymmetrical situations allow only an interpretation of power when involvement strategies are used. It is the upper or benevolent one who has rights to strategies of solidarity and involvement. Expressions of involvement, then, are most likely to be heard or read as assertions of power.

Here, as in many other cases, it is well to go back a bit to something written by Edward Sapir. He noted that there is a general tendency to see the behavior of others as evidence of "culture," but to see our own behavior or the behavior of those close to us as evidence of "personality" or individuality (Sapir, 1949; original 1934). In other words, what is close is the personality of the individual, what is distant is culture. This by itself is an important observation that it would be well not to forget because it has a corollary. The corollary is that a description of someone else's behavior is likely to be perceived as setting one off at a distance. Just imagine the difference in your reactions to someone saying, "That's just like Jane!" as opposed to "That's just like an American!" There is a clear tendency for the first to be felt as positive because it shows closeness, intimacy, personal knowledge. The second sounds stereotypical, hostile, and distant.

There is a second observation Sapir (1949) makes in the same article. He notes a general tendency for those who study culture as opposed to those who study personality to do so partly along lines of their own sense of identity:

> The study of culture as such, which may be called sociology or anthropology, has a deep and unacknowledged root in the desire to lose oneself safely in the historically determined patterns of behavior. The motive for the study of personality, which we may term indifferently social psychology or psychiatry, proceeds from the necessity which the ego feels to assert itself significantly (p. 198).

We believe that at least one aspect of the problem of stereotyping in cultural descriptions is that researchers may well share some of the sense suggested by Sapir (1949) of comfort in such historically motivated generalizations about human behavior. One might well describe that interest in "losing oneself" in the study of culture as a perception of involvement with the people one is studying. What student of culture has not "gone native" to some degree? On the other hand, as Sapir has suggested, descriptions of cultural behavior are inherently distancing; they display and assume independence. Perhaps, then, it is not surprising that when researchers do not belong to the populations they study, there should be a major tension between their personal sense of involvement and the inherently distancing aspect of their descriptions. One has the perennial dilemma of demonstrating that one knows the population and its behavior closely enough for descriptive accuracy while at the same time demonstrating to that population that one is, in fact, not a member. Paradoxically, it seems that the better the description, and therefore the more accurate the "exposure" of the behaviors of members, the more those same members are likely to perceive the involvement of the researcher as the exercise or expression of power.

Those of us who do such research have an inherent problem; it is not likely to go away easily. We believe that in any such work it is necessary to acknowledge the power base from which researchers work. In making reports outside of the research population it seems that strategies of independence (or deference) are more likely to mitigate the worst aspects of this problem than strategies which emphasize one's involvement or solidarity. At the same time, it is important to be quite clear about just what one's membership claims really are. In a way that parallels interpersonal communication, while Western researchers have taken the central function of a research report to be informational, at least some readers have looked at such research reports as conveying or establishing asymmetries of power between the researcher and the group studied. Where this has not been done with a clear expression of deference of independence, the interpretation has been critiqued as exercising power and is read as potentially stereotyping and hostile.

Problems for the Cross-Cultural Study of Face

Confusion and even negative responses in communication between Asians and Westerners arises as a natural outcome of universals of the face relationship coupled with differences in assumptions about three factors in communication, the relative emphasis given to information and relationship, the hierarchical nature of interpersonal roles, and the contrast between negotiation and ratification of such roles. Researchers in intercultural communication have themselves not been immune from these miscommunications. The problem as we have described it is a conflict between the requirement to show involvement (solidarity or positive face) and to show independence (deference or negative face) in the relationship between the researcher and members of the group the researcher has studied. The closeness to the group (involvement) required to achieve accuracy is in direct opposition to the distance (independence) required to achieve objectivity.

Sapir (1949) has suggested that researchers tend to choose their topics of study along lines of their own personal tendencies to either submerge their own sense of self or to assert it. Researchers with the former tendency prefer cultural research, while those with the latter tendency prefer research into personality.

We do not know that this idea of Sapir's (1949) has been followed up in more recent analyses of cultural and psychological research. We do think, however, that it is very suggestive of a problem which will need to be addressed directly in future studies of face—that is, the problem of the concept of the self assumed by participants in communication. A corollary is that the concept of the self held by facework researchers will also have to be more closely examined.

The Concept of the Self

The study of the self as a problem in studies of face is not a new concept, of course. Tracy (1990) has pointed out that a major weakness in the politeness-theory approach to face (exemplified best by Brown and Levinson, 1978) is that it does not take into account the complexity of the problems surrounding identity in analyses of face. Such complexities have been demonstrated for cross-cultural studies of the person (Marsella, DeVos, and Hsu, 1985). Ting Toomey (1988) has pointed out, for example, that at a minimum, a distinction must be made between *individualistic* and *collectivistic* concepts of the self. This distinction would be critical in understanding face in Western-Asian intercultural communication.

Hall and Ames (1987) suggest that any understanding of traditional Chinese use of language needs to take into account the fundamental assumption of a moral basis for communication. Our own ethnographic research in Asia leads us to believe that a relatively clear contrast can be made between this moral assumption held in Asia with a more transactional assumption held in the West. From Goffman, to pick a scholar not entirely at random, down to this essay, the presuppositional basis is that both the actions of participants in communication and the actions of researchers *can be* (though not necessarily always are) understood entirely transactionally without taking into serious consideration either the moral positions of the participants (and researchers) or the social outcomes of those communications. We believe that such an assumption is not generally held by Asians who, since Confucius, have been concerned with the outcomes of communications in the social world.

In many ways Goffman made the opening move in contemporary studies of face with his article "On Face-work" (Goffman, 1967). In that article he directed our attention to an even more fundamental study of Chinese face, that of Hu (1944). Since that article is well known to researchers concerned with concepts of face, we will not here recapitulate its argument beyond mentioning the distinction between *mien-tzu* and *lien* in Chinese thinking about face. The former distinction refers to the outer sense of person which is achieved in one's reputation; the latter refers to one's inner qualities or sense of character, quite apart from the reputation that one might have. Hu notes that the term *lien* itself is relatively new, dating to the K'ang-Hsi dictionary of 1716[9]. It would require further research to establish the antiquity of a clear distinction between these inner and outer senses of face in China. What we suggest, however, is that such a distinction has not been followed up in Western analytical studies of face and that it is likely to prove fruitful to do so. It seems likely to us that our Western concentration on face as an outer phenomenon (*mien-tzu* as opposed to *lien*) fits well with our generally transactional position. A more inner, permanent, character-based understanding of face is more consistent with a moral analysis and that is, generally, not currently in favor in Western analytical practice.

Quite beyond the inner and outer senses of face presented by Hu (1944), there is a further distinction between "inside" and "outside" that we believe will be fruitful in future studies of face both East and West. We have been able to show that in Asia such discourse phenomena as the introduction of topics are governed by a more basic distinction between "inside" and "outside" (*nei* and *wai*) relationships (Scollon & Scollon, 1991). Tracy (1991) has argued that studies of face must take into consideration that "the face wants (i.e., identity claims) to which people orient are dependent on situation, personality, and culture" (p. 218). "Inside" and "outside" relationships constitute one such situational dependency. Classically, the five Confucian relationships (ruler-ruled, father-son, husband-wife, elder-younger, friend-friend) as well as a host of "*tong*" relationships (same school, same town, same employer) are "inside;" while such occasional relationships as those with bank tellers or taxi drivers are "outside." Future research will need to clarify whether Chinese concepts of *mien-tzu* apply equally to relationships within such inside relationships and to those considered outside relationships. We assume that such further clarifications will then provide a richer set of tools for the analysis of face (inner *mien-tzu* and outer *lien*, inside *nei* and outside *wai*) universally, not just in regard to communication among Asians.

We are still left, however, with what may be the most interesting, although most difficult, aspect of the comparative analysis of the concept of the person in communication between East and West. As mentioned earlier, Ting-Toomey (1988) has pointed to the need to distinguish between *individualistic* and *collectivistic* cultures. The individualism of the concept of the self in the West is well known. Unfortunately, when it comes to analysis of discourse and especially the study of face, there has been relatively little close analysis of how this individualism plays out in moment-by-moment aspects of communication. The recent work of Carbaugh (1989, 1990), however, provides a beginning for such an analysis. The self presented in U.S. American discourse and as analyzed by Carbaugh is part of (and contained within) the individual. This self is unique and inaccessible to outside observation. As a result, it is displayed as it is realized through communication with others. In other words, two crucial aspects of the contemporary U.S. American concept of the self are (1) it is unique (and therefore autonomously separated from others), and (2) it is realized through communication.

We know of no comparable studies of the Asian self, but the work of Francis Hsu (1985) leads us to believe that such a study will disclose a concept of self which is significantly different from such an autonomous, communication-based self. Hsu contrasts a Western and a Chinese sense of self as being a distinction not so much in the basic elements of which the self and the world are constructed as in the aggregation of those elements as self and as other. For Hsu, the self is consisted of seven layers.

Hsu (1985) argues that the first crucial distinction between the Chinese sense of self and the Western sense of self lies in the placing of the boundary between the self and others. The Chinese sense of self places that boundary between layers 3 (intimate society and culture) and 2 (operative society and culture). For the Chinese self, the contents of layer 3 (those things with which one senses a strong feeling of intimacy) are *within* one's self. Westerners, in contrast, place such entities as intimate friends, spouses, children, and pets *outside* the strong boundary of the self. Hsu argues that the contents of layer 3 are as important for the individual's survival as the requirement for food, water, and air. He argues that "if human beings are not available for layer 3, the individual is likely to fill it with gods or things or certain cultural rules (such as ideals) on which he will lavish his affect" (Hsu, 1985, p. 34).

This latter accounts for Hsu's (1985) second major distinction between the Western sense of self and the Chinese. Since the Chinese (he argues) have intimate relationships within the strong boundary of the self, ideals and issues tend to be placed on the far outer ring, layer 1 (wider society and culture). Westerners, he argues, tend to hold strongly to not only pets, but pet ideals and issues because their boundary of the self is located closer to the core of the unique, conscious or unconscious self.

There is much of interest in Hsu's analysis which we cannot deal with here. For our purposes it is sufficient to suggest that if he is correct in his core notion of a different placement of the boundary of the self, surely any cross-cultural analysis of face phenomena in general or of facework in intercultural communication must take such a difference seriously. It is also clear that taking such an idea seriously will not be simple. While Hsu's analysis is reasonably complex, Stover's (1974) analysis of Chinese society convincingly argues that a minimal distinction between "high" and "low" culture must be made in coming to an understanding of traditional cultural conditions. As a further complication, Chu (1979, 1985) shows that the concept of the self itself is undergoing considerable contemporary change on both sides of the Taiwan Strait.

It is possible that in some fundamental sense, cross-cultural communication theory, like cross-cultural communication is an oxymoron, a term that is contradictory in itself. Perhaps it is ultimately not possible to have a theory of face which is simple enough to be analytically meaningful and at the same time encompass such radically different conceptions of the self. In concluding this essay, it is only possible to say for certain that current conceptions of face (ours included) are at best heuristic; they are helpful in understanding some of the ways in which linguistic phenomena and sociopsychological phenomena interact. More important to us is that we hope that such studies of Asian-Western intercultural facework communication are helpful in some practical sense in understanding how miscommunication between Asians and Westerners occurs. We are also hopeful that these studies are helpful in alleviating some of the worst consequences of such miscommunication.

Notes

General note: An earlier version of this paper was presented at the American Association for Applied Linguistics, New York, March 1991. The research on which this paper is based was carried out while the authors were teachers first at Providence University (Ching Yi Ta Hsueh), Shalu, Taiwan and then at the Sogang Institute for English as an International Language, Sogang University, Seoul, Korea. Our research project has received continued funding from the Alaska Humanities Forum, Anchorage, Alaska (a program of the National Endowment for the Humanities) and Lynn Canal Conservation, Haines Alaska. We wish to thank the two universities as well as the two funding agencies for their support of our work. Of course, the ideas expressed in this paper are not the responsibility of any of these agencies.

1. It is no simple matter to define or to label our populations in this analysis. Our research has focused most directly on Chinese in Taiwan and on Koreans in South Korea. We have also made further observations in such places as Hong Kong, Macao, Zhongsan, and Tokyo. We believe that what we have to say here applies quite generally throughout those parts of Asia which have historically been strongly influenced by Confucian (or Sinographic) literacy. See Scollon and Scollon (1990) for a discussion of this problem and these terms.

2. A letter from a reader in New Jersey came to us a year or so after the publication of our *Narrative, Literacy, and Face* (Scollon and Scollon, 1981) which congratulated us on finally putting in print all of the reasons why Indians were inherently inferior to Caucasians. Perhaps we are not the only researchers in this field to be championed by the very camps we had worked so hard to undermine.

3. We temporarily set aside the problem of the more complex rhetorical structures of writing (but also of more fixed spoken forms). These may ultimately derive from considerations given by the primary nature of face-to-face spontaneous communication.

4. We believe that further comparative study will show that the assumption of egalitarian communicative roles in Western society is more a matter of foregrounded self-perceptions that objective analysis. This is, nevertheless, the story we Westerners like to tell about

ourselves and it does, we believe, have a major impact on our assumptions about communication.

5. We can also approach this difference from another direction, the direction of deconstructionist theory. The dictum of Derrida that all language is writing seems so perverse, so counter-intuitive to Western thinkers that academic wars have raged over the very legitimacy of deconstructionist criticism and yet in Taiwan the problem with deconstructionist criticism is not in understanding this fundamental point of Derrida's; the problem is in understanding why Western critics have any problems with this idea. A teacher who finds himself as one of us did in the position of trying to teach both Saussurean linguistics with its emphasis on speech and deconstructionist criticism with its emphasis on writing finds himself in a paradoxical experience.

6. From Mo Tzu of the fifth century b.c. to Li Peng of the twentieth century it does not seem such a great distance. Mo Tzu is quoted as saying, "The sources of our knowledge lie in what is written on bamboo and silk, what is engraved on metal and stone, and what is cut on vessels to be handed down to posterity." In the troubled aftermath of the June 1989 Tiananmen deaths political activists were set to the diligent study of a letter of Li Peng as part of their punishment (or re-education, choose the word you prefer) in a fashion that these days is all but unimaginable outside of Asia.

7. Hall and Ames (1987) give an extended discussion of the differences between individuality as taken in the West and in China. The contrast they make is between a rational concept of individuality in which the abstract characteristics of the individual are emphasized and an aesthetic individuality in which the particularistic and concrete attributes of the individual are emphasized. They believe it is this difference between rational (or transcendent) analysis and aesthetic analysis that is significant, not individuality itself.

8. Such highly formal uses of language in oral traditions tend to be relatively unknown to scholars working exclusively within literate traditions. For an example and a discussion of such language use see Dauenhauer and Dauenhauer 1987, 1990.

9. Incidentally, Hu's dating of the K'ang Hsi dictionary as Yuan dynasty (thirteenth century) is incorrect. This most famous of all Chinese dictionaries was published under the K'ang Hsi Emperor (1661–1722). This, in turn, means that the term *lien* is not seven centuries old but no more than, perhaps, three centuries. Jodi Yeh (personal communication) has suggested that the term *mien-tzu* contained within it both the inner and outer meanings and that it was the "foreign" (i.e., non-Han Chinese) occupation of the Ch'ing dynasty which gave rise to an awareness of inner and outer face values. She further suggests that Hu's inadvertent attribution of the term to Yuan rather than Ch'ing was because that was the only other dynasty of foreign occupation.

References

Brown, P., and Levinson, S. (1978). Universals in language usage: Politeness phenomena. In E. Goody (Ed.), *Questions and politeness: Strategies in social interaction.* New York: Cambridge University Press.

Carbaugh, D. (1989). *Talking American: Cultural discourses on Donahue.* Norwood, NJ: Ablex Publishing Corporation.

Carbaugh, D. (1990). Communication Rules in *Donahue* discourse. In D. Carbaugh (Ed.), *Cultural communication and intercultural contact.* Hillsdale, NJ: Lawrence Erlbaum.

Chang, K. C. (1983). *Art, myth, and ritual.* Cambridge: Harvard University Press.

Chen, J. (1986). On Kaplan's idea concerning the Chinese eight-legged essay. *Studies in Language Education, 5,* 71–79.

Chou, H. L. (1989). Contrastive rhetoric: Chinese and English. In S. Chang, D. Tseng, and B. Hwang (Eds.), *A collection of papers presented in the sixth conference on English teaching and learning in the Republic of China.* Taipei: The Crane Publishing Co.

Chu, G. (1979). Communication and cultural change in China: A conceptual framework. In G. Chu and F. Hsu (Eds.) *Moving a mountain: Cultural change in China.* Honolulu: University Press of Hawaii.

Chu, G. (1985). The changing concept of self in contemporary China. In A. Marsella, G. DeVos, and F. Hsu (Eds.), *Culture and self: Asian and Western perspectives.* New York: Tavistock Publications.

Dauenhauer, N. and Dauenhauer, R. (1987). *Haa Shuka, our ancestors: Tlingit oral narratives.* Seattle: University of Washington Press.

———. (1990). *Haa Tuwunaagu Yis, for healing our spirit: Tlingit oratory.* Seattle: University of Washington Press.

Goffman, E. (1967). *Interaction ritual.* Garden City, NY: Doubleday.

Goody, J. (1977). *The domestication of the savage mind.* New York: Cambridge University Press.

Gumperz, J. (1982). *Discourse strategies.* New York: Cambridge University Press.

Hall, D. and Ames, R. (1987). *Thinking through Confucius.* Albany, NY: State University of New York Press.

Hsu, F. (1985), The self in cross-cultural perspective. In A. Marsella, G. DeVos, and F. Hsu (Eds.), *Culture and self: Asian and Western perspectives.* New York: Tavistock Publications.

Hu, H. (1944). The Chinese concept of "face". *American Anthropologist, 46,* 45–64.

Hu, S. (1953). The tendency of world culture in the last three hundred years and the way china has to follow. In C. Yang (Ed.), *The political thoughts of Dr. Hu Shih*. Taipei: Bookman Books.

Kaplan, R. B. (1966), Cultural thought patterns in intercultural education. *Language Learning, 16*, 1–20.

Legge, J. (1967). *Li Chi: Book of Rites*, vol. 1. New York: University Books.

Levinson, S. (1990). Interactional biases in human thinking. Working paper no. 3, Project Group Cognitive Anthropology, Max-Planck-Gesellschaft, Berlin.

Lin, C. (1987). A second thought on Robert Kaplan's theory of Chinese thought pattern. Paper presented at the Third Conference on English Teaching and Learning in the Republic of China.

Marsella, A., DeVos, G., and Hsu, F. (1985). *Culture and self: Asian and Western Perspectives*. New York: Tavistock Publications.

Sapir, F. (1949). The emergence of the concept of personality in a study of cultures. In D. Mandelbaum (Ed.), *Culture, language and personality*. Berkeley: University of California Press.

Schegloff, E. (1972). Sequencing in conversational openings. In J. Gumperz and D. Hymes (Eds.), *Directions in sociolinguistics*. New York: Holt, Rinehart and Winston.

Scollon, R. (1991a). The people of the book: Are the Chinese really the most bookish people on earth? Working Papers on China, Literacy, and American/East-Asian Intercultural Communication. Haines, AK: Black Current Press.

———. (1991b). China and literacy: Does Sinographic Asia tell us anything new or useful about literacy? Working Papers on China, Literacy, and American/East-Asian Intercultural Communication. Haines, AK: Black Current Press.

———. (1991c). Eight legs and one elbow: Stance and structure in Chinese English compositions. Paper presented at the Second North American Conference on Adult and Adolescent Literacy, Banff, Canada.

Scollon, R. and Scollon, S. W. (1981). *Narrative, literacy and face in interethnic communication*. Norwood, NJ: Ablex Publishing Corporation.

———. (1983). Face in interethnic communication. In J. C. Richards and R. Schmidt. *Language and communication*. London: Longman.

———. (1990). The post-Confucian confusion. Report submitted to the Alaska Humanities Forum on our research grant entitled "Post-Confucian Asians in contemporary Alaska."

———. (1991). Mass and count nouns in Chinese and English: A few further Whorfian considerations. In R. Blust (Ed.), *Currents in*

Pacific linguistics: Papers on Austronesian languages and eth-nolinguistics in honour of George W. Grace. Canberra: Pacific Linguistics.

———. (in press). Topic confusion in English-Asian discourse. *World Englishes.*

Scollon, S. W. (1989). Literacy and face relations in teaching English in China. In S. Chang, D. Tseng, and B. Hwang (Eds.), *A collection of papers presented in the sixth conference on English teaching and learning in the Republic of China.* Taipei: The Crane Publishing Co.

Stover, L. (1974). *The cultural ecology of Chinese civilization.* New York: Pica Press.

Tannen, D. (1986). *That's Not What I Meant!* New York: Ballantine Books.

———. (1989). *Talking voices.* Cambridge: Cambridge University Press.

———. (1990). *You just don't understand.* New York: Morrow.

Ting-Toomey, S. (1988). Intercultural conflict styles: a face-negotiation theory. In Y. Kim and W. Gudykunst (Eds.), *Theories in intercultural communication.* Newbury Park, CA: Sage.

Tracy, K. (1990). The many faces of facework. In H. Giles and W. P. Robinson (Eds.) *Handbook of language and social psychology.* Chichester, UK: John Wiley and Sons.

Tsien, T H. (1962). *Written on bamboo and silk.* Chicago: The University of Chicago Press.

Young, L. W. L. (1982). Inscrutability revisited. In J. Gumperz (Ed.), *Language and social identity.* New York: Cambridge University Press.

-6-

Gender Perspective on Facework: Simplistic Stereotypes vs. Complex Realities

SUSAN B. SHIMANOFF

"When to Speak Like a Lady"—Always
"Learning What It Means to Talk Like a Lady"
"Genderlect, Powerlect, and Politeness"

Although one might expect to find titles like those above in magazines at the grocery store, in Dear Abby, or in one of Amy Vanderbilt's etiquette books; they were in fact drawn from serious, scholarly investigations. In 1975, Robin Lakoff, a linguistic professor at the University of California, Berkeley wrote:

> Women are supposed to speak more politely than men. . . .
> Women are the repositories of tact and know the right things
> to say to other people, while men carelessly blurt out whatever
> they are thinking. Women are supposed to be particularly
> careful to say "please" and "thank you" and to uphold the
> other social conventions; certainly a woman who fails at these
> tasks is apt to be in more trouble than a man who does
> so. . . . In a woman, it's social death in conventional circles to
> refuse to go by the rules. (pp. 55–56)

Lakoff's pronouncement—that women are not only more polite than men, they have to be—prompted extensive examination into the communication of females and males. But before I review that research, I would like to describe how politeness and facework are related and in what ways they are different.

Facework may be defined as behaviors which establish, enhance, threaten, or diminish the images/identities of communicators. The images/identities of communicators have been

159

linked to the basic needs of approval and autonomy (Brown & Levinson, 1978). Facework may be directed toward oneself or another. Politeness consists of behaviors which honor another's need for approval and autonomy. Actions directed toward threatening or diminishing another's needs are not acts of politeness though they may be considered facework, and facework directed toward oneself is not an act of politeness. Thus the concept of facework includes politeness, but politeness does not incorporate all types of facework.

In this chapter I will (1) review the previous research which has made explicit references to politeness or facework and gender; (2) compare various approaches to facework and gender; (3) demonstrate how facework theories might be extended to other types of research on gender and communication; and (4) identify some challenges for future investigations.

The role of gender in facework research began, and in most cases remains, focused on politeness. Table 1 provides a summary of research that explicitly compared males and females on various measures of facework. Since most of this research has focused on politeness, I will review that literature first and then discuss other applications of face-needs approaches to research involving gender.

Examinations of Gender and Politeness

Researchers who have investigated politeness and gender have been primarily concerned with the following questions: (1) Who do people think is more polite, males or females? (2) Whose behavior is more polite, females or males? (3) Who is addressed more politely, females or males? (4) Are males and females evaluated similarly when they use the same behavior? (5) Do females and males evaluate the politeness of utterances in a similar fashion? (6) Is the speaking style which is stereotypically associated with one gender evaluated more politely than the one associated with the other gender?

Who do people think is more polite, males or females?

Clearly, Lakoff (1975) believed that females are more polite than males. Edelsky (1977) found that for the most part third graders, sixth graders, and adults in the United States shared Lakoff's assumptions. The response of one of the sixth graders in Edelsky's study was particularly revealing:

Table 1. EXPLICIT EXAMINATIONS OF GENDER AND FACEWORK

Researcher (Country)	Findings	Explanation
Axia (1989) (ITALY)	1. When asked what a F or a M character would say in certain situations, both boys and girls made F speakers more polite, especially if addressing a M or an older addressee.	1. None
Baroni (1984) (ITALY)	1. Intonationally polite F rated more likable and desirable as a friend than an intonationally polite M.	1. Sex-role stereotypes
	2. F speaker using "excuse me" and "thank you" was rated as more polite than a F speaker not using these forms. The use of these forms made no difference in the likability scores of males.	2. None
	3. Regardless of the presence or absence of polite forms males were perceived as having higher occupations.	3. None
Bates (1977) (USA—CO)	1. Preschool boys and girls produced and comprehended (im)polite requests equally in a role-playing task.	1. The situation may have contributed to Ms and Fs being equal.
Baxter (1984) (USA—OR)	1. Fs reported that they were less likely to use face-threatening messages than Ms.	1. Sex-role socialization concern for the feelings of others; lower social power of Fs compared to Ms
	2. Fs reported that they were more likely to use negative politeness than Ms.	2. Same as 1
	3. Fs reported that they were more likely to use positive politeness than Ms.	3. Same as 1

Table 1 (continued)

Researcher (Country)	Findings	Explanation
Becker (1984) (USA—FL)	1. Adults generally believe girls and boys acquire politeness skills at the same rate: girls were expected to acquire 2 out of 8 skills before boys but the researcher did not specify what those 2 were.	1. None
Becker (1986) (USA—FL)	1. Preschool boys and girls did not differ in their production of polite features or structures for either "bossy" or "nice" requests.	1. None
	2. Pre-school boys (ages, 4, 5, 6 yrs.) were able to distinguish bossy requests from nice requests slightly more than girls of the same age.	2. None
	3. Finding 2 was not replicated in a follow-up study with 5 and 10 years; in this study boys and girls were equally skilled in distinguishing bossy and nice requests.	3. None
Becker (1986) (USA—FL)	1. Preschool girls said "thank you" spontaneously more than preschool boys when receiving a sticker from a F gift giver.	1. Expectations for politeness may be higher for females.
Bell (1984) (USA—NC)	1. Fs got higher scores on the James' (1978) scale of politeness.	1. None
	2. Politeness scores were particularly low for males who scored high on masculinity and were speaking to males.	2. None

Study	Findings	Interpretations
Bellinger (1982) (USA—MA)	1. Fathers and sons produce more directives than mothers and daughters.	1. The authoritarian role of males may explain the fathers' behavior and the sons may be modelling their father's behavior.
	2. Fathers and sons used more directive imperative forms (e.g., "Take your hat off") than mothers and daughters.	2. See 1 above
	3. Fathers and sons used more implied indirect requests (e.g., "Your hat is blocking my view") than mothers and daughters.	3. Father's may be using this form as a way of teaching logical reasoning with sons modelling this behavior.
	4. Mothers and daughters used more conventional indirect forms (e.g., "Could you take off your hat?") than fathers and sons.	4. No direct explanation given, but the implication was that females are more polite and less authoritarian.
	5. Findings 1 through 4 occurred regardless of the hearer's gender.	5. Modelling is the best explanation for children's behavior.
Bradac (1984) (USA—CA)	1. When using politeness Fs and Ms were rated equally authoritative and sociable.	1. "Connections between power of style and gender appear weak and obscure at this point."
Brouwer (1979) (DENMARK)	1. A M clerk was addressed more politely than a F clerk.	1. The sex or the personality of the clerk might have influenced the findings; fewer males serve in this occupation.
	2. When asking for tickets and directions Ms and Fs were equally polite.	2. The situation may have limited the gender differences.

Table 1 (continued)

Researcher (Country)	Findings	Explanation
Brouwer (1982) (DENMARK)	1. Fs and Ms used an equal no. of polite forms (e.g., please, thank you, greetings, modals).	1. The situation, buying a train ticket may have reduced gender differences.
	2. M clerks were addressed more politely than F clerks.	2. M clerks are more rare; Ms may get more respect.
	3. M clerks were more polite than F clerks, but there was not a correlation between the clerk's politeness and the politeness received.	3. 70% of M clerks but only 10% of F clerks are promoted within 2 yrs; perhaps the greater hope of promotion influences the politeness
Broverman (1972) (USA—NY)	1. Respondent indicated that they thought Fs are more tactful than Ms and that Ms more blunt than Fs.	1. Sex-role stereotypes
Brown (1980) (MEXICO)	1. In same-sex dyads Fs use more positive and negative politeness than Ms.	1. Fs marry into husband's family creating more distance between Fs than Ms.
	2. Overall Fs are more polite than Ms.	2. Ms have more power in the culture.
Buikema (1982) (NETHERLANDS)	1. Fs made more threats toward negative face (e.g., suggestions, offers, promises, reminders) than Ms.	1. Conversants didn't seem to react to these as face-threatening acts.
	2. Ms made more threats toward positive face (e.g., disagreements, criticisms, disapproval, noncooperation) than Fs.	2. None
	3. Ms spoke more baldly on-record than Fs.	3. "Possibly women think they cannot afford to do so."
	4. Fs used more politeness (e.g., approval and interest) than Ms.	4. Ms have more social power.
	5. Fs were more polite to Ms than Fs.	5. None

Cashion (1985) (USA—CA)	1. The constrains of courtroom interaction influence politeness more than gender. 1. F and M judges were equally polite.
Cashion (1987) (USA—CA)	1. Fs are more polite. 1. Fs report using more face-maintenance strategies in prefacing a joke than males
Edelsky (1977) (USA—NM)	1. Sex-role stereotypes are learned. 1. Across various linguistic variables there is a progression of association with one gender over another from 1st, 3rd, and 6th grade to adult; such that 6th graders agreed most with adults and 1st graders only saw 2 out of 12 linguistic features as sex-marked. 2. Sex-role stereotypes are learned and they become overgeneralized until later in adulthood they contextualized and thus less extreme. 2. The phrase "won't you please" was associated more with Fs than Ms by 3rd and 6th graders and adults; but this association was stronger for 6th graders than adults. 3. See 2 above 3. In interviews children would say "men swear but ladies don't" and "ladies are polite"; adults said this as well, but they also qualified with contextual features.
Franzblau (1980) (USA—NY)	1. Deference is perceived as a female trait 1. If a request contained the word "please," people thought the speaker was most likely to be a F and the listener a M than any other gender combination. 2. Nondeference is perceived as a male trait. 2. If a request did not contain "please," people thought the speaker was most likely to be a M, but the sex of the hearer was less clear.

Table 1 (continued)

Researcher (Country)	Findings	Explanation
	3. If a request contained the word "please," people rated the speaker as more cooperative, more polite, more likable, smarter, and less demanding than when a request did not contain "please."	3. None
	4. Fs rated a speaker using "please" as more cooperative and less demanding than Ms; Fs tend to rate a speaker who does not use "please" as more demanding than Ms rate the same speaker.	4. Males may see themselves as the recipient of the request (chore) and thus view it as less cooperative and more demanding.
	5. Fs rated their own requests more polite and more effective than Ms rated their own requests.	5. Politeness is stereotypically associated with Fs more than Ms
	6. Fs rated themselves as more polite when speaking to a M and more effective when speaking to a F; Ms rate themselves as more polite when speaking to F than a M.	6. None
	7. In actual request behavior, Ms were more likely to use "please" than females in mixed-sex dyads.	7. None
	8. Ms rated actual requesters as less demanding and more convincing than Fs rated these same requesters.	8. None
	9. Actual requests from mixed-sex dyads were rated as more polite than requests from same-sex dyads.	9. None

Fine (1981) (USA—FL)	1. Fs were more polite in 7th grade classrooms than Ms.	1. None
Gleason (1980) (USA—MA)	1. Boys and girls produced an equal no. of spontaneous thank yous. 2. Parents were equally insistent that their sons and daughters say thank you. 3. Mothers were more likely than fathers to thank the person who gave their child a gift.	1. Thanking is an important ritual regardless of gender. 2. Thanking is an important ritual regardless of gender. 3. Mothers are modelling politeness more than fathers.
Gleason (1983) (USA—MA)	1. Fathers are less polite with their children than mothers.	1. Fathers' speech may serve as a bridge to the world outside the family.
Gleason (1984) (USA—MA)	1. Girls produced more spontaneous and prompted politeness routines than boys; boys produced more "whinny" politeness.	
Goodwin (1980) (USA—PA)	1. The request forms of 8-13 yr. girls making rings were more polite than requests from 8-13 yr. boys making slingshots. 2. Boys accused more directly than girls. 3. Boys criticized braggards in person, while girls did it when the braggard was absent.	1. The social organization of girls and boys is different. 2. Same as 1 above. 3. Same as 1 above.
Hartman (1976) (USA—ME)	1. Fs used more polite forms than Ms.	

Table 1 (continued)

Researcher (Country)	Findings	Explanation
Herbert (1990) (USA—NY)	1. Fs use more personal forms of compliments than Ms.	1. Fs employ a more personal focus in their language behavior.
	2. The syntactical form "I love X" occurred as a compliment in the speech of Fs only.	2. Sex-role stereotypes
	3. Compliments by Ms are more likely to be accepted than compliments by Fs.	3. Compliments by Ms are more "purely" praise, while those by females signal solidarity.
Holmes (1986) (NEW ZEALAND)	1. Fs use "you know" to signal affirmation of the hearer's knowledge and to emphasis their own knowledge more than Ms.	1. Inconsistent with sex-role stereotypes.
	2. Ms use "you know" to signal their uncertainty about the linguistic precision of their own utterances more than Fs.	2. None
Holmes (1988) (NEW ZEALAND)	1. Fs give and receive more compliments.	1. Fs view compliments as signals of solidarity and thus they value them; while Ms are more likely to view compliments as face-threatening acts.
	2. The syntactic patterns used by Ms and Fs are more similar than different.	2. Compliments are fairly formulaic.

3. M-M dyads produced the fewest compliments about appearance; F-F dyads produced the most compliments on appearance.	3. Appearance compliments communicate solidarity and Fs value this.
4. F-F dyads produced the fewest compliments about ability/performance.	4. None
5. M-M dyads produced the most compliments about possessions.	5. Ms view compliments as face-threatening acts.
6. Fs complimented Ms on their personality more than any other complimenting group.	6. None
7. High status Fs are more likely to be complimented than high status Ms.	7. Fs are probably perceived as less intimidating than Ms.
8. Fs and Ms accept/reject compliments equally.	8. None
9. Fs are more likely to deflect a compliment and Ms are more likely to ignore it.	9. Deflecting a compliment is treating it less like a face-threatening act than ignoring it.
Holmes (1989) (NEW ZEALAND) 1. Fs give and receive more apologies than Ms.	1. Fs regard apologies as more important and more relevant to maintaining relationships than Ms.
2. Ms apologized for intrusions into another's space, for interrupting and for talking too much more than Ms; Ms apologized more for time violations and possession offenses.	2. Fs typically take-up less space, interrupt less, and talk less so they may be especially sensitive to these factors.
3. Fs apologize for less serious offenses.	3. See 1 above

Table 1 (continued)

Researcher (Country)	Findings	Explanation
	4. Ms are more likely to apologize to a stranger than a friend; Fs are equally likely to apologize to a friend as a stranger; Fs apologize to their friends more than Ms apologize to their friends.	4. Ms view apologies as distancing markers, while Fs see them as devices to maintain a relationship. It appears as if Ms regard offenses toward strangers as more serious than those toward friends or as at least requiring an apology more. Among M friends, saving one's own face may be more important than apologizing for an offense.
Holtgraves (1991) (USA—IN)	1. Fs and Ms were equally likely to interpret an indirect hint or question according to its literal or implied meaning regardless of the degree of face-threat.	1. None
	2. Fs were more likely than Ms to interpret an indirect response according to its implied meaning than were Ms.	2. None for this particular finding, but in comparing findings 1 and 2 the author asserted that gender differences may be more likely as the ambiguity increases.
Ide (1982) (JAPAN)	1. Fs are more polite than Ms in four areas: (1) women use more honorifics, (2) women use higher level honorifics than men under the same conditions, (3) women do not use vulgar forms, and (4) women use "softening" (less imposing) forms more than men.	1. Sex-role expectations
Ide (1986) (JAPAN)	1. Fs rate the same utterances as less polite than Ms.	1. Sex-role expectations that Fs should be more polite than Ms.

Study	Findings	Explanation
	2. Fs report using politer forms than Ms.	2. Rating utterances as less polite may prompt Fs to select more polite forms than Ms.
	3. Fs and Ms report a similar hierarchy as to whom they address more or less polite.	3. Fs and Ms may be more similar than previously thought.
Keenan (1974) (MADAGASCAR)	1. Fs are less polite than Ms.	
Kemper (1984) (USA—KA)	1. Fs were rated as more appropriate using more polite forms regardless of the type of request than if Fs used less polite forms.	1. Sex-role stereotypes
	2. Ms were rated as more appropriate using more polite forms than less polite ones if requesting someone to perform a feminine task; but more appropriate using less polite forms than more polite ones requesting masculine behavior, especially if the hearer is a male.	2. Sex-role stereotypes
	3. Fs received higher appropriateness ratings than Ms for using the most polite form (e.g., "please" + an imperative.)	3. Sex-role stereotypes
Kirsh (1981) (USA—NJ)	1. Preschool boys used more all types of directive more than preschool girls.	1. None
	2. Popular girls spoke more like popular boys than unpopular girls.	2. Social variables may be more important than gender in predicting behavior.
Kramer (1977) (USA—IL)	1. Respondents indicated that they thought polite speech was more typical of Fs than Ms.	1. Sex-role stereotypes
Leonard (1988) (AUSTRALIA)	1. Preschool girls and boys were equally polite in role playing negotiation episodes.	1. None

Table 1 (continued)

Researcher (Country)	Findings	Explanation
Loveday (1981) (ENGLAND AND JAPAN)	1. In Japan Fs use a higher (more polite) pitch than Ms.	1. "In Japanese a high pitch level serves to express a stereotypically female role while in British English high pitch level is a means of expressing politeness by both sexes" (p. 86)
	2. In England Ms and Fs use similar levels of polite intonation (higher pitch).	2. See 1
Metts (1984) (USA—IL)	1. Fs were more polite than males in six dyadic conversations where 91% of the politeness was positive politeness.	1. Sex-role stereotypes
	2. Fs used more negative politeness than Ms, though neither the Fs nor Ms used much negative politeness.	2. None
	3. Ms used more negative politeness and less positive politeness in same-sex dyads than mixed-sex dyads; Fs did not vary the type of politeness with the type of dyad.	3. Ms may be more reluctant to impose on Fs, Ms may offer less redress to Fs, Ms offer less positive politeness to Ms, Ms threaten the positive face of Fs more.
	4. Fs and Ms differ in the type of positive politeness: Fs attended to the hearer's needs and presence, avoid disagreement, and expressed approval (summarized as "cooperative identity validation"); Ms used slang and jargon and presupposed the hearer's knowledge (summarized as "efficiency").	4. Sex-role stereotypes

Study	Findings	
Milan (1976) (PUERTO RICO)	1. Ms used the most polite form of "you're welcome" when addressing Fs and least polite form when addressing Ms; Fs' use of polite forms fell in the middle. "You're welcome" was a response to a "thank you" for giving directions.	1. Sex-role socialization
Ogino (1985) (JAPAN)	1. Fs used more polite terms and humble forms than Ms. 2. Ms pay more attention to age differences than Fs in choosing their politeness markers. 3. Fs pay more attention to intimacy level than Ms in choosing their politeness markers.	1. Sex-role expectations; Fs are held to higher standards of politeness. 2. None 3. None
Ogino (1986) (JAPAN)	1. Fs are more polite than Ms toward all hearers. 2. Ms pay more attention to age differences than Fs in choosing their politeness markers. 3. Fs pay more attention to intimacy level than Ms in choosing their politeness markers.	1. Sex-role expectations; Fs are held to higher standards of politeness. 2. None 3. None
Quina (1987) (USA—WI)	1. A "female" style of speech was judged as more socially warm than a "male" style of speech. The measure of socially warm included the following scales: polite, soft spoken, mild, sensitive, friendly, sincere, indirect, altruistic, and sociable. A "female" style of speaking was associated with a "feminine" person.	1. Sex-role stereotypes
Rasmussen (1986) (USA—IN)	1. Fs and Ms using (im)polite features were rated equally on a socially positive scale.	1. None

Table 1 (continued)

Researcher (Country)	Findings	Explanation
Shimanoff (1974) (USA—CA)	1. Tactfulness is associated equally with Fs and Ms.	1. None
Shimanoff (1977) (USA—CA)	1. Fs and Ms were equally polite in using politeness features identified by Brown and Levinson.	1. None
	2. Fs used more positive politeness than negative politeness; Ms did not used one type more than another.	2. Fs may be more supportive than Ms; status and gender were confounded in this study and the results might be due to status.
	3. Fs acknowledged the hearer's wants more and used exaggeration more than Ms; Ms used indirectness, in-group markers, and hedges more.	3. None
Shimanoff (1985) (USA—CA)	1. Wives report that they disclose more face-threatening emotions than husbands' self-reports.	1. Sex-role stereotypes
	2. Wives and husbands do not differ in their reported disclosure of face-honoring and face-compensating emotions.	2. These types of disclosures equally important to Ms and Fs.
	3. The actual disclosures of emotions by wives and husbands are largely the same.	3. Fs and Ms may be the same; or the conversations may not be representative.
Shimanoff (1987) (USA—CA)	1. Wives and husbands evaluated the face-value of different types of emotional disclosures in request the same.	1. Face-needs transcend gender

Shimanoff (1988) (USA—CA)	1. Even though Fs report that they disclose emotions more than Ms, which emotions they disclose is consistent with the face-needs model for both best friends and acquaintances.	1. Face-needs transcend gender ʹ
Shimanoff (1989) (USA—CA)	1. Fs and Ms did not differ in evaluations of the face-value of compliments or criticisms regardless of their emotional content.	1. If the sex-role appropriateness of a comment is neutral Ms and Fs will respond in a similar manner; the face-value is more salient than sex-role stereotypes.
	2. Fs indicated a greater willingness to perform desired behaviors than Ms.	2. Sex-role stereotypes
Shimanoff (1992) (USA—CA)	1. Fs rate affirmatively worded requests more positively than Ms.	1. None
	2. Fs rate requests with explicit politeness markers (e.g., "please" and "excuse me") as more polite than Ms.	2. Consistent with Franzblau's (1980) study.
	3. Fs varied their politeness ratings more than Ms on the basis of relational type.	3. Fs are more sensitive to relational factors.
	4. There was a six-way interaction between 3 linguistic and three social variables.	4. Judgments about politeness are complex.
Sigelman (1986) (USA—KY)	1. Girls and boys rated polite characters as more likable than rude characters in hypothetical scenarios (3rd, 4th, 7th, 8th, 11th, and 12th graders participated in the study); however, high school students were more accepting of rudeness in a boy than a girl.	1. None
Smith (1990) (USA—DC)	1. Ms were more likely to use an imperative form than Fs in sermons and Fs were more likely to use the construction "Let's."	1. Not stated in the abstract.

Table 1 (continued)

Researcher (Country)	Findings	Explanation
Smith-Hefner (1988) (JAVA)	1. Fs more polite among family members.	1. Fs are of lower social status; the Fs themselves say it is because they are more refined than Ms.
	2. Ms use the politeness markers more appropriately than Fs in public.	2. Politeness markers are also symbols of refinement, prestige, superior status authority, and a speaker's skill.
	3. Fathers are addressed more polite than mothers.	3. Fathers are socially more distant.
	4. Mother model polite address toward the father more than the fathers model polite speech toward the mother for children.	4. Mothers are the primary caregivers and a more distant relationship with fathers is expected.
Stafford (1984) (USA—TX)	1. Fs ask more questions.	1. Fs are more polite; working to keep the conversation going.
	2. Fs talk centered on her M partner more than Ms talk about his F partner.	2. Fs are more polite.
	3. Fs and Ms spoke for an equal amount of time.	3. Fs and Ms are the same
	4. Fs and Ms talk about themselves for an equal amount of time.	4. Fs and Ms are the same

Steffen (1985)
(USA—IN)

1. Fs and Ms were perceived to be equally likely to use po-
lite/impolite or direct/indirect requests within an organization; organizational status rather than gender
predicted the type of request expected.

1. Status was a better predictor than gender.

Walters (1979)
(PUERTO RICO)

1. Girls and boys generally use the same level of politeness
in their requests.

1. None

Note:: Only the first author is listed. Complete bibliographic information is provided in the bibliography. Only the results related to facework and gender are presented here. This table reports the findings as indicated by the original author. No attempt has been made to compensate for great variation in the sample size and the quality of the research design. For studies conducted in the United States of America (USA), the abbreviation for the state in which it was conducted is also given.

> She *has* to be polite because we won't do it if she doesn't say
> "please," but if a man doesn't say it, we sure will anyway, and
> the man is thought of as the king of his house or something
> and he can tell you what to do, and the lady just *wants* you to
> close the door while the man tells you to and expects you to do
> it. (p. 238)

First graders, on the other hand, had not yet developed many sex-role biased folklinguistics; that is, they largely believed that males and females communicated in the same manner. This research demonstrated that attitudes regarding the gender appropriateness of specific communication behaviors is acquired rather than innate.

Several researchers have reported that people believe females are more polite than males (Axia & Argenti, 1989; Broverman, Vogel, Broverman, Clarkson, & Rosenkrantz, 1972; Franzblau, 1980; Kramer, 1977), but in other studies respondents stated that they thought that males and females would be equally polite (Becker, 1984; Shimanoff, 1974; Steffen & Eagly, 1985). I found no studies in which people indicated that they thought males would be more polite than females.

While the above studies were connected with what people assume about males and females in general, a few studies asked males and females to assess or predict their own politeness behavior. In all of these studies women rated their own behavior as more polite than males rated themselves (Baxter, 1984; Bell, 1984; Franzblau, 1980).

Whose behavior is more polite, females or males?

Various measures have been used to assess the politeness level of the actual behavior of females and males (e.g., use of formal politeness markers ("please," "thank you," "excuse me," "you're welcome"); direct versus indirect requests; utterances that enhanced or detracted from another's need for approval or autonomy). The results of these studies are quite mixed. Some reported that the behavior of females was more polite (Becker & Smenner, 1986; Bellinger & Gleason, 1982; Brown, 1980; Buikema & Roeters, 1982; Cashion, Cody, & Erickson, 1986; Fine, 1981; Gleason, 1980; Gleason, 1983; Gleason, 1984; Goodwin, 1980; Hartman, 1976; Loveday, 1981; Metts & Bryan, 1984; Ogino, Misono, & Fukushima, 1985; Smith, 1990; Smith-Hefner, 1988; Stafford, 1984). Some report that males were more polite (Brouwer, 1982; Franzblau, 1980; Keenan,

1974; Smith-Hefner, 1988), and others that the behavior of females and males was equally polite (Bates & Silvern, 1977;
Becker, 1986; Brouwer, 1982; Brouwer, Gerritsen, & DeHaan,
1979; Cashion, 1985; Gleason, 1980; Leonard, 1988; Loveday,
1981; Shimanoff, 1977; Stafford, 1984; Walters, 1979). These
inconsistencies were found in studies of both adults and children, and in domestic and foreign investigations.

Even the same researchers have found conflicting results.
For example, Becker and Smenner (1986) found that girls produced more spontaneous "thank you's" than boys, but in another study, published in the same year, Becker (1986) found
that girls and boys did not differ in their production of polite or
rude requests. Gleason (1980) found that boys and girls produced an equal number of "thank you's," but that mothers were
more likely to model politeness rituals than fathers. Females in
Franzblau's (1980) study rated their requests as more polite
than males rated their own requests, and yet in mixed-sex dyads males actually used "please" more than females. Smith-
Hefner (1988) reported that the context made a difference in
Java where females are more polite in more private settings
and males are more polite in public arenas, but no other research has tested for nor attempted to explain the contradictions in the research.

Some researchers have compared the amount of different
types of politeness by females and males. In particular, they
have examined naturally occurring discourse to determine if
gender affects the number of messages that address approval
or autonomy needs. Shimanoff (1977) found that males and females were equally polite, but that women spent most of their
politeness-time honoring approval needs while males divided
their time equally between approval and autonomy needs.
However, in this field study, gender and status were confounded in that there were far more high-status males than females. Having greater status may have given the males more
legitimacy to impose on someone else's autonomy and this may
have prompted more autonomy-based politeness by males.

Metts and Ryan (1984) studied males and females who were
presumed to be status equals and found that both males and
females spent far more time on politeness aimed at approval
needs (91%) than autonomy needs (9%), and in their study
women were more polite than males. Buikema and Roeters
(1982) also studied status equals. They found that males were
more likely to threaten a hearer's need for approval than fe-

males and that females were more likely to express interest and approval in another's ideas than were males. All three of these studies indicate that politeness which expresses approval of another has been more common among women than men. Still, all three of these studies had very small sample sizes and therefore it is not clear whether the results would generalize to larger samples of males and females.

Who is addressed more politely, females or males?

In two separate studies in Denmark, Brouwer and colleagues (1979; Brouwer, 1982) reported that male clerks are addressed more politely than female clerks. She hypothesized that since male clerks are rare, they may receive additional respect. Brouwer's observation is consistent with the other studies where male tokens were treated especially well (Floge & Merrill, 1986; Ott, 1989). But tokenism is not an "equal opportunity" marker. In general, female tokens have been treated less favorably (Ott, 1989; Woman & Frank, 1975). So Brouwer's explanation is not as likely to apply to female tokens.

Other researchers have reported that males talking to males are the least polite (Bell, 1984; Milan, 1976) or that mixed-sex dyads were more polite than same-sex dyads for both males and females (Franzblau, 1980) or for males alone (Metts & Bryan, 1984). Collectively this line of research suggests that males are generally less polite to other males than females.

Are males and females evaluated similarly when they use the same behavior?

High school students reported greater tolerance for rudeness from boys than girls (Sigelman, Carr, & Begley, 1986). In interpersonal settings, polite women compared to polite men were rated more likable and desirable as a friend (Baroni & Durso, 1984) and more appropriate when requesting a male to perform a masculine tasks (e.g., "Please rake the leaves"— Kemper, 1984). But Bradac and Mulac (1984) found that in a job interview females and males who were equally polite were rated equally authoritative and sociable, and in another study male and female characters were rated equally on a social positiveness scale when their level of (im)politeness was the same in short stories (Ramussen & Moely, 1986). These four studies used different forms of politeness and different measures of effects so it is difficult to compare them directly. Still, they suggest that setting (e.g., interpersonal versus organizational) may alter the expectations and evaluations.

Do females and males evaluate the politeness of utterances in a similar fashion?

Japanese women rated the same request form as less polite than Japanese men (Ide, Hori, Kawasaki, Ikuta, & Haga, 1986). The researchers argued that this difference in judgment might provide a partial explanation for why Japanese women use a politer form. They wrote: "Women's use of politer forms appears to be politer only when observed from the hearer's point of view, but from the female speaker's point of view she is simply using forms with her own politeness level" (p. 31).

Shimanoff, West, and Bruno (1992) sought to replicate and extend the Japanese study in the United States. In contrast to the Japanese study, females in the United States rated affirmatively worded requests (e.g., "can you" rather than "can't you") and words with explicit politeness markers (e.g., "please" and "excuse me") as more polite than males. But females rated the same utterance as less polite if it were addressed to an acquaintance than to most other groups, while males did not make a similar distinction. Thus in the context of addressing acquaintances, the ratings of U.S. females and Japanese females were more similar than they were in other contexts. Shimanoff, West, and Bruno also found a six-way interaction involving three linguistic variables (valence, modal, and type of request) and three social variables (gender of rater, friendship level, and communication role (speaker/hearer). Hence, while gender influenced the results, it alone was not an adequate predictor. It is just more complex than that.

In somewhat related studies, women were more likely than men to assign an implied, rather than literal, meaning to an utterance (Holtgraves, 1991; Tannen, 1981). This finding as well as its relationship to facework can be made clearer by drawing upon a dialogue example found in Holtgraves' (1991) research:

A: Did you notice my new coat?
B: I think it takes so much effort to shop for clothes.

Women were more likely than men to interpret B's response as meaning B did not like the coat; they interpreted utterances like B's as attempts not to threaten A's need for approval. This finding suggests that at least in some contexts, females may be more sensitive to potentially face-threatening acts.

Is the speaking style which is stereotypically associated with one gender evaluated more politely than the one associated with the other gender?

Lakoff's pronouncements about what she believed were the "female" and "male" styles of speaking stimulated numerous investigations into the possible effects of using one style more than the other. The most prolific researcher in this area is Anthony Mulac (e.g., Mulac, Bradac, & Mann, 1985; Mulac, Incontro, & James, 1985; Mulac, Lundell, & Bradac, 1986; Mulac, Studley, & Blau, 1990; Mulac, Wiemann, Widenmann, & Gibson, 1988). This line of research has found that the feminine style of speaking is viewed as more aesthetic and of higher socio-intellectual status than the masculine style of speaking and that the masculine style is viewed as more dynamic. However, this research has not included measures of politeness.

On the other hand, Quina, Wingard, and Bates (1987) found that the feminine style was judged as socially more warm than a masculine style of speaking. In their study, social warmth was measured with the following scales: polite, soft spoken, mild, sensitive, friendly, sincere, indirect, altruistic, and sociable. In addition to the explicit politeness scale, many of these other scales seem related to honoring another's need for approval and autonomy.

Based on their study, then, the stereotypically feminine style would seem to be more polite than the stereotypically masculine style. Similarly, Liska, Mechling, and Stathas (1981) reported that a feminine style was reviewed as more interpersonally warm (e.g., friendly, caring, and sincere), and one might expect these attributes to be associated with the need for approval. In these studies the masculine style was rated as more competent (Quina et al., 1987) and more assertive (Liska et al., 1981).

Summary

Research on gender and politeness has not produced consistent results. Many of these studies, though certainly not all, have measured attitudes or counted the occurrence of specific behaviors in the absence of theoretical underpinnings. That is, the research has often sought to determine if males and females differed in their politeness behaviors or if they are evaluated differently, without positing reasons why they should or should not differ. Frequently, researchers have made references to assumed sex-role expectations, but these explanations seem rather circular (e.g., females do X because they are females) and do not account for why such expectations exist. Later in this chapter I will indicate some ways this problem might be remedied.

Even with these limitations, the following summary statements can be offered as partial answers to the questions raised above:

1. Generally, people are more likely to report that they believe females are more polite than males than to report the opposite, but some times respondents say both genders are equally polite. Females rate themselves as more polite than males rate themselves.

2. In those studies which measured the sheer volume of politeness the results are quite mixed. There is limited evidence that females may be more concerned with honoring another's need for approval than males.

3. Generally, it would appear as if the talk in male-male dyads is less polite than in mixed-sex or female-female dyads.

4. It appears as if setting (e.g., formal vs. informal) may influence whether males and females are rated similarly when using politeness.

5. In Japan, women rated the same politeness form as less polite than men. In the United States, the perceived politeness of an utterance is influenced by a multitude of factors including interactions among the gender of the rater, the level of friendship, various linguistic features, and whether one is the speaker or hearer.

6. Stereotypical "feminine" speech is rated as more polite than stereotypical "masculine" speech.

In the section that follows I will review the research by Janet Holmes, Robert Herbert, and myself. Each of us has applied a facework model to speech acts that have not been explicitly labelled as acts of politeness.

Other Applications of Face-Needs Models to Gender Research

Janet Holmes (1986, 1988, 1989) has conducted a series of studies using Brown and Levinson's model of facework to analyze the role of gender in various types of speech in New Zealand English: "you know," compliments, and apologies.

"You Know"

Holmes (1986) found that women used "you know" more than men to signal their confidence in both the hearer's knowledge and their own. She associated this use of "you know" with positive politeness in as much as it can acknowledge the hearer's competence as well as the speaker's and it expresses "solidarity by generously attributing relevant knowledge to the addressee" (p. 18).

Compliments

Similarly, compliments can signal both approval of another and solidarity with that person (Holmes, 1988). Yet compliments can also be face-threatening acts in that they imply that another has the right to judge the hearer or to proscribe the desired behavior; that one is envious of another; or that one is indebted to another (Brown & Levinson, 1978; Holmes, 1988; Kissling & Kramarae, 1991; Kramarae, 1986; Wilensky, 1991; Wolfson, 1984). Several researchers have examined the role of gender in compliments (Barnlund & Araki, 1985; Herbert, 1990; Holmes, 1988; Knapp, Hopper, & Bell, 1984; Sims, 1989; Turner & Edgley, 1974; Wolfson, 1984), but only Holmes (1988) and Herbert (1990) have used a facework model to explicate their findings.

Holmes (1988) maintained that women tend to use compliments as face-honoring acts, while men tend to view them as face-threatening acts. In her study, New Zealand males were least likely to compliment each other on their appearance, but most likely to compliment possessions; females are least likely to compliment each other's ability or performance; and females are most likely to compliment males on their personality than any other group. Holmes argued that appearance compliments are solidarity comments, while possession remarks are face-threatening because they communicate envy. She used these assumptions to argue that females view compliments as face-honoring and males consider them face-threatening, but she did not ask males or females to rate the face-value of different types of compliments.

Another explanation for Holmes' (1988) findings is also possible. Sex-role stereotypes stress the importance of a female's appearance and a male's material success (possessions). Thus, sex-role stereotypes could account for the findings as well as differences in the perceived face-value. The low occurrence of ability compliments in female-female dyads might be related to maintaining equilibrium (solidarity) in the relationship, but it might also be a function of sex-role stereotypes.

Unlike Holmes (1988), Herbert (1990) treated the compliments of both males and females as face-honoring. Still, he argued that the focus of the compliments were different. He asserted that compliments by males serve primarily to praise others, while those by females were aimed at creating greater solidarity. In his study, compliments by males were more often accepted than those by females. He argued that the greater deflection of compliments by females served to reestablish the similarity of the interactants. This same deflection did not occur with the same frequency when males complimented. Herbert's explanation for this occurrence was that because the compliments by males were not offered primarily as symbols of solidarity, deflection was not the appropriate response. Like Holmes, Herbert did not test his suppositions about the differences in the types and meanings assigned to compliments by males and females.

Apologies

Holmes' (1989) research on apologies had some similarities with her research on compliments and "you know." She found that females both offered and received more apologies and compliments. Her data led her to argue that it was likely that males and females view apologies differently: "Use of more formal formulae suggest that men may regard apologies as signals of social distance or as devices to be used only in cases of relatively serious offenses . . . women's motivation for apologies may be related to their perception of what is necessary to maintain the relationship with the person offended" (p. 199). Only the apologies of women contained statements indicating that they did not intend the offending behavior and that the hearer had a right to an apology. Males were more likely to apologize to strangers than friends, while females were equally likely to apologize to friends and strangers. Holmes maintained that males view apologies among other male friends as a distancing device.

Collectively, Holmes' (1988, 1990) studies led her to conclude that New Zealand women use "you know," compliments, and apologies to communicate solidarity (one type of face-honoring messages) more often than males. And further, that the use of "you know," compliments, and apologies may be linked to face-threatening acts more for males than females, especially when males are speaking with their male friends. Additional research is needed to test these hypothesized functions more directly and to explore their application to males and females in other countries.

Emotional Expressiveness and Responsiveness

I have conducted a serious of studies aimed at developing a face-needs model of emotional expressiveness (Shimanoff, 1985, 1987, 1988, 1989). This line of research differs from the politeness literature in that it is concerned with both the speaker's and the hearer's face-needs and it examines face-honoring, face-compensating, face-neutral, and face-threatening messages, while politeness is concerned only with messages which honor the hearer's face-needs. These studies have demonstrated considerable and predictable differences in emotional disclosures on the bases of a face-needs model.

The research has also shown that the face-value of a particular emotional disclosure varies with the communication role (i.e., speaker versus hearer) and the level of intimacy (e.g., spouses, best friends, and acquaintances). For example, telling one's spouse how other people have made you feel vulnerable or angry makes one's spouse feel honored and trusted, but the teller's face is threatened (e.g., she/he has admitted vulnerabilities). Further, while spouses and best friends feel honored that they are trusted enough to hear about these vulnerabilities and hostilities, such disclosures make acquaintances feel uneasy. Intimate relationships provide a "we vs. they" framework for interpreting such messages, but among acquaintances where this perspective does not yet exist, hearers may wonder whether the speaker will be critical of them in their absence.

Because a multitude of studies support the sex-role stereotype that females are more emotionally expressive than males and because different types of emotions have been associated with females and males (see also Shimanoff, 1983), I thought it was important to determine whether a face-needs model of emotional expressiveness would be the same for males and females.

Females have reported that they disclose more face-threatening emotions than males, but in actual conversations males and females in these studies have talk about emotions equally. Furthermore, in both their actual behavior and self-reports males and females produce the same hierarchy of disclosure. That is, males and females have the same rank order for the relative face-value of different types of emotional disclosures, even when women report that they express more emotions. And they demonstrate the same complexities regarding communication role (speaker/hearer) and relationship (spouse, best friend, acquaintance). Where there have been gender differences, they were better explained by sex-role stereotypes than facework (e.g., females report disclosing more emotions because the society says females are more emotionally expressive). But the studies have also shown far more similarities than differences between the genders and these similarities were predictable on the basis of a face-needs model.

Summary
The studies of Holmes (1988, 1989), Herbert (1990), and Shimanoff (1987, 1988, 1989) have demonstrated that a face-needs approach to discourse can offer explanations for data that go beyond a simple indication as to whether males and females differ. By using a face-needs model each of these researchers have offered reasons for why males and females have or have not differed from each other in the type and amount of facework produced. Holmes and Herbert account for their data by hypothesizing that that males and females approach "you know," compliments, and apologies with different assumptions about their face-value. Additional research is needed to verify whether the data is in fact produced according to the principles hypothesized by Holmes and Herbert. Shimanoff has shown that even when the amount and type of emotional disclosures vary, males and females still share the same hierarchical model for producing and evaluating emotional disclosures and that this model is predictably related to the face-needs of speakers and hearers.

Although these studies have made strides in giving reasons for differences and similarities among females and males, they do not offer accounts for why sometimes males and females assign the same face-value to utterances and in other contexts they apparently differ in their interpretation. The earlier distinction of public/private will not work here because all the studies involved interpersonal communication.

The research on gender has demonstrated that the facework behavior of females and males is much more complex than simple stereotypes. But how are we to get at this complexity in future research? To address that question I will evaluate three approaches that have been used to assess the role of gender in facework. They include examinations of (1) isolated behaviors, (2) discourse functions, and (3) sociological factors. The strengths and weaknesses of each will be discussed so that major challenges and directions for future research might be identified.

Isolated Behaviors

Lakoff (1974) specified three rules of politeness: (1) don't impose, (2) allow the addressee options, and (3) make the addressee feel good. These rules are compatible with the two basic needs that politeness is expected to meet. That is, rules 1 and 2 address the need for autonomy, while rule 3 is related to the need for approval. Lakoff (1975) also identified several linguistic features that she believed represented the female style of speaking. Her assertions, as well as those of others, lead to numerous investigations of isolated behaviors. The results were less than satisfactory. I will illustrate why this was the case by reviewing the research on two such behaviors, interruptions and tag questions.

Some scholars viewed interruptions as a violation of Lakoff's politeness rules 1 and 2 (e.g., Sacks, Schegloff, & Jefferson, 1974; Zimmerman & West, 1975). From their perspective, interruptions impose on one's conversational partner, limit his/her options, and hence reduce her/his autonomy. Some studies of interruptions have found that men interrupted women more often than the reverse (e.g., Brooks, 1982; Octigan & Niederman, 1979; Porter, Geis, Cooper, & Newman, 1985; West & Zimmerman, 1983; Zimmerman & West, 1975), and thus in these studies females were reviewed as upholding rules 1 and 2 more than males.

But other studies have reported no differences in the interruptive behavior of males and females (e.g., Dindia, 1987; Kennedy & Camden, 1983), and still other scholars have demonstrated that interruptions are not always impositions; in fact, they can be a means of communicating solidarity or involvement with one's conversational partner (Dindia, 1987; Jefferson, 1978; Kennedy & Camden, 1983; Tannen, 1984, 1986, 1990). In other words, interruptions can be a way of fulfilling Lakoff's (1975) politeness rule 3.

Tag questions were also initially identified as politeness markers. Lakoff (1975) explained how tag questions can be viewed as fulfilling politeness rules 1 and 2: "A tag question, then might be thought of as a declarative statement without the assumption that a statement is to be believed by the addressees: one has an out, as with a question. A tag gives the addressee leeway, not forcing him to go along with the views of the speaker" (p. 16). Lakoff (1975) claimed that women use more tag question (i.e., questions tagged on to the end of assertions) than men.

Several researchers sought to test Lakoff's claim. Some found that indeed women used more tag questions than men (Fishman, 1978; Hartman, 1976; McMillan, Clifton, McGrath, & Gale 1977; Mulac & Lundell, 1986), but others reported that men used more (Dubois & Crouch, 1975; Lapadat & Seesahai, 1978), and still others found no differences (Baumann, 1976; Martin & Craig, 1983). In a summary of this literature, Throne, Kramarae, and Henley (1983) point out that tag questions can have multiple functions (e.g., to convey uncertainty, to solicit participation, to sustain interaction, and to forestall opposition). Bradley (1981) found that males who use tag questions were liked better and rated more dynamic than females who use tag questions, and this led her to speculate that tag questions may be perceived as nonassertiveness when uttered by women and polite when uttered by men.

In citing literature on interruptions and tag questions it is not my intent to provide definitive answers as to who uses more. Rather I wish to illustrate problems that have arisen when researchers have taken the rules of politeness and have attempted to measure their relative enactment by females and males by simply counting the occurrence of a particular behavior. Such a procedure erroneously assumes that there is a one-to-one correspondence between linguistic or nonlinguistic symbols and their meaning, or in this case, their relative politeness or face value. Several scholars have warned against such practices (e.g., Brown, 1980; Holmes, 1986, 1988; Shimanoff, 1977; Throne, Kramarae, & Henley, 1983). Still, much of the work testing Lakoff's (1975) assertions used this method, and predictably the data produced mixed answers regarding gender and politeness. A much more promising perspective can be found in the functional approaches to facework.

Discourse Functions

Several writers have argued that the socialization of males and females within the family, peer groups, and beyond, have led females and males to emphasize two different approaches to interactions with others (Bloom, 1990; Chodorow, 1978; Gilligan, 1982; Gilligan & Attanucci, 1988; Tannen, 1986, 1990). For females the emphasis seems to be placed on caring, intimacy, and interconnectedness; for males the emphasis tends to be on fairness, hierarchy, and independence. These emphases are described as relative preferences rather than absolute differences.

These presumed preferences have strong parallels with the two needs Brown and Levinson (1978, 1987) argued are addressed by politeness: the need for approval and the need for autonomy. Given this, one would expect that males and females might differ in their facework vis-à-vis these two needs. The research in this area has been limited, but there is some support for this supposition.

In some studies females produced more messages which were concerned with approval needs of others than males (Baxter, 1984; Buikema & Roeters, 1982; Metts & Bryan, 1984; Shimanoff, 1977). The data for autonomy needs is much more mixed. Females in Baxter's (1984) study reported they would honor autonomy needs more than males. Shimanoff (1977) reported that in their politeness males were proportionally more concerned than females with autonomy over approval needs, but Metts and Bryan (1984) found the opposite pattern. The status and social distance of the communicators may have influenced the differences in these studies. In Shimanoff's study several males had higher status and were more distant from the hearer than females, while in the other two studies the status of males and females was the same. The importance of considering social variables will be discussed more fully in the section on sociological factors in facework. However, before leaving our discussion on functions, Lim and Bowers' (1991) extension of Brown and Levinson's (1978) model should be probed for potential applications to gender-related research.

Lim and Bowers' Extension

Lim and Bowers (1991) maintained that the need for approval should be conceptualized as two separate needs, the need for inclusion ("fellowship-face") and the need for respect ("competence-face"). Explicit investigations of facework and gender predate Lim and Bowers, so their model has not been applied to gender research, but I believe it has potential utility for that research. In support of my optimism I will give a few examples of how it might be used by reexamining some previous gender research.

In looking at specific features that distinguished the politeness behaviors of females and males, Metts and Bryan (1984) described the politeness of females as being primarily a validation of the communicators' "cooperative identity," and they characterized the politeness of males as "efficiency." These labels seem parallel enough to Lim and Bower's needs of inclusion and competence to warrant further investigation. Similarly, Shimanoff (1977) reported that females acknowledged the hearer's wants more than males which would seem to be consistent with fulfilling solidarity needs, while males used more in-group markers. In-group markers could be a signal of inclusion or competence (e.g., knowing the jargon). Finally, Stafford (1984) reported that females were more likely to produce talk centered on her conversational partner than were males (potentially honoring his need for inclusion), but they were just as likely as males to talk about themselves (potentially demonstrating their competence). Lim and Bowers' model would encourage explorations of these types of distinctions.

As noted above, Herbert (1990) maintained that compliments by males are aimed at praising others, while compliments by females are designed to create greater solidarity. If this is the case, one would expect compliments by females to be viewed as enhancing fellowship-face and those by males to be viewed as supporting one's competence-face. Holmes (1989) maintained that females view apologies as enhancing solidarity needs, while males consider them evidence of the lack of solidarity and as threatening to their own face-needs (their competence). Both Herbert and Holmes base their interpretations on the frequency of different types of compliments/apologies, recipients, and responses. Neither of them directly asks males or females what meaning they assign to compliments or apologies. Lim and Bowers' model could be used as a vehicle for testing the viability of Herbert's and Holmes' claims against the reactions of speakers and hearers of both genders.

Other Areas of Gender-Related Research

Lim and Bowers' face-needs model may also have applications for other areas of gender research that have not typically employed a facework perspective. To illustrate that possibility I will give a few brief examples from gender research on story-telling, humor, and self-disclosure. When gender differences have been found in storytelling and humor, they tend to support the conclusion that males see storytelling and humor as more of a performance (a demonstration of competence) and females see it as more of a sharing and bonding (a way of increasing intimacy) (Jenkins, 1984, 1986; Johnstone, 1989; Tannen, 1990). Similarly, when comparing reasons for not self-disclosing, Rosenfeld (1979) reported that males seemed more concerned about losing control (an issue of competence) and females were more concerned about hurting the relationship.

These are just a few examples of how other types of gender-related research might benefit from Lim and Bowers' (1991) model. The examples also point to the importance of distinguishing facework which enhances needs or detracts from them, and work which is hearer or speaker centered. Most of the explicit work on facework and gender has focused exclusively on the enhancement of the hearer's needs.

In addition, the concept of competence-face may need refinement in gender-related research. In some contexts, what is considered competent for one gender is not seen by some as the most competent for the other gender. For example, Kemper (1984) found that to be perceived as appropriate, females needed to always use the most polite form, but males were viewed as more competent when using a less polite form to ask another male to perform a masculine task. Research has also shown that in some contexts the type of messages which are most persuasive (competent) differs from males and females (Burgoon, Dillard, & Doran, 1983; Burgoon, Jones, & Stewart, 1975; Haccoun, Haccoun, & Sallay, 1978; Rosen & Jerdee, 1975).

Other examples can be found in the self-disclosure literature. Shaffer and Ogden (1986) reported that for initial meetings of task-oriented dyads males disclosed more if they thought they would be meeting with their partner several times, while females disclosed less. The researchers argued that this occurred because both sexes have to overcome different stereotypes. Males feared they might not be seen as cooperative and friendly and hence the greater self-disclosure, and females feared they might not be seen as serious task partners and hence the limited self-disclosure. Further, the sex-role appropriateness of self-disclosure has affected men's and women's willingness to self-disclose (Snell, Belk, Flowers, & Warren, 1988; Snell, Belk, & Hawkins, 1986). Both females and males are concerned with appearing competent (i.e., enhancing one's own positive-face), but what constitutes competence for males and females may be different.

Summary

In general, research from a functional approach has indicated that females may be more concerned than males in producing utterances which support another's need for approval, or more particularly, the need for fellowship/solidarity. The evidence regarding autonomy needs is more mixed. Perhaps some of the inconsistency in this latter research can be resolved by more refinements in the research design (e.g., distinctions between the autonomy needs of oneself versus those of others, autonomy needs across different levels of social distance and status, and autonomy regarding different types of actions). Explicit investigations of gender and facework have not yet employed Lim and Bowers' concept of a competence-face, but the application of such a concept, with some refinements, seems quite promising. Further, the gender-related research indicates that males and females might be expected to differ in their response to the needs for fellowship, competence, and autonomy, and that they may even define these needs differently.

The functional approach seems more promising that the isolated-variables approach because the functional approach is concerned with the purpose of utterances rather than merely their linguistic form. In spite of its strengths, however, a functional approach is not by itself efficient. Focusing on the purpose of utterance helps to more accurately get at its meaning, but this knowledge is not adequate for predicting when such a message will be sent or for explaining why it was sent. Studies which examine both the functional aspects of discourse and the sociological factors which influence choices and meaning are needed to meet those goals.

Sociological Factors

As the table on pp. 161–177 indicates, many studies provide no explanation for the gender-related findings. When an explanation is provided, it is most often a reference to sex-role expectations. However, an appeal to sex-roles is not a very satisfying explanation because it does not indicate why or when such roles are relevant. The inconsistencies in the previous research point to the importance of understanding when and why gender is a salient variable and when it is not. In her chapter on "Indexing Gender," Ochs (in press) described this problem cogently:

> Knowledge of how language relates to gender is not a catalog of correlations between particular linguistic forms and sex of speakers, referents, addressees, and the like. Rather, such knowledge entails tacit understanding of (1) how particular linguistic forms can be used to perform particular pragmatic work (such as conveying stance and social action), and (2) norms, preferences, and expectations regarding the distribution of this work vis-à-vis particular social identities of speakers, referents, addressees.

Brown (1980) posited several social conditions under which we might expect females to be more polite than males. In particular, women will be more polite if compared to men they (1) speak more with status superiors, (2) speak more with socially distant persons, (3) are more sensitive to face-threatening aspects of acts, or (4) produce more face-threatening acts. To my knowledge, no one has examined the last two criteria directly, but there has been direct evidence that such criteria might be relevant. For example, Holtgraves' (1991) finding that females are more likely than males to recognize an implied face-threat suggests that females may be more sensitive to potentially face-threatening aspects of messages.

Two different studies have commented on a possible relationship to the rate of face-threatening acts and politeness. Shimanoff (1977) hypothesized that the higher proportion of autonomy-based politeness for higher status males compared to females might be attributed to their status which permits them more autonomy-based face-threats. Similarly, in contrast to the general assumption that the higher the status the lower the politeness (Brown & Levinson, 1978), Cashion (1985) reported that courtroom judges use a great deal of politeness. She argued that their high production of politeness features was directly related to the substantial number of face-threatening acts their job requires them to perform. Other studies have examined the interplay between gender and status or social distance.

Status

In her investigations of Tenejapa society, Brown (1980) demonstrated that in general women were viewed as status inferiors to men, that in joining her husband's family's household rather than the reverse greater distance is created for women than men, and that these two factors made women more polite and more apt to avoid face-threatening acts. Brown (1980) encouraged researchers to

> attempt to show how the ways in which women choose to express themselves reveals truths about their social relationships and their social status in the society. . . . By linking behavior to social structure we are thereby enabled to ask the question *why* do women talk the way they do in this society and what social-structural pressures and constraints are molding their behavior. (p. 133)

In a later analysis, Brown (1990) contrasted the usually polite behavior of women in Tenejapa with highly confrontative behavior found in court cases involving women. Her investigation revealed that polite forms combined with sarcasm were used by the women to be especially confrontative and that in this context "Face was saved by face being thrown to the winds." In comparing polite speech used by women in everyday interactions with their highly confrontative court behavior, Brown wrote: "This provides clear evidence, for Tenejapan society, that gender is not a unified one-dimensional feature of one's social identity; one's gender has different applicability (and different effects) in different kinds of situations" (p. 139).

Smith-Hefner's (1988) investigation of facework in Java also pointed to the importance of context in understanding "politeness" and gender. In Java women were more polite in private settings, particularly within the family where they are viewed as status inferiors. In contrast, men were more polite in certain public spheres. Smith-Hefner maintained that men cultivated politeness in public arenas "as a means of expressing superior status and authority." Keenan (1974) also found that politeness was a mark of status and superiority among Malagasy men.

Smith-Hefner (1988) argued that if polite markings are relatively complex, they can be used to signal one's skill and hence one's status superiority: "Skill in polite language use signals that the speaker has had the proper upbringing and education and is a cultivated or refined speaker" (p. 550). Her data demonstrated that males in Java were more effective than females in manipulating the politeness system to increase their perceived status. The different functions of polite features in private and public settings led Smith-Hefner to write: "Where politeness is expressed by the use of a stable, formal register, a formulaic speech style, or special vocabulary, as in Javanese and Keenan's Malagasy example, these codes may play a dual role, serving as expressions of politeness and deference, and also as mechanisms of social control and refinement" (p. 552).

In Smith-Hefner's (1988) study politeness in public settings was used as means of communicating high status, but in more private settings researchers have tended to associate politeness with deference or lower status (e.g., Brown, 1980; Lakoff, 1975; Smith-Hefner, 1988). One explanation for the differences in these studies is the context, and other researchers have pointed to gender differences in the public and private spheres (e.g., Tannen, 1990).

But an alternative hypothesis is that the social status of the person speaking frames how the utterance is interpreted. In a study where the social status of males and females was held constant, respondents indicated that they expected the same level of politeness from males and females (Steffen & Eagly, 1985). Since gender and status are often correlated (i.e., males often have higher social status), if status and gender are not controlled for separately, one might erroneously attribute differences in facework to gender when they are really a function of status differences.

Social Distance

Several researchers have demonstrated that differences in the level of relational intimacy will influence facework (e.g., Baxter, 1984; Brown & Levinson, 1978; Leichty & Applegate, 1991; Roloff, Janiszewski, McGrath, Burns, & Manrai, 1988; Shimanoff, 1988). There has also been limited evidence that females may be more sensitive to this social variable than males.

For example, in Japan females varied their politeness more on the bases of relational intimacy than males (Ogino, 1986; Ogino, Misono, & Fukushima, 1985), and in the United States females placed greater emphasis on relational factors when judging the politeness of various utterances (Shimanoff, West, & Bruno, 1992). Females also reported more sensitivity to the possible relational consequences of conversations than males (Duck, Rutt, Hurst, & Strejc, 1991), and females included more relationally-based strategies in their conflict resolutions than males (Carrocci, 1985).

Other studies have indicated that males and females may view the facework obligations for various relationships differently. For example, Holmes (1988, 1989) found that among same-sex friends females were much more likely to compliment and to apologize to their friend than were males. She maintained that for females such messages reinforce their connectedness, but for males such messages portend distances (i.e., among friends apologies and compliments are unnecessary). Holmes pointed out that males may view apologies as self-oriented face-threatening acts, while females "may perceive them as 'other oriented' speech acts and as ways of facilitating social harmony" (p. 208).

Even different aspects of a relationship may vary in their importance to males and females. For example, in Japan age differences were a better predictor of the facework of males than females, while the level of relational intimacy was a better predictor for females than males (Ogino, 1986; Ogino, Misono, & Fukushima, 1985).

Summary

Research which has examined sociological variables has been able to offer some predictive and explanatory power in the research on facework and gender. Specifically, it has generally indicated that women will exceed men in politeness when women are considered status inferiors to men or when women place more emphasis on behaviors aimed at maintaining or increasing relational intimacy. In contrast, there is limited evidence that men may exceed women in politeness when politeness registers are associated with status superiority or when their status permits them to perform more face-threatening acts which they still mitigate with politeness markers. Researchers have also argued that one needs to consider possible gender differences in sensitivity to face-threatening messages and the degree to which one has opportunity, obligation, or inclination to perform face-threatening acts. Because so little of the research on gender and facework has incorporated sociological variables, there are probably more questions than answers.

Major Challenges

There is much to be done in examining the role of gender in facework. This research needs to go beyond the examination of isolated symbols because (1) single symbols fulfill multiple meanings, (2) the assignment of meaning may vary with gender and other social variables, and (3) males and females may need or want to achieve different face needs. Still, one strength that came out of the isolated-variable approach was a list of behaviors that are associated with facework under certain conditions. By combining functional and sociological approaches we might be able to identify what those conditions are, when they are relevant, and what the behaviors mean to speakers and hearers.

Preliminary evidence suggests that there may be gender differences related to different types of face-needs (solidarity, competence, and autonomy) and how those face-needs are enacted. Most of this work has largely consisted of the researcher making inferential associations between the data and face-needs models or post hoc analyses on my part. Future research could be aimed at assessing more directly how speakers and hearers themselves interpret the facework of females and males.

Some studies have demonstrated that gender interacts with other sociological variables (e.g., status, relational intimacy, context, age) to determine what kind of facework is done, how much is done, and how it is interpreted. An analysis of these studies leads to several other questions: Does the facework of males and females vary with public and private encounters, and if yes, why? Do "politeness" markers count as deference in some contexts and status in others? If yes, why? Is gender or social status a better predictor of facework, and does this vary with context? How does gender or social status serve as an interpretative frame for shaping the meaning of facework? Are some social variables more important to males or females (e.g., relational intimacy versus social status or age), and why? Do females and males have different systems for doing facework (e.g., enacting solidarity via the presence or absence of apologies, compliments, etc.), and if so why? Do males and females differ in their need for, appreciation of, or sensitivity to various types of facework?

Collectively, the research on gender and politeness/facework has addressed the rather simplistic question, who does more facework, males or females? Based on our current research one cannot answer that question without addressing the following questions: In self-report or actual behavior? What kind of facework? With whom? Directed toward self or other? In what setting? In what kind of discourse? For what purpose? According to what interpretative frame? The data shows that the facework behavior of females and males is much more complex than the simple stereotype—females are more polite. By combining both functional and sociological approaches we have a better chance of providing the complex answers the questions deserve.

References

Axia, G., and Argenti, E. (1989). Context and linguistic politeness in 7- and 9-year-old Italian children. Paper presented at the Biennial Meeting of the Society for Research in Child Development. Kansas City, MO. ERIC Doc. No. = 306034.

Barnlund, D. C., and Araki, S. (1985). Intercultural encounters: The management of compliments by Japanese and Americans. *Journal of Cross-Cultural Psychology, 16*, 9–26.

Baroni, M. R., and Durso, V. (1984). Some experimental findings about the question of politeness and women's speech. *Language in Society, 13*, 67–72.

Bates, E., and Silvern, L. (1977). Social adjustment and politeness in preschoolers. *Journal of Communication, 27*, 104–111.

Baumann, M. (1976). Two features of women's speech? In B. L. Dubois and I. Crouch (Eds.), *The Sociology of the Languages of American Women*. San Antonio, TX: Trinity University.

Baxter, L. (1984). An investigation of compliance-gaining as politeness. *Human Communication Research, 10*, 427–456.

Becker, J. A. (1984). Adult beliefs about the acquisition of pragmatic skills. Paper presented at the Biennial Meeting of the Southeastern Conference on Human Development, Athens, GA. ERIC Doc. No. = 245809

———. (1986). Bossy and nice requests: Children's production and interpretation. *Merrill-Palmer Quarterly Journal of Developmental Psychology, 32*, 393–413.

Becker, J. A., and Smenner, P. C. (1986). The spontaneous use of "thank you" by preschoolers as a function of sex, socioeconomic status, and listener status. *Language in Society, 15,* 537–546.

Bell, K. M. (1984). The relationship of gender and sex role identity to politeness in speech behavior. *Dissertation Abstracts International,* 45 *8,* 2678B.

Bellinger, D. C., and Gleason, J. B. (1982). Sex differences in parental directives to children. *Sex Roles, 8,* 1123–1139.

Bloom, M. M. (1990). Sex differences in ethical systems: A useful framework for interpreting communication research. *Communication Quarterly, 38,* 244–254.

Bradac, J. J., and Mulac, A. (1984). A molecular view of powerful and powerless speech styles. *Communication Monographs, 51,* 307–319.

Bradley, P. H. (1981). The folklinguistics of women's speech: An empirical examination. *Communication Monographs, 48,* 73–90.

Brooks, V. R. (1982). Sex differences in student dominance behavior in female and male professors' classrooms. *Sex Roles, 8,* 683–690.

Brouwer, D. (1982). The influence of the addressees sex on politeness in language use. *Linguistics, 20,* 697–711.

Brouwer, D., Gerritsen, M., and DeHaan, D. (1979). Speech differences between women and men: On the wrong track. *Language in Society, 8,* 33–50.

Broverman, I. K., Vogel, S. R., Broverman, D. M., Clarkson, F. E., and Rosenkrantz, P. S. (1972). Sex-role stereotypes: A current appraisal *Journal of Social Issues, 28,* 59–78.

Brown, P. (1980). How and why are women more polite: Some evidence from a Mayan community. In S. McConnell-Ginet, R. Borker, and N. Furman (Eds.), *Women and language in literature and society.* New York: Praeger.

———. (1990). Gender, politeness, and confrontation in Tenejapa. *Discourse Processes, 13,* 123–141.

Brown, P., and Levinson, S. (1978). Universals in language usage: Politeness phenomena. In E. N. Goody (Ed.)., *Questions and politeness: Strategies in social interaction.* Cambridge: Cambridge University Press.

———. (1987). *Politeness: Some universals in language use.* Cambridge: Cambridge University Press.

Burgoon, M., Dillard, J. P., and Doran, N. E. (1983). Friendly or unfriendly persuasion: The effects of violations of expectations by males and females. *Human Communication Research, 10,* 283–294.

Burgoon, M., Jones, S., and Stewart, D. (1975). Empirical investigations of language intensity: I. The effects of sex of source, receiver, and language intensity on attitude change. *Human Communication Research, 1,* 244–248.

Buikema, R., and Roeters, A. (1982). Politeness strategies in the interaction of women and men. Paper presented at the Annual Meeting of the World Congress of Sociology, Mexico City. ERIC = ED229324.

Carrocci, N. M. (1985). Perceiving and responding to interpersonal conflict. *Central States Speech Journal, 36,* 215–228.

Cashion, J. (1985). Politeness in courtroom language. Paper presented at the Annual Meeting of the Western speech Communication Association, Fresno, CA. ERIC = ED254882.

Cashion, J., Cody, M. J., Erickson, E. V. (1986). "You'll love this one": An exploration into joke-prefacing devices. *Journal of Language and Social Psychology, 5,* 303–312.

Chodorow, N. (1978). *The reproduction of mothering.* Berkeley: University of California Press.

Dindia, K. (1987). The effects of sex of subject and sex of partner on interruptions. *Human Communication Research, 13,* 372–385.

Dubois, B. L., and Crouch, I. (1975). The question of tag questions in women's speech: They don't really use more of them, do they? *Language in Society, 4,* 289–294.

Duck, S., Rutt, D. J., Hurst, M. H., and Strejc, H. (1991). Some evidence truths about conversations in everyday relationships: All communications are not created equally. *Human Communication Research, 18,* 228–267.

Edelsky, C. (1977). Acquisition of an aspect of communication competence: Learning what it means to talk like a lady. In S. Ervin-Tripp and C. Mitchell-Kernan (Eds.), *Child Discourse.* New York: Academic Press.

Fine, J. T. (1981). Sex similarities in behavior in a seventh grade classroom. *Journal of Early Adolescence, 1,* 234–243.

Fishman, P. M. (1978). Interaction: The work women do. *Social Problems, 25,* 397–406.

Franzblau, S. H. (1980). Traits or strategies: An analysis of perceptions of an actual speaker-listener roles in the issuance of deferent and non-deferent requests. Unpublished dissertation, State University of New York, Stony Brook.

Gilligan, C. (1982). *In a different voice: Psychological theory and women's development.* Cambridge, MA: Harvard University Press.

Gilligan, C., and Attanucci, J. (1988). Two moral orientations: Gender differences and similarities. *Merrill-Palmer Quarterly, 34,* 223–237.

Gleason, J. B. (1980). The acquisition of social speech routines and politeness formulas. In H. Giles, W. P. Robinson, and P. M. Smith (Eds.), *Language: Social psychological perspectives.* Oxford: Pergamon.

Gleason, J. B., and Grief, E. B. (1983). Men's speech to young children. In B. Thorne, C. Kramarae, and N. Henley (Eds.). *Language, gender and society.* Rowley, MA: Newbury House.

Gleason, J. B., Perlmann, R. Y., and Greif, E. B. (1984). What's the magic word: Learning language through politeness routines. *Discourse Processes, 7,* 493–502.

Goodwin, M. H. (1980). Directive-response speech sequences in girls' and boys' task activities. In S. McConnell-Ginet, R. Borker, and N. Furman (Eds.), *Women and Language in Literature and Society.* New York: Praeger.

Haccoun, D. M., Haccoun, R. R., and Sallay, G. (1978). Sex differences in the appropriateness of supervisory styles: A nonmanagement view. *Journal of Applied Psychology, 63,* 124–127.

Hartman, M. (1976). A descriptive study of the language of men and women born in Maine around 1900 as it relates to the Lakoff hypotheses in *Language and woman's place.* In B. L. Dubios and I. Crouch (Eds.), *The sociology of the language of american women.* San Antonio, TX: Trinity University.

Herbert, R. K. (1990). Sex-based differences in compliment behavior. *Language in Society, 19,* 201–224.

Holmes, J. (1986). Functions of *you know* in women's and men's speech. *Language in Society, 15,* 1–22.

———. (1988). Paying compliments: A sex-preferential politeness strategy. *Journal of Pragmatics, 12,* 445–465.

———. (1989). Sex differences and apologies: One aspect of communicative competence. *Applied Linguistics, 10,* 194–213.

Holtgraves, T. (1991). Interpreting questions and replies: Effects of face-threat, question form, and gender. *Social Psychology Quarterly, 54,* 15–24.

Ide, S. (1982). Japanese sociolinguistics: Politeness and women's language. *Lingua, 57,* 357–385.

Ide, S., Hori, H. Kawasaki, A., Ikuta, S., and Haga, H. (1986). Sex difference and politeness in Japanese. *International Journal of the Sociology of Language. 58,* 25–36.

Jefferson, G. (1978). A case of precision timing in ordinary conversation. *Semiotica, 9,* 47–93.

Jenkins, M. M. (1984). The story is in the telling: A cooperative style of conversation among women. In S. Tromel-Plotz (Ed.), *Gewalt durch sprache: Die vergewaltigung van Frauen in gesprachen.* Frankfurt am Main: Fischer Taschenbuch Verlag.

———. (1986). What's so funny: Joking among women. In S. Bremner, N. Caskey, and B. Moonwomon (Eds.), *Proceedings of the first Berkeley women and language conference 1985*. Berkeley, CA: Linguistics Department, University of California, Berkeley.

Johnstone, B. (1989). Community and contest: How women and men construct their worlds in conversational narrative. Paper presented at Women in America: Legacies of race Ethnicity, Georgetown University, Washington, DC. Cited in Tannen, 1990.

Keenan, E. O. (1974). Norm-makers, norm-breakers: Uses of speech by men and women in Malagasy community. In R. Bauman and J. Sherzer (Eds.), *Exploration in the ethnography of speaking*. Cambridge: Cambridge University Press.

Kemper, S. (1984). When to speak like a lady. *Sex Roles, 10*, 435–444.

Kennedy, C. W., and Camden, C. T. (1983). A new look at interruptions. *Western Journal of Speech Communication, 47*, 45–58.

Kirsh, B. (1981). Status and verbal power assertion: Does gender or popularity better predict directive use? *Dissertation Abstracts International, 42*, (1), 394–395A.

Kissling, E. A., and Kramarae, C. (1991). Stranger compliments: The interpretations of street remarks. *Women's Studies in Communication, 14*, 75–93.

Knapp, M. L., Hopper, R., and Bell, R. A. (1984). Compliment: A descriptive taxonomy. *Journal of Communication, 34*, 12–31.

Kramer, C. (1977). Perceptions of female and male speech. *Language and Speech, 20*, 151–161.

Kramarae, C. (1986). Speech crimes which the law cannot reach or compliments and other insulting behavior. *Proceedings of the first Berkeley women and language conference 1985*. Berkeley, CA: Linguistics Department, University of California, Berkeley.

Lakoff, R. (1974). What you can do with words: Politeness, pragmatics, and performatives. *Berkeley Studies in Syntax and Semantics, 16*, 1–55.

———. (1975). *Language and woman's place*. New York: Harper and Row.

Lapadat, J., and Seesahai, M. (1978). Male versus female codes in informal contexts. *Sociolinguistics Newsletter, 8*, 7–8. Abstracted in Thorne, Kramarae, and Henley, 1978.

Leichty, G., and Applegate, J. L. (1991). Social-cognitive and situational influences on the use of face-saving persuasive strategies. *Human Communication Research, 17*, 451–484.

Leonard, R. (1988). Exploring the roles of requests, refusals and reasons in preschoolers' negotiations. Paper presented at the Australian Developmental Conference, Sydney, Australia. ERIC Doc. No. = 301312.

Lim, T. S., and Bowers, J. W. (1991). Facework: Solidarity, approbation, and tact. *Human Communication Research, 17,* 415–450.

Liska, J., Mechling, E. W., and Stathas, S. (1981). Differences in subject's perceptions of gender and believeability between users of deferential and nondeferential language. *Communication Quarterly, 29,* 40–48.

Loveday, L. (1981). Pitch, politeness, and sexual role: An exploratory investigation into the pitch correlates of English and Japanese politeness formulas. *Language and Speech, 24,* 71–89.

Martin, J. N., and Craig, R. T. (1983). Selected linguistics sex differences during initial social interactions of same-sex and mixed-sex student dyads. *Western Journal of Speech Communication, 47,* 16–28.

McMillan, J. R., Clifton, A. K., McGrath, D., and Gale, W. S. (1977). Women's language: Uncertainty or interpersonal sensitivity and emotionality. *Sex Roles, 3,* 545–559.

Metts, S., and Bryan, G. (1984). Politeness: A conversational indicator of sex roles. Paper presented at the Central States Speech Association Convention, Chicago, IL. ERIC Doc. No. = ED246500.

Milan, W. G. (1976). The influence of the sex and age factors in the selection of polite expressions: A sample from Puerto Rican Spanish. *The Bilingual Review, 3,* 99–121.

Mulac, A., Bradac, J. J., and Mann, S. K. (1985). Male/female language differences and attributional consequences in children's television. *Human Communication Research, 11,* 481–506.

Mulac, A., Incontro, C. R., and James, M. R. (1985). Comparison of the gender-linked language effect and sex role stereotypes. *Journal of Personality and Social Psychology, 49,* 1098–1109.

Mulac, A., and Lundell, T. L. (1986). Linguistic contributions to the gender-linked language effect. *Journal of Language and Social Psychology, 5,* 81–101.

Mulac, A., Lundell, T. L., and Bradac, J. (1986). Male/female language differences and attributional consequences in a public speaking situation: Toward an explanation of the gender-linked language effect. *Communication Monographs, 53,* 115–129.

Mulac, A., Studley, L. B. and Blau, S. (1990). The gender-linked language effect in primary and secondary student's impromptu essays. *Sex Roles, 23,* 439–469.

Mulac, A., Wiemann, J. M., Widenmann, S. J., and Gibson, T. W. (1988). Male/female language differences and effects in same-sex and mixed-sex dyads: The gender-linked language effect. *Communication Monographs, 55,* 315–335.

Ochs, E. (in press). Indexing gender. In B. Miller (Ed.), *Gender Hierarchies.*

Octigan, M., and Niederman, S. (1979). Male dominance in conversations. *Frontiers, 4,* 50–54.

Ogino, T. (1986). Quantification of politeness based on the usage patterns of honorific expressions. *International Journal of the Sociology of Language, 58,* 37–58.

Ogino, T., Misono, Y., and Fukushima, C. (1985). Diversity of honorific usage in Tokyo: A sociolinguistics approach based on a field survey. *International Journal of the Sociology of Language, 55,* 23–39.

Porter, N., Geis, F. L., Cooper, E., and Newman, E. (1985). Androgyny and leadership in mixed-sex groups. *Journal of Personality and Social Psychology, 49,* 808–823.

Quina, K., Wingard, J. A., and Bates, H. G. (1987). Language style and gender stereotypes in person perception. *Psychology of Women Quarterly, 11,* 111–122.

Ramussen, J. L., and Moely, B. E. (1986). Impression formation as a function of the sex role appropriateness of linguistic behavior. *Sex Roles, 14,* 149–161.

Roloff, M. E., Janiszewski, C. A., McGrath, M. A., Burns, C., and Manrai, L. A. (1988). Acquiring resources from intimates: When obligation substitutes for persuasion. *Human Communication Research, 14,* 364–396.

Rosen, B., and Jerdee, T. H. (1975). Effects of employee's sex and threatening versus pleading appeals on managerial evaluations of grievances. *Journal of Applied Psychology, 60,* 442–445.

Rosenfeld, L. B. (1979). Self-disclosure avoidance: Why I am afraid to tell you who I am? *Communication Monographs, 46,* 63–74.

Sacks, H., Schegloff, E. A., and Jefferson, G. (1974). A simplest systematics for the organization of turn-taking for conversation. *Language, 50,* 696–735.

Shaffer, D. R., and Ogden, K. (1986). On sex differences in self-disclosure during the acquaintance process: The role of anticipated future interaction. *Journal of Personality and Social Psychology, 51,* 92–101.

Shimanoff, S. B. (1974). An experimental examination of English lexical gender and the perception of sex markedness. M.A. Thesis, San Diego State University.

———. (1977). Investigating politeness. In E. O. Keenan and T. L. Bennet (Eds.), *Discourse across time and space.* Los Angeles: University of Southern California Press.

———. (1983). The role of gender in linguistic references to emotive states. *Communication Quarterly, 31,* 174–179.

———. (1985). Rules governing the verbal expression of emotions between married couples. *Western Journal of Speech Communication, 49,* 147–165.

———. (1987). Types of emotional disclosures and request compliance between spouses. *Communication Monographs, 54,* 85–100.

———. (1988). Degree of emotional expressiveness as a function of face-needs, gender, and interpersonal relationship. *Communication Reports, 1,* 43–53.

———. (1989). Responses to compliments and criticisms: From accuracy to legitimacy. Paper presented at the Western Speech Communication Association, Spokane, WA.

Shimanoff, S. B., West, D. L., and Bruno, J. (1992). Linguistic and social influences on perceived politeness. Unpublished paper, San Francisco State University.

Sigelman, C. K., Carr, M. B., and Begley, N. L. (1986). Developmental changes in the influence of sex-role stereotypes on person perception. *Child Study Journal, 16,* 191–205.

Sims, A. L. (1989). The compliment sequence. *Southern Communication Journal, 54,* 171–184.

Smith, F. (1990). Gender and the framing of exegetical authority in sermon performances. Ph.D. dissertation, Georgetown University.

Smith-Hefner, N. J. (1988). Women and politeness: The Javanese example. *Language in Society, 17,* 535–554.

Snell, W., Jr., Belk, S. S., Flowers, A., and Warren, J. (1988). Women's and men's willingness to self-disclose to therapists and friends: The moderating influence of instrumental, expressive, masculine, and feminine topics. *Sex Roles, 18,* 769–777.

Snell, W., Jr., Belk, S. S., and Hawkins, R. C., II. (1986). The masculine and feminine self-disclosure scale: The politics of masculine and feminine self-presentation. *Sex Roles, 15,* 249–268.

Stafford, L. (1984). Politeness: Differences in the language of men and women. Paper presented at the Speech Communication Association Convention, Chicago, IL.

Steffen, V. J., and Eagly, A. H. (1985). Implicit theories about influence style: The effects of status and sex. *Personality and Social Psychology Bulletin, 11,* 191–205.

Tannen, D. (1981). Indirectness in discourse: Ethnicity as conversational style. *Discourse Processes, 4,* 221–238.

———. (1984). *Conversational style: Analyzing talk among friends.* Norwod, NJ: Ablex.

———. (1986). *That's not what I meant! How conversational style makes or breaks your relations with others.* New York: William Morrow.

———. (1990). *You just don't understand: Women and men in conversation.* New York: William Morrow.

Thorne, B., Kramarae, C., and Henley, N. (1983). *Language, gender and society.* Rowley, MA: Newbury House.

Turner, R. E., and Edgley, C. (1974). Manners—you're too kind: The consequences of compliments. *Psychology Today, 8,* 43.

Walters, J. (1979). Strategies for requesting in Spanish and English: Structural similarities and pragmatic differences. *Language Learning, 29,* 277–293.

West, C., and Zimmerman, D. H. (1983). Small insults: A study of interruptions in cross-sex conversations between unacquainted persons. In B. Throne, C. Kramarae, and N. Henley (Eds.), *Language, gender, and society.* Rowley, MA: Newbury House.

Wilensky, J. (1991). Such a pretty face: An examination of compliments and criticisms received by women in the weight loss process. Unpublished master's thesis, San Francisco State University, San Francisco, CA.

Wolfson, N. (1984). Pretty is as pretty does: A speech act view of sex roles. *Applied Linguistics, 5,* 236–244.

Zimmerman, D. H., and West, C. (1975). Sex roles, interruptions and silences in conversations. In B. Throne and N. Henley (Eds.), *Language and sex: Difference and dominance.* Rowley, MA: Newbury House.

-7-
Facework and Interpersonal Relationships

TAE-SEOP LIM

Since a facework message conveys one's assessment of the social qualities of one's self or the other, it usually bears certain implications on the relationship. For example, an expression of solidarity, as a type of facework (Leech, 1983; Lim and Bowers, 1991; Scollon and Scollon, 1983), implies that one values the other as a member of an in-group, which signals one's intention to establish or maintain a close relationship with the other. Absence of an expected enactment of solidarity or an expression of indifference, in contrast, conveys one's disregard for the other as a member of an in-group, which indicates one's intention to increase the relational distance temporarily or permanently.

Facework, therefore, is an integral part of managing interpersonal relationships. In this chapter, I will discuss the relationship between facework and interpersonal relationships. Specifically, I will (1) characterize face and facework, and (2) delineate how individuals' intentions to establish or maintain certain interpersonal relationships affect their use of facework strategies.

Face and Facework

Persons universally have face and the desires to maintain or even gain face (Brown & Levinson, 1987; Goffman, 1967). Facework, the actions which are taken to support these desires to maintain or gain face, can also be found universally. While the universality of face and facework seems to be evident (Brown &

209

Levinson, 1987), the specific elements of face and the specific facework strategies seem to vary across different societies or across different situations even in the same society. The general characterizations of face and facework that are delineated in this chapter should be universal. However, the specific tactics of face enactment and the degrees of face supported by these tactics are specific to Northern American English-speaking and interpersonal situations.

Face

Face is defined as the positive public image that a person claims for him/herself. There are at least three important characteristics of face that need to be explicated. First, face is not private but *public* (Brown & Levinson, 1987). In other words, face is not what one thinks of oneself, but what one thinks others should think of one's worth. Since the claim of face is about one's image held by others, one cannot claim face unilaterally without regard to the other's perspective. For example, "No matter what you think of me, I know I'm good at this" is not a claim for face. The claim for face is the claim that the other should acknowledge, whether explicitly or implicitly, that one possesses the claimed virtues. Since face is public, one cannot gain face from a great feat that is not witnessed by others, and cannot lose face from blunders made in private. Face, in this sense, is different from such psychological concepts as self-esteem, self-concept, ego, and pride, which can be claimed without regard to the other's perspective, and can be gained or lost in private as well as public.

Second, face is one's projected *image* which may or may not be concurrent with others' assessment of one's real self. The claim for face, therefore, is not necessarily about the real opinions of others (i.e., real esteem), but sometimes is about the manifested opinions of others. In other words, the bottom line of face want is "no matter what you really think of me, you must act as if you respected me," so that one's projected image can be preserved.

Finally, face is in terms of positive social values (Goffman, 1967). Persons do not claim face for what they think are negative. Different societies and different groups have different values. Thus, a positive attribute in one society or group may not be valued at all or may even be considered negative in another.

Since any positive social value can be an element of face, face is as complex as the value system of a society. As specific values vary across different cultures, so do specific elements of face. However, it seems to be universal that individuals have three basic types of face: autonomy, fellowship, and competence (Lim & Bowers, 1991).

Autonomy-face is persons' image that they are in control of their own fate, that is, they have the virtues of a full-fledged, mature, and responsible adult. This type of face includes such values as "independent," "in control of self," "initiative," "creative," "mature," "composed," "reliable," and "self-sufficient." When persons claim these values for themselves, they want to be self-governed and free from others' interference, control, or imposition (Brown & Levinson, 1987). The claim for autonomy-face, in other words, is embodied in the want not be imposed upon (Lim & Bowers, 1991).

Fellowship-face is persons' image that they are worthy companions. It is concerned with the social aspect of a person, that is, how desirable a person is as a member of the group. Fellowship-face includes such values as "likeable," "accepted and loved," "friendly," "agreeable," "cooperative," "alike," and "affiliated." When persons claim these values for themselves, they want to be thought of as a member of an in-group. Thus, fellowship-face brings about the want to be included (Lim & Bowers, 1991).

Competence-face is the image that one is a person of ability. It is concerned with past accomplishments, good reputations, and the capabilities to perform successfully in the future. This type of face-claims emphasize such values as "knowledgeable," "intelligent," "wise," "experienced," "influential," "prosperous," "accomplished," "attractive," and "distinguished." When persons claim these values for them, they want others to acknowledge their success and capabilities. Thus competence-face produces the want that one's abilities be respected (Lim & Bowers, 1991).

In short, people have three distinct face-wants: the want not to be imposed upon (autonomy-face), the want to be included (fellowship-face), and the want that their abilities be respected (competence-face). These face wants of people are addressed by the line of actions called facework.

Facework

Facework is broadly defined as the actions taken to deal with the face-wants of one and/or the other. Facework, therefore, includes the actions oriented toward one's own face as well as the actions oriented toward the other's face. In this chapter, however, I will limit my discussion to other-oriented facework, or the actions that one takes to promote, maintain, threaten, or ignore the face-wants of the other.

Since the three types of face-wants are distinct human needs (Craig, Tracy, & Spisak, 1986; Lim 1988, 1989, 1990; Lim & Bowers, 1991), supporting one particular type of face does not necessarily support or undermine other types of face, nor does it compensate for the loss of other types of face. Hence, speakers need to see to it that all the three face-wants of the other be properly attended. Different types of face are supported by different kinds of facework.

Autonomy-face is addressed by *tact* facework (Leech, 1983; Lim & Bowers, 1991), which expresses that to some degree one respects the other's freedom of action or autonomy. Tact facework is characterized by the effort to maximize the freedom of action of the other and minimize the impositions that restrict the other's freedom of action. Thus, tact facework strategies often ask for suggestions and directions, avoid explicit directives, and use pleas and conventional indirectness.

Fellowship-face is supported by *solidarity* facework (Lim & Bowers, 1991; Scollon & Scollon, 1983), which expresses to some degree that one accepts the other as a member of an ingroup. Solidarity facework minimizes the differences and maximizes the commonalities between the speaker and the addressee. Thus, strategies of solidarity facework tend to use informal or intimate language, and emphasize the necessity to cooperate, similarities, shared fate, and mutual trust.

Competence-face is addressed by *approbation* facework (Leech, 1983; Lim & Bowers, 1991), which shows to some degree that one appreciates and respects the other's general abilities and accomplishments. Approbation, therefore, is characterized by the effort to minimize blame and maximize praise of the other. Strategies of approbation, therefore, tend to ignore or understate negative aspects of the other, and notice and exaggerate positive aspects of the other.

All three types of facework vary in the extent to which they support the relevant types of face-wants. At the most supportive extreme, facework actually gives face to the other; at the opposite extreme, facework directly threatens the face of the other; and in between these two extremes are those actions taken to mitigate the threat to the other's face. Literature suggests four basic strategies of facework that vary in the amount of face that is extended to the other: face-giving, withdrawal, moderation, and disregard.

Face-giving, which is "approach-based" (Brown & Levinson, 1987) facework, actively promotes the given face want of the other, thus being the most supportive facework of the four. Specifically, the face-giving strategy of tact gives autonomy to the other; the face-giving strategy of solidarity actively includes the other in the in-group, and the face-giving strategy of approbation shows admiration for the other's achievement or abilities. The face-giving strategy is normally used when there is no direct threat to the particular type of face. Since the face-giving strategies actively acknowledge the positive attributes of the other, they are more supportive when they are more directly expressed. "It's nice," for example, is more supportive than "I think it's kind of nice."

Withdrawal, moderation, and disregard are used when persons perform certain face-threatening acts. They, in other words, are "avoidance-based" (Brown & Levinson, 1987) facework, which are used to mitigate the threat to the face of the other. Withdrawal, which is equivalent to the "don't do the face-threatening act" strategy of Brown and Levinson, gives up performing the intended face-threatening act in order to avoid threatening the face of the other. Disregard, on the other hand, does not pay any attention to the face want of the other. It is "baldly on record" (Brown & Levinson, 1987), and the lowest in the amount of face support. Moderation, which falls in between withdrawal and disregard in terms of face support, performs the intended face-threatening act but attempts to mitigate the possible face-threat. Indirectness has been proposed as the most important principle for moderating face-threat.

There are different ways of enacting disregard, moderation, and face-giving strategies of tact, solidarity, and approbation. Table 1 presents some important tactics of disregarding the other's autonomy, moderating the threat to the other's freedom of action, and giving more autonomy face to the other. "Imperative," which expresses the intended imposition without any redressive effort, ignores the other's want not to be imposed on.

Moderating tactics of tact facework attempt to express one's wish to avoid imposing upon the other. Thus, the tactics vary in the amounts of face-support dependent upon the indirectness of expressing the intended imposition. "Pleading," "advice," "conventional indirectness," and "debt incurrence" are

Table 1. TACTICS OF TACT FACEWORK

	Disregard
Imperative	(To state the imposition directly.) "Do it."

	Moderation
Pleading	(To use the conventional marker "Please" along with the Imperative.) "Please do it.'
Advice	(To emphasize the benefit of accepting the imposition.) "It'll be a good idea for you to do it."
Conventional Indirectness	(To ask a question instead of giving an order.) "Would you do it?"
Debt Incurrence	(To imply that one will owe to the other for the favor.) "I'd appreciate it if you could do it for me."
Unconventional Indirectness	(Not to state the imposition. To be off record.) "I think you are the best candidate."
Experimenting	(To check the possibility for the other to volunteer.) "Do you think you can take time to do it?"

	Withdrawal Face-Giving
Nomination	(To put the other person in charge.) "You are in charge."
Volunteering	(To expand the other's domain of control by offering service.) "Is there anything you want me to do?"
Submission	(To limit one's own autonomy to accept the other's imposition.) "Your wish is my command."

indirect. However, due to conventions, their meanings are more or less direct (Brown & Levinson, 1987). Thus, this group of conventionally indirect tactics do not moderate the face-threat greatly.

On the other hand, "unconventional indirectness," which gives hints or association clues, and "experimenting," which explores the possibility for the other to volunteer, are very indirect, thus significantly mitigating the threat to the other's autonomy face. Autonomy face-giving strategies are not intended to avoid threatening the other's face, but purported to give leeway to the other. "Nomination" dedicates, endows, or transfers the leadership to the other; "volunteering" expands the other's domain of control by offering service; and "submission" gives relative autonomy to the other by limiting one's own.

Table 2 presents some widely used tactics of solidarity. "Exclusion," which separates or expels the other from the group, "dissimilarity," which emphasizes the lack of commonality or actual differences, and "apathy," which demonstrates the lack of compassion, show little concern for the other's want to be included. Moderating tactics of solidarity are used when one needs to threaten the other's fellowship-face, but wants to avoid directly depreciating the other as a member of in-group. "Disagreement," which implies that the one thinks differently from the other, "self-liability," which openly discusses relational problems, and "formality," which creates relational distance by acting formally and using formal language style, express more or less indirectly one's want not to include the other.

Fellowship-face-giving tactics are used when one wants to actively promote the other's want to be included. As mentioned earlier, face-giving tactics are more supportive, when they are more direct. "Similarity," "Informality," "Agreement," and "presupposition" actually imply, but not directly state, that one approves of the other as a member of an in-group. On the other hand, "appreciation," which approves of the other's character, "empathy," which shows compassion, "cooperation," which emphasizes the obligation to cooperate, and "affirmation," which reaffirms the close relationship, express one's intention to include the other more or less directly.

Table 3 shows the tactics of approbation facework, that is, disregarding, moderating the threat to, and actively promoting the competence-face of the other. "Disapproval," which bluntly disapproves of the other's abilities or performances, and "comparative disapproval," which disapproves of the other for not meeting certain standards, show little concern for the other's competence face. Moderating tactics of approbation facework expresses one's intention to avoid disapproving of the other. The tactics, therefore, are more face-supportive if they are more indirect in expressing the disapproval. "Resentment," which disapproves of the other's performance, but leaves the

Table 2. TACTICS OF SOLIDARITY FACEWORK

	Disregard
Exclusion	(To expel the other from the in-group.) "I don't like you."
Dissimilarity	(To emphasize the lack of similarity or commonality.) "You and I do not have much in common."
Apathy	(To act indifferently toward the other.) "I don't care. It's your problem."

	Moderation
Disagreement	(To imply that the other is wrong.) "I don't think so."
Self-Liability	(To attribute the relational break-down to self.) "Well, it's not really you, but me. I'm so occupied by my work that I don't think I can go out with you."
Formality	(To act formally and use formal language style.)

	Withdrawal Face-Giving
Similarity	(To emphasize the similarities and commonalities.) "That's my favorite, too."
Informality	(To act informally and use informal language style.)
Agreement	(To imply that the other is right.) "Right."
Presupposition	(To claim that one knows about the other.) "You had a date last night, didn't you?"
Appreciation	(To approve of the other's character.) "You're a nice guy."
Empathy	(To show compassion.) "I'm so happy for you."
Cooperation	(To emphasize the cooperative relationship.) "We gotta help each other."
Affirmation	(To affirm the friendship.) "You've been such a good friend, so I know I can trust you."

other's competence intact, "aspiration," which implies that the performance is not bad, and "diminutive," which understates the problem, are still more or less direct in the expression of disapproval. On the other hand, "suggestion," which suggests the ways to make the performance perfect, "contradiction," which approves of some related aspect and moderates the problem, and "encouragement," which approves of the potential of the other, are very indirect in disapproval because they also express certain approval. Competence-face-giving tactics, "comparative approval," "positive comments," and "admiration" actually promote the other's want to be respected by giving approvals.

Facework in Interpersonal Relationships

When engaged in an interpersonal interaction, persons are expected to satisfy each other's face-wants (Goffman, 1967). Persons, therefore, need to honor the other's face-wants by including the other in their group, respecting the other's abilities, and limiting constraints on the other's freedom of action. The degree to which persons honor the other's face-wants are not only affected by such external factors as relational intimacy and power differences, but it is also greatly influenced by the person's intention to renegotiate the natures of their relationships. This section will delineate the processes in which these relational factors and various intentions determine the degrees of facework manifested in interpersonal interactions.

Face Threat and Legitimacy of Face Threat

The degree of facework is dependent upon one's assessment of face-threat that is posed by performing the given face-threatening act or not performing a certain face-giving act (Brown & Levinson, 1987). Persons are expected to select more face-saving strategies as the threat to the face-want of the other increases. One's assessment of face-threat (or the negative implications of the act upon the positive public image of the other), in turn, is affected by one's assessment of the legitimacy to threaten (or ignore) the other's face by performing a certain face-threatening act or not performing a certain face-giving act. When the legitimacy is high, the behavior has little threat to the face of the other; however, when the legitimacy is low, the behavior poses a strong threat to the face of the other. In short, persons are expected to use more facework when they have less legitimacy to threaten the other's face-want.

Table 3. TACTICS OF APPROBATION FACEWORK

	Disregard
Disapproval	(To disapprove bluntly or ridicule.) "It's bad."
Comparative Disapproval	(To disapprove in comparison to certain standards.) "It's not up to par."

	Moderation
Resentment	(To imply that the other has better abilities.) "You could've done a much better job."
Aspiration	(To imply that the work is not bad, but can be bettered.) "It can be improved."
Diminutive	(To understand the problem.) "I found a few problems in it."
Suggestion	(To suggest the ways to make the work complete.) "It needs a little more evidence to be really good."
Contradiction	(To approve of some related aspect, then moderate the problem.) "You're a good writer, but it needs more evidence."
Encouragement	(To approve of the potential that needs to be cultivated.) "It has good potential but needs to be reorganized a bit."

	Withdrawal Face-Giving
Comparative Approval	(To approve in comparison to certain standards.) "You are better than many other people."
Positive Comments	(To approve moderately.) "I think it was pretty good."
Admiration	(To approve without reservation.) "You did a very good job."

However, the effect of the legitimacy of face-threat on face-work is not direct, but mediated by one's intentions to manage the relationship and/or the situation. For example, if persons' primary goal is to present themselves as nice persons, they may employ highly face-saving strategies even when they are quite justified in ignoring the other's face-want. Or, if persons want to expand their authority over the other, they may use little face-saving facework even when they lack the legitimacy to threaten the other's face (Brown & Levinson, 1987).

In summary, the selection of facework strategies is determined interactively by one's legitimacy to threaten the face of the other and one's intention to manage the relationship or the situation. The legitimacy of face-threat is determined by a number of relational and situational factors. This chapter will discuss three of the most essential determinants of legitimacy—status difference, relational intimacy, and role right. There also are a variety of goals and intentions that influence the selection of facework strategies. The discussion in this chapter will include the intentions to renegotiate relational distance (or intimacy) and relational power and to present oneself as a desirable person.

Status Difference and Facework

Status Difference and Legitimacy. The status difference has been referred to as power difference by most facework researchers including Brown and Levinson (1987) and Goffman (1967). It is the difference in overall abilities to control the other's behavior including the abilities to reward and punish the other. Status, therefore, is closely related to the relative rank one has over the other in the given organization. Supervisors, for example, have higher status than their subordinates.

As one's status over the other increases, one tends to claim more right to perform acts that threaten the other's autonomy, fellowship, and/or competence face. Most societies and social groups have explicit regulations or implicit conventions to differentiate between a superior and a subordinate, and their relative rights to ignore the other's wish to maintain a positive public image. Superiors across cultures are endowed with more legitimacy to ignore subordinates' face-wants, and subordinates generally believe that it is their virtue not to claim too much face. This disparity in legitimacy of performing face-threatening acts is more obvious in a more authoritarian society. In a highly authoritarian society, superiors believe that it is their way of maintaining their status to threaten subordinates' face-wants, and subordinates have virtually no resources to retaliate to a superior's abusive face-threat.

Proposition 1: As one's status over the other increases, one has more legitimacy to ignore the threat to the other's face-wants.

Moderators of Status-Based Legitimacy. The manifestation of the status-based legitimacy to ignore the other's face-wants is moderated by one's intention to manage one's relationship or impression in certain ways. First, studies (Brown & Gilman, 1960; Lim & Bowers, 1991) have found that persons, who intend to maintain or develop a close relationship with the other, tend to downplay the status difference. Since status difference constitutes a dissimilarity between communicators (Brown & Gilman, 1960), its display signals one's want to make the dissimilarity salient, which hinders the accomplishment of relational closeness or solidarity. Thus, persons in friendly relationships refrain from exerting the status-based legitimacy to perform face-threatening acts.

Proposition 2: The effect of status difference on facework will be moderated by the intent to develop or maintain a close relationship.

Second, research on politeness suggests that persons with higher status employ high degrees of facework towards persons with lower status when they want to present themselves as kind and pleasant persons. Lakoff (1973) argues that high degrees of facework used by subordinates towards superiors simply reflect the status difference, but highly face-supportive strategies used by superiors towards subordinates are usually attributed to the pleasant personalities or good will of the superiors. On the contrary, superiors' outright display of their status-based legitimacy is perceived as negative, that is, as the sign of a "mean" and "power-hungry" personality. Thus, superiors who want to be perceived as nice persons make considerable efforts to save the face of their subordinates.

However, when superiors want to emphasize the status difference, they will make little effort to refrain from displaying the status-based legitimacy to ignore the face-wants of their subordinates. In other words, superiors with the intent to show off their power tend to make less effort to save the face of subordinates as the status difference becomes larger. The need to emphasize the status difference is not limited to superiors. Subordinates sometimes also need to show that they are aware of the status difference. Particularly, when subordinates want to express their respect to superiors, or when subordinates want to show their resentment of superiors' maltreatment, they attempt to remind superiors of the difference by employing high degrees of facework.

Proposition 3: Superiors' use of high degrees of facework towards subordinates is marked by their intent to present themselves as nice persons.

Proposition 4: The tendency that persons use more face-saving strategies as the relative status of the other increases is marked by their intent to emphasize the relative status.

Role Right and Facework

Role Right and Legitimacy. Role right here refers to one's claim that the relational contract, either explicitly or implicitly, authorizes one to perform the given social act. Whereas the rights and obligations associated with status difference or relational intimacy are generic to all social acts, the rights and obligations specified by role relationships are particular to the given social act. In other words, the role right is not solely dependent on the nature of the act or the nature of the relationship, but interactively determined by the nature of the act *and* the nature of the relationship (Craig Tracy, & Spisak, 1986).

Thus, status difference or relational intimacy do not necessarily constraint role rights and obligations. Suppose, for example, that a professor asks her teaching assistant and her research assistant to type in to a computer file the data generated from a research project in which both she and her research assistant are involved and the teaching assistant is not. In spite of the similar status differences and relational intimacy, the professor will have less role right over the teaching assistant.

The specification of role rights and obligations are not always clear. While some role rights and obligations are specified on a written contract or conventionally taken for granted, some other role rights and obligations are not defined or discussed at all. Thus, relational partners are not always sure whether performing a certain act is within the domain of their rights. When persons are confident that they have undisputable right to perform the given act, they tend to feel that they have certain legitimacy to ignore the other's face-wants. However, when persons are not sure about their role right due to the lack of role clarification, they cannot claim high legitimacy to perform the face-threatening act.

Proposition 5: Persons have more legitimacy to ignore the threat to the face of the other as it is clearer that the act belongs to their domain of role right.

Moderators of Role-Based Legitimacy. The ways in which role-based legitimacy influences people's facework behavior are very similar to those in which status-based legitimacy affects people's facework behavior. Specifically, when persons lack role-based legitimacy to threaten the face of the other, they will make more attempts to mitigate the face-threat as the legitimacy becomes less clear. However, persons would not ignore the other's face-want simply because they have the role right unless they want to emphasize only the "role" relationship. When persons emphasize the rights and obligations based on the role relationship, they tend to be impersonal. Thus, persons who want to be considered friendly or considerate will attempt to show their concern for the other's face, even though they have a very high role right to ignore the threat to the other's face.

Proposition 6: The effect of role rights on facework will be moderated by the intent to maintain a friendly relationship.

On the contrary, when persons want to expand their role rights, that is, when persons intend to make it clear that it is their role rights to perform a given face threatening act or not to perform an expected face-giving act, they become less face-supportive. Relational partners continuously renegotiate their role rights and obligations, and most renegotiation processes are initiated by one party's intention to expand his/her role right. This intention is usually signaled through one's use of facework strategies that are normally expected to be used by those who already have the role right (Scotton, 1983). Thus, persons use less facework than normal expectations.

Proposition 7: The tendency that persons use less face-saving strategies due to higher role rights will be marked by their intent to emphasize their role relationship.

Relational Intimacy and Facework

Relational Intimacy and Legitimacy. As a relationship gets closer, relational partners attain better understandings of each other's real self. Thus, their public images, that is, face-wants, become less consequential. Relational partners, in other words, give to each other a greater amount of exemption from facework as the relationship becomes more interpersonal. Specifically, persons put up with more criticisms of personality or integrity (fellowship-face), more criticisms of performance, abilities, and possessions (competence-face), and more impositions or interference (autonomy-face) as they get to know each other better.

However, this tolerance for face-threat has its limit. Even in extremely intimate relationships, partners draw lines that the other is not supposed to cross. In other words, any interper-

sonal relationship distinguishes between the domain of tolerance and/or cooperation and the domain of sacredness (Lim &
Bowers, 1991). When a face-threatening act falls within the domain of tolerance, the hearers tend to tolerate more or less dependent upon the nature of the relationship. However, when
the face-threat is so high that it falls outside the domain of tolerance, hearers react negatively regardless of the nature of the
relationship. In this case, persons tend to become more sensitive to the other's face-wants as relational intimacy increases,
since persons do not wish to be disliked by closer relational
partners. Thus, when the face-threat is outside the domain of
tolerance, persons have lower legitimacy as relational intimacy
increases, whereas when the face-threat is within the domain
of tolerance, persons have higher legitimacy as relational intimacy increases.

The domain of tolerance is established by two different
rules: sociocultural and idiosyncratic rules (Miller & Steinberg,
1975). Sociocultural rules regulate what kinds of face-
threatening or face-giving acts are conventionally practiced in
the relationships with the same or similar natures. The rules,
therefore, determine the normality of a given act in a given relationship. Idiosyncratic rules stipulate what kinds of face-
threatening acts are uniquely acceptable or unacceptable in
the given relationship. These unique conventions are established through the repeated practice of certain face-threatening
acts with or without explicit agreements between the relational
partners. Thus, idiosyncratic conventions are more legitimate
as they have been more practiced, that is, as they are more familiar to the relational partners. In short, as a face-threatening
act is more normal due to social conventions and more familiar
due to repeated practice, it is more likely to be within the domain of tolerance. Thus, when the normality and/or familiarity
of an act are high, relational partners have more legitimacy to
threaten the other's face-want, as the relationship is closer;
when the normality and familiarity of an act are both low,
relational partners have less legitimacy as the relationship
is closer.

Proposition 8a: When performing normal and familiar
acts, persons have more legitimacy to
ignore the threat to the face of the
other as relational intimacy increases.

Proposition 8b: When performing abnormal and unfamiliar acts, persons have less legitimacy to ignore the threat to the face of the other as relational intimacy increases.

Moderators of Intimacy-Based Legitimacy. The manifestation of one's intimacy-based legitimacy is affected by one's intentions to change the relationship either temporarily or permanently. The exaggeration of intimacy-based legitimacy, that is, displaying more legitimacy than what is normally allowed in the given level of relational intimacy, is prompted by one's intention to make the relationship closer. In contrast, the suppression of intimacy-based legitimacy, that is, not displaying as much legitimacy as is normally expected in the given level of intimacy, is prompted by one's intention to create more distance in the relationship or to emphasize the existing relational distance.

The intent to make a relationship closer, or the approaching move, is characterized by less than expected facework for normal and familiar acts and more than expected facework for abnormal and unfamiliar acts. Approaching moves can be either short-term or long-term. Short-term or temporary approaching moves are often motivated by such action goals as compliance-gaining or mental support. For example, the "liking" which is proposed by Marwell and Schmitt (1967) as one of compliance-gaining strategies is characterized by decreasing the relational distance temporarily. Long-term approaching moves are intended to increase relational intimacy permanently. These moves, therefore, are frequently observed in developing relationships.

Proposition 9: The tendency that persons use the facework strategies that are normally used in more intimate relationships is marked by their intention to increase the relational intimacy.

The intent to increase relational distance or the distancing move is characterized by higher degrees of facework for normal and familiar acts and lower degrees of facework for abnormal and unfamiliar acts than what are expected in the given level of relational intimacy. The distancing move is motivated by a variety of intentions including power display, role emphasis, display of negative emotion, and regressing the relationship. First, when persons want to emphasize, remind the other of, or amplify the status difference, or when they want to emphasize or increase their role rights, they tend to downplay the relational intimacy. As mentioned earlier, status difference and role rights tend to be moderated by relational intimacy, since persons in closer relationships want to be considered more caring and less impersonal. Thus, persons who intend to emphasize their status and role rights need to lower the relatively high relational intimacy or emphasize the existing low degree of intimacy.

Second, when persons intend to lower the relational intimacy temporarily or permanently, they suppress the use of the legitimacy that is based on the current relational intimacy. The intent to lower intimacy temporarily is often produced by the want to express one's anger toward the other (if not by the intent to show status difference or role rights). When persons want to show that they are irritated by the other, they need to show that their psychological distance from the other has been increased. Thus, they forsake the privilege that stems from the relational intimacy. The intent to lower intimacy permanently is often generated by the plan to regress the relationship. Thus, relational partners who are in intimate, but now deteriorating relationships tend to avoid using their intimacy-based legitimacy.

Proposition 10: The tendency that persons use the facework strategies that are normally used in more distant relationships is marked by their intention to decrease the relational intimacy.

Conclusion

In this chapter, I have attempted to delineate the processes in which persons in interpersonal interactions select facework strategies. Although the picture of the interpersonal facework theory presented here is sketchy, the challenge this chapter offers to the traditional studies of interpersonal facework is substantial.

First, facework studies including those on politeness have grossly underspecified the key concepts, face and facework. No studies have offered any tangible definition of face beyond Goffman's (1967) highly abstract conception of the terms. In addition, although the claim that both face and facework are multidimentional constructs has been repeatedly made (Brown & Levinson, 1978; Craig et al., 1986; Lim, 1988, 1990). few systematic efforts have been made to find the exact dimensions of face and facework. This chapter has attempted to offer a tentative answer to the problem of underspecification that hinders a more objective and scientific approach to facework. The conceptualizations of face and facework, including their dimensions and interrelationships, which are presented in this chapter are by no means conclusive. To make the conceptualizations more specific, systematic, and accurate is the first challenge that we all have to meet.

Second, the traditional approach to facework has understood facework as an instance of social appropriateness. In other words, the function of facework in this perspective has been to meet appropriately one's obligation to save the other's face. Thus, the study of facework strategy selection has focused on the processes in which persons select the facework strategies that properly mitigate the threat to the other's face. In this chapter, I have attempted to redefine the function of facework. Facework is not a social requirement that must be always satisfied, but a means of manipulating a given relationship and/or situation. Facework, therefore, should be understood as a reflection of one's relational intentions and action goals.

This perspective differs from the traditional one in two respects. First, it assumes that no relationships are stable or constant enough to dictate the natures of appropriate facework. The selected facework strategy changes the relationship as much as the relationship influences the selection of the facework strategy. Second, since facework is not the product of external or contextual factors, but the product of internal purposes, its value should be measured in terms of effectiveness not appropriateness.

The discussion in this chapter of the processes in which internal purposes or intentions affect facework behavior is incomplete. However, it will serve its purpose when more facework researchers turn their attention to the study of the effectiveness of facework. To develop a more comprehensive account of the processes in which persons manifest their intentions or accomplish their goals through facework is the second challenge that we all have to meet.

References

Brown, R., and Gilman, A. (1960). The pronouns of power and solidarity. In T. A. Sebeok (Ed.), *Style in language.* Cambridge: MIT Press.

Brown, P., and Levinson, S. (1978). Universals in language usage: Politeness phenomena. In E. Goody (Ed.), *Questions and Politeness: Strategies in social interaction.* Cambridge: Cambridge University Press.

————. (1987). *Politeness: Some universals in language use.* Cambridge: Cambridge University Press.

Craig, R. T., Tracy, C., and Spisak, F. (1986). The discourse of requests: Assessment of a politeness approach. *Human Communication Research, 12,* 437–468.

Goffman, E. (1967). *Interaction ritual: Essays on face-to-face behavior.* Garden City, NY: Doubleday.

Lakoff, R. T. (1973). The logic of politeness; or minding your p's and q's. In C. Colum et al. (Eds.), *Papers from the Ninth Regional Meeting of the Chicago Linguistic Society.* Chicago: Chicago Linguistic Society.

Leech, G. N. (1983). *Principles of pragmatics.* London: Longman.

Lim, T. S. (1988). A new model of politeness in discourse. Paper presented at the annual convention of the Speech Communication Association, New Orleans, LA.

————. (1989). Positive and negative politeness in performing face-threatening acts. Paper presented at the annual meeting of the International Communication Association, San Francisco, California.

————. (1990). Politeness behavior in social influence situations. In J. P. Dillard (Ed.), *Seeking compliance: The production of interpersonal influence messages.* Scottsdale, AZ: Gorsuch Scarisbrick Publishers.

Lim, T. S., and Bowers, J. W. (1991). Facework: Solidarity, approbation, and tact. *Human Communication Research, 17,* 415–450.

Marwell, G., and Schmitt, D. R. (1967). Dimensions of compliance-gaining behavior: An empirical analysis. *Sociometry, 30,* 350–364.

Miller, G. R., and Steinberg, M. (1975). *Between people: A new analysis of interpersonal communication.* Chicago: Science Research Associates.

Scollon, R., and Scollon, S. W. (1983). Face in interethnic communication. In J. C. Richards and R. W. Schmidt (Eds.), *Language and communication.* London: Longman.

Scotton, C. M. (1983). The negotiation of identities in conversation: A theory of markedness and code choice. *International Journal of Sociology of Language, 44,* 115–136.

-8-
Embarrassment and Blushing: Factors Influencing Face-Saving Strategies

ROBERT J. EDELMANN

"Whatever else, embarrassment has to do with the figure the individual cuts before others felt to be there at the time. The crucial concern is the impression one makes on others in the present—whatever the long range or unconscious basis of this concern may be" (Goffman, 1956, p. 265). When a person perceives that he/she has projected an undesired impression to others present, a state of uncomfortable arousal called embarrassment ensues. Embarrassment typically causes discomfort for the person concerned and can have a severely disruptive effect upon social interaction. As Goffman, (1967) again remarks, "face-to-face interaction in any culture seems to require just those capacities that flustering seems guaranteed to destroy" (p. 101). Although there are occasions when people intentionally embarrass themselves (Miller, 1986) or others (Sharkey, 1991; Sharkey & Waldron, 1990), because of its aversive and disruptive nature people generally attempt to avoid embarrassing situations when possible. We are rarely able to completely avoid such situations. Hence, following an embarrassing event, attempts are often made to redress the situation in an attempt to maintain face, regain social approval, and restore the interaction. Embarrassment is thus essentially a state in which a person has failed to maintain an appropriate identity and has, in short, lost face. It is thus a central "face" construct within social interaction.

Goffman (1967) has used the term facework to describe "the actions taken by a person to make whatever he [or she] is doing consistent with face" (p. 12) or to take the necessary re-

231

medial action to restore a desired identity. Facework in such circumstances has been variously labelled "remedial tactics" (Schlenker, 1980), "remedial strategies" (Cupach & Metts, 1990), "excuses" (Snyder, 1985), "impression management strategies" (Tedeschi & Riess, 1981), "motive talk" (Semin & Manstead, 1983) and "coping strategies" (Edelmann, 1990a, 1990b). For present purposes face-saving will be taken to refer to all those coping actions both verbal and nonverbal taken by both the actor and observer to overcome feelings of embarrassment in an attempt to regain social composure and the smooth flow of interaction. The experience of embarrassment thus clearly illustrates both the dramatic effect of a loss of face and the subsequent attempts made by the person concerned to restore their identity or save face. Because it is a common, if unpleasant, everyday experience, it is a particularly useful vehicle for studying clusters of "face" issues.

Because most models of embarrassment assume that embarrassment is generated by some clearly defined event (i.e., a faux pas, gaffe, or impropriety), remedial actions taken to restore face are usually assumed to be verbal apologies or accounts which focus upon the event. It is clear, however, that some people experience embarrassment even in the absence of a clearly defined antecedent event (Edelmann, 1987a, 1990a, 1990b, 1990c, 1990d, 1991; Timms, 1980). First, it is possible to elicit embarrassment by informing the person that he or she looks embarrassed even if this is not the case and/or the situation is not defined as embarrassing. Second, it is possible to become embarrassed as a result of blushing, even in a situation that is not deemed by others present or by the embarrassed person to be intrinsically embarrassing. There are individuals for whom it appears that internal and expressive cues, notably blushing, are sufficient to provoke extreme embarrassment. Any conceptualization of embarrassment must therefore be able to explain the multiplicity of the phenomenon. In order to place the current account into perspective the present chapter will briefly overview recent conceptualizations of the process underlying embarrassment emphasizing both internal and external eliciting circumstances. The relationship between type of embarrassing event and the use and success of verbal or nonverbal face-saving strategies in addition to mediating factors such as gender and culture will then be examined.

Conceptualizing Embarrassment

There have been numerous attempts to conceptualize the process underlying embarrassment largely derived from Goffman's writing (e.g., Edelmann, 1985a, 1987a, 1990a, 1990b; Modigliani, 1968, 1971; Semin & Manstead, 1982; Silver, Sabini, & Parrott, 1987). Although differing in focus, the basic framework for such conceptualizations is to view embarrassment as first, occurring in only real or imagined social situations; second, to be the result of an undesired and unintentional social predicament that has occurred or that the person fears may occur; third, the person anticipates or perceives a discrepancy between his or her current self-presentation and his or her standard for self-presentation. This basic framework has recently been extended to incorporate both internal or expressive cues in addition to external cues. This model has been described in detail elsewhere (Edelmann, 1987a, 1990a, 1990b) and will only be reiterated briefly here.

Embarrassment is characterized by a well-defined behavioral display. Eye contact is reduced, body movement and speech disturbances increase (Edelmann & Hampson, 1979, 1981), and blushing may occur. Although it is possible to feel embarrassed without visibly blushing and to visibly blush without experiencing embarrassment, blushing and embarrassment have been inextricably linked by a number of authors. Buss (1980), for example, describes blushing as the hallmark of embarrassment. Indeed, it seems that in certain circumstance blushing clearly precedes the experience of embarrassment, the latter emotion being experienced in the absence of any clearly defined external antecedent event. There seem to be individual differences in the propensity to blush (Leary & Meadows, 1991) with chronic blushers being overconcerned with internal cues and thoughts and observers' subsequent reactions to their blushing to such an extent that the very fact of blushing is sufficient to provoke extreme embarrassment (Edelmann, 1990c, 1990d, 1991). Embarrassment can thus be elicited by either external cues (a faux pas, impropriety, social transgression) or internal cues (bodily, facial cues, and associated cognitions.)

The notion that feedback from one's facial and expressive behaviors gives rise to the experience of the emotion has a long and checkered history, and a wealth of contradictory evidence exists. There are those who support, or who claim that the evidence supports, some version of the feedback hypothesis and those who feel that there is a lack of evidence to support such a notion (see reviews by Buck, 1980; Laird, 1984). While there may be little evidence to support the more extreme view that facial expression is the emotion, it seems quite reasonable to assume that expressive behavior adds to or accentuates emotional experience. Tomkins (1981), for example, comments that "I have come to regard the skin in general and the skin of the face in particular as of the greatest importance in producing the feeling of affect" (p. 386).

Although such a supposition remains to be empirically verified, skin blood-flow changes associated with blushing could therefore influence the intensity of reported embarrassment. The perception and interpretation of such cues is also likely to play an important part in influencing the extent of experienced embarrassment. The emotional state will result from the perception of some internal state discrepant from one's baseline state, the focusing of attention towards this state and the use of existing knowledge structure to interpret it.

The amount of attention we are able to allocate to internal or external cues is often assumed to be limited (Duval & Wicklund, 1972; Scheier, Carver, & Matthews, 1983). Thus if one source of information is particularly salient, our attention will be directed towards this at the expense of decreasing attention to other less salient stimuli. Therefore, if attention to the self increases, attention towards external cues will decrease.

One assumption is that our attention is shifting between ourselves and environmental cues on a continual, but nonrandom basis (Hull & Levy, 1979; Scheier, Carver, & Matthews, 1983). Following a faux pas or social accident, attention may initially be directed towards an appraisal of the event itself. Subsequent inward focus of attention may be directed towards those factors assumed by prior experience to be associated with embarrassment (blushing, gaze aversion, trembling, stammering). When attention is again directed towards the environment, the person may specifically be directed towards the reactions and views of others. Such subjective and environmental appraisal may partly alternate and partly operate in parallel. Repetition of the process with focus directed towards negative aspects of oneself and others' reactions may lead to an escalation of experienced embarrassment. Some people may by nature be more inclined to focus upon their own bodily cues so that minor facial reddening is interpreted as blushing with the fear that this will be interpreted by others as embarrassment.

Subsequent appraisal of the situation by the embarrassed person will be directed towards attempts to deal with or cope with his or her predicament. These attempts to excuse, explain away, minimize, or correct the behavior (either externally or internally elicited) form the face-saving component of the experience of embarrassment. The use of a particular strategy may be influenced by a number of factors including the nature of the eliciting circumstances, the degree of felt embarrassment, and the observer's reaction. Although there is an extensive literature on strategies for remediating damaged encounters in general (see below), it is only recently that researchers from both psychology and the communication field have begun to systematically investigate remedial strategies used in embarrassing encounters in particular. A number of differing methodologies have been used in this search for a greater understanding. Some have asked subjects to recall personally embarrassing situations and the strategies used to deal with them; others have used experimenter generated situations and remedial strategies for subjects to evaluate; while still others have evaluated such strategies in relation to experimentally manipulated events.

In addition to varying methodologies, different studies have used different systems for categorizing both embarrassing events and the face-saving tactics used to deal with them. These categorization systems do, however, have a flavor of evolving from a common underlying theoretical theme so that although they may differ in content, the difference is one of degree rather than of fundamental substance. Indeed, in spite of the differing methodologies and categorization systems used, a general picture is beginning to emerge of the relationship between the causes of embarrassment and the resultant face-saving strategies. In order to evaluate this fully, a brief summary of schemes for classifying both embarrassing and remedial strategies will be presented followed by an evaluation of the relationship between event and strategy use in addition to other factors influencing the use of a particular strategy. The relationship between internal and external eliciting circumstances and remedial strategies will also be discussed.

Categories of Predicament

There have been a number of attempts to categorize embarrassing predicaments on the basis of the actions or situations
involved (see Edelmann, 1987a; Miller, 1986). In one of the first
of such attempts, Gross and Stone (1964) collected over a thousand instances of embarrassing events which they classified
into three broad categories: inappropriate identity (an inability
to perform one's role), loss of poise, and disturbance of assumptions persons make about one another in social transactions. The latter two categories have been referred to by Argyle
(1969) as "failure of social skill" (i.e., failure of social graces or
failure of skilled social performance) and "failure of meshing"
(i.e., disagreement over the definition of the situation or failure
to agree on the roles played by those present).

In a further study investigating recollections of embarrassing events, Sattler (1965) collected over three thousand descriptions from over three hundred subjects. Three of the
categories derived were subsequently incorporated by Buss
(1980) into his five categories of embarrassing events. These
involve inpropriety (e.g., improper dress), lack of competence
(e.g., failure of social skill), conspicuousness (e.g., being sin-
gled out for attention by others), breaches of privacy (e.g.,
touching or coming too close to another), and overpraise (e.g.,
discomfort occasioned by excessive compliments). Sharkey and
Stafford (1990) have also adapted Sattler's classification
scheme into the following five broad categories: violation of privacy (e.g., bodily exposure, invasion of personal space), forgetfulness or lack of knowledge/skill (e.g., forgetting someone's
name), positive or negative criticism (e.g., praise or teasing),
awkward acts (e.g., verbal blunders or clumsiness), and image
appropriateness (e.g., concern about clothing and possession).
In an analysis of 387 responses, awkward acts was the most
frequently reported embarrassing situation (reported by
33.1%) followed by violations of privacy (22%), forgetfulness
(22%), criticism (12.1%), and image appropriateness (6.2%).
As discussed elsewhere (Edelmann, 1987a), while such classification systems are useful, there is often no clear rationale for
deciding on categories. One such rationale would involve taking into account both the nature of the rule-breaking episode
and the actor's and/or observer's interpretation of this event.

Sattler (1965), for example, found that embarrassing
events could be organized into three groups in which the embarrassed person is either (1) the agent in, (2) the recipient of,
or (3) an observer of an embarrassing act. A further such at-

tempt is offered by Weinberg (1968) who proposed two orthogonal dimensions: the intended or unintended nature of the act and the correct or incorrect definition of the situation. This has been adapted by Metts and Cupach (1989) to identify four categories of embarrassing event: faux pas (intentional behavior subsequently found to be inappropriate); mistake (intentional acts which would be appropriate to the situation but are not because they are incorrectly or inappropriately executed); accidents (unintentional acts which are also inappropriate); and recipient acts (those in which embarrassment is caused by the behavior of others). As Sharkey and Stafford (1990) point out, however, this classification system also has its drawbacks as three categories refer to acts while one relates specifically to the agent of that act. Interpreting or measuring the concept of intentionality is also not without its difficulties; how, for example, does an observer of the embarrassed person know whether the act was or was not intentional?

In a further study, Miller (in press) has incorporated both dimensions of embarrassing circumstances involving individual, interactive, audience and bystander behavior, and eight specific categories of social predicaments. These were derived from descriptions of recent embarrassments obtained from 350 high school and college student respondents. The categories and their frequency of mention were as follows: Within the individual behavior dimension there were three categories: (1) normative public deficiences (inept performance, loss of control, etc.) (mentioned by 57% of respondents), (2) abashed harm-doing (embarrassed by harming others) (mentioned by 2%), and (3) conspicuousness (suffering the attention of others when not deficient) (mentioned by 7%). Categories within the interactive behavior domain include both (1) awkward interactions (mentioned by 8%), and (2) "team" embarrassment (mentioned by 7%). Categories within the audience provocation dimension involve both (1) real trangressions (others publicizing one's past predicaments) (mentioned by 5%), and (2) no real transgressions (teasing by others) (mentioned by 13%). Finally, the dimension of bystander behavior involving empathic embarrassment was mentioned by 2%.

Cupach and Metts (1990) have also recently extended and revised their typology to include actor-responsible and observer-responsible categories, each of which is subdivided into broad categories of social predicament. Within the former, subcategories involve behavior that is incongruent or inappropriate to one of three levels of competence: the idealized social actor (e.g., failure of physical or emotional control), the accomplished role performer (e.g., skill failure), and the idealized self-image (e.g., creating a false image). Incidents in which the observer is responsible can be direct (e.g., drawing attention to someone or making someone look clumsy) or indirect (e.g., through association or empathy).

Certainly, these two recent schemes from Miller (1987) and Cupach and Metts (1990) seem to provide the way forward for future research. Both have developed a dimensional approach rather than merely attempting to classify incidents into types of behavior. Both incorporate what can be viewed as "higher level" categories (individual, interactive, audience, and bystander from Miller; and actor-responsible and observer-responsible from Cupach and Metts), and "lower level" categories (Miller's eight specific categories of social predicament and Cupach and Metts' broad classes of social predicament). Both have also been used by the authors concerned to effectively quantify embarrassing episodes and to relate them to such factors as reported intensity of embarrassment and coping strategies employed. As Cupach and Metts (1990) note about their own scheme: "the taxonomy . . . is an initial step toward formalizing a comprehensive and reliable method for classifying types of embarrassing predicaments. We think it merits elaboration and refinement through additional research" (p. 348).

Indeed, the Cupach and Metts' (1990) and Miller's (1987) classifications overlap sufficiently for a common scheme to be derived from them. The following is a suggested combined scheme with four main categories: (1) Individual behavior, actor responsible: this includes (a) normative public deficiencies from Miller's scheme and encompasses indealized social actor and accomplished role performer from Cupach and Metts' scheme, (b) abashed harm-doing from Miller's scheme, and (c) idealized self-image from Cupach and Metts' scheme. (2) Interactive behavior, shared responsibility: this includes (a) awkward interactions and (b) team embarrassment from Miller's scheme. (3) Audience provocation, observer responsible: this includes (a) conspicuousness from Miller's individual behavior category, in addition to (b) real transgression, audience provocation, and (c) no real transgression, audience provocation, also from Miller's scheme. The real transgression, audience-provocation category encompasses the observer responsible by direct action from Cupach and Metts' scheme, referring to the intentional embarrassment discussed by Sharkey (1991) and

Sharkey and Waldron (1990). (4) Audience behavior, observer responsible: this includes the bystander behavior from Miller's scheme which encompasses the observer responsible by indirect action from Cupach and Metts' scheme. Certainly, great strides have been made within the last few years and further research should enable the development of a reliable classification scheme which would enable greater comparability across studies.

Face-Saving Strategies

A number of authors have attempted to delineate the strategies a person can use to mitigate an undesired or unwanted identity following an undesirable behavior (Austin, 1970; Schlenker, 1980, 1982; Semin & Manstead, 1983; Schonbach, 1980; Scott & Lyman, 1968; Tedeschi & Riess, 1981; Tedeschi, Riordin, Gaes, & Kane, 1983). Two broad categories are generally recognized: apologies and accounts, the latter of which is additionally subdivided into excuses and justifications. With regard to specifically dealing with embarrassing events a number of further categories have also been discussed involving avoidance and escape (evasive facework), the use of humor (e.g., Cupach & Metts, 1990; Edelmann, 1985c; Fink & Walker, 1977; Sharkey & Stafford, 1990), describing the incident, reacting with aggression or offering or requesting help (remediation) (Cupach & Metts, 1990; Sharkey & Stafford, 1990). As noted below, providing a description of the incident can generally be encompassed within the account category, while remediation can be included as a subcategory of apology. It is also useful to think of escape and avoidance as related categories. There thus seem to be five main categories involving apologies (including remediation), accounts (including excuses and justifications), avoidance (including escape), humor (including laughter), and aggression.

Apologies

Apologies are statements which accept responsibility for an untoward or inappropriate act and acknowledge blameworthiness (Goffman, 1967). As Schlenker and Darby (1981) note an apology can range from a simple "pardon me" or "I'm sorry" to a rather more elaborate expression of remorse, sorrow, or embarrassment, offers of help (i.e., remediation), self-castigation, or direct attempts to obtain forgiveness. At its simplest an apology can be used in a ritualistic way to allow minor indiscretions to be passed over quickly and forgotten by the interactants.

Indeed, the very act of being embarrassed can itself serve as an apology, providing a visual sign that the person acknowledges responsibility for the untoward act. This notion has been developed by Castelfranchi and Poggi (1990) with specific regard to blushing, which they suggest serves an appeasement function acting as an involuntary apology to observers of one's embarrassment. An interpretation of embarrassment as an apology most likely occurs in situations in which the person's undesired behavior may have caused discomfort to someone else who was present. Brazening out the situation may serve to increase both actor and observer discomfort, while a display of embarrassment accompanied by laughter may diffuse the situation. This is illustrated in an experimental study in which a subject was required to inform a confederate of the experimenter that he had performed badly on a task (Edelmann, 1982). The confederate responded with either a defiant stare or a look of embarrassment accompanied or unaccompanied by laughter. Ratings of liking for the confederate and degree of comfort felt by the subject were higher when the confederate looked embarrassed than when he stared, with laughter further increasing ratings of both comfort and liking.

Accounts

"An account is a linguistic device employed whenever an action is subjected to evaluate enquiry. . . . By an account we mean a statement made by a social actor to explain unanticipated or untoward behavior (Scott & Lyman, 1968, p. 46). Accounts are generally of two types: excuses and justifications. An excuse is an attempt to play down the importance of, and minimize one's responsibility for, the embarrassing event, while at the same time admitting that the behavior was wrong, bad or inappropriate. A justification, while admitting that the embarrassing event has occurred and that the actor was at least partly responsible for it, at the same time denies that it has negative consequences attached to it.

In their analysis of excuses, Scott and Lyman (1968) distinguish four main categories. The first involves an appeal to accidents which highlights external environmental factors. The second involves an appeal to defeasability which highlights one's lack of intent in performing the untoward behavior. The third involves an appeal to biological drives which highlights one's own personal characteristics. The fourth involves scape-goating which locates the cause of failure in the actions of someone else. Schonbach (1980), Schlenker, (1980), Tedeschi and Riess (1981), and Semin and Manstead (1983) all offer modifications of Scott and Lyman's classification scheme (see Edelmann, 1987a). Schonbach's (1980) modification lies more in the expansion of categories rather than in any marked alter-ation of specific categories themselves. Schlenker (1980) dis-tinguishes between unforeseen consequences and extenuat-ing circumstances (the former showing close correspondence with Scott and Lyman's first two categories the latter with their third and fourth categories). Tedeschi and Reiss (1981) identify three main categories of excuse: denial of intention, lack of volition, and denial of agency, to which Semin and Manstead (1983) add a fourth category, appeal to mitigating circumstances.

In their analysis of justifications, Scott and Lyman distin-guish six main categories; in each case the act is acknowledged but justified. First, in denial of injury the act is justified on the grounds that no harm was done. Secondly, in denial of victim the action is seen as permissable because the victim deserved to be a victim. Third, in condemnation of condemners, the act is justified on the grounds that others would get away with this and worse. Fourth, in appeal to loyalties the act is justified be-cause it served someone else to whom the actor is committed. Fifth, in sad tales the actor uses an unfortunate past experi-ence to explain his/her present state. Finally, in self-fulfillment the actor justifies the action on the grounds that it leads to some form of enlightenment. Schonbach (1980), Schlenker, (1980), Tedeschi and Riess (1981), and Semin and Manstead (1983) all offer modifications of Scott and Lyman's classification scheme (see Edelmann, 1987a). Schonbach's (1980) modifica-tion contains only two categories which cannot be subsumed by Scott and Lyman's scheme: minimizing damage and appeal to positive intentions. Of Schlenker's (1980) three categories, direct minimization and justification through higher goals cannot be easily subsumed by Scott and Lyman's typology, al-though their third category, justification through comparison, is comparable to Scott and Lyman's category of condemnation of the condemner. Tedechi and Reiss's (1981) typology with ten major categories of justification and which is presented in slightly revised form by Semin and Manstead (1983) is effec-tively a combination of those referred to above.

Avoidance

Avoidance refers both to withdrawal subsequent to an embarrassing event (i.e., escape) as well as attempts to avoid encounters in which embarrassment might occur (i.e., avoidance).
With regard to the former, although a verbal apology or an account may be used frequently, they may fail to redress the situation or may be perceived by the embarrassed person as
inappropriate. In these instances the embarrassed person may
use evasive rather than preventive facework. However, physically retreating from an encounter may actually draw further
undue attention to the embarrassed person rather than achieving the desired goal of averting attention. There may, however,
be instances when averting an awkward event can be achieved
by changing the topic or by remaining silent rather than by
escape per se (McLaughlin, Cody, & Rosenstein, 1983;
McLaughlin, Cody, & O'Hair, 1983).

It is also clear that for some people a chronic fear of embarrassment can lead to anxiety about, or avoidance of social encounters. This is particularly true for chronic blushers who
seem overconcerned with internal cues and thoughts and observers' subsequent reactions to their blushing. Avoidance in
this instance is more an attempt to avoid losing face through
blushing inappropriately (as perceived by the actor) than an attempt to save face. It does seem, however, that fear of blushing
serves to impede the use of verbal face-saving strategies, a
point discussed later.

Humor

A further general category of acts that are used in coping with
predicaments involves the use of humor or laughter and smiling. Clearly a number of facets of the situation will influence
the extent to which such responses will occur. For example, in
one study, Fink and Walker (1977) found that there was more
laughter between people of equal status than between people of
unequal status in response to an embarrassing interaction.
There are many occasions, however, when humor or laughter
can be used to diffuse an otherwise difficult situation as a
number of reports in medical settings illustrate. Robinson
(1983) writing about health and humor refers to jokes about
bedpans, bodily functions, and sex as a way of coping with or
forestalling embarrassment, while Emerson (1970) discusses
the use of humor as a strategy for neutralizing embarrassment
during a gynaecological examination. While laughter may

serve to reduce tension inherent in a difficult situation joking has the additional advantage of turning a potential loss of social approval into a gain in social approval.

Aggression

Reacting with hostility or anger as a way of coping with predicaments generally seems to be restricted to situations in which another party has caused the embarrassment, particularly if it was caused intentionally (Metts & Cupach, 1989; Sharkey, in press; Sharkey & Stafford, 1990; Sharkey & Waldron, 1990). Thus deliberate criticism, teasing or violation of privacy the intention of which is to embarrass another person may be particularly likely to generate an aggressive response from the victim of such acts. Clearly, the perception of intentionality will be a function of the embarrassor's and embarrassed person's interpretation of events (Sharkey & Waldron, 1990; Stamp & Knapp, 1990). Thus a perception that one has been intentionally embarrassed even if this was not perceived as intentional on the part of the "perpetrator" may result in aggressive behavior from the person who perceives himself or herself to be the "victim."

Embarrassment and the Use of Remedial Strategies

The earliest studies rather than examining the links between embarrassment and remedial strategies emphasised the lengths to which the actor might go to avoid embarrassing situations. Brown (1970), for example, found that subjects were prepared to sacrifice tangible rewards in order to avoid looking foolish (i.e., performing a potentially embarrassing act). This was particularly true if the audience was high status and if there was a likelihood that the subject would have to meet them afterwards (Brown & Garland, 1971; Garland & Brown, 1972). In a more recent report Froming, Corley, and Rinker (1990) found individual differences in likely withdrawal from both hypothetical and real embarrassing situations in front of audiences composed of friends or strangers. Subjects low in public self-consciousness withdrew sooner from an audience of strangers they would have to interact with than from either an audience of friends or strangers they would never see again. Subjects high in public self-consciousness tended to withdraw quickly no matter who the audience was. In another recent study, Miller (1988) found that actors, particularly those of high embarrassibility, faced with the threat of embarrassment described themselves in modest, self-effacing terms. This "admission of faults" strategy adopted by threatened actors was apparently perceived positively by others. In first creating a lowered image consistent with the image resulting from embarrassment and secondly exceeding this lowered image in subsequent actions, actors are serving to protect themselves from failure. In a similar vein, subjects may use impediments as excuses for possible failure (cf. self-handicapping strategies, Jones & Berglass, 1978). Clearly individual difference variables are likely to play a part in determining face-saving strategies following embarrassment.

The first attempts to investigate face-saving subsequent to an embarrassing event were presented in studies by Aspler (1975) and Modigliani (1971). Modigliani constructed a "facework" index which contained any statements made by the embarrassed person which were intended to improve his image in the eyes of a confederate. Items excusing their performance or offering redeeming or self-enhancing information that might compensate for their failure were included in the index. Modigliani did not look specifically at the different techniques used but found that the more embarrassed subjects were the higher the "facework" index and hence the more techniques they used. In a more recent report, however, Sharkey and Stafford (1990) report no association between either the type of embarrassing situation or the degree of embarrassment reported and the number of face-saving responses.

Aspler (1975) found that subjects who had just performed a potentially embarrassing task complied more with a subsequent request for help than nonembarrassed subjects. It seems plausible to assume that the negative effects associated with embarrassment can be relieved by the action of compliance with requests for help. As Aspler comments: "compliance produces positive feelings that counteract the negative affect created by the embarrassing incident. . . . Embarrassed subjects' compliance could be interpreted as an attempt to improve the image they presented to an observer of their embarrassing incident" (p. 151).

It is only within the past few years that researchers have begun to systematically investigate the relationship between various parameters associated with embarrassing incidents, such as type and severity of incident, gender and status of those involved, and use of specific remedial strategies. It seems reasonable to assume that different remedial strategies will be more or less effective depending upon the nature of the incident. Scott and Lyman (1968), for example, suggest three criteria which are implicated in making an explanation successful. First, it must be acceptable (i.e., it must fit the prevailing ideas and beliefs of a particular society or sub-group); second, it must be reasonable (i.e., it must fit the facts that are known about the event by the audience); and third, it must be adequate (i.e., it must be appropriate to the offensiveness of the situation). For example, humor and/or laughter may be used to minimize the importance of the least threatening or damaging events; for somewhat more serious events an apology may be appropriate, while for even more serious events an excuse or justification may be more appropriate, perhaps added to an apology (Edelmann, 1987a).

Studies have also evaluated the part played by the observer of the embarrassing predicament. As Cupach and Metts (1990) note, "Structurally, the roles of social interactants are inter-dependent. When an individual becomes embarrassed, other persons who witness the embarrassment are often drawn into the predicament" (p. 326). Thus, various strategies can be used by both the actor and the observer as face-saving strate-gies which can be particularly effective if the audience clearly "plays along" with the actor.

Coping with One's Own Embarrassment
Although verbal strategies are commonly used by the actor to remedy the situation following an embarrassing event and have been the most frequent topic for research, nonverbal strategies in the form of laughter and smiling are also used. Laughter can be a purposeful strategy used to change the meaning and focus of the situation. "By diminishing the im-portance of the event the identity 'victim' can be transformed to 'co-actor' and the label 'embarrassing' transformed to 'hu-morous' " (Edelmann, 1987a, p. 86). Frequently, however, laughter is used in conjunction with joking. In one study jok-ing and laughter were used as methods of coping with embar-rassment on 5 percent of occasions by socially anxious subjects and 8.5 percent of occasions by nonsocially anxious

subjects (Edelmann, 1985b). Verbal strategies other than joking have tended to form the focus for research.

Embarrassing Event and Gender Differences. In two studies,
Cupach, Metts, and Hazleton (1986) examined the use of remedial strategies dependent upon the type of embarrassing event
and the gender of the observer. Subjects were presented with
two scenarios, one representing loss of poise (someone spilling
gravy on themselves at a formal dinner party) and one representing an inappropriate identity display (not having enough
money to pay for groceries). In the first study, subjects were
presented with four researcher-generated strategies representing excuse, avoidance, apology, and justification, which they
rated for perceived efficacy and appropriateness. In the second
study, subjects were asked to generate their own remedial
strategies in response to the scenarios used in study one. In
addition to the remedial categories of excuse, apology, and justification, further categories involving humor, escape, remediation (behavioral action taken to remedy the situation) and
description were added. In the first study apologizing was
rated as significantly more appropriate as a response to embarrassment, as more likely to reduce embarrassment, and as
most satisfying to others in comparison to excuses, justifications, and avoidance. In the second study, excuses and justification were used infrequently (approximately 2% of responses),
while, in contrast, apologies (approximately 18%) and remediation (approximately 31%) were highly preferred strategies. Results from the first study indicated that females viewed excuses
as more appropriate and apologies as more satisfying to others
than did males, although in the second study there was little
difference between males and females in their descriptions of
what they would do following an embarrassing event.

Gender differences in face-saving strategies used to reduce
embarrassment have also been reported by Petronio (1984) using a similar methodological approach. She asked respondents
to describe the most embarrassing incident they could remember after which they were presented with a list of face-saving
strategies. Subjects were then asked to rate each strategy to indicate how useful it would be in reducing their embarrassment. Women tended to find more communication strategies
representing excuses helpful, while men tended to find communication strategies representing justifications helpful. As
Cupach, Metts, and Hazleton (1986) note, however, although

there are gender differences, they could be interpreted as re-flecting dimensions other than excuses and justifications. The item which most characterized men ("person laughs at own be-havior") could reflect the use of humor or joking rather than justification of one's actions; while the item which most char-acterized women ("person criticizes own behavior") could re-flect an apology rather than an excuse.

A further interesting gender difference is noted by Sharkey (personal communication) from an re-analysis of data pre-sented in Sharkey (1991). When a person intentionally embar-rassed a person of the opposite gender, there was a tendency for the embarrassed person to respond with hostility; when the two people were of the same gender the use of hostility was less usual.

Embarrassing Event and Degree of Felt Embarrassment. In a further study by Metts and Cupach (1989), subjects were asked to describe an incident in which they were significantly embar-rassed, to rate their degree of felt embarrassment and to de-scribe what they and others present did to try to reduce the respondent's embarrassment. Remedial strategies used by the actor were coded into eight categories. Avoidance (representing 23% of the total strategies coded) was the strategy used most frequently by the embarrassed person, followed by remediation (17%), humor (15%), excuse (13%), apology (11%), escape (11%), justification (6%), and aggression (4%). Use of a partic-ular strategy varied according to the type of situation. Apolo-gies were more likely to be used in escape situations and less likely in situations in which someone else caused the embar-rassment. Justifications were more likely in faux pas situa-tions; humor and remediation were more likely in situations involving accidents while aggression was used exclusively in situations in which someone else caused the embarrassment. In addition, there was a tendency for actors to use multiple strategies; 35 percent of respondents reporting combinations of two, three, or four remedial strategies to deal with an embar-rassing event. Similar use of multiple strategies is reported by Sharkey and Stafford (1990), with 33.5 percent of their respon-dents reporting use of two or more remedial strategies.

The study by Metts and Cupach (1989) has been criticized on a number of grounds by Sharkey and Stafford (1990). They suggest, for example, that the situation by response analysis used was inappropriate for the data as the response rather than the respondent was treated as the unit of analysis and respondents reported multiple responses. They thus conducted a replication and extension. Subjects were asked to report three situations in which they were personally embarrassed (one highly, one moderately, and one slightly embarrassing); how they dealt with each situation, and how others present dealt with the situation. Responses were coded into seven categories derived from Metts and Cupach (1989). The categories were (1) accounts (including excuses, justifications, apologies, and descriptions of the act), (2) remediation, (3) hostility/agression, (4) escaping or avoiding, (5) objective symptoms (such as laughing, smiling, blushing, exclaiming), (6) concealing symptoms (such as suppressing a reaction or pretending nothing had happened), and (7) subjective symptoms (reporting one's reaction—this category was not used in subsequent analysis as it was taken as representing a person's internal feeling rather than an a communicative response). The most common responses to embarrassment were objective symptoms (representing 23% of the total strategies coded) and accounts (representing 24% of the total strategies coded). Frequency of other strategies used by actors were remediation (15%), avoidance (15%), escape (14%), subjective symptoms (6%), and aggression (3%).

As with findings reported by Metts and Cupach (1989), the type of situation was predictive of the reaction of the embarrassed person. With situations involving a violation of privacy, objective symptoms, or remediation predominated; when forgetfulness was the cause, the embarrassed actor tended to respond with an account; when criticism was the cause, objective symptoms, escape, or aggression were the most common responses; finally, in awkward situations or when image appropriateness was problematic, the embarrassed actor reported using accounts or avoidance. Interestingly, if the embarrassed actor was responsible for the embarrassment, then that person was more likely to try to account for the event; if someone else was perceived to be responsible for the embarrassment, the embarrassed actor was more likely to respond with escape or aggression although remediation was also used. While the embarrassing situation was related to the actor's response, there was no relation between degree of embarrassment and response by the embarrassed actor.

In a further report, Sharkey and Waldron (1990) examined remedial action undertaken by subordinates intentionally embarrassed by their supervisors. One hundred of 550 people (18 percent) sampled in the workplace reported that they had been intentionally embarrassed by a superior. Hostility, which included protest and complaint, was the most common response reported by 30 percent of subjects. Twenty-one percent of subordinates attempted to conceal their embarrassment, 20 percent reported using a form of escape, remediation was reported by 11 percent and 9 percent reported using accounts such as excuses, while 6 percent responded with objective symptoms such as crying. In a study of responses to intentional embarrassment with a student population, Sharkey (in press) found that the most common response was objective symptoms followed by aggressiveness.

Gender, Status and Seriousness of the Event. In contrast to the above studies, all of which used self-report methodology, a recent study by Gonzales, Pederson, Manning, and Wetter (1990) used an experimental manipulation to examine the effects of offender sex, offender status, and consequent severity on accounts following an embarrassing incident. Subjects were induced to believe that they had committed a "gaffe" (spilling a cup of water into a confederates bag), with either mild or serious consequences for the confederate/victim (the contents of the bag appeared to contain either expensive items such as a camera or, of less consequence, computer paper). They were also induced to believe that the confederate was either of higher or lower status than they were. Subject's subsequent reactions were recorded on videotape through a one-way screen. Verbal responses were classified according to Schonbach's (1980) typology and included two mitigating elements: concessions (expression of regret or guilt) and excuses: and two aggravating elements—justifications and refusals (denial or evasion of the event). In each case the number of phrases in each account and the account type were recorded. A verbal helping index (rated from 0 to 4) and a behavioral helping index (rated 0 to 3) were also calculated.

With regard to gender differences, women offered longer accounts than men and were more likely to offer mitigating accounts, particularly concessions. Women were also more likely to offer meaningful verbal offers of help as well as being more likely to act on their offers. Women were also much more likely to use explicit "I'm sorry's" and statements of feelings (e.g., "I feel bad" or "I'm so embarrassed"). These findings match to some extent the gender differences suggested by Cupach, Metts, and Hazleton (1986), that is, women "assign more positive value to deferential (mitigating) strategies" (p. 197). With regard to the seriousness of the event and perceived status of the subjects, in the case of events with serious consequences, subjects in both high and low status conditions offered accounts of similar length; however, when the event was less serious, subjects in the high-status condition were less likely to acknowledge responsibility for the event and made less effort to account for their actions in comparison to subjects in the low-status condition.

Effect of Culture. In a series of studies, verbal coping strategies and observer's reactions derived from the theoretical analysis described above were examined in questionnaire data collected from over one thousand subjects in seven countries (Edelmann et al., 1987; Edelmann & Iwawaki, 1987; Edelmann & Neto, 1989). All subjects had lived since childhood in the countries concerned—namely Greece, Italy, Japan, Portugal, Spain, the United Kingdom, and West Germany—and were native speakers of the language in question. Equivalent forms of the questionnaire were developed in Greek, Italian, Japanese, Spanish, Portuguese, English, and German. Respondents were asked to describe an embarrassing event which had happened to them within the past few weeks and were then asked a series of questions about that event. One part of the questionnaire asked specifically for respondents verbal coping strategies and observer's verbal reactions. Subjects were asked to describe what they said or did to deal with their embarrassment and to describe the verbal and behavioral reaction of others present or witnesses to the event.

Verbal coping strategies were coded into eight categories derived from the theoretical analyses of Austin (1970); Scott and Lyman (1968); Tedeschi and Reiss (1981); Schlenker (1980 1982), and Semin and Manstead (1983) described previously. The categories used were: excuse, comment on feelings, exclamation, apology, justification, joking, and would not respond verbally with a final category where a response was not specified. Table 1 gives the frequencies with which a particular verbal reaction was recorded.

In each country two-thirds to three-quarters of the subjects either stated that they would not respond verbally or failed to indicate that they would make a verbal response. With regard

Table 1. VERBAL RESPONSES AS ATTEMPTS TO DEAL
WITH EMBARRASSMENT (FIGURES REPRESENT
PERCENTAGE CODED IN THE RESPECTIVE
CATEGORY FOR EACH NATION)

	Greece	Italy	Japan	Portugal	Spain	U. K.	West Germany
Not specified	57	65	63	59.2	37	35	43
Would not respond verbally	16	11	2	6.7	29	27	21
Excuse	2	3	7	3.3	5	8	3
Comment on own feelings	2	2	8	4.2	6	8	8
Exclamation	2	3	5	8.3	3	6	1
Apology	3	2	8	3.3	2	6	7
Apology + excuse	1	–	–	1.7	1	4	1
Apology + justification	–	–	–	–	–	–	2
Justification	13	8	6	1.7	14	3	10
Joking	4	6	1	1.7	3	3	4

to specified verbal responses, no particular strategy was used with any great regularity, although justification was the most frequently used verbal strategy in Greece, Spain, and West Germany. There is, however, little evidence for variation in face-saving strategies used within the countries studied; there was also no relationship between perceived intensity and duration of embarrassment experienced and coping strategy used. The large number of subjects who failed to indicate whether a verbal response would be made may simply represent a reporting omission on the part of respondents or it could indicate that verbal coping is not the most effective way of dealing with embarrassment (these issues are discussed fully in the original papers). Certainly a specific statement that no verbal response would be offered was given by almost one-third of respondents in Spain and the United Kingdom. This suggests that many of these subjects may have simply withdrawn from the situation or used behavioral remediation (e.g., picking up spilled items) rather than making a verbal response.

Remedial Strategies Used by Observers

As noted above, others present are likely to react to and become involved in the actor's embarrassment and may assist the actor either by offering their own account for the event or "playing along" with them in reciprocating the embarrassed person's response. For example, by laughing at an embarrassed person's joke or acknowledging an apology with a comment such as "it's not important" or "it does not matter," the embarrassment inherent in the situation can be diffused. Laughter from an observer will clearly have a different meaning dependent upon whether the observer laughs alone or if laughter is reciprocal with both observer and actor laughing. Clearly it is important for the observer and actor to "collude" if laughter is to serve as a remedial strategy. If the actor fails to join in with the observer in his/her attempt to help, they may well end up being the butt of the joke rather than making light of the event. It is only when reciprocal laughter occurs that Miller's (1986) comment: "Paradoxically, to help the person, they may laugh" (p. 303) is likely to apply. Both Coser (1960) and Oleson and Whittaker (1966) note from observational studies that an audience often responds to a person's embarrassment with laughter, a response which is intended to assist the embarrassed actor rather than impede the interaction. As with laughter by the embarrassed person, laughter by an observer to the embarrassing event can serve to make light of it. As Harris (1981) notes with regard to accounts and joking: "As long as the audience agrees to accept these as releases, the interaction will continue. If the audience refuses to forgive, then the error takes on even greater significance" (p. 60).

Verbal strategies used by the observer have been the more frequent focus of research. In a study referred to above (Metts & Cupach, 1989), respondents were asked to describe an incident in which they were significantly embarrassed and to describe what they and others present did to try to reduce the respondent's embarrassment. With regard to respondent's perceptions of observer's reactions, the most frequently cited remedial strategy was support (representing 32% of the total strategies coded), followed by empathy (19%), humor (16%), avoidance (12%), justification (9%), excuse (7%), and remediation (5%). Unlike the actor's responses, the strategies used by others present were not strongly related to the type of situation in which the embarrassment occurred.

In a replication and extension of this study also referred to above (Sharkey & Stafford, 1990), respondents were again asked to describe what others present did to try to reduce the respondent's embarrassment. The most common responses to embarrassment by others present were objective symptoms (representing 34% of the total strategies coded) and accounts (representing 20% of the total strategies coded). Frequency of other strategies reported as used by observers were escape (17%), remediation (13%), avoidance (8%), subjective symptoms—which were regarded as an index of internal feelings rather than a communicative response (4%) and aggression (4%). There was no association between degree of embarrassment and response by others present. However, in contrast to findings reported by Metts and Cupach (1989), the type of situation was predictive of the reaction of others in the situation. With situations involving a violation of privacy, objective symptoms predominated; when criticism was the cause objective symptoms and escape were the most common responses reported; with situations involving awkward acts, objective symptoms predominated. There was also evidence of the interdependent nature of the interaction. When an embarrassed actor responded with remediation, the observer was likely to respond with objective symptoms of remediation. When an embarrassed actor responded with an account, a form of remediation was most likely to be provided by the observer. Perhaps the most notable examples of "cooperative face-saving" involved avoidance and objective symptoms: when the embarrassed party responded with avoidance, others responded with avoidance; similarly, when the embarrassed party responded with objective symptoms (e.g., laughter), others responded with objective symptoms.

In the studies referred to above, observer's reactions reported by the actor to their embarrassment was examined in seven countries (Edelmann, et al., 1987; Edelmann & Iwawaki, 1987; Edelmann & Neto, 1989). The observer's reactions were coded into nine categories which partially reflect the code system used for actors' verbal coping attempts referred to above, with some of the categories combined and with additional categories covering an empathic response, starting/continuing a conversation and pretending nothing has happened. The remaining six categories were: comment on actor's embarrassment/stupidity, apology, joking, exclamation, and saying nothing with a final category where a response was not specified. Table 2 gives the frequencies with which a particular verbal reaction was recorded.

Over half the respondents in each of the seven samples either specified that the observer did not respond verbally or failed to indicate a verbal response for the observer. As with the actor's reported response, the large number of subjects who failed to indicate a verbal response from the observer may reflect a reporting omission on the part of subjects or it could indicate that a verbal response from an observer is not particularly helpful. Certainly, a specific statement that no verbal response was offered by the observer was referred to by one-fifth to one-quarter of all respondents in each country, with the exception of the lower rate in Japan. In these instances, a nonverbal rather than a verbal response may be offered by the observer. For example, between one-fifth and one-half of respondents across the countries studied noted that observers their embarrassment smiled, grinned, or laughed. For those who did indicate an observer's verbal response, an empathic reaction was mentioned most frequently in Greece, the United Kingdom, and West Germany; a comment on the actor's embarrassment/stupidity was mentioned most frequently in Japan (referred to by over a quarter of the sample); and starting/continuing the conversation was mentioned most frequently in Spain.

Table 2. OBSERVER'S VERBAL RESPONSE TO ACTOR'S EMBARRASSMENT (FIGURES REPRESENT PERCENTAGE CODED IN THE RESPECTIVE CATEGORY FOR EACH NATION)

	Greece	Italy	Japan	Portugal	Spain	U. K.	West Germany
Not specified	39	38	45	37.5	29	37	43
Nothing	22	16	7	25.8	26	17	19
Joking	2	6	—	0.8	5	9	3
Empathic	15	9	6	9.2	10	19	20
Exclamation	3	2	9	7.5	1	5	1
Comment of actor's embarrassment/stupidity	7	6	28	1.7	7	5	6
Apology (i.e., if the observer is the cause of the embarrassment)	2	4	2	1.7	3	2	1
Starting/continuing conversation	7	10	—	13.3	15	6	6
Pretending nothing has happened	3	9	3	2.5	4	—	1

Coping With Chronic Blushing

Discussion has so far focused upon actor/observer face-saving attempts associated with embarrassment elicited by identifiable external events. Until recently there was little attempt to examine embarrassment generated by internal cues. As noted above, people with a chronic fear of blushing may be overattentive to internal and expressive cues and may experience embarrassment even in the absence of an external eliciting circumstances. The feeling state of embarrassment is being generated by a negative evaluation of one's perceived alteration in facial skin temperature, sweating, or other physiological markers. In one study, data concerning self-reported coping attempts were generated from a sample of self-defined chronic blushers (Edelmann, 1987b, 1990a). The sample consisted of 100 subjects who completed a questionnaire sent to an initial pool of 500 people who had written requesting a fact sheet entitled "Blushing: What it is and what to do about it" that was advertised with an article published in a well-known British women's magazine. Given the method of respondent recruitment and the fact that only a small number of potential subjects returned the completed questionnaire, it is possible that the subjects are not representative of the population of chronic blushers. Nevertheless, the respondents provide some interesting data relating to coping with blushing. Each respondent was asked to answer ten questions, two of which concerned coping attempts. Subjects were first asked about methods used for making a blush to go away, and second about methods for coping with the problem of blushing.

Coping with a current blush was coded into four main categories reflecting either an inability to cope or one of three coping strategies either used alone or in combination; these were behavioral avoidance (e.g., leaving the room), cognitive strategies (e.g., distraction), and physiological strategies (e.g., relaxation, slow breathing). Coping with a current blush seems to present extreme difficulty: 62% of respondents stated that they were unable to cope and did not have an available strategy. A total of 17% chose behavioral avoidance, 10% cognitive, and 9% physiological strategies, with 2% using some combination of strategies. Verbal coping was not referred to by any of the respondents.

Coping with blushing in general was coded into seven categories. In addition to the four categories referred to above, responses also included hypnosis, mention of medication, and makeup. Coping with blushing in general also seems to present extreme difficulties. Twenty-two percent were unable to cope, 22% resorted to tranquilizers, 22% wore makeup, physiological strategies were reported by 13%, cognitive strategies by 12%, hypnosis by 11%, and behavioral avoidance by 3%. (Some subjects used more than one strategy so that the percentages are not cumulative.) Again, verbal remediation attempts were not referred to as a coping strategy.

The fact that many chronic blushers are unable to cope with their difficulty is no doubt partly due to the lack of knowledge about how to cope and the use of inappropriate strategies. It is likely that coping is made more difficult by a predisposition to blush and cognitive distortions concerning the likely cue salience of blushing. Given that a predisposition to blush is closely related to social anxiety (Edelmann, 1990a, 1991) and that clinically socially anxious subjects report more embarrassment in specified situations than nonsocially anxious subjects (Edelmann, 1985b), it seems reasonable to assume that chronic blushing represents the extreme endpoint of embarrassability. In this regard, Miller (in press) has reported that embarrassable subjects seemed to respond more intensely than did less embarrassable subjects to essentially the same social predicaments. Chronic blushing and extreme embarrassability may then be related to a tendency to freeze in social situations even if these are not intrinsically embarrassing. A desire to withdraw rather than confront the situation may predominate.

Integration and Future Directions

Recent research endeavors have led to a clearer rationale for categorizing embarrassing events and associated face-saving strategies. Taxonomies developed by Cupach and Metts (1990), Miller (in press), and Sharkey and Stafford (1990) represent an important step in recognizing "higher level" dimensions of importance in addition to "lower level" situational categories. These taxonomies have already resulted in a significant advance in our understanding of the interaction between the embarrassing situation, moderating variables, and both actor and observer reactions to the event. They clearly merit further refinement, possibly in the way suggested here, and use in future research studies. The continued use of varying methodologies emphasizing both self-report data and experimental manipulation also seems of importance, particularly given the inherent difficulty of observing naturally occurring embarrassment. The replication of results from studies using different methodologies clearly adds weight to the strength of findings derived from any one research method.

In attempting to construct a model of the interaction between the embarrassing situation, moderating variables, and actor and observer reactions, a number of factors need to be taken into account. The first issue relates to whether strategies which may be appropriate for remedying damaged encounters in general are of equal appropriateness for remedying embarrassing events in particular. Results from a number of studies both within and across countries suggest that justifications are rarely used to remedy embarrassing situations, whereas apologies, physical remediation attempts (e.g., picking up spilled objects), and escape are common reactions.

The second issue concerns the relationship of such remedial strategies to specific embarrassing events. There seems to be general agreement within the literature that the type of situation influences the reaction of the embarrassed person. One dimension of importance suggested by Sharkey and Stafford (1990) relates to the agent of embarrassment. If the embarrassed person is responsible for the embarrassment, then an attempt by them to explain or account for their action seems appropriate; if someone causes another person to be embarrassed, then escape or aggression from the embarrassed person seems appropriate although objective symptoms are also commonly reported (Sharkey, in press). Future research could usefully be directed at further investigating the dimensions of relevance to embarrassment suggested by recent taxonomies and their relation to specific remedial strategies. Related to the type of situation is the extent to which intensity of embarrassment experienced influences the use of face-saving strategies. Studies have approached this issue in somewhat differing ways and it is thus not surprising that results are contradictory. Self-report data from studies both within and across cultures tends to suggest that degree of embarrassment is not related to strategy used. As Sharkey and Stafford (1990) note, however, studies relying upon recall may only generate situations reflecting a relatively narrow range of embarrassment intensity. Certainly, when examining individual differences in fear of blushing (i.e., those who are likely to experience extreme embarrassment even in mildly or nonembarrassing situations), escape or avoidance seem to be the strategy of choice. One might assume therefore a change in strategy from mild embarrassment (laughter and/or apology) through moderate embarrassment (apology plus excuse) to extreme embarrassment (escape or avoidance), although this would clearly be influenced by other factors such as the perceived seriousness of the event itself.

In addition to individual differences in embarrassability, there is a range of moderating variables that might influence the choice of remedial strategy following embarrassment. These include the gender, status and relational distance or intimacy of interactants, the observer's reaction, and number of observers present. There is, however, limited research in this area and thus conclusions are of necessity tentative. Gender seems to influence choice of strategy, women placing more weight on apologizing or use of deferential strategies in comparison to men. This may reflect differences in normative behavior for men and women or may be a reflection of the fact that both laboratory and self-report studies have found that women experience more embarrassment than men (Miller, 1987, in press) a differential which may of itself demand varying reactions. Status also seems to influence face-saving activity. In laboratory studies respondents are more likely to sacrifice tangible rewards if asked to perform an embarrassing task in front of a high-status audience (Brown & Garland, 1971; Garland & Brown, 1972). This may reflect the use of social withdrawal as face-saving. In the one study which has investigated this factor subsequent to an embarrassing event, status was found to interact with seriousness of the event with high-status subjects being less likely to account for their actions when the embarrassing event was less serious (Gonzales, Pederson, Manning, & Wetter, 1990). Degree of intimacy among the embarrassed person and observers is also likely to influence face-saving, although there is a surprising lack of research pertaining to this issue. One might assume, however, that intimacy would be related to cooperative face-saving attempts and a tendency to make light of the situation through the use of humor or laughter. Indeed, one might expect a similar response with strangers whom we are unlikely to meet again, while embarrassment in front of acquaintances whom we may well encounter subsequently might generate the most discomfort with apologies, excuses, or even avoidance predominating. Certainly, the findings of Froming, Corley, and Rinker

(1990) that embarrassed respondents were less likely to withdraw from an audience of friends or strangers they were unlikely to meet again than from an strangers they were likely to meet again supports this contention. Clearly, the influence of gender, status, and intimacy as determinants of face-saving strategies subsequent to embarrassment are factors which warrant further investigation.

Finally, it is clear that the observer plays an important role in determining the embarrassed person's reaction to their embarrassment. With the exception of situations in which the observer intentionally embarrasses another (when hostility, concealment of felt embarrassment, or avoidance may be appropriate reactions by the embarrassed person, Sharkey & Stafford, 1990; Sharkey & Waldron, 1990) it is generally assumed that the observer will collude with the embarrassed person in helping to remedy the situation. Self-report data suggests that this is indeed the case (Sharkey & Stafford, 1990). As with responses by the embarrassed person there seem to be certain appropriate observer responses, a reaction of empathic embarrassment being frequently reported both within and across countries (Metts & Cupach, 1989; Miller, 1987; Edelmann, 1990). Indeed, there is evidence that empathic embarrassment on the part of an observer is more likely with greater observer embarrassability and increased familiarity with the embarrassed actor (Miller, 1987).

With regard to the relationship between the embarrassing situation and the observer's reaction, there is some inconsistency of findings between studies. Thus, Sharkey and Stafford (1990) suggest that the situation is predictive of the observer's response, while Metts and Cupach (1989) report no such relationship. These researchers have also noted that multiple responses to embarrassment might be used by both actor and observer with certain responses being more likely to co-occur than others. Sharkey and Stafford (1990) report no association between combinations of responses with different situations or severity of embarrassment, although, as noted previously, studies relying upon recall may only be tapping a relatively narrow range of embarrassment intensity. Clearly, these are issues that warrant further investigation.

The interaction between the embarrassing situation and moderating variables such as agent, gender, intimacy, intensity of embarrassment, audience characteristics, and audience reaction to remedial strategies is a complex one. Empirical investigation of this interrelationship is in an embryonic stage, and yet significant advances have already been made. The challenge for future research is twofold: first, to extend the range of research findings so that the interrelationship between variables can be more clearly delineated, and, second, to extend the range of empirical studies beyond those relying upon self-report data. With regard to the first issue, findings to date suggest a possible relationship between factors which increase perceived distress from embarrassment and face-saving strategies used. It seems that less intense feelings of embarrassment are more likely to be dealt with by humor, moderately intense with apologies or accounts, and high-intensity embarrassment by escape or avoidance. Factors associated with low distress include situations where the actor is responsible for causing their own embarrassment which is observed by friends. Factors associated with high-intensity embarrassment include situations where the actor is responsible for causing his/her own embarrassment (particularly if this is internally generated as with chronic blushers) which is witnessed by a large, high-status audience of acquaintances whom we are likely to encounter subsequently. Clearly, the audience's role and reaction also play an important part. If the audience is responsible for causing another's embarrassment, then aggression from the embarrassed party might be the typical response. If responsibility for the embarrassment lies with the actor and the audience reacts with humor, then humor from the embarrassed party is more likely.

Such suppositions are largely derived from self-report data. It is, of course, impossible to say whether self-report data is representative of reactions to actual embarrassment. Even manipulating variables experimentally may not mirror reaction to naturally occurring embarrassment. Inducing embarrassment for experimental purposes is not without its ethical constraints, while observing naturally occurring embarrassment is inherently difficult. Studying observer reactions to "naturally occurring" embarrassment is less difficult. A number of studies have investigated reactions to embarrassment by using a confederate who commits a faux pas; these have tended to use one specific situation (e.g., Levine and Arluke [1982] used a female confederate who "accidentally" dropped a large quantity of papers). Such a procedure could be used to investigate observer reactions to a range of embarrassing events varying gender, perceived status, and so on of the embarrassed actor.

Given the advances made in the past few years, the next decade is likely to be one of exciting new developments.

Note

I am extremely grateful to William F. Sharkey and Rowland Miller who made excellent criticisms of an earlier version of this chapter which led to significant improvements. I also thank Stella Ting-Toomey for her help in this respect. However, in the final analysis I must take responsibility for the views expressed, together with any errors or omissions contained within this chapter.

References

Argyle, M. (1969). *Social interaction.* London: Methuen.

Aspler, R. (1975). Effects of embarrassment on behavior toward others. *Journal of Personality and Social Psychology, 32,* 145–153.

Austin, J. L. (1970). *Philosophical papers.* 2nd ed. New York: Oxford University Press.

Brown, B. R. (1970) Face-saving following experimentally induced embarrassment. *Journal of Experimental Social Psychology, 6,* 255–271.

Brown, B. R., and Garland, H. (1971). The effect of incompetency, audience acquaintanceship, and anticipated evaluative feedback on face-saving behavior. *Journal of Experimental Social Psychology, 7,* 490–502.

Buck, R. W. (1980). Nonverbal behavior and the theory of emotion: The facial feedback hypothesis. *Journal of Personality and Social Psychology, 38,* 811–824.

Buss, A. (1980). *Self-consciousness and social anxiety.* San Francisco: Freeman.

Castelfranchi, C., and Poggi, I. (1990). Blushing as discourse: Was Darwin wrong? In Crozier, R. (Ed.), *Shyness and embarrassment: Perspectives from social psychology.* Cambridge: Cambridge University Press.

Coser, R. (1960). Laughter among colleagues: A study of the social functions of humor among the staff of a mental hospital. *Psychiatry, 23,* 81–95.

Cupach, W. R., and Metts, S. (1990). Remedial processes in embarrassing predicaments. In J. A. Anderson (Ed.), *Communication yearbook 13.* Newbury Park, CA: Sage.

Cupach, W. R., Metts S., and Hazleton, V. (1986). Coping with embarrassing predicaments: Remedial strategies and their perceived utility. *Journal of Language and Social Psychology*, 5, 181–200.

Duval, S., and Wicklund, R. A. (1972). *A Theory of Objective Self-awareness*. New York: Academic Press.

Edelmann, R. J. (1982) The effect of embarrassed reactions upon others. *Australian Journal of Psychology*, 34, 359–367.

———. (1985a). Social embarrassment: An analysis of the process. *Journal of Social and Personal Relationships*, 2, 95–213.

———. (1985b). Dealing with embarrassing events: Socially anxious and non-socially anxious groups compared. *British Journal of Clinical Psychology*, 24, 281–288.

———. (1985c). Embarrassment, laughter and humour. Paper presented at the Fifth International Conference on Humour at University College, Cork, Ireland.

———. (1987a). *The psychology of embarrassment*. Chichester, UK: John Wiley.

———. (1987b). Chronic blushing: A model and some preliminary descriptive data. Paper presented at the British Psychological Society London Conference.

———. (1990a). Embarrassment and blushing: A component-process model, some initial descriptive and cross-cultural data. In R. Crozier (Ed.), *Shyness and embarrassment: Perspectives from social psychology*. Cambridge: Cambridge University Press.

———. (1990b). Coping with embarrassment and blushing. In J. A. Anderson (Ed.), *Communication yearbook 13*. Newbury Park, CA: Sage.

———. (1990c). *Coping with blushing*, London: Sheldon Press.

———. (1990d). Chronic blushing, self-consciousness, and social anxiety. *Journal of Psychopathology and Behavioral Assessment*, 12, 119–127.

———. (1991). Correlates of chronic blushing. *British Journal of Clinical Psychology*, 30, 177–178.

Edelmann, R. J., Asendorpf, J., Contarello, A., Georgas, J., Villanueva, C., and Zammuner, V. (1987). Self-reported verbal and non-verbal strategies for coping with embarrassment in five European cultures. *Social Science Information*, 26, 869–883.

Edelmann R. J., and Hampson, S. E. (1979). Changes in nonverbal behaviour during embarrassment. *British Journal of Social and Clinical Psychology*, 18, 385–390.

———. (1981). Embarrassment in dyadic interaction. *Social Behavior and Personality*, 9. 171–177.

Edelmann, R. J., and Iwawaki, S. (1987). Self-reported embarrassment and consequences of embarrassment in the United Kingdom and Japan. *Psychologia, 30,* 205–216.

Edelmann, R. J., and Neto, F. (1989). Self-reported expression and consequences of embarrassment in Portugal and the U. K. *International Journal of Psychology, 24,* 351–366.

Emerson, J. P. (1970). Behaviour in private places: Sustaining defintions of reality in gynecological examinations. In H. P. Dreitzel (Ed.), *Recent sociology.* Vol. 2: *Patterns of communication* behavior. New York: Macmillan.

Fink, E. L., and Walker, B. A. (1977). Humorous responses to embarrassment. *Psychological Reports, 40,* 475–485.

Froming, W. J., Corely, E. B., and Rinker, L. (1990). The influence of public self-consciousness and the audience's characteristics on withdrawal from embarrassing situations. *Journal of Personality, 58,* 603–622.

Garland, H., and Brown, B. R. (1972). Face-saving as affected by subjects' sex, audiences' sex and audience expertise. *Sociometry, 35,* 280–289.

Goffman, E. (1956). Embarrassment and social organisation. *American Journal of Sociology, 62,* 264–271.

———. (1967). *Interaction ritual: Essays on face-to-face behavior.* New York: Pantheon.

Gonzales, M. H., Pederson, J. H., Manning, D. J., and Wetter, D. W. (1990). Pardon my gafee: Effects of sex, status, and consequent severity on accounts. *Journal of Personality and Social Psychology, 58,* 610–621.

Gross, F., and Stone, G. P. (1964). Embarrassment and the analysis of role requirements. *American Journal of Sociology, 70,* 1–15.

Harris, T. E. (1981). The "faux pas" in interpersonal communication. In S. Thomas (Ed.), *Studies in communication.* Vol 2: *Communication Theory and Interpersonal Interaction.* Norwood, NJ: Ablex.

Hull, J. G., and Levy, A. S. (1979). The organizational function of the self: An alternative to the Duval and Wicklund model of self-awareness. *Journal of Personality and Social Psychology, 37,* 756–768.

Jones, E. E., and Berglas, S. (1978). Control of attributions about the self through self-handicapping strategies: The appeal of alcohol and the role of underachievement. *Personality and Social Psychology Bulletin, 4,* 200–206.

Laird, J. D. (1984). The role of facial response in the experience of emotion: A reply to Tourangeau and Ellsworth, and others. *Journal of Personality and Social Psychology, 47,* 909–917.

Leary, M. R., and Meadows, S. (1991). Predictors, elicitors, and con-comitants of social blushing. (submitted).

Levin, J., and Arluke, A. (1982). Embarrassment and helping behav-ior. *Psychological Reports, 51,* 999–1002.

McLaughlin, M. L., Cody, M. J., and O'Hair, H. D. (1983). The man-agement of failure events: Some contextual determinants of accounting behavior. *Human Communication Research, 9,* 208–224.

McLaughlin, M. L., Cody, M. J., and Rosenstain, N. E. (1983). Ac-count sequences in conversation between strangers. *Communi-cation Monographs, 50,* 102–125.

Metts, S., and Cupach, W. R. (1989), Situational influence on the use of remedial strategies in embarrassing predicaments. *Communi-cation Monographs, 56,* 151–162.

Miller, R. S. (1986). Embarrassment: Causes and consequences. In W. H. Jones, J. H. Cheek, and S. R. Briggs (Eds.), *Shyness: Per-spectives on research and treatment.* New York: Plenum Press.

Miller, R. S. (1987). Empathic embarrassment: Situational and per-sonal determinants of reactions to the embarrassment of another. *Journal of Personality and Social Psychology, 53,* 1061–1069.

———. (1988). Embarrassability and reactions to the threat of em-barrassment. Papar presented at the meeting of the American Psychological Association, Atlanta.

———. (in press). The nature and severity of self-reported embarrass-ing circumstances. *Personality and Social Psychology Bulletin.*

Modigliani, A. (1968). Embarrassment and embarrassability. *Sociom-etry, 31,* 313–326.

———. (1971). Embarrassment, facework, and eye contact: Testing a theory of embarrassment. *Journal of Personality and Social Psy-chology, 17,* 15–24.

Oleson, V. L., and Whittaker, E. W. (1966). Adjudication of student awareness in professional socialization: The language of laughter and silences. *Sociology Quarterly, 7,* 381–396.

Petronio, S. (1984). Communication strategies to reduce embarrass-ment: Differences between men and women. *The Western Jour-nal of Speech Communication, 48,* 28–38.

Robinson, V. M. (1983). Humor and health. In P. E. McGhee and J. H. Goldstein (Eds.), *Handbook of humor research.* Vol 2: *Applied Studies.* New York: Springer-Verlag.

Sattler, J. M. (1965). A theoretical, clinical, and developmental inves-tigation of embarrassment. *Genetic Psychology Monographs, 71,* 19–59.

Scheier, M. F., Carver, C. S., and Matthews, K. A. (1983). Attentional factors in the perception of bodily states. In J. T. Caccioppo and

266   EDELMANN

R. E. Petty (Eds.), *Social psychophysiology: A sourcebook.* New York: Guildford.

Schlenker, B. R. (1980). *Impression management: The self-concept, social identity, and interpersonal relations.* Monterey, CA: Brooks/Cole.

————. (1982). Translating actions into attitudes: An identity analytic approach to the explanation of social conduct. In L. Berkowitz (Ed.), *Advances in experimental social psychology,* vol 15. New York: Academic Press.

Schlenker, B. R., and Darby, B. W. (1981). The use of apologies in social predicaments. *Social Psychology Quarterly, 44,* 271–278.

Schonbach, P. (1980). A category system for account phases. *European Journal of Social Psychology, 10,* 195–200.

Scott, M. B., and Lyman, S. B. (1968). Accounts. *American Sociological Review, 33,* 46–62.

Semin, G. R., and Manstead, A. S. R. (1982). The social implications of embarrassment displays and restitution behaviour. *European Journal of Social Psychology, 12,* 367–377.

————. (1983). *The accountability of conduct: A social psychological analysis.* London: Academic Press.

Sharkey, W. F. (in press). The use of and responses to intentional embarrassment. *Human Communication Research.*

Sharkey, W. F., and Stafford, L. (1990). Responses to embarrassment. *Human Communication Research, 17,* 315–342.

Sharkey, W. F., and Waldron, V. R. (1990). The intentional embarrassment of subordinates in the work place. Paper presented at the seventy-sixth annual conference of the Speech Communication Association, Chicago, IL.

Silver, M., Sabini, J., and Parrott, W. G. (1987) Embarrassment: A dramaturgical account. *Journal for the Theory of Social Behaviour, 17,* 47–61.

Snyder, C. R. (1985). The excuse: An amazing grace? In B. R. Schlenker (Ed.), *The self and social life.* New York: McGraw-Hill.

Stamp, G. H., and Knapp, M. L. (1990). The construct of intent in interpersonal communication. *Quarterly Journal of Speech, 76,* 282–299.

Tedeschi, J., and Riess, M. (1981). Verbal strategies in impression management. In C. Antaki (Ed.), *The psychology of ordinary explanations of social behaviour.* London: Academic Press.

Tedeschi, J., Riordan, C. A., Gaes, G. G., and Kane, T. (1983). Verbal accounts and attributions of social motives. *Journal of Research in Personality, 17,* 218–225.

Timms, M. W. H. (1980). Treatment of chronic blushing by paradoxical intention. *Behavioural Psychotherapy, 8,* 59–61.

Tomkins, S. S. (1981). Affect theory. In P. Ekman (Ed.), *Emotion in the human face*, 2nd ed. Cambridge: Cambridge University Press.

Weinberg, M. S. (1968). Embarrassment: Its variable and invariable aspects. *Social Forces, 46,* 382–388.

-9-
Face Dynamics: From Conceptualization to Measurement

DAVID YAU-FAI HO

In this chapter, I propose to take a journey through the territory of research in face dynamics. The cognitive map for this territory is based on two strands of analysis previously conducted, one concerning the concept of face (Ho, 1976), and the other concerning the methodological implications of relational orientation (Ho, 1991).

The thesis of relational orientation, or *relationalism* (a newly coined term), is that social behavior invariably takes place in relational contexts, regardless of social class or cultural variations. Accordingly, the unit of analysis is not the individual, but the *individual-in-relations*. By relational contexts, I mean social, particularly interpersonal, contexts. Among the most important relational contexts are those involving role and/or status relationships. Relational orientation confronts the bias toward methodological individualism in contemporary mainstream psychology. It makes a demand on the theorist to consider how social relationships are defined, before attempting to interpret the behavior of individuals. An adequate explanation entails, therefore, making explicit the normative expectations and behavioral rules governing interpersonal relationships.

The intellectual tools employed in theory building guided by methodological relationalism are relational concepts, such as reciprocity, interdependence, interrelatedness, and dyads. More so than individualistic concepts (e.g., actor, ego, and self), relational concepts lend themselves to analytic exercises that reflect the relational contexts within which social behavior takes place. Face is a relational concept par excellence. Indeed, the development of relationalism owes much to analytic studies of the face concept.

A Relational Conception of Face Dynamics

As a first step, a clarification of the scientific vocabulary concerning face would be useful. I propose to use the term *face dynamics* to refer generically to social processes, directly observable or inferred, involved in face enhancement, maintenance, protection, restoration, and derogation. Interactions directly observable may be called simply *face behavior;* aspects of interaction not directly observable are inferred from face behavior. Of particular interest are the dynamics arising from: (*a*) incongruences among a person's self-concept, the projection of his/her social self in the public domain, and his/her social image publicly and collectively perceived by others, and (*b*) discrepancies between the face claimed by a person from others and the face extended to him/her by others.

The term *facework* is more restricted in meaning than face dynamics. As used by Goffman (1955), facework refers to the subtle style in interpersonal encounters, found in all societies, calculated to avoid personal embarrassment, or loss of poise, and to maintain for others an impression of self-respect. I shall restrict my use of this term to refer specifically to the strategies, social maneuvers, and/or coping mechanisms an actor employs in face dynamics.

A conceptualization of face dynamics based on relationalism gives particular emphasis to three aspects: (*a*) face as a field concept, (*b*) reciprocity, and (*c*) social influence and social control.

Face as a field concept
Accepting that the unit of analysis is the individual-in-relations, the relational context within which face dynamics take place has to be taken into account. For instance, face may be lost not only from one's failure to meet social expectations, but also from the failure of: (*a*) people closely associated with him/her to meet expectations, and (*b*) others to act in accordance with one's expectations of how one and one's associates should be treated. That is, face may be lost not only from one's

own actions but also from the actions of other people. This line of inquiry leads to a delineation of social consequences over which an actor has little or no control and for which he/she may have no responsibility.

Face is a field concept: it takes full recognition of the individual's embeddedness in the social network. A methodological consequence is that the analysis of face behavior, even when pertaining to a single individual, must extend its domain to include: (a) actions by the individual, either self-initiated or in response to those of others; (b) actions by other people closely associated with the individual; (c) actions directed at the individual by people with whom the individual is interacting; (d) actions directed at the individual by people closely associated with those with whom the individual is interacting; and, finally, (e) actions directed at people closely associated with the individual by those with whom the individual is interacting directly or indirectly.

Clearly, the domain of social actions to be included for analysis is more encompassing and more complicated than what has traditionally been envisioned. It is a dynamic field of forces and counterforces in which the stature and significance of the individual appear to have diminished. The individual, no longer at center stage, is not the measure of all things; and the world is not seen through his/her eyes. This altered perspective cannot be characterized by anything short of psychological decentering, as dramatic as the historic change of worldview from the Ptolemaic to the Copernican.

Relationalism does not negate the individual, but it does counter egoism. It considers the perspective of each actor; more importantly, it insists on the necessity of including the participation of others in the individual's perspective. We may use an analogy from music. One might say that the ultimate self-expression is the solo virtuoso playing without accompaniment and without an audience. But, even here, the participation of the audience in the mind of the virtuoso is an integral part of his/her musicianship. The ensemble exemplifies a relational arrangement—one, unlike the orchestra, is not hierarchically organized under the direction of a conductor. The individuality of each member's musicianship has to be subjugated. Yet individuality reemerges collectively to mark the ensemble's unique identity, not reducible to the sum of its members' musicianship.

Reciprocity

Inherent in face dynamics, reciprocity concerns the need to show regard for not only one's face but also the face of others. Each interacting party expects to be given face by others and is expected to give face to others. Indeed, a failure to give face to others may occasion a loss of one's own face. This idea of reciprocity is embodied in Ho's (1976) definition of face: "In terms of two interacting parties, face is the reciprocated compliance, respect, and/or deference that each party expects from, and extends to, the other party" (p. 883). Ting-Toomey (1988) also speaks of the self-other dimension in her conceptualization of facework: self-face concern and other-face concern (the other dimension being positive-face and negative-face). Unfortunately, most investigators, especially those from Western cultures preoccupied with individualism, have not recognized the importance of other-face concern. It must be added, though, a conception of face dynamics which gives full recognition to reciprocity would be met with a congenial reception by communication researchers (e.g., Tracy, 1990)—for whom a nonrelational conception would be quite unnatural indeed.

Social influence and social control

Having face means both commanding social influence over others as well as being influenced by others—another aspect of reciprocity. A person who has face is in a position to exercise considerable influence, even control, over others indirect or indirect ways; at the same time, he/she is under a strong constraint to act in accordance with the requirements for maintaining his/her face. The more face, the greater the social visibility and public scrutiny over one's actions, and hence the stronger the constraint imposed on one's actions. Examples are abundant: candidates seeking high public office in the United States run the risk of having their private life, past and present, exposed to microscopic scrutiny by the public.

Thus the concern for face exerts a reciprocated constraint upon each member of the social network. It delimits individual volition: much of the time, the individual's actions are dictated by the necessity of meeting the expectation of others. In short, the concern for face is a pervasive social sanction; it generates pressure toward conformity; and it is a powerful mechanism underlying other-directedness, that is, acting in ways that reflect a high degree of sensitivity for how one's actions are perceived and reacted to by others.

It has often been said that the avoidance of losing face is an overriding concern in Asian cultures. What about Westerners? In response to this question, Riesman's (1950) characterization of other-directedness in American society comes to mind. Other-directed people are said to have a paramount need to seek approval and direction from, and hence the tendency to act in conformity with, their contemporaries, especially their peers. In the Asian context, other-directedness differs from Riesman's characterization in one fundamental respect. In American society, the driving motive is to seek approval, recognition, and popularity. In Asian societies, the imperative is to avoid disapproval. The dynamics involved in avoiding disapproval versus seeking approval are quite dissimilar. Here we are reminded of the basic difference between gaining face and losing face (Ho, 1976). Face is not lost merely on account of a failure to gain it; and regaining face that has been lost is not gaining face, but merely a restoration of the face to which the individual is originally entitled. To gain face is an intricate social game; the actor may choose not to play it. But to maintain face, to avoid losing face, and to regain face lost are essential for effective social functioning.

From Conceptualization to Measurement

Definition

A critical review of the literature reveals that two distinctions in the definition of face should be made explicit. First, face may be defined in terms of the projection of one's social self in the public domain; that is, aspects of one's self that a person reveals to others. Thus, Goffman (1955) defines face as "the positive social value a person effectively claims for himself by the line others assume he has taken during a particular contact. Face is an image of self delineated in terms of approved social attributes" (p. 213). But face may also be defined in terms of one's social image that is publicly and collectively perceived by others—an image is not necessarily the same as that one reveals to others. Clearly, these are two different approaches to definition, and hence to measurement. Correspondingly, the face that a person expects or claims for himself/herself from others should be distinguished from the face accorded him/her by others. Potential conflicts arise when these two are discrepant. This is a gold mine for research—one that has not been fully exploited.

Second, face may be defined situationally, referring to specific instances of social encounter. Goffman (1955) states: "The person's face is clearly something that is not lodged in or on his body, but rather something that is diffusely located in the flow of events" (p. 214). His seminal ideas have generated research on facework and several closely related topics, such as embarrassment (e.g., Edelmann, 1990), impression management (e.g., Leary and Kowalski, 1990), and negotiation in conflict situations (e.g., Ting-Toomey, 1988; Ting-Toomey & Cole, 1990). Nevertheless, it is important to point out that Goffman's conception of face differs from the Chinese conception, which is not restricted to situational encounters.

According to the Chinese conception, face may be defined in terms of the more enduring, publicly perceived attributes that function to locate a person's position in his/her social network. Thus defined, a person's face is largely consistent over time and across situations, unless there is a significant change in public perceptions of his/her conduct, performance, or social status. It goes wherever the person goes, and would not change, for instance, on account of a change in jobs that signify no change in status. As Ho (1976) states: "Face is attached to persons" (p. 874)—not externally to their position, rank, or office. It would then be meaningful to ask how much face a given individual has and what changes in his/her face are perceived, apart from specific social events. (But it would not be meaningful to ask how much face is attached to the individual's rank or office.) This question would lead to a fruitful line of investigation, which researchers have yet to pursue in depth.

Although face is attached to persons, it is not a personality variable (Ho, 1976). Unlike personality, face is not to be regarded as a construct pertaining to personal attributes inferred from behavior. Measurements of face are sociometric, not psychological, in nature. They would not be based upon a direct study of the individual; rather, a person's face would be ascertained by conducting inquiries on the opinions that others have of him/her. That is, a person's face is assessed in terms of what others think of the person. The assessment does not include what the person thinks of himself/herself (i.e., self-perceptions), but may include what the person thinks other people think of him/her. Of course, misjudgments may be made, and will act as a source of strain in one's interpersonal relationships.

The two distinctions identified above have direct method-ological implications for the measurement of face, to which I now turn.

Quantification

How much face does a person have? On one occasion, I raised this question in a graduate seminar where face was discussed. A knowledgeable Westerner familiar with the scholarly litera-ture on face, also a contributor to this book, said: "The ques-tion doesn't make sense." I responded: "You must have been misled by Goffman." If the question were put to a Chinese au-dience, no one would have difficulty understanding it. Further-more, it would be immediately understood that the question demands two answers: one concerning how much face a per-son expects/claims from others, and the other concerning how much face people give him/her (or how much face the person receives from others).

Nonetheless, face is a universal. As Ho (1976) argues: "While it is true that the conceptualization of what constitutes face and the rules governing face behavior vary considerably across cultures, the concern for face is invariant" (pp. 881–82). What is culturally invariant is the inevitability of judg-ment; and, therefore, anyone who does not wish to renounce the social nature of his/her existence must show a regard for face. Of course, the criteria by which a person's face is judged are rooted in cultural values, and are hence culture specific. The challenge now is to demonstrate how face may be mea-sured in different cultural contexts. In the following, I outline a scheme for the steps to be followed in face measurements. The scheme is stated at a sufficiently high level of generality so that it is invariant across cultures, that is, applicable regardless of cultural variation.

Defining a domain of attributes. To ask how much face a per-son has is to quantify face. Quantification makes sense when face is defined in terms of the more enduring, publicly per-ceived attributes that locate a person's standing in his/her so-cial network, unrestricted to specific social encounters—that is, defined according to the Chinese conception. In general, a person's face is a function of his/her standing or social position within a defined group. The higher the standing, the greater the claim or entitlement to face. The question of how much face a person has then translates into one concerning a person's respectability and the social influence that he/she can exercise over others. This would be a concrete, yet rare, example of following a conception that is non-Western in origin in behavioral science—there being nothing preordained about Western conceptions.

In operational terms, the measurement problem translates into one of defining a domain of attributes that may be considered important for face judgments in various cultural contexts. This domain includes the following classes of attributes.

1. Biographical variables, such as age, sex, birth order, and generational rank.
2. Relational attributes based on birth, blood or marriage ties.
3. Social status indicators based on personal effort or achievement: (a) educational attainment, occupational status, and income; and (b) social connections and influence; membership in clubs, associations, and/or other organizations.
4. Social status indicators not based on personal effort or achievement, such as wealth and/or social connections acquired through marriage.
5. Formal title, position, rank, or office acquired through personal effort or awarded in recognition of personal achievement.
6. Formal title, position, rank, or office acquired through ascription (e.g., inheritance).
7. Personal reputation based on the amoral (e.g., skill-related or task-oriented) aspects of social performance.
8. Personal reputation based on moral character, judged on the basis of personal conduct.
9. Integrity of social being: freedom from stigmata.

The domain defined is by no means exhaustive. Even then, it is far more inclusive than the traditional indices of socioeconomic class (i.e., education, occupation, and income—3a). Again, it illustrates how the face concept is more inclusive than, and hence cannot be reduce to, socioeconomic status; and it points to the inadequacy of relying on the traditional indices when it comes to face research.

The attributes in the domain may be recategorized in different ways: for instance, along the intrinsic-extrinsic, achievement-ascription, moral-amoral, and individual-relational dimensions. Classes 7 through 9 are attributes intrinsic to the individual; classes 1 through 6 are attributes extrinsic to the individual. Classes 3, 5, 7, and 8 are based on personal effort, achievement, and/or conduct; classes 1, 2, 4, 6, and 9 (to be explained later) are based on ascription. Class 7 concerns evaluative judgments of personal conduct made on the basis of moral criteria (e.g., good vs. evil); class 8 concerns evaluative judgments of social performance made on the basis of amoral criteria (e.g., efficiency, skill, and competence). Finally, comparing class 3a and class 3b illustrate most clearly the distinction between individual (e.g., education) and relational attributes (e.g., social connections).

The last class, what I call *integrity of social being* (9), requires a more extended discussion. It is more encompassing than moral character, because it includes judgments of actions or circumstances not under the individual's control and hence beyond the domain of personal responsibility. Here we are concerned with the avoidance of something negative in the extreme, rather than the pursuit of something positive. Consider the case of a woman who has been raped (or widely suspected of being raped) in a culture where chastity is considered more important than life; a patient who has fallen victim to a hideous disease like leprosy in ancient times or AIDS in contemporary life; or being a member of a ethnic minority group that is considered inferior by the community. In each of these cases, the negative consequence amounts to no less than a massive assault on the person's social identity that renders him/her "unclean" in the eyes of others. The person's face is violated, shamed, and stigmatized; his/her social being has lost its integrity. Face is thus far more profound than just politeness, embarrassment, or impression management—the favorite topics of researchers. At rock bottom, face as the integrity of one's social being is not something that has to be earned, but is an inalienable right to human dignity.

Of course, different cultures attach varying degrees of importance to different attributes; and the attachment may change within cultures as a result of cultural change through time. These are facts that invite, respectively, synchronic and diachronic cross-cultural research. A comparison between Chinese and U.S. American cultures would be illuminating. Given its traditional-collectivistic values, Chinese culture would put more weight than American culture on generational rank (1), birth, blood or marriage ties (2), social connections (3, 4), and formal title, position, rank, or office (5, 6). U.S. American culture, which champions individualism, would put the most weight on attributes that reflect personal effort or achievement (3, 5) and personal reputation (7). A permissible generalization is that Chinese culture tends to emphasize relational attributes, whereas U.S. American culture tends to emphasize individual attributes. Moral character (8) is vital in both cultures; but it would be rated higher in importance, reflecting a greater emphasis on moral judgments than on evaluating the amoral aspects of social performance (7), in Chinese than in U.S. American culture. (Note that this statement says nothing about moral behavior per se in either culture.) Finally, under ordinary circumstances, everyone is entitled to integrity of social being (9) in both cultures.

Mien-tzu and lien. In the literature on face, many authors have accepted Hu's (1944) distinction between two Chinese concepts of face, based on two different sets of judgment criteria: *mien-tzu* achieved through success and ostentation, and *lien*, representing the confidence of society in the integrity of one's moral character. Concerning this distinction, three points should be made. First, conceptually we can distinguish one class of attributes considered important for face judgments from another. The moral and the amoral (e.g., success and ostentation) attributes, for instance, may be distinguished from each other. But this conceptual distinction does not correspond exactly to the semantic distinction between the two terms. It is not entirely accurate to say that *mien-tzu* is based on only the amoral attributes; the concept is not altogether devoid of moral content. Moreover, the terms of *mien-tzu* and *lien* are used interchangeably in some contexts, as their meanings vary according to the context of usage. Thus, it is hardly surprising that, even among Chinese subjects, many find it difficult to differentiate one term from the other (Chu, 1983). This result simply reflects a lack of clear differentiation at the semantic level; and it would be wrong to conclude from it that the respondents had difficulty making a distinction between the moral and the amoral attributes at the conceptual level.

The second point is that Hu (1944) described *lien* primarily in terms of moral character (8). The concept is actually more encompassing; it includes integrity of social being (9) as well. An important implication is that *lien* may be lost not only through unacceptable conduct, but also through circumstances beyond one's control. As the cases mentioned above indicate, the stigmata leading to a fatal damage of *lien* may not be due to personal misconduct for which one is held responsible, but to life's misfortunes for which one cannot be held responsible.

The third point concerns Hu's (1944) claim that "all persons growing up in any community have the same claim to *lien*, an honest, decent 'face' " (p. 62). Admittedly, in every society, members are normally entitled to the claim of a basic, decent face, regardless of how humble their social status may be. It is the minimum, irreducible, and inviolate face that one must maintain for adequate functioning as a social being. The loss of this basic face would seriously threaten the integrity of one's social being or, worse, one's acceptability as a member of human society. We are tempted to claim that the entitlement to a basic face is universal. Tragically, we cannot. I was wrong when I stated: "*Lien* is something to which everyone is entitled by virtue of his membership in society and can be lost only through unacceptable conduct" (Ho, 1976, p. 870). History is replete with instances where some members of a society are by definition excluded from the entitlement of *lien:* invalids, slaves, and members of an "inferior race" or a lowly caste (e.g., the untouchables in traditional India). Such exclusion is an expression of prejudice in its deepest form: the negation of *humanhood* (a newly coined term). An individual is judged and treated solely on the basis of group membership—given a number, but nameless, as in a concentration camp. There is no individuality and no individual self. Individual identity is reduced, and becomes identical, to collective identity—defective, unclean, even subhuman.

Despite stigmatization, some people are able to survive psychologically without self-stigmatization—a fascinating subject for study. Their inner sense of self remains healthy, even when their outer social identity is marked with indelible insults. These people are living examples of the resiliency of the human spirit. They also demonstrate why the concept of self, as distinct from that of social identity, is necessary—a point that seems too obvious to make; yet, in cultural contexts clouded with prejudice, it is far from reaching public consciousness.

Delineating the audience. The next step is to delineate the audience or specific group concerned. The audience may comprise members of a clan, institution, or social group, formal or informal. The person may or may not be a member of the group, and no face-to-face interaction is necessary at this stage of analysis. Obviously, however, the person must be known to members of the group; and the person must have some knowledge of how he/she is regarded by the group, if the analysis includes his/her perceptions of how he/she is perceived by the group.

How much face a person has is not fixed in amount, but varies largely according to the audience making a judgment about the target person's face—an important point that has largely escaped due attention by researchers. A different audience, even within the same culture, may attach different weights to differing attributes in face judgments. For instance, an academic community would presumably put more weight on intellectual accomplishment, scholarship, and academic rank, whereas a business community would put more weight on social connections important for the promotion of business activities. In quantitative terms then, face is a composite measure that reflects the relative weights attached to attributes by the audience. This measure serves to locate the individual's position within his/her social network. It should be added, though, that weights attached to intrinsic attributes (classes 7 through 9) are much less likely to vary across audiences than weights attached to extrinsic attributes (classes 1 through 6). That is because intrinsic attributes form the core of the individual's face, regardless of the group by whom it is judged. They reveal what the individual is really like as a person.

Information gathering. In table 1, I summarize the kinds of information that are useful and should be gathered in research studies. (The specific techniques of data gathering, e.g., actual wording of the questions to be asked, need not concern us here.) Let X be the target person and Y be members of the group concerned. The X and the Y within parentheses represent X's and Y's perception (or perspective), respectively. For example, "Perception of X's expectation (Y)" reads as: "Y's Perception of X's expectation."

Derived measures of discrepancies. The information gathered will yield different measures of the target person's face. Measures derived from the information obtained from members of Y are aggregate measures. (Individual variation among

Table 1.   CATEGORIES OF INFORMATION TO BE
OBTAINED FROM X AND FROM Y

	Information to be obtained from X
1. Entitlement (X)	How much face are you entitled to in relation to Y?
2. Actual (X)	How much face do members of Y actually give you?
3. Expectation/ entitlement (Y)	How much face do members of Y think that you expect to receive from them? Or, how much face do members of Y think you are entitled to?
4. Actual (Y)	How much face do members of Y think they actually give you?
5. Perception of X's expectation (Y)	How much face do members of Y think that you think you are entitled to? How do they perceive your expectation/claim?
	Information to be obtained from Y
6. Entitlement (Y)	How much face is X entitled to in relation to Y?
7. Actual (Y)	How much face do members of Y actually give X?
8. Expectation/ entitlement (X)	How much face does X expect/claim from Y? Or, how much face does X think he/she is entitled to receive from Y?
9. Actual (X)	How much face does X think members of Y actually give him or her?
10. Perception of Y's judgment(s) (X)	How much face does X think that members of Y think X is entitled to? How does X perceive Y's judgment(s) of X's expectation/claim, or more generally of X's face?

members of Y need not concern us here.) Of particular theoretical interest are the derived measures: discrepancies as perceived by X, discrepancies as perceived by Y, and discrepancies between perceptions by X and Y. These are summarized in table 2.

We begin with an analysis of the information obtained from X, illustrated with an example. X feels that he/she is entitled to a great deal of face vis-à-vis Y and, therefore, expects to be treated accordingly by members of Y. Discomfort is likely to result when X perceives that they do not give him or her face as expected (1 vs. 2) or, probably worse, do not think that he or she deserves it (1 vs. 3). The discomfort may be reduced if X

Table 2.   DERIVED MEASURES OF DISCREPANCIES

Discrepancies as perceived by X

---

1 vs. 2	Entitlement claimed by X from Y vs. actuality
1 vs. 3	Entitlement claimed by X from Y vs. Y's judgment(s) of X's expectation
1 vs. 4	Entitlement claimed by X from Y vs. Y's perception of actuality
3 vs. 2	Y's judgment(s) of X's expectation vs. actuality
3 vs. 4	Y's judgment(s) of X's expectation vs. Y's perception of actuality
4 vs. 2	Y's perception of actuality vs. actuality

Discrepancies as perceived by Y

---

6 vs. 7	Entitlement accorded X by Y vs. actuality
6 vs. 8	Entitlement accorded X by Y vs. X's expectation
6 vs. 9	Entitlement accorded X by Y vs. X's perception of actuality
8 vs. 7	X's expectation vs. actuality
8 vs. 9	X's expectation vs. X's perception of actuality
9 vs. 7	X's perception of actuality vs. actuality

Discrepancies between perceptions by X and by Y

---

1 vs. 6	X's vs. Y's assessment of X's entitlement
2 vs. 7	X's vs. Y's perception of actuality
3 vs. 6	X's perception of Y's judgment(s) of X's expectation vs. Y's judgment(s) of X's expectation
3 vs. 8	X's perception of Y's judgment(s) of X's expectation vs. Y's perception of X's expectation
4 vs. 9	X's perception of Y's perception of actuality vs. Y's perception of X's perception of actuality
5 vs. 8	X's perception of Y's perception of X's expectation vs. Y's perception of X's expectation

---

perceives that members of Y merely made a misjudgment or social blunder: they thought they gave X more face than X
thought they actually did (1 vs. 4).

A socially sensitive X would also consider how members of
Y perceive his or her expectation/claim (1 vs. 5). Our analysis
would then include X's perception of Y's perception of X's ex-

pectation/claim (5), an instance of what a person thinks others think of him/her. The information obtained from X (5) may be gauged against that obtained from Y on X's expectation/entitlement (8); that is, the derived measure (5 vs. 8) reflects how accurately X perceives Y's perception of how much face X expects from Y.

Similarly, we analyze the information obtained from Y. Members of Y will usually give X the face they consider X is entitled to (6 vs. 7): People generally give—or at least say they would give—as much face to another person as what they feel he/she deserves. However, members of Y may feel that X expects/claims more, or less, than what they think X is entitled to (6 vs. 8), or what X thinks they give him or her in actuality (6 vs. 9). Person X expects more, perhaps because of X's arrogance or exaggerated sense of self-importance. He/she may claim less face, perhaps because of X's humility. In a culture where arrogance is eschewed and humility is held in high esteem, one has to be careful not to appear arrogant, but humble—otherwise, one's face would suffer. Paradoxically, people perceived by others to be claiming more face than is justified weakens their claim, and may even run the risk of losing face. And people perceived to be claiming less than is deserved strengthens their claim and may even gain face. Such people may be said to have understood the underlying principle involved: face is not to be demanded from others; it is given by others and, therefore, the important thing is how others judge you and what they are willing to give you.

We would also include in our analysis Y's perception(s) of how X perceives their judgment(s) of his/her face (6 vs. 10). This is an instance of what other people think a person thinks of their judgment(s) of him/her. Again, the information obtained from Y (10) may be gauged against that obtained from X on Y's judgment(s) of X's expectation/entitlement (3). The derived measure (3 vs. 10) reflects how accurately members of Y perceive X's perception of how much face they think X expects/claims from them.

The next set of comparisons pit the perceptions of X and Y against each other. Derived measures are obtained from comparing the information obtained from X and that from Y. The derived measure (1 vs. 6) reflects the discrepancy between X's and Y's assessments of X's face entitlement in relation to Y; the measure (2 vs. 7) reflects the discrepancy between X's and Y's perceptions of how much face members of Y actually give X;

the measure (3 vs. 8) reflects the discrepancy between X's perception of Y's judgment(s) of X's expectation/entitlement and Y's own perception of X's expectation/entitlement; and the measure (4 vs. 9) reflects the discrepancy between X's and Y's perceptions of each other's perception (i.e., X's perception of Y's perception and Y's perception of X's perception) concerning how much face members of Y actually give X. Finally, the measure (5 vs. 10) reflects the discrepancy between X's perception of Y's perception of X's expectation/entitlement, and Y's perception about X's perception of Y's judgment(s) of X's expectation/entitlement.

The information derived from this set of comparisons enhances an external observer's understanding of the social dynamics involved in measuring X's face in relation to Y. However, it may or may not be known to either of, or both, X and Y. Consider a rather common example, that of a professor who feels that he/she is slighted by his/her students. The office of a professor ordinarily commands respect, and its occupier would have face vis-à-vis an audience of students. In our example, the professor likewise thinks highly of himself/herself, and expects students to give him/her face (1). He/she also assumes that the students understand that he/she has a high expectation (3). Unfortunately, the professor has not taken the students' reactions to his/her high expectation into his/her face calculation (5). In actuality, the professor is judged by students to be undeserving (6)—perhaps on account of being widely suspected to be guilty of sexual harassment, resulting in his/her claim to face being seriously undermined. A comparison of the professor's and the students' perceptions reveals that the professor expects much more from the students than they think he/she is entitled to (1 vs. 6). But the professor is unaware of this discrepancy, on account of his/her overestimating the face that the students think he/she deserves (3 vs. 6). In this way, the professor sets himself/herself up for disappointment, upon discovering that the face he/she receives from the students falls short of expectation (1 vs. 2).

In general, large discrepancies between perceptions of the two interacting parties will act as a source of strain in their relationship. An adequate analysis would, therefore, need to consider not only the perceptions of each party toward the other, but also how accurate and/or congruent these perceptions are.

Conclusion

In analyzing face dynamics, we gain insight into the significance of interrelatedness and interdependence between individuals. Social actions follow not so much from the individual's own inclinations, sentiments, or needs as they do from the individual's perception of his or her relationships with other people—largely conditioned by cultural definitions. The social presence of others, real or imaginary, is always entered into the calculus of social actions. Moreover, this process is bidirectional. One assumes that one's own presence is taken into consideration by others; in the same way one also assumes that others assume that their presence is considered by oneself.

In conclusion, the analysis above, guided by methodological relationalism, serves to illustrate both the richness and the complexity of the face concept; that it is not reducible to other constructs currently employed in the social sciences, such as personality, status, and prestige; and that it is a potent intellectual tool for the analysis of complex social interaction. Clearly, relationalism promises to open a new direction of research into face dynamics, which will, in turn, give substance to the development of relationalism as a viable theoretical position on human behavior.

References

Chu, R. L. (1983). An empirical investigation into psychological and behavioral phenomena related to "face." Ph.D. dissertation, National Taiwan University, Taipei. (In Chinese)

Edelmann, R. J. (1990). Coping with embarrassment and blushing. In J. Anderson (Ed.), Communication yearbook 13. Newbury Park, CA, Sage.

Goffman, E. (1955). On face-work: An analysis of ritual elements in social interaction. Psychiatry, 18, 213–231.

Ho, D. Y. (1976). On the concept of face. American Journal of Sociology, 81, 867–884.

———. (1991). Relational orientation and methodological individualism. Bulletin of the Hong Kong Psychological Society 26/27, 1–15.

Hu, H. C. (1944). The Chinese concepts of "face." American Anthropologist, 46, 45–64.

Leary, M. R., and Kowalski, R. M. (1990). Impression management: A literature review and two-component model. *Psychological Bulletin, 107,* 34–47.

Riesman, D. (1950). *The lonely crowd.* New Haven, CT: Yale University Press.

Ting-Toomey, S. (1988). Intercultural conflict styles: A face-negotiation theory. In Y. Kim and W. Gudukunst (Eds.), *Theories in intercultural communication.* Newbury Park, CA: Sage.

Ting-Toomey, S., and Cole, M. (1990). Intergroup diplomatic communication: A face-negotiation perspective. In F. Korzenny and S. Ting-Toomey (Eds.), *Communication for peace: Diplomacy and negotiation.* Newbury Park, CA: Sage.

Tracy, K. (1990). The many faces of facework. In H. Giles and W. P. Robinson (Eds.), *Handbook of language and social psychology* Chichester, UK: John Wiley.

-10-
The Case for Case Studies of Facework

KAREN TRACY
and
SHERYL BARATZ

Facework has many faces. It can be respectful and deferential; it can be friendly; it can be forthright; it can be hostile. Facework may be oriented to enhancement of the self and/or other; it may be oriented to self-defense and other-attack. (Tracy, 1990, p. 221)

In a review chapter titled "The many faces of facework" (1990), we provided the definitions of face and facework that ground this chapter. As we see it, face is a social phenomenon created through communication when people come into each others' presence. Within this conception, face and facework are highly interdependent constructs. Face refers to the identities people claim or attribute to each other in specific social situations, whereas facework refers to the "communicative strategies that are the enactment, support, or challenge of those situated identities" (Tracy, 1990, p. 210).

Our central purpose in this chapter is to argue for the advantages of studying face and facework using a case study approach. We do so by first contrasting this approach with the politeness-theory approach to facework (Brown & Levinson, 1978, 1987), the face perspective that has most influenced the conceptualization and development of our work. After reviewing politeness theory, and critiquing the main ways scholars have extended Brown and Levinson's work, we highlight the general advantages of approaching the study of face through specific cases. In the second part of the chapter, we illustrate the case study approach, drawing upon our ongoing study of intellectual discussion among faculty and graduate students in

287

academic settings (Tracy & Baratz, 1992; Tracy & Photopoulos, 1991). In the final section, we identify the fundamental challenges facing a case study approach to face and facework.

An Overview of Politeness Theory

Developed by Brown and Levinson (1978, 1987), politeness theory offers a culture and context-general perspective on face. Face, in their theory, refers to the identity or image each person wants to claim in interactions with others and consists of two types. The first type, "positive face" refers to a person's wants to be appreciated and approved of, that is, a person's desire for selected others to regard him or her as competent and likable. The second type, "negative face" refers to a person's want to have his or her autonomy respected and not imposed or infringed upon.

The way people talk in communicative situations, Brown and Levinson (1978, 1987) argue, can be explained by the fact that everyone has these face-wants and simultaneously recognizes that interactional partners have similar wants. Thus, whenever people are performing communicative acts that may threaten a partner's face-wants, they will use linguistic strategies that attend to and attempt to respect part of these wants. For instance, recognition of existing face wants explains why a college student who wanted to borrow a classmate's notes typically would not ask for them baldly ("Lend me your notes, would you?"), but more frequently would ask in a manner that paid attention either to a person's negative face-wants ("Would it be at all possible for me to borrow your notes for just an hour? I'll xerox them and get them back to you right away.") or positive ones ("Jim, good friend, how would you like the opportunity to do a big favor for little old me? Can I borrow your notes?").

In a nutshell, politeness theory seeks to explain why speakers select the particular facework strategies they do. That is, it seeks to explain why a speaker would use a positive politeness strategy (orientation to positive face) rather than a negative politeness, baldly stated, or indirect one. According to politeness theory, strategy selection will depend on the relative face-threat of the communicative act that a speaker is considering performing, where the face-threat is not inherent in the act but influenced by three situational factors: (1) the social distance between speaker and recipient; (2) the relative power of the speaker compared to the recipient; and (3) the degree of imposition of an act. In essence, the greater the social distance, the larger the relative power of the speaker over the recipient; and the bigger the imposition of an act, the more face-threatening a communicative act will be. Communicative acts that are highly other face-threatening will be carried out using facework strategies that are highly face-supportive, such as negative politeness, as opposed to ones that are less face-supportive (positive politeness or bald-on-record acts).

Brown and Levinson (1978, 1987) maintain that while instantiation of their three situational variables are culturally influenced, the relationship between the face-threat of an act and the selected strategy is universal. This means, for instance, that while one culture may see a teacher speaking to a student as a relationship in which the speaker has high power over a listener, and another may see that same relationship is one of modest power difference, across cultures wherever there is a large power difference, speakers will use similar strategies.

Critique of Politeness Theory

Since its inception, politeness theory has garnered considerable empirical and analytic attention, providing the central theoretical touchstone for researchers interested in connecting face-concerns to interactive talk. Brown and Levinson's (1978) theory makes sense of a wide range of linguistic phenomena that had seemed unexplainable. By linking discourse markers to facework, their theory made language central to the study of face. It highlighted the notion that one's identity is *not* merely in the head; facework is conducted through talk. Undoubtedly, politeness theory has functioned as this theoretical touchstone, because it is formulated as a universal theory, applicable to all contexts and cultures. Such a universal formulation provides a ready theoretical foil for whatever a researcher observes in a particular culture and context, an advantage if the theory provides a good description. An obvious concern, then, is the degree to which politeness theory has provided a reasonable description of facework processes.

Research using and assessing the theory can be divided in two camps: studies which call for revisions and/or extensions to the current model and studies which call for abandoning

Brown and Levinson's (1978) framework entirely. Revisionists, for instance, have advocated that politeness theory needs to reconceptualize: (1) the way social distance affects the face-threat of an act (Brown & Gilman, 1989; Slugoski & Turnbull; 1988); (2) the nature of positive politeness (Lim & Bowers, 1991); (3) the salience of speaker-oriented face-strategies (Penman, 1990) and salient third parties (Aronsson & Rundstrom, 1989; Penman, 1990); and (4) the expected relationship between the occurrence of positive and negative face-strategies (Aronsson & Saterlund-Larson, 1987; Myers, 1989; Penman, 1990). Each revision taken individually seems modest, but when viewed collectively, they call into question the value of proceeding within the politeness theory framework.

In line with several others (Coupland, Grainger, & Coupland, 1988; Hymes, 1982; Katriel, 1986; Tracy, 1990) we think it is time to abandon Brown and Levinson's (1978) framework entirely. Besides the ever-increasing list of needed revisions, there are two other factors that point to the need for a new theoretical and methodological approach to face.

First, if we view the goal of theory as helping us understand what is going on interactionally rather than predicting facework strategy use by situational factors, then it seems obvious that politeness theory cannot do a good job. The current model forces researchers a priori to impose face-concerns on interactants. While it may in fact be the case that interactants in a given setting are orienting to the two types of face-concerns dictated by Brown and Levinson's (1978, 1987) theory, it is likely, as pointed out by Tracy (1990), that participants' concerns about identity will be much more specific to the context of a given interaction. In other words, dividing face-concerns into positive and negative face is but one way of dividing the pie, and this way may be irrelevant to the talk in a given context. For example, imagine a woman trying to carry several heavy packages as her friend walks by. In this situation the woman may want to be seen as helpless or unable to handle herself and the packages in order that the friend will offer to help her with the packages. She may not be concerned about appearing competent or getting respect.

It may also be the case that the framing of face-concerns (e.g., positive face as defined as the desire to be seen as desirable and competent) may be too general to capture the face-concern most central to an interactant. This same woman in an interaction with her daughter's teacher may want to be seen as a good mother, while at her league basketball game she may want to be seen as a good athlete. To say that in both these situations, this woman wanted to be seen as competent glosses over the important differences between what it means to be seen as a good mother and what is involved in being seen as a good athlete.

Thus, Brown and Levinson's model (1978) is built around preconceived categories of face-concerns which are presumed to be universally-relevant. This premise detracts from the potential value of the theory because it forces researchers to ignore what may be the central face-concerns for the individuals in the interactions.

Second, Brown and Levinson's (1978) type of model cannot take into account the situated nature of facework. As a theoretical model, it decontextualizes individual utterances and facework strategies, and promotes the assumption that the relationship between discourse strategies and face concerns is universally fixed and unproblematic. Craig and colleagues (1986) first pointed out that "the assessment of an act's face threat is highly context-dependent" (p. 463), using the example of being asked to type a paper in two different settings. They argue that according to Brown and Levinson's (1978) model, one cannot explain the difference in the significance of typing a paper when a boss asks his/her secretary from when a professor asks a student. If we assume that power and social distance are equal, how can we understand the difference in the rank of imposition when the request is the same? Essentially, Brown and Levinson's model leads researchers to assess acts (in terms of their threat to face) out of their context.

In their model, Brown and Levinson (1978) describe the linguistic output devices that serve to maintain positive and negative face. These linguistic strategies, however, are often described as discursive markers, which when added to the talk, serve one particular function—all the time. As Coupland and colleagues (1988) pointed out in their analysis of nurses' talk to elderly patients at a long-stay hospital, the positive and negative politeness markers used by nurses do not actually serve the same functions that Brown and Levinson claim these markers will serve. Thus the nurse's reference to the drink as "little" (a negative politeness marker serving to minimize the imposition), "does not necessarily impinge upon the patient's perception of the extent of the imposition" (p. 261). In fact, they argue, "at a deeper level of analysis, such orientations in talk are more rather than less likely to impose and threaten face, more fundamentally" (p. 261).

In addition to the problem of ignoring the potential for multifunctionality of these markers, as pointed out by Baxter (1984) and Craig and colleagues (1986), other researchers' findings (Coupland et al., 1988; Penman, 1990) have indicated that a given linguistic device may serve different functions in different settings when used at different times or when repeated more than once.

Brown and Levinson's (1978) model, according to Hymes (1982) and Katriel (1986), also has serious limitations in terms of its sensitivity to the level of cultural meanings. Katriel shows through her analysis of *dugri* speech in Israeli Sabra culture that *dugri* speakers "interpret the interactional dance Goffman refers to as 'facework' within a culture specific framework in which respect and not considerateness is the issue" (p. 47). *Dugri* speech, Katriel explains, is speaker-focused and shows great concern for one's autonomy or what one owes him/herself, which in *dugri* is speaking one's mind. It also, however, shows a concern for identification which according to Hymes (1982) is other-focused, that is, on union. Interactants share a relationship in which it is appropriate to speak *dugri*. Framed this way, it might be said that *dugri* is to the Sabras what indirectness is to Americans, namely the way we balance the conflicting needs for involvement and independence (Tannen, 1986). Indirectness, however, in *dugri* speech is highly avoided and interpreted negatively. As such, it appears that the hierarchy of strategies illustrated by Brown and Levinson's model does not effectively capture the complex relationship between *dugri* speech and face in this culture. These findings call into question the starting assumption that the relationship between discourse strategies and face are fixed.

Our position need not to be construed simply as viewing interpretive goals of social science as better than predictive and explanatory ones. In fact, we are arguing that a solid understanding of facework is required for both sorts of goals. In order to develop a clearer sense of facework, then, we are proposing a case study approach to face which will take account of the socially situated nature of identity. Based on the existing body of literature on face and politeness, we have learned that people put forth claims about their own and each other's identity as they communicate with others, and that these claims are challenged, supported, and negotiated in interaction with others.

A case study approach would enable researchers to develop a better understanding of the following: How do interactants in a particular setting want to be seen or *not* want to be seen? How do these interactants get this across or try to get this across? What is the relationship between certain communicative behaviors and attributions of identity? What misunderstandings, problems, and/or contradictions arise in the setting that relate to facework?

Case Study Approach to Face:
An Overview

The case study approach calls for qualitative methods applied to naturally occurring interactions. It can be distinguished from other approaches in terms of three features: (1) the end-goal of the research; (2) the selection of what to study; and (3) the investigative procedures used.

The end-goal of case study research is to unpack a complex interesting case. We assume that if we do it well, it may not only shape our scholarly discussions about communication issues but the conduct of the communicative activities we study. We *do not* accept as an end-goal that research should be seeking to create increasingly abstract ideas capable of explaining communicative action in all contexts and cultures.

Selection of what to study is guided by practical and intellectual interests. Stated at its simplest, a researcher must determine what real-world situation deserves detailed attention. For instance, the decision to study the faculty-student colloquia, described in the section below, arose out of our own interest in intellectual communicative situations that people experienced as problematic. The decision stemmed from a sense that intellectual talk was interesting and not easily describable, and a belief that the event was consequential for the degree to which individuals were evaluated as successful academics and intellectuals. Our case selection then, while shaped by communicative ideas and issues we found interesting, was not primarily theoretically-driven.

The final feature of our case study approach is its investigative procedures. In general thrust, the research can be characterized as "theoretically influenced induction." Thus, we use our grounding in communication writings to identify activities and issues in this particular case that might be generally interesting. Data sources such as interviews, audiotapes of interactions at the setting, and field notes taken by participant-observers are useful in analyzing a setting. Ethnographic, conversation analytic, and discourse analytic methods may each be used to highlight various aspects of facework.

Exemplar: Intellectual Discussion at State U

Background
"State U" is a large urban university on the east coast, In the communication department, which was the focus of our study, weekly colloquia are held. The typical colloquium format involved a presenter speaking for approximately forty-five minutes followed by an equally long discussion period. The work presented in the weekly colloquia varied from papers in the beginning stages to already published work. Participants were primarily graduate students and faculty from the department, but visitors from other departments and universities also attended. Attendance was voluntary, varying from 10–25 participants. Doctoral students were expected to make one presentation at the colloquium.

In addition to participating in this group for an extended amount of time, we collected audiotapes of colloquia over an eighteen-month time period, took extensive field notes, and conducted ten in-depth interviews. The discourse of the interview transcripts was analyzed to uncover what participants' face-concerns were (see Tracy & Baratz, 1992 for details about setting and analytic method).

Summary of Case Study Findings
The participants in the colloquium understood the group's goals in similar ways and repeatedly identified two purposes. Participants saw the central purposes of the group as fostering idea development and developing and maintaining intellectual community. Against the backdrop of these group-level goals, individual participants brought self-specific face-concerns.

One of the most noticeable concerns of individual participants was to be seen as intellectually competent. In response to a question about likely face-concerns, a faculty member and graduate student said the following:

Extract 1
I think there's a concern about appearing intelligent, appearing like you know you're doing something worthwhile and that you're doing a fairly good job of it. (Faculty)

Extract 2
Whether what I have to say is worth saying, is important, ah what, "so what" is the big question. (Graduate student)

A prominent face-concern, then, was to appear intellectually competent. Another concern that co-existed with this one, although not acknowledged in a straightforward way, was a concern to be *not* seen as trying to be seen as smart. Put somewhat differently, while people wanted to be seen as smart they wanted to avoid appearing as if they were concerned about displaying their smartness. This second concern was one that participants did not claim for themselves but was visible in their implied criticisms of others' actions. For instance, when asked if colloquium served unofficial purposes, one participants said:

Extract 3
Well, I suppose there are individual agendas . . . , ways of showing how bright and knowledgeable and incisive they are.

For this situation, then, a central face-concern of participants was to be seen as intellectually able without being seen as a show-off or overly concerned with displaying intellectual ability.

To claim this face successfully, participants' communicative moves had to take account of three aspects of the other to whom a comment might be directed: (1) whether the person was inside or outside the department group, (2) his or her institutional status, and (3) the person's characteristic ability to "take it." The relationship between these factors and how a person should talk to enact the desired face was a complex one. At the simplest level, it seemed that when the presenter was a member of the group, the higher in status the presenter was, and the more he or she could "take it," the more strongly a person should work to challenge the recipient. The difficulty was, however, that while rank was a relatively easy judgment call, ability was not. When participants were required to make judgments about other's ability and deciding what to say, they have the choice of giving strong, tough criticism and with it the implication that the other was seen as intellectually and interactively able.

This view of criticism contrasts with the everyday notion of criticism as an act that is inherently face-threatening as well as the view articulated in politeness theory (Brown & Levinson, 1987). Brown and Levinson argue that when a person gives tough criticism to someone, she/he is questioning that person's competence and thereby threatening his/her positive face. In this community, however, the understanding of criticism was not so straightforward. Not only was criticism often *not* viewed as face-threatening, it was viewed as suggesting that the other *was* competent and intellectually able. Therefore, in this community, criticism could be a face-supportive move. It was also the case that asking tough questions had identity implications for self as well as the person questioned. One faculty member, in commenting on the judgments he made about others, said:

Extract 4
I see them reacting to things; I think the way they react to issues is a pretty good clue to how they think, to what their interests are.

In this setting specifically, participants who asked tough and challenging questions were often seen as smart and competent. However, when the asking of tough questions lead to someone being humiliated, the question-asker could be seen as self-aggrandizing and into unwarranted egoism. At the same time, asking nice questions which might seem to solve the "ego" problem potentially suggest that the *other* had limited ability and should be handled gently. In addition, the questioner might be seen as less intellectually able and unconcerned about intellectual standards.

The communicative problem left for any speaker in this setting then was to adequately judge the other's status and ability and then to design their questions and comments in such ways that they were seen as appropriate or reasonable.

Analysis of the audiotaped interactions, did, in fact reveal noticeable differences in the "toughness" of the comments and questions. On the one end were questions that asked for repetition or nonthreatening information:

Extract 5
In the work that you did on checking to verify the Rogers and
Farace's scheme, could you say it again, I think you said it
near the end but I didn't quite catch it. How did people's interpretations map against the claims they were making?

On the other, were comments which asserted that the presenter was not carrying out the basic task that presenters had.
Comments that accused the presenter of having "no news"
functioned this way:

Extract 6
I noticed that most of the literature that you review is from
the eighties (uh huh) and some of it goes back to the seven-
ties, but nothing goes back to the ancient period of the fifties
(group laughter). There's some rhetoric that you go back
2,500 years and we think that's just the beginning. Uh, there
does seem to be a neglect of origins here and I'm wondering
whether or not it's any different. . . . Are the research questions any different?. . . . Didn't we have a human relations
model back in the fifties? Well, what's new here since Roeth-
lisberger and Rogers? What's new in the way of these variables? We're hearing the same stuff.

A comment that asserts that the speaker's talk has "no news"
can be seen as challenging whether the presenter has met the
minimum situational expectations to present an idea of his or
her own. Such a challenge must be clearly dealt with if the person is to avoid being seen as incompetent. The challenge is a
tough one but if it is successfully countered, it is likely to be
strong support for the presenter's claim to be intellectually able.
    Someplace in the middle of the toughness continuum were
comments that use discourse work to identify the reasonableness of the speaker's position before explicitly disagreeing with
it. Such a move is illustrated in a faculty member's comment to
a graduate student presenter.

Extract 7
Uh, this is kind of following, I guess you could see it as following Ted's question about perceptions. Uh, using perceptions as the gauge or measure of competence, that seems to
be a pretty common move these days in writing about communicative competence, to write about it as a perception or
judgment or something. Uh, there are a couple of things

about that that bother me. One is. . . . Uh that winds up being a fairly long speech but the point is, to, it seems to me
that it all kind of converges to raise a question about whether
it makes sense fundamentally to see competence as a matter
of assessments or judgments or perceptions.

Comments that begin by identifying the reasonableness of another's position may seem more supportive of the presenter's
claim to be intellectually able than a "no news" kind of move.
But, we would argue, it depends on the identity of the other. If
the other is of high institutional rank or ability, prefacing a disagreement with explicit support of the reasonableness of the
other's position, may be seen as, or meant as, a condescending,
nonpositive assessment of the presenter's intellectual skill. If
the other were a novice, such conversational moves might be
expected and seen as appropriate.

It was also the case that presenters did work in their opening comments to claim a particular level of intellectual competence. In the face claimed through their opening comments,
speakers could be seen as instructing others as to why they
were and how they were to be treated in the questioning period. In making their initial identity claim, speakers faced a
dilemma. If a speaker claimed high ability level, he or she
implicitly licensed the most difficult of questions and potentially risked discrediting his or her initial claim. On the other
hand, if a speaker claimed a more limited ability level (a less
desirable identity), he or she decreased the likelihood of being asked questions he or she could not answer well. As with
most facework, the establishment of a face was done through
implication.

Claims to a high level of intellectual competence were made
when speakers referred to large amounts of time and energy invested in the project about which they were speaking ("This
book was based on research I was involved in while still a graduate student and then a postdoctoral at Indiana University, uh
where we had a major grant to do a study . . ."). It was also
done by referencing socially valued by-products of involvement
with ideas such as books or grants.

More modest claims were visible when presenters described
their work drawing upon temporal and spatial metaphors that
suggested their involvement with the ideas had only been for a
short time ("a pilot study," "in the beginning stages," "in
progress") or that the ideas were tangential to self's main concerns ("a spin-off of," "a tangent to the main project").

Finally, at the other end were opening comments which marked the presenter as far removed from the ideas he or she was talking about. Most typically this was done indirectly, and almost always by novices (graduate students). Consider what one graduate student said in her opening comments in the presentation she used to satisfy the departmental requirement for Ph.D. students.

> Extract 8
> Thank you Rich, uh first of all I'd like to begin by thanking the faculty for reviewing my manuscript and giving me so many nice criticisms and suggestions (group laughter). Uh, I know it's your job (group laughter) but I also know that my paper came at the time. . . . I hope that I've addressed your criticisms and suggestions as best as I can.

Notable in this opening is a sense that the presenter sees herself as completing a task given to her by someone else where she is trying to meet their specifications. This is especially highlighted by her referencing the obligations in the faculty-student role—faculty are required to give feedback; students are expected to use it to improve. This task framing, while not an unreasonable assumption in the situation, de-emphasizes the student's own investment in the ideas. Thus, while it seems plausible that the student's main motive in creating such a distance between self and ideas was to instruct discussants to be gentle in their questioning and minimize the impact of whatever criticism was made, the moves simultaneously mark her as a novice, someone not involved with ideas in the ways expected of an academic (see Tracy and Photoupolus, 1991 for more detail).

To summarize, our study of State U revealed participants to be concerned that others see them as intellectually able (or at least not intellectually limited), while at the same time not wanting to be seen as overly concerned with displaying intellectual ability. Participants used opening remarks, comments, and questions as a central vehicle to enact their own desired face; these conversational moves simultaneously had implications for the other, and sometimes nonintended implications for their own.

Beyond this State U Case

Based on study of this case, we (Tracy & Baratz, 1992) offered a model of one part of the identity-attribution process operat-

Table 1.   THE ATTRIBUTION PROCESS IN
INTELLECTUAL DISCUSSIONS

Comment-Response Assessments			Intellectual Attributions	
Comment Difficulty	Comment Fairness	Response	Discussant	Presenter
(1) tough	fair	adequate	"able"	"able"
(2) tough	unfair	adequate	"able" "self-serving"	"able"
(3) tough	fair	inadequate	"able"	"limited"
(4) tough	unfair	inadequate	"able" "self-serving"	indeterminate
(5) easy		adequate	"limited" or indeterminate	indeterminate
(6) easy		inadequate	indeterminate or "limited"	"limited"

ing generally in intellectual discussions. The model is an attempt to extrapolate from this particular case to a broader description of facework processes in intellectual discussion. We think that what we have observed in this one department may be generalizable to many intellectual discussion situations in higher education. The focus of the model is on discussions among academics (professors and graduate students) where one person has presented his/her ideas to a group of peers (and near-peers).

How we ask, do participants in such discussions arrive at judgments about the intellectual ability of the presenter (the recipient of questions and comments) and the others who make comments and ask questions (potentially anybody in the group)? The model is built on the assumption that talk has simultaneous implications for both presenters' and respondents' faces, although not always equally (table 1).

We suggest that when observers make attributions about presenters and discussants, they first make judgments about the questions or comments and their response. Judgments about comments and responses provide the scaffolding upon which inferences about the presenter and discussant abilities are made. In particular, three judgments are made about questions and responses.

The first judgment by observers is about the difficulty of the question asked or the comment that must be responded to. That is, how easy or tough is the question? How much does the comment require? If a comment is assessed as difficult, a second judgment is made: Is the comment fair? While the assessment of question difficulty is tied primarily to topical knowledge and the complexity of the thinking level inherent in the question, the judgment of fairness is made by considering whether there is a reasonable match between the socially understood identity of the recipient and the assessed "toughness" of the comment. The final judgment observers make is of the adequacy of the response to the question or comment. A judgment that a recipient has responded adequately is an assessment that he or she has responded to the comment/question suitably.

Judgments about these three issues become the basis upon which attributions are made about the discussant's and the presenter's intellectual identities. Table 1 summarizes the process. If a question is posed (1) that is perceived to be tough and fair, and the response is adequate then both the discussant and the presenter are seen to be intellectually able. Discussion however, does not always proceed as smoothly as identified in scenario 1. Not all comments are tough and fair; not all responses are adequate. In all the other cases, a negative attribution is made about one or both parties. If the response to a difficult comment is perceived as adequate, but the comment is judged unfair (2), then while both parties will be seen as intellectually able, the discussant will also be seen as self-serving, a person who is trying to look smart, potentially, at the other person's expense. If the question/comment is perceived tough and fair, but the response is inadequate (3), then the presenter will be seen as possessing intellectual limitations. When the response to a tough question or comment is inadequate, but the question is judged unfair (4), intellectual attributions will not be made about the recipient.

Finally, consider what happens when an easy-to-deal-with comment is made. The first thing to note is that fairness becomes irrelevant; only when a comment is difficult does it make sense to inquire whether it is fair. If an easy comment is addressed adequately (5), the attributional picture is the most complex. It may be that the discussant is unable to pose a more complex or demanding question, "intellectually limited." Yet it could also be the case that the discussant could but has chosen not to because of concerns about embarrassing the other. If an observer judges the discussant to be motivated by other-concern, then a judgment will not be made about the asker's intellectual ability. For the recipient, addressing easy comments adequately says little about his or her intellectual ability. It could be that the recipient could not handle anything more difficult, but it could also be that the asker cannot pose anything more difficult.

The last case is when a comment that is perceived to be easy is addressed inadequately (6). Here, the strongest attribution about the recipient's intellectual limitations are undoubtedly made. Attributions about the discussant may be indeterminate or, possibly, limited. In both scenarios 5 and 6, it is possible for either no judgments to be made or the discussant to be judged as limited. While we think the attributions can go either way in each situation, there is a slightly different bias in each. When a response is inadequate to an easy question or comment, it heightens the possibility that the question asker was "trying to be nice." Thus, it seems more likely that a discussant will be judged limited when an easy question elicits an adequate response than when it does not.

Advantages to the Case Study Approach

The first advantage of the case study approach is that the emphasis is on the identification of specific face concerns as they are oriented to by participants in a setting. Face concerns are meaningless if they are not seen as relevant to interactants in a given context. In the colloquium at State U, participants expressed their concerns to be seen as intellectually able and to *not* be seen as trying to be seen as smart. We were able to come to understand these face concerns through analysis of the interview transcripts.

A second advantage of this approach is the expansion in scope of facework strategies and the more thorough analysis of the not-so-straightforward nature of the functions of these strategies. For example, a participant's choice to give strong, tough criticism carried with it the implication that the other was seen as intellectually, interactively able; it also implied that the participant was intellectually able, and under certain circumstances, self-aggrandizing. Similarly, the giving of "easy" criticism had several possible face implications. It could mean that the discussant was a novice or possessed a low level of intellectual ability; it could also mean that the discussant was a thoughtful person working to avoid humiliating the other, who appeared to have limited intellectual competence.

The facework strategies identified as significant in this setting were not at the level of markers added to the discourse, as is the case with politeness strategies. Rather, the strategies which impacted most for participants were at the level of the choice of act, more specifically the choice of question or comment type. As this study illustrates, tough questions do not always carry the same face implications for speaker or discussant. In sum, the case study approach resists the tendency to oversimplify—a tendency fostered when research begins with an overarching theoretical framework—and fosters the goal of achieving a detailed understanding of the situationally relevant facework strategies.

A third advantage yielded by this approach to face is that it enables researchers to gain a better understanding of how participants in a setting come to make attributions of identity. In particular, the open-ended interviews allowed us to uncover the dimensions of judgment people routinely use in the situation. In addition, the in-depth familiarity with the situation, acquired through participant observation, permits the case study researcher to unpack the relationship between identity attributions and the situational factors and actions that create them.

Major Challenges

Theories of facework, we argue, must be built from the ground up. We must avoid prematurely developing abstract general theories to insure that we capture what is most important and interesting about the interactions studied. For this reason, we have argued for an abandonment of Brown and Levinson's (1978, 1987) framework and the use of a case study approach. The major challenge the case study approach faces is the building of links among cases. There is undoubtedly a potential within the case study approach for individual cases to stand as isolated units, disconnected from broader communicative issues. This is something the case study approach must work to overcome. We need to build middle-range, domain-specific theories if we are to advance our understanding of face and facework. The model of the identity-attribution process described in this chapter is a first step. It needs, however, to be reexamined following study of other intellectual discussion cases. Does the model apply to all academic disciplines? Does it apply to discussion where no one person is presenting? Does it apply to mediated discussion such as on computer hot-line? Does it apply to nonacademic discussion in a book club or film society? Does it apply in non-U.S. cultures? Extending the scope of the case and reconsidering the broader facework processes are two important next steps.

References

Aronsson, K., and Rundstrom, B. (1989). Cats, dogs, and sweets in the clinical negotiation of reality: On politeness and coherence in pediatric discourse. *Language in Society, 18,* 483–504.

Aronsson, K., and Satterlund-Larsson, U. (1987). Politeness strategies and doctor-patient communication: On the social choreography of collaborative thinking. *Journal of Language and Social Psychology, 6,* 1–28.

Baxter, L. A. (1984). An investigation of compliance-gaining as politeness. *Human Communication Research, 10,* 427–456.

Brown, R., and Gilman, A. (1989). Politeness theory and Shakespeare's four major tragedies. *Language in Society, 18,* 159–212.

Brown, P., and Levinson, S. C. (1978). Universals in language usage: Politeness phenomena. In E. N. Goody (Ed.), *Questions and politeness: Strategies in social interaction.* Cambridge: Cambridge University Press.

———. (1987). *Universal in language usage: Politeness phenomena.* Cambridge: Cambridge University Press.

Coupland, N., Grainger, K., and Coupland, J. (1988). Politeness in context: Intergenerational issues. *Language in Society, 17,* 253–262.

Craig, R. T., Tracy, K., and Spisak, F. (1986). The discourse of requests: Assessment of a politeness approach. *Human Communication Research, 12,* 437–468.

Hymes, D. (1982). *Ethnolinguistic study of discourse in the classroom.* Final report to the National Institute of Education: University of Pennsylvania.

Katriel, T. (1986). *Talking straight: Dugri speech in Israeli Sabra Culture.* London: Cambridge University Press.

Lim, T., and Bowers, J. W. (1991). Facework, solidarity, approbation and tact. *Human Communication Research, 17,* 415–450.

Myers, G. (1989). The pragmatics of politeness in scientific articles. *Applied Linguistics, 10,* 1–35.

Penman, R. (1990). Facework and politeness: Multiple goals in courtroom discourse. *Journal of Language and Social Psychology, 9,* 15–38.

Slugoski, B. R., and Turnbull, W. (1988). Cruel to be kind and kind to be cruel: Sarcasm, banter, and social relations. *Journal of Language and Social Psychology, 7,* 101–121.

Tannen, D. (1986). *That's not what I meant!* New York: William Morrow.

Tracy, K. (1990). The many faces of facework. In H. Giles and P. Robinson (Eds.), *Handbook of language and social psychology.* Chichester, UK: John Wiley.

Tracy, K., and Baratz, S. (1992). Face concerns and attributions in intellectual discussion. Paper presented to the annual meeting of the International Communication Association, Miami.

Tracy, K., and Photopoulos, J. (1991). Identify enactment in intellectual discussion. Paper presented to the 4th International Conference on Language and Social Psychology, Santa Barbara, CA.

-11-
Face and Facework:
Theoretical and Research Issues

STELLA TING-TOOMEY
and
BETH-ANN COCROFT

Face is an intoxicating metaphor that connects communication with social life. It is a multifaceted construct that takes on dimensions of identity issues, social cognitive issues, affective issues, and communication issues. It is a construct that captivates the interest of scholars from diverse disciplines.

The objective of this chapter is twofold: (1) to explore the role of culture in face and facework interaction, and (2) to map out some issues and directions for future researching into face and facework process.

Culture, Face, and Facework

In order to address some of the conceptual difficulties involved when examining face and facework in different cultures, the role of culture in face conceptualizations and specific facework enactment strategies are reviewed in this section. While authors have reviewed selective conceptualizations of face or facework schemata, this section provides an overview and an extension of some of the existing approaches to face and facework strategies.

The Role of Culture in Face Conceptualizations

According to Ho (1976), face is inherently interactional and is only meaningful when perceived in relation to others. It is through communication behavior, called facework, .that face is negotiated. For example, Ho (1976) argues that in most cases face loss can be restored. Communication provides the means through which face can be restored. A clear working conceptualization of face is important because how the domain of face is specified will affect how facework strategies are conceived and interpreted. Thus, face and facework are closely interlinked and inseparable. The meaning of face has profound influence on the conceptual and operational dimensions of facework enactment strategies. Face constitutes the ritualistic basis of everyday social interaction.

As Ho (1976) states, "it is virtually impossible to think of a facet of social life to which the question of face is irrelevant" (p. 883). A construct with such widespread heuristic value deserves systematic scrutiny. Furthermore, facework researchers argue that the construct of face exists in all cultures (Brown & Levinson, 1978; Goffman, 1971; Hill, Ide, Ikuta, Kawasaki, & Ogino, 1986; Ho, 1976; Hu, 1944; Ting-Toomey, 1988). We must understand the basic conceptualization of face before we can understand how face is enacted and invoked in different cross-cultural interpersonal settings.

According to Hu (1944) and Ho (1976), the concept of face originated with the Chinese. Hu describes two Chinese conceptualizations of face—*lien* and *mien-tzu. Lien* is "the confidence of society in the moral character of ego" (p. 61), while *mien-tzu* refers to identity-related interaction across time. According to Ho, *lien* is "something to which everyone is entitled by virtue of his [or her] membership in society and can be lost only through unacceptable conduct" (p. 870). *Mien-tzu*, however, is more dependent on social interaction and varies according to the social situation of the interaction. For example, if an individual was sent to prison for robbery, he or she would lose *lien* face; if, however, an individual was not properly deferential toward an elder, he or she would lose *mien-tzu* face. Thus, while *lien* is a prescribed concept, *mien-tzu* is a dynamic, interactive construct. Ho argues that the conceptualization of *mien-tzu* face is interactional because face is closely related to social expectations as enacted through communicative performance. As Ho suggests, the possibility of losing face (i.e., *mien-tzu*) can be a result of an individual's failure to communicate in accordance with the expectations of others. Ho (1976) provides the following conceptualization of face:

> Face is the respectability and/or deference which a person can claim for himself [or herself] from others, by virtue of the relative position he [or she] occupies in his [or her] social net-

work and the degree to which he [or she] is judged to have
functioned adequately in that position as well as acceptability
in his [or her] general conduct. . . . Face is the reciprocated
compliance, respect, and/or deference that each party expects
from, and extends to, the other party. (p. 883)

Face, as described by Ho (1976), is inherently social because it
is dependent upon the perceptions of other people. In addition,
Ho argues that people in all cultures value pride, honor, and
dignity. They wish to avoid embarrassment, maintain self-
respect, and project a positive self-image in social interaction.

Indeed, people in all cultures internalize the mutual support of face. Failure by individuals to mutually support each
other's face may result in face loss and embarrassment. Ritualistic everyday politeness is one mechanism of mutual face-
support. The notion of face as interactional is also evident in
Western conceptualizations.

Western researchers such as Goffman (1959) have offered
definitions of face which are influenced by the Chinese conceptualization. Goffman (1959) described face as something that
can be lost, maintained, or enhanced. According to Goffman,
face is "the positive social value a person effectively claims for
himself [or herself] by the line others assume he [or she] has
taken during a particular contact" (p. 213). Goffman defines a
line as "a pattern of verbal and non-verbal acts by which he [or
she] expresses his [or her] evaluation of the participants, especially himself [or herself]" (p. 213). According to Goffman, during social interactions, one protects self- and other-face.
Goffman points out that facework is an attempt to defend one's
self-face when it is threatened.

Holtgraves (1992) concurs with Goffman's (1959, 1967)
conceptualization of face when he argues that face, by its very
basic nature, is a social rather than a psychological construct. In addition, he observes that while face "involves self-
presentation, face is not the same as situated identity. . . .
Rather, face is a more basic and more abstract construct that is
entailed in the projection of any identity or line. Insofar as one
successfully projects *any* identity, one can be said to have face"
(p. 142). He continues:

Face, therefore, is not an objective of interaction but rather a
condition for interaction, or a ritual constraint. Moreover, because face (and deference) can be given only by others, it is in

each other person's best interest to maintain the other's face. Acting with demeanor (supporting one's own face) entails acting with deference to the other (supporting the other's face); hence threats to another's face become threats to one's own face. Thus, although insults, challenges, and so on occur, facework is (and must be) a cooperative venture. (p 142)

Holtgraves' concept of ritual constraint closely echoes that of Penman's (this volume) concept of social order. In addition, his emphasis on how face is "given by others" closely resembles that of Lim's (this volume) concept of claimed sense of public image. Finally, his concept of deference-demeanor is similar to Penman's (this volume) respect-contempt dimension of face. Face is, in essence, a cooperative discourse game with ad infinitum rules. These rules, however, are grounded in the sociocultural norms of the speech community.

From the politeness-theory approach, Brown and Levinson (1978, 1987) conceptualize face as the public image that everyone wants to claim. Face is a pancultural phenomenon. Facework strategies are also thought to contain "negative face" and "positive face" dimensions. Negative face refers to the need for autonomy and the desire not to be imposed on by others. Positive face refers to the need for approval, inclusion, social validation, and the need to be held in positive regard by others. In addition, they propose that the amount of face-threat carried by a particular speech act in a particular situation is a function of the social distance between the interactants, the power distance, and the normal or absolute imposition inherent to the speech act.

While Brown and Levinson (1978) have presented an original linguistic model to conceptualize face and facework, their work has been challenged by researchers such as Baxter (1984), Coupland, Grainger, and Coupland (1988), Craig, Tracy, and Spisak (1986), O'Keefe (1992), Hymes (1986), Lim and Bowers (1991), Matsumoto (1988), Penman (1990, 1991), and Tracy (1990). The criticisms include the problem of unit of analysis, the multifunctional nature of a speech act, the use of the unfortunate "negative face" and "positive face" labels, the unidimensional nature of the face propositions, the avoidance-approach distinction concerning negative face and positive face, the oversight on self-concern and other-concern issue, and the limited explanatory power of the model.

On a more specific level of critique, the universality of Brown and Levinson's (1978) notion of negative face (the need to be free from imposition) has been disputed. Matsumoto (1988), for example, in reviewing countless studies on Japanese society and culture, concludes that Brown and Levinson's concept of negative face is not relevant to Japanese culture. According to Matsumoto the most important concern for a Japanese is his or her position relative to members of the in-group and the responsive acceptance by members of the in-group. As Matsumoto argues, the desire for acceptance is instilled into Japanese children at a very young age. Consequently, "one's commitment to the social structure and to the other members of a group is so strong that one's actions become meaningful and comprehended only in relation to others" (Matsumoto, 1988, p. 408). In comparing Matsumoto's perspective with Ho's (this volume) viewpoint on face, Ho would probably concur with Matsumoto's point concerning the important of social hierarchical position in governing face-claim. However, Morisaki and Gudykunst (this volume) would refute the notion of autonomy face or negative face not existing in the Japanese culture. According to Morisaki and Gudykunst's perspective, autonomy face, for the Japanese, exists on the in-group/out-group dimension rather than on the interindividual, self/other dimension. In addition, the concept of imposition/nonimposition takes on long-term reciprocal obligations rather than stands as a situated, interactive construct.

Furthermore, Matsumoto (1988) also discusses problems with some of Brown and Levinson's (1978) strategies of negative politeness. Matsumoto explains that to a Japanese hearer, the English example (e.g., "it's not much, it's just a little thing I picked up in a bargain basement sale in Macy's last week. I though maybe you could use it") provided by Brown and Levinson sounds rude and insulting, rather than deferential. Matsumoto explains that the primary value of the Japanese politeness system is to recognize the interpersonal relation. Thus, Matsumoto concludes by stating, "in the absence of emphasis of what Brown and Levinson call 'negative face,' their theory can only with great difficulty, if at all, be seen as satisfactorily embracing the politeness system in Japan" (p. 425). Although Brown and Levinson (1978) do assume that cultural calculations enter into facework enactment, the functional role of culture is not fully explicated in their politeness framework.

Scollon and Scollon (this volume) are able to bring in the face default parameters of relationship, hierarchy, and ratification of face relationship from the Western and the Asian cultural persectives, to extend Brown and Levinson's (1978) discourse model. On a positive note however, Brown and Levinson's (1978, 1987) work is groundbreaking and original, and they are able to use the politeness theory to account for a wide range of linguistic phenomena. By grounding their work via the politeness theory, many researchers in diverse disciplines have systematically refined and updated the Brown and Levinson's politeness model in different arenas.

In fact, drawing from both Goffman's (1967, 1971) and Brown and Levinson's (1986) ideas, Holtgraves (1992) proposes a face management theory in which he derives five basic propositions; (1) When individuals are ready to perform face-threatening acts, they will construct their utterances so as to encode face-concerns; (2) the more threatening the act (as a function of power, distance, imposition, and possibly other interpersonal variables), the greater extent to which face-concerns will be encoded; (3) only when the speaker's own face is not an overriding concern will the hearer's face be supported; (4) salient face concerns will increase the likelihood that an utterance will be interpreted indirectly; and (5) individuals may differ in their assessment of the degree of face-threat—these differences may be related to cultural and subcultural assumptions, and, by implication, cross-cultural misunderstandings (p. 155; see also Holtgraves & Yang, 1992). While Holtgraves' (1992) theory incorporates the role of culture in the face-enactment process and emphasizes the interdependent nature of speaker's face and hearer's face, many questions remain unaddressed. For example, the emphasis in proposition 3 concerning self-face focus overriding other-face focus is derived from an individualistic, Western perspective to the neglect of a collectivistic, Eastern perspective. The work by Chang and Holt (this volume) concerning the mutual-face focus in the Chinese culture, the East-West discourse analysis by Scollon and Scollon (this volume), and the gender analysis by Shimanoff (this volume) concerning the role of other-face focus in females suggest different boundary conditions for this proposition.

Holtgraves' (1992) proposition 4 which concerns the relationship between perceived face-salience and the use of indirect face-strategies, has not be supported by the work of some scholars (Irvine, 1979; Katriel, 1986, 1991). Irvine (1979), for example, in studying the speech community of Wolof in the West African country of Senegal, finds that a direct request or demand is actually perceived as more face-polite than the use of hedges and indirect request. Thus, the phrase "give me a drink" is perceived to be a much more polite expression than "I wish to have a drink." In using lingusitic marker like "I think or I wish," the Wolof perceive this as putting one's ego before a simple assertion, hence, expresses arrogance. In addition, the norm for direct assertion or bald on-record utterance typically applies to the *griots'* (the lower caste who sings and performs for entertainment) interaction with the nobles, while the nobles typically respond with a benevolent gesture or a succinct expression.

Katriel (1986), in analyzing facework strategies in Israeli Sabra culture, also argues that the cultural communication orientation has a profound influence in the use of direct and indirect facework strategies. She finds that the use of *dugri* speech or "speaking straight to the point" (p. 10) invokes a set of cultural meanings that is both self-face affirming and other-face affirming in the Israeli Sabra community. Direct facework strategies do not necessarily correspond with a high face-threat level. The use of direct and indirect facework strategies is highly contingent on how face is being conceptualized, what face topic is being raised, how salient is the face issue, and how cultural norms influence the meanings of face and facework.

To summarize, past literature in face conceptualization has typically viewed face as: (1) a claimed sense of identity in an interactive situation, (2) a symbolic, interactive resource, (3) a resource that is highly vulnerable that can be threatened, honored, maintained, and bargained over, (4) a resource that entails the threat or enhancement of a claimed sense of self-respect or self-esteem, and (5) a resource that is grounded in the webs of interpersonal and sociocultural variability.

Cultural Variability and Facework Typologies

A typology is a classification scheme in which phenomena are grouped based on some common attributes or patterns. If we want to develop a coherent theory of facework, we need to understand the functional dimensions of face, and the relationship between these face dimensions and facework strategies. In addition, any facework typology used in a cross-cultural interpersonal communication study must include strategies which are applicable to the cultures of the study. In order to understand how facework operates in different cultures, it is necessary not only to describe differences, but to explain them. Dimensions of cultural variability can be used as explanatory mechanisms.

While there are many dimensions in which cultures differ, one dimension that has received consistent attention from both cross-cultural communication researchers and psychologists around the world is individualism-collectivism. Countless cross-cultural studies (Chinese Culture Connection, 1987; Gudykunst & Ting-Toomey, 1988; Hofstede, 1980, 1991; Hui & Triandis, 1986; Schwartz & Bilsky, 1990; Ting-Toomey, 1991; Triandis, 1988, 1990; Triandis, Brislin, & Hui, 1988; Wheeler, Reis, & Bond, 1989) have provided theoretical and empirical evidence that the value orientations of individualism and collectivism are pervasive in a wide range of cultures.

Basically, *individualism* refers to the broad value tendencies of a system in emphasizing the importance of individual identity over group identity, individual rights over group rights, and individual needs over group needs. In contrast, *collectivism* refers to the broad value tendencies of a system in emphasizing the importance of the "we" identity over the "I" identity, group rights over individual rights, and in-group—oriented needs over individual wants and desires. In individualistic cultures, the recognition of "self" is based on personal achievements and the self-actualization process. In collectivistic cultures, the recognition of "self" is based on ascribed status, role relationships, family reputation, and/or workgroup reputation. According to Triandis and colleagues (1988), when respondents were asked to give twenty descriptions of themselves by completing twenty sentences that started with "I am . . . ," people from individualistic cultures used only 15 percent of group-related attributes to define themselves, while people from collectivistic cultures used 35—45 percent group-related attributes (e.g., I am the third daughter of my family, etc.) to describe their sense of personhood (for a detailed discussion on individualism-collectivism, see Morisaki and Gudykunst, this volume).

A review of facework strategies from both an individualistic and a collectivistic perspective is a necessary starting point for facework behavior research. While authors in different chapters have reviewed their own strategy schema, no chapter in this volume has provided a review of different facework typologies (although almost every chapter covers Brown and Levinson's politeness typology). This section presents a summary review of various facework typologies that appear useful in linking face and facework. The strategies reviewed are based on discourse analysis as well as self-report data.

Individualistic facework strategies are those strategies developed and tested with Western respondents, and appear to reflect primarily individualistic value tendencies. The reviewed facework typologies include: Penman (1990), Shimanoff (1987), and Lim and Bowers (1991). The reviewed collectivistic facework strategies include Japanese strategies described by Lebra (1976) which appear to reflect predominant collectivistic value tendencies. Individualistic and collectivistic strategies are those described by Ting-Toomey (1988; Ting-Toomey, Gao, Trubisky, Yang, Kim, Lin, & Nishida, 1991) and Kim (1992, 1993).

Penman's Model of Facework. Drawing from Brown and Levinson's (1978, 1987) politeness theory, Penman (1990, 1991) developed a model of facework strategies based upon studies of discourse in courtrooms. Penman (1990) assumes that the major goal of facework is the maintenance of respect for self and avoidance of contempt. She assumes that respect and contempt can operate as continuous parallel dimensions. Her model also assumes that respect and contempt are equally applicable to negative and positive facework. Penman further posits that people can and do distinguish between threats to self-face and other-face and between negative and positive face. Penman argues that the means to achieve face-claims vary in degrees of directness. Finally, it is assumed that utterances of communicators can be multifunctional; in other words, different facework strategies can serve different facework functions in the same message.

Based on these assumptions, Penman (1990) developed a model of facework in which various microstrategies fall into one of two dimensions: respect-contempt, direct-indirect. Out of these two dimensions, four facework options are deduced: mitigate/enhance face, protect face, threaten face, and aggravate/depreciate face. In addition, specific facework microstrategies are further developed based on self-directed negative or positive face, and other-directed negative or positive face. According to Penman's facework model, threatening the face-needs of self or the other is characterized by self-attribution strategies indicating some degree of contempt or lack of respect. Protecting face-needs of self or the other is brought about by indirect strategies indicating some degree of respect. The model also accounts for utterances in which facework does not appear to be involved, but over time could have a cumulative effect on the self and other. This category is termed indeterminate.

In addition to presenting the model, Penman (1990) describes the practices used in coding when applying the model interactions. The unit for coding was full utterances regardless of completion; attempts at interruption were included; and any particular utterance could be coded more than once because it was assumed that there could be strategies aimed towards the self and other and/or strategies aimed towards negative and positive face.

Overall, Penman's (1990) facework model is a coherent typological attempt at identifying facework strategies which account for self and other, distinguish between negative and positive face, and account for the dual nature of effect and face strategies (i.e., strategies directed toward self and other and strategies directed toward negative and positive face). Penman's model allows for the possibility of facework strategies that protect the face of the self and the other, protecting self-face while threatening other-face, and threatening other-face while protecting self-face. Furthermore, data from Penman's (1990) case studies in courts provide substantial support for the method.

However, Penman notes that "full confidence cannot be placed in the current method until further testing and development occurs in other contexts" (p. 29). Because Penman's strategies were developed from courtroom discourse, the typology may or may not be applicable to interpersonal interaction in other contexts. The courtroom is a very specialized context in which interaction is highly formal and structured. The typology has not yet been tested in other contexts. In addition, the strategies included in Penman's model were tested mainly with respondents in an individualistic culture, and, therefore, the applicability of the typology in other cultural settings await to be tested and refined.

Penman (this volume) expands the conceptual parameters of face and facework as reflective and constitutive of the larger social order and the moral domain of human interaction. For her, facework refers to the implicit social knowledge that the facework partners conjointly conceived and enacted. In addition, the dimension of justice and order poses dialectical tensions in facework exchange, courtroom drama process.

Shimanoff's Facework Typology. Extending Brown and Levinson's (1978) work, Shimanoff (1985, 1987, 1988, this volume) develops a face-needs' model which is concerned with both the speaker's and the hearer's face-needs, and it examines face-honoring, face-compensating, face-neutral, and face-threatening messages in marital interactions. Using her face-needs model, Shimanoff consistently has found predictable differences in emotional disclosures along the lines of communication roles (i.e., speaker versus hearer) and intimacy level (i.e., acquaintances, best friends, and spouses). Interestingly though, mixed results emerge concerning male and female differences in emotional disclosures. While females tend to self-report more emotional disclosures than males, in actual conversations, no such distinctions are observed. Shimanoff's typology focuses on other-face honoring and threatening process, while self-face is not a locus of concern. However, her typology (see also Edelmann, this volume) comes closest to consider the role of emotion as a critical part of facework discourse process by emphasizing close attention to the disclosure of both pleasant and unpleasant emotions toward other or about a third person.

Shimanoff (this volume) advocates the conjoint perspective of functional and sociological directions in studying politeness discourse in females and males. While a functional direction emphasizes the goal functions of facework utterance, a sociological direction examines the tacit sociocultural knowledge of the relationship among social status, social distance, and gender-related issues in facework enactment. For example, research from a sociological orientation generally indicated that "women will exceed men in politeness when women are considered status inferiors to men or when women place more emphasis on behaviors aimed at maintaining or increasing relational intimacy. In contrast, there is limited evidence that men may exceed women in politeness when politeness registers are associated with status superiority." Shimannoff ends her chapter by raising an intriguing question: "Is gender or social status a better predictor of facework, and does this vary with context?"

Lim and Bowers' Facework Typology. Lim (this volume) and Lim and Bowers (1991) developed a facework typology in the context of the U.S. culture. According to Lim (this volume), individuals have three types of face-needs—autonomy, fellowship, and competence face. Autonomy face refers to the need to be free from the imposition of others. Fellowship face is the need for approval and social inclusion. Competence face refers to the need to uphold an image of ability. This last type of face is described by Lim as a type of positive face and includes past accomplishments, a good reputation, and the capability to perform successfully in the future. Lim and Bowers (1991) describe three types of facework which correspond to the three types of face. Tact is facework which addresses autonomy face. Solidarity is facework which involves fellowship face, and approbation is facework which concerns competence face. Lim (this volume), and Lim and Bowers (1991) assume that it is possible to give face, threaten face, and mitigate face-threat to the other's face. While the authors acknowledge the self aspect of face, the facework strategies developed are strategies directed toward other-face. No rationale is provided concerning the exclusive focus on other-face.

Lim and Bowers (1991) used their facework typology to examine the effects of relational intimacy, power difference, and the right to perform a given act in a given situation on tact, solidarity, and approbation facework. The relationships among different types of facework were also examined. The respondents were given a hypothetical situation with twelve possible variations. The situation involved a group research project in which one member did his (it was a male) part poorly and the respondent had to ask this member to redo it or ask another member of the group to redo the other's work. Intimacy was addressed by informing the respondents that the addressee was either a friend or an acquaintance. Power difference was manipulated by telling the respondents that they were undergraduate teacher's assistance in charge of the group or just a group member. The different levels of right to criticize varied between negative comment and direct request to redo the work.

Results indicated that in distant and close relationships, tact and approbation were affected by power difference. The right to impose affected the level of tact for both the intimate and nonintimate relationship, while the right to criticize influenced the level of approbation in the distant or nonintimate relationship. Multiple types of facework were used when the respondents threatened multiple face-wants. Furthermore, the study showed that "the co-occurrence of different types of face-work is not only possible but sometimes required of a socially competent person" (Lim & Bowers, 1991, p. 448).

Lim and Bowers (1991) did develop a typology of facework rather than a list of strategies. Unfortunately, the typology does not account for strategies which have implications for self-face in a discourse situation. The typology applies only to other-oriented facework strategies and is applicable to self-report data situation. It seems logical, however, that interactive face-work strategies would have implications for both self-face and other-face. For example, the tact strategy of order (to demand forcefully) could protect self autonomy face by conveying to the other that the other must comply with the request without help from the person giving the order. Thus, the person who gives the order ensures freedom from imposition and at the same time threatens the other's autonomy face. By attempting to direct the actions or behavior of another, it impinges on the other's freedom of choice.

To summarize, Lim (this volume) and Lim and Bowers (1991) include the autonomy and approval types of face-claims and also provide a third type of face-claim referred to as competence face. They also describe the facework strategies of tact, solidarity, and approbation which correspond to each of the three types of face. Although Lim and Bowers recognize the self and other dimensions of facework, their typology focuses on face-strategies which function to either protect or threaten the other's face to the neglect of self-face concern. However, their study provides some very useful evidence concerning the role of relational intimacy in the use of different types of facework strategies. In addition, while the corresponding relationship between face-claims and face-strategies may be applicable to the mainstream U.S. community, other facets of face-claims and facework strategies may need to be incorporated in their typology in the future.

Lebra's Japanese Facework Typology. Lebra (1976) discusses the Japanese cultural ideal of balancing face-concerns in ritu-alistic interactive situations. She provides a description of facework strategies from a collectivistic perspective. According to Lebra, Japanese strive to maintain a balance between humility and dignity. As Lebra (1976) states, "one should be humble, modest, and polite but at the same time maintain one's dignity" (p. 129). When an individual's attempt at maintaining dignity goes too far, he or she is considered arrogant and a civilized face is violated. Likewise, when an individual's attempt at maintaining humility goes too far, he or she is considered to have a lack of dignity, and hence, face is also lost. Lebra describes several communication strategies used by the Japanese to maintain face in a "ritual situation"—a ritual situation is defined as a communicative situation in which a person takes the opinion of the other person or a third person into face calculation.

According to Lebra, ritual behavior in the Asian or collectivistic culture context is defined situationally. Interaction in a ritual situation is characterized by communication attempts to maintain face. The strategies used in such a situation have implications for both the self and other. *Mediated communication* refers to speaker A asking someone else to transmit a message to speaker B. This strategy protects both self and other face. *Refracted communication* is when speaker A communicates with speaker B by talking to a third person in speaker B's presence. It is expected that speaker B will understand that speaker A is communicating to him or her through the third person. This strategy also protects the self and other's face. A third strategy described by Lebra is that of *acting as delegate;* this strategy refers to one person who pretends to be a messenger from a third person. For example, the individual says, "She wants this," or "I really don't care but the group is pressuring me to do this." *Anticipatory communication* is when one person does not express his or her wish explicitly, but expects the other person to understand. Although it may seem as though this strategy protects only other-face, self-face is protected because a direct expression of a desire might be perceived as inappropriate, resulting in a loss of face. Thus, this strategy also protects the face of both individuals. One strategy which does not involve spoken communication is that of *correspondence*—communication through the sending of a letter. Correspondence is another communication strategy which protects the face of both the self and other. *Conspicuous generosity* is the final strategy which protects self and other's face. This strategy refers to offering help or giving gifts.

In addition to describing strategies which protect one's face, Lebra (1976) describes strategies which protect self-face while threatening other-face. According to Lebra, *self-praise* is a communication strategy which is disapproved of by most Japanese. *Arrogance* is another communication strategy that threatens other-face. Lebra describes this strategy as the least sociable form of self-display. This strategy is an attempt by one person to threaten and downgrade the face of another. Both *self-praise* and *arrogance*, according to Lebra, enhance one's own face by demoting the other's face.

Lebra's (1976) strategies do account for both self- and other-face. However, she does not discuss in-depth the parameters that constitute a ritualized situation. Although Lebra (1976) does not discuss specifics regarding the contexts or types of relationship which affect face-concern, her facework typology provides new insights into a collectivistic orientation to facework. For example, categories such as mediated communication, acting as delegate, correspondence, and the gift-giving aspect of conspicuous generosity have not been discussed in previous Western or individualistic literature on facework strategies. Overall, Lebra's facework typology emphasizes strategies which protect self-face and other-face, and strategies which protect self-face while threatening the face of the other. In addition, her facework strategies emphasize heavily the use of intermediaries to cement or diffuse face-concern, thus, interactants who are directly involved with face issues can save face and avoid to lose direct face in a face-threatening situation.

Underlying Similarities of Lebra and Penman. Although Lebra's (1976) work is from a collectivistic perspective and Penman's (1990) is from an individualistic perspective, there are some interesting similarities. Both researchers recognize facework strategies which have implications for both self-face and other-face. Additionally, both authors describe an underlying continuum regarding concern for face. Lebra's notion of humility and dignity is similar to Penman's dimensions of contempt and respect. Penman explains that in order for there to be a demonstration of respect or contempt, at least two people must publicly relate to each other. Lebra also assumes that attempts to maintain a balance between humility and dignity are dependent upon interpersonal interaction. Although neither scholar elaborates on the meaning of their constructs, Penman's dimension of respect seems similar to Lebra's notion of dignity. In attempting to maintain one's dignity an individual is attempting to maintain respect. According to Lebra, if a person demonstrates too much humility, he or she is disgraced. Disgrace seems to be a similar construct to Penman's notion of contempt. Disgrace seems to be brought on by an awareness of the other's contempt for the self. Thus, the dimension of dignity-humility or respect-contempt can be one facet of facework functions that cuts across individualistic and collectivistic boundaries. Future theoretical work can use this dimension as a base to conceptualize the relationship between face and facework dynamics.

Individualistic and Collectivistic Strategies. Using a cultural variability approach to the study of face and facework, Ting-Toomey (1988) proposes an interactive model of facework which consists of a self-concern and other-concern dimension and an autonomy-face (negative face) and approval-face (positive face) dimension. More specifically, she argues that the need for autonomy-face entails both self-concern and other-concern aspects, and the need for approval-face includes both self-concern and other-concern aspects. In relating facework with conflict styles across cultures, Ting-Toomey's typological framework emphasizes that while members of individualistic cultures are predominantly concerned with self-face maintenance for the purpose of asserting and defending the "I" identity, members of collectivistic cultures are predominantly concerned with both self-face and other-face maintenance for the purpose of maintaining relational harmony and diffusing shame and interactive anxiety. While members in the individualistic cultures orient themselves in a "face-saving" mode, members in the collectivistic cultures orient themselves in both "face-saving" and "face-giving" modes.

In a nutshell, Ting-Toomey's (1988) conflict face-negotiation theory assumes that: (a) people in all cultures try to maintain and negotiate face in all communication situations; (b) the concept of "face" is especially problematic in uncertainty situations when the situated identities of the interactants are called into question; (c) conflict, as a class of face-threatening situations, demands active facework management by both conflict parties; (d) conflict parties, in a conflict situation, will engage in two types of facework management: self-face concern and other-face concern, and autonomy-face and approval-face maintenance; and (e) the cultural variability dimension of individualism-collectivism will influence members' selection of one set of facework strategies and conflict styles (such as face-avoiding and face-obliging strategies) over others (such as face-threatening and face-defensive strategies).

While Ting-Toomey's (1988) facework typology accounts for self- and other-face, autonomy and approval face, and the role of culture in facework enactment, no specific microstrategies are discussed in the framework. While her typology emphasizes the conceptual relationship between cultural meanings of face and facework, no specific behavioral strategies are identified. Finally, it seems clear that from the results of her research program (Ting-Toomey & Cole, 1990; Ting-Toomey et al., 1991), a third category "mutual-face" should be added to the self-face and other-face dimension. Her typology, however, does treat culture as playing the anchoring role for face conceptualization and facework. In addition, her face-negotiation perspective emphasizes the embedded aspects of face, such as face-giving and face-honoring, in conjunction with face-threatening or face-defensive acts.

Ting-Toomey (1988; Ting-Toomey & Cole, 1990) further argues that facework strategies are used under the conditions that the individual's face-identity is perceived to be challenged, threatened, and the face-identity has tipped its civilized balance. They are also being used when one wants to advance a courteous front or smooth/upgrade a relationship. Face dynamics also serve as an ideal testing ground for the rigidity or flexibility of cultural norms, relational rules, and self/other distance boundary issues, and respect and approval signalling issues.

Kim's (1992, 1993) Facework Strategies. Kim (1992, 1993) studied requests as face-threatening acts and developed three main strategy types. According to Kim, the strategy types all pertain to the interactive constraint construct. Interactive constraints are criteria used to choose strategies. The interactive constraint of concern for face-support is further separated into three different constraints. Concern for minimizing imposition is the degree to which an utterance does not impose on the other's autonomy-face. The concern for avoidance to hurt the other person's feelings refers to the speaker's perceived obligation to comply with the other's need for approval or need for a positive face. The concern for avoiding negative evaluation by the other refers to the desire to protect one's own need for approval and inclusion. This constraint is the desire to protect one's own positive face. The concern for effectiveness is the final constraint identified by Kim and refers to an individual's desire for getting end results from an interaction.

The strategy types which Kim (1992) describes are the results of using the interactive constraints for choosing how to construct a message: hint, query, and direct statement. The strategies were developed from an integration of previous classifications of requests in different languages. Kim (1992) tested the relationship between these strategies and the interaction constraints with Koreans and North Americans. Respondents were provided with six situations describing a wide variety of requests including obtaining permission, borrowing goods, and soliciting agreement. Two utterances were provided to represent each strategy. Results indicate that to both Koreans and North Americans, hint showed the most consideration for the other's feelings, query the next, and direct statement showed the least consideration for the feelings of the other. Thus, the North Americans and Koreans of this study viewed hint as enhancing other positive face, queries as protecting other positive face, and direct statements as threatening the other's positive face. In terms of self-face, both cultures ranked the direct statement highest in disapproval for self's positive face, query the next highest, and hint the least. Results also indicate that to Koreans, face-maintenance consideration plays a more central role in interaction than North Americans. Koreans rated concern for other's feelings as more important than North American respondents, and also rated minimizing impositions as higher in importance than the North American respondents. Complementing Kim's (1992) study, Holtgraves and Yang (1992) uncover that the Korean respondents weighted power and relational distance more heavily than did North Americans in the use of politeness requests. It appears that the Korean respondents were much more responsive to the interpersonal features of politeness than North Americans.

Overall, while Kim (1992) does mention self- and other-face when discussing constraints, self-face autonomy threat is not included. Furthermore, the strategies are not organized in typology form, but are simply a list of strategies. The strategies are not categorized in terms of their face dimension implications. Thus, it is difficult to analyze facework using only a list of strategies because results cannot be meaningfully interpreted as concerning the functions of face strategies in relationship to specific dimensions of face.

Summary. The study of facework from both individualistic and collectivistic orientations suggest that the following strategy combinations may operate for both approval and autonomy face-needs: (1) strategies which protect one's self-face, while also protecting the other's face (Lebra, 1976; Penman, 1990), (2) strategies which downgrade one's self-face, while supporting/protecting the other's face (Lebra, 1976; Penman 1990), (3) strategies which protect one's self-face while threatening the other's face (Lebra, 1976; Penman 1990), and (4) strategies which encode low concern for one's self-face and low concern for the other's face (Holtgraves, 1992; Holtgraves & Yang, 1992).

Although many researchers acknowledge the importance of cultures, the existence of self-face as well as other-face, and the multifunctionality of facework strategies, few researchers attempt to incorporate all of these issues in their studies. Overall, the communication-oriented literature on facework suggests that: (1) individuals negotiate over the need for face-approval and face-autonomy, (2) facework strategies have implications for self-face, other-face, and mutual-face, (3) individuals typically use facework strategies to maintain, to mitigate, to threat, and/or to honor self- and other-face, (4) facework negotiation process can take place beyond the parties who are directly involved in the face episode, and (5) facework strategies derive their meanings and functions through gender and/or culture as the larger frame of reference. In addition, drawing from the ideas of the chapters in this book, facework strategies can be used to invoke a moral order, a cultural sense of personhood, rectify social structure, reflect social expectation, identify social network, metacommunicate about the relationship, and finally, mediate the boundaries between persons.

Future Directions and Challenges

In summarizing the recent approaches to face and facework, face is viewed by all researchers as a fundamental communication phenomenon. Facework refers to the "ways particular communicative moves speak to the identity claims of self and other in specific social situations. And while face concerns are not necessarily focal, they are always immanent" (Tracy, 1990, p. 215). While the facework typologies developed by many of these researchers represent a significant step towards conceptualizing various facework strategies, many theoretical questions remain to be answered. For example, what is the role of culture in framing face and facework strategies? How should we prevent our ethnocentric biases from interfering with theorizing about face and facework? How can we uncover the culturally relevant, situated domains of face? Does a one-to-one correspondence exist between a particular face domain and a strategy cluster? How does culture interact with situational parameters in influencing the meanings, functions, and outcomes of a particular set of facework strategies? How does culture interact with interpersonal features in the facework discourse process?

The goal of this section is twofold: (1) to explore some of the basic issues and challenges that confront face and facework theorizing process, and (2) to examine the fundamental steps that are needed in researching cross-cultural facework interaction process.

Theoretical Issues

Drawing from the work of previous research and the ideas presented in this book, three sets of cross-cultural interpersonal issues concerning face and facework stand out that warrant close attention. These issues are: (a) face as identity claim, (b) social cognitive/affective construction of face and facework, and (c) facework competence.

Identity Claim Issues. Positive identity claim provides the motivational key to situated facework actions. Individuals desire a positive public image in order to feel good about their interactive selves. However, the idea of public versus private images is deeply grounded in the cultural ideals of the sense of personhood. What constitutes a competent or effective public image varies from situation to situation, and from culture to culture. Thus, claiming a competent "interactive self" in a facework episode is, in it most basic form, a situated cultural phenomenon. Cultural variability influences the situational parameters and the "locus" of the claimed sense of face identity.

As LeVine (1982) observes, "cultures vary in the attributes of the ideal self over the life course, in the actions with which pride and shame are associated and in expectancies for autonomy or interdependence in the domains of social action" (p. 295). Individuals can vary in their claims of face-protection boundary—depending on whether they are influenced by the individualistic value tendencies, collectivistic value tendencies, or mixed value tendencies. For example, for individualists, the face-protection boundary is likely to be associated with individual attributes, traits, abilities, and competence. For collectivists, face boundary regulation is likely to be associated with appropriate role enactment, in group face-boundary, and in group face approval and disapproval. Interpersonal face constraints probably also extend more to obligatory, in group relationships than transitory, in group/out group relationships. In collectivistic, group-oriented cultures, the concept of face typically moves beyond the immediate "situated" parameter and extends across relationship nets and across spatio-temporal dimensions (see for example, Chang & Holt, Scollon & Scollon, and Ho, this volume). The cultural factors, however, are moderated by interpersonal features such as relational intention, power/status, intimacy, and relational familiarity on face and facework process.

In addition, the claimed sense of situated identity is closely tied to the concept of self-esteem. Both cultural and gender variations influence self-esteem or "face-saving" construction issues (see Shimanoff, Edelmann, this volume). Protecting a claimed sense of self-esteem or self-respect is viewed as occupying a pivotal role in competent facework negotiation. Again, self-esteem is grounded in the evaluational criteria of the "ideal model person" in the sociocultural webs of the community. As Harre (1984) observes, "a person is not a natural object, but a cultural artifact. A person is a being who has learned a theory, in terms of which his or her experience is ordered. . . . There are two primary realities in human life: the array of persons and the network of their symbiotic interactions" (p. 20). A claimed sense of self-esteem, which relies heavily on the approval or disapproval of others' perceptions and reactions, is a fundamental cultural creation. For example, while the locus of self-esteem stemming from independent construal of self may emphasize the individual-oriented self-esteem issues, the locus of self-esteem generating from an interdependent construal of self may emphasize the collective membership esteem issues (Luhtanen & Crocker, 1992; Markus & Kitayama, 1991; see also, Morisaki & Gudykunst, this volume).

From a cross-cultural orientation in studying face and facework, the theoretical challenges of studying identity claims in relationship to face include: First, delineating the boundary conditions that trigger the face and facework negotiation process in different cultural communities; second, uncovering the different facets of the claimed sense of self-esteem construct across cultural and gender lines; third, examining in more

depth the role of culture in defining face-salient situations and
how facework strategies encode such situations; fourth, identifying the common grounds and the differences in which face
signals in different ethnic and sociocultural communities;
and fifth, identifying the conditions and the meanings among
situational features and terms such as face-saving, face-
giving, face-mitigating, face-compensating, face-threatening,
and face-honoring.

Social Cognitive and Affective Issues. The second set of issues concerns the roles of social cognition and affect in the
facework management process. While most politeness discourse approaches to facework emphasize the linguistic aspects of the enactment of face, the social cognitive level of
facework construction has been largely ignored (O'Keefe,
1992). In order to gain a comprehensive picture of face calculation and the facework management process, we need to develop the theoretical linkage between the social cognitive level
of face and the linguistic aspects of facework. In most instances, facework management process involves strategic communication moves and countermoves. This strategic process
entails the level of interpersonal intention, expectations, multiple goal orientations, and message effects in the facework
negotiation episode. Lim (this volume) has explored systematically the role of intention and interpersonal features in the
facework bargaining process.

In addition, the theoretical perspective of Burgoon and
Hale (1988) on expectancy violations (which includes constructs such as expectancy violations, arousal, communicator
reward valence, behavior interpretation and evaluation, and
violation valence) can perhaps help to account for the face-
expectation and face-violation process. More recently, Burgoon (1992) has added a cultural dimension to the expectancy
violations theory. In addition, the constructivism approach
(O'Keefe, 1988, 1992) in connecting message design logics (expressive, conventional, and rhetorical) with multiple goal strategies may also help to give a fuller explanatory picture of the
theoretical linkage between social cognitive beliefs and facework management process on the interindividual level.

It appears that while researchers have started to pay close
attention to the social cognitive level of facework message design, the role of affect has been continuously ignored by most
facework researchers. When one's face or sense of self-respect

is being violated, feelings of anxiety are inevitable. According to Lazarus (1991), anxiety is generated by an existential threat. Anxiety always entails existential vulnerability and insecurity. At the most basic level, face-threat involves anxiety arousal, shame issue, and pride issue on both the cultural and the interpersonal levels of analysis. However, it is amazing that the fundamental face-related emotions have not been discussed with much depth in the facework literature.

When one's face is threatened or attacked, identity anxiety is aroused and facework strategies are used to diffuse, protect, compensate, or defend one's face, and at the same time, manage other's face-attack. Likewise, when one's face is being embarrassed, upgraded, or honored, blushing (see Edelmann, this volume) also occurs. Blushing signals affective anxiety arousal. Anxiety, together with pride and shame, probably serves as the basic emotional architecture of facework management process. According to Scheff (1990), pride and shame basically revolve around the issue of "self's perception of the evaluation of self by other(s)" (Scheff, 1990, p. 72). Thus, face, which entails strongly the dimension of other-evaluation, is deeply tied with the emotions of pride and shame. When pride is aroused or challenged, or shame is activated or anticipated in a social or interpersonal situation, face-concern is immanent. Cocroft's (1992) research indicates that pride concern is closely related to the selection of facework strategies. Morisaki (1992) also found a strong association between shame and various face-concerns.

However, while either pride or shame can be experienced continuously by all individuals, the degree of emotional salience experienced by persons in reacting to different facework episodes varies from the intergender level to the intercultural level. As Scheff (1990) notes, "pride and shame serve as instinctive signals, both to self and other, to communicate the state of the bond. We react automatically to affirmations of, and threats to our bonds. However, if a culture is sufficiently insistent, it can teach us to disguise and deny these signals" (p. 15). Bonds, in this context, refer to webs of social connection. Scheff's (1990) perspective concerning the relationship among emotion, discourse, and social structure serves as a solid foundation in which we can start theorizing about affect, face, and facework. Scheff's point of view, in addition to the work of Cocroft (1992) and Morisaki (1992), indicates that pride and shame may operate as the underlying emotional dimension of facework. Future challenges of face and facework research include the importance of: incorporating the role of affect in facework management process, connecting emotional facets with specific facework strategy enactment, examining the hidden affect dimensions of face in relationship to respect-contempt issue (Penman, this volume) or dignity-humility issue (Lebra, 1976), and examining the role of culture in the display or the masking of emotions during different types of facework negotiation situations. In short, both the cultural construction of emotion (Harre, 1986; Lutz, 1988) and the gender construction of emotion (Shimanoff, this volume; Gilligan, Ward, & Taylor, 1988) should be systematically integrated into face and facework research design. In addition, the relationship between social cognition and affect should also be systematically incorporated in a coherent perspective of face and facework management process.

Facework Competence Issues. Competent facework emerges from the conjoint perceptions of the interactants based on the communicative actions of the participants in the facework negotiation process. The general objective of competent facework interaction is to achieve both individual and mutual face-concern goals and, at the same time, adhere to the ideals and standards of the discourse community. Competent facework process requires face co-orientation, facework coordination, and facework attunement.

Facework co-orientation involves conjoint knowledge of each other's face-expectations, face-claims, and face-intentions. It requires cultural-sensitive knowledge, gender-relevant knowledge, and interpersonal knowledge of face vulnerability and face threshold level. Facework coordination refers to the synchrony in the meanings and on the behavioral level of facework management process. Smooth and competent facework coordination signals interest and willingness between interactants to develop "intact social bonds." For Scheff (1990), the need for the "maintenance of social bonds" serves as the most important driving force for human interaction. He explains:

> Secure social bonds are the force that holds a society together . . . this force involves a balance between closeness and distance. . . . Optimal differentiation defines an intact social bond, a bond which balances the needs of the individual and the needs of the group. It involves being able to main-

> tain ties with others who are different from self. . . . Optimal
> differentiation involves closeness since it requires knowledge
> of the other's point of view. . . . An intact social bond does not
> imply agreement but knowledge of both agreement and dis-
> agreement. (p. 4)

Intact social bonds provide a sense of communal webs in which
face-claim can be centered, anchored, and tested.

Competent facework attunement emerges out of accurate
facework co-orientation and smooth facework coordination. Attunement refers to the "joint attention to thoughts, feelings,
intentions, and motives between individuals and also between
groups" (Scheff, 1990, p. 199). In addition, attunement consists of not only "joint knowledge of meanings evoked during
contact, but long-range considerations involving intentions
and character. The same kind of attunement between groups is
referred to as social solidarity" (p. 201). Interactive facework attunement refers to a coherent sense of understanding of the
self/other-situated identity-construction issue, a knowledgeable sense of the culturally grounded self-esteem process, a
sensitive awareness of the interpersonal dynamics in facework management, and a good working knowledge of the relationship among social cognition, emotion, and discourse. A
competence-based perspective in theorizing about face and
facework can help to capture outcome-related dimensions of
face and also tap into the practical utilities of face and facework research. Competent facework process, in short, requires a high degree of cognitive, affective, and communicative
resourcefulness (Ting-Toomey, 1993). A resourceful communicator learns when to engage in effective and appropriate facework, and at the same time, knows when to transcend, modify,
and meta-frame the face issues through the dynamic role of human communication.

Research Issues
The research issues pertaining to face and facework include:
(1) establishing conceptual equivalence in face and facework
concepts across cultures, (2) uncovering the multiple dimensions of face and facework, and (3) cultural testing issues of
face and facework constructs.

Conceptual Equivalence Issues. Conceptual equivalence is
extremely important to future facework studies. According to

Lonner (1979), conceptual equivalence involves the common meanings people attach to stimuli across cultures. Conceptual equivalence is important to the study of face and facework because a particular strategy in one culture could be considered face-threatening, while the same strategy might be considered face-protective in another culture depending on the norms and rules of the culture. For example, acknowledging the achievements of another publicly may considered face-protective or face-enhancing in one culture, but face-threatening in another culture. Additionally, types of face may not be equivalent from one culture to another.

In order to achieve conceptual equivalence so that meaningful cross-cultural research comparisons can be made, it is important first to determine the meaning of face in various cultures. Constrastive case study methods (see Tracy & Baratz, this volume), videotaped stimulated recall methods (Waldron & Cegela, 1992), and ethnographic open-ended interviews (Spradley, 1979) in which people within the culture respond to questions designed to elicit the meaning of face are critically needed. Such studies are necessary to identify commonalities and differences in conceptualizing face, and subsequently, facework strategies.

Once derived-etic conceptualizations of face are established, it is important to determine the contextual parameters of face in different cultures. Contextual parameters can involve delineating the boundaries of the facework situated episode, the facework topic (such as request, embarrassment, or ritualistic politeness issue), and the participants who are directly or indirectly involved in the episode. In addition, in order to determine which situations involve face, determination of common emotions associated with face is necessary.

As discussed in the previous section, two emotions which may indicate the salience of face in a particular situation are pride and shame. Scheff (1990) begins his discussion of pride and shame by assuming that all human beings desire secure social bonds via approval and inclusion. Since face involves the need for approval and inclusion, respect for face is one way to maintain secure social bonds. According to Scheff, pride and shame communicate the state of our social bond to the self and the other. Pride and shame then would be associated with both self- and other-face. Scheff describes pride as the sign of a secure bond, while shame is a sign of a broken bond or an emotional response to a threat of the loss of connection to another person or persons. Thus, it seems logical that shame is experienced when face is threatened.

In addition, Scheff's (1990) notion of shame is similar to Lebra's (1976) discussion of dignity and disgrace. Scheff discusses the need for human pride and the need to diffuse shame, and Lebra explains that the Japanese strive to maintain a balance between dignity and disgrace. If the balance is not maintained, face is lost. Finally, in discussing cases of overt shame, Scheff (1990) links face and shame and states, "one becomes painfully embarrassed and flustered when one 'loses face' in public" (p. 170). Collaborative discussions by researchers concerning the role of emotion on face conceptualization from multiple cultures can move toward building a possible underlying logic of the facework emotion management process. The emotions of pride and shame as universal indications of face deserve further attention. In addition, the nonequivalent aspects of face also deserve extra attention from researchers because the nonequivalent aspects of face are probably the areas that contribute to intercultural or intergroup miscommunication.

Multiple Dimensions of Face. Once common emotions are identified, future researchers should also attempt to uncover the relationship between emotions and common underlying dimensions of face across cultures. Research is needed to determine if face operates along a continuum of respect and contempt as Penman (1991) suggests or along a continuum similar to Lebra's (1976) description of the Japanese balance point between disgrace and dignity or a mixture of the two continuums. It is also possible that face operates along a continuum of pride and shame. There appears to be multiple overlaps regarding possible face dimensions. Identifying common multiple dimensions of face would help researchers to better operationalize face on both the social cognitive and the affective levels.

The underlying dimensions of face become most important when linked to facework. Without the link to facework, the dimensions of face are only social psychological or affective constructs. It is the link between face and the strategies used to negotiate face that make the study of face an exciting area of inquiry for communication scholars. Without a meaningful conceptual linkage between face and any facework typology, it is difficult to determine whether a particular strategy is face-protective, face-enhancing, face-threatening, or face-depreciating. Discourse analytic method (Tracy, 1991) and interaction observation method (Sillars, 1991) in conjunction with retrospective self-report method (Metts, Sprecher, & Cupach, 1991) may help to link the relationship between the logic of face-salient issues and the patterns of facework discourse. In addition, while researchers have typically paid close attention to the linguistic aspects of facework, the role of nonverbal facework encoding has been totally ignored by all facework researchers. The nonverbal level, however, is the one that carries the relational meanings of facework. The relational meanings can involve the respect-contempt dimension or the dignity-humility dimension.

Linguistic Equivalence and Sample Equivalence Issues. Linguistic equivalence and sample equivalence are the remaining issues to be discussed here. Linguistic equivalence or translation equivalence refers to the language used in an interview session, or the wording in a survey. For open-ended interviews on face and facework, it is critical that researchers use the native language of the interviewees. Since face and facework have such culturally loaded meanings in different cultures, it is critical that the native language be employed in eliciting narratives or accounts in the interview sessions. As Gudykunst and Ting-Toomey (1988) argue, it is important that interview protocols or surveys used in cross-cultural studies be linguistically equivalent because if linguistic equivalence is not achieved, problems with conceptual equivalence may arise.

Cultures used in a study should represent the underlying values of the dimensions of cultural variability. If the sample of the study does not represent the dimensions of cultural variability employed in a study, it is impossible to explain the results using the cultural variability dimension. Regarding specific facework studies which use the dimensions of individualism and collectivism, it is critical to remember that relationships with one's in group in a collectivistic culture are maintained throughout one's life. Facework management in group-oriented cultures typically extends beyond the immediate situation to a concern for the life of the relationship and an individual's social networks. Most current studies have examined facework within the context of the immediate situation.

Because facework negotiation involves more than the immediate situation, researchers should examine the facework process from a longitudinal perspective by asking about face strategies used throughout the life of the relationship instead of focusing on a specific situation. In addition, social network analysis (see Ho, this volume) surrounding face and facework issues should also be incorporated in the future study of face and face dynamics.

In brief, in a comprehensive study of face and face dynamics, we need multicultural collaborative research efforts to determine the conceptual equivalence of face and facework. Such research must involve pluralistic comparative research methods in eliciting the meanings, functions, situations, emotions, and social attributions of face and facework strategies. In addition, close collaboration among researchers in different cultures in sifting through the conceptual and linguistic equivalence (or nonequivalence) of face and facework-related terms is critical to develop a relatively ethnocentric-free understanding of face and facework as two fundamental communication phenomena.

Conclusions

To conclude, face is a dialectical metaphor. From the ideas presented in this book and the work in previous research, face appears to represent the civilized, balanced point of situated interaction in a given culture. While it appears that too much humility is detrimental to one's self-presentation, too much self-esteem turns to self-focused attention and arrogance. In addition, in translating the dimension of respect-contempt to other-face interaction, too much displayed respect for another person's face can be perceived as too ingratiating, while too little respect can be construed as interactive irreverence. Thus, facework is a communication dance that tiptoes between appropriate respect for one's self-face dignity, while at the same time according appropriate respect to the other person's face.

Facework miscommunication occurs when interactants operate from different ends of the dialectical metaphor, or use strategies that are culturally inappropriate or insensitive. In addition, facework miscommunication arises when parties from different cultures uphold different norms of what constitute the delicate, "civilized point" of appropriate facework presentation and effective facework management.

Overall, we believe this book contributes to a more dynamic understanding of face and facework from multiple cultural, interpersonal perspectives. These cultural interpersonal perspectives include some in-depth discussions on moral, cultural, gender, identity, relational, affective, social cognitive, and discourse issues. It is evident that although the concepts of face and facework (as scholarly concepts) have existed for more than fifty years now, there is still much to be learned, uncovered, and refined. We advocate that since the study of face and facework is still at its fermenting stage, researchers should engage in a continuous, open dialogue concerning the prospects or challenges of face and facework across disciplinary, cultural, ethnicity, gender, theoretical, and methodological lines. By engaging in a cross-boundary dialogue, perhaps we can touch upon the convergent point of the study of human communication from a connectedness perspective.

Note

We want to extend our grateful appreciation for the insightful comments Bill Gudykunst provided on an earlier version of this manuscript.

References

Baxter, L. (1984). An investigation of compliance-gaining as politeness. *Human Communication Research*, *10*, 427–457.

Brown, P., and Levinson, S. (1978). Universals in language usage: politeness phenomenon. In E. Goody (Ed.), *Questions and politeness: Strategies in social interaction*. Cambridge: Cambridge University Press.

———. (1987). *Politeness: Some universals in language usage*. Cambridge: Cambridge University Press.

Burgoon, J. (1992). Applying a comparative approach to expectancy violations theory. In J. Blumer, J. McLeod, and K. Rosengren (Eds.), *Comparatively speaking: Communication and culture across space and time*. Newbury Park, CA: Sage.

Burgoon, J., and Hale, J. (1988). Nonverbal expectancy violations: Model elaboration and application to immediacy behavior. *Communicataion Monographs*, *55*, 58–78.

Burnett, R. (1991). Accounts and narratives. In B. Montgomery and S. Duck (Eds.), *Studying interpersonal interaction.* New York: Guilford.

Chinese Culture Connection (1987). Chinese value and search for culture-free dimensions of culture. *Journal of Cross-Cultural Psychology, 18* 143–164.

Cocroft, B. (1992). Facework in Japan and the United States: A cross-cultural comparison. Unpublished master's thesis, California State University, Fullerton, Ca.

Coupland, N., Grainger, K., and Coupland, J. (1988). Politeness in context: Intergenerational issues. *Language in Society, 17,* 253–262.

Craig, R., Tracy, K., and Spisak, F. (1986). The discourse of requests: Assessment of a politeness approach. *Human Communication Research, 12,* 437–468.

Gilligan, C., Ward, J., and Taylor, J. (Eds.) (1988). *Mapping the moral domain.* Cambridge, MA: Harvard University Press.

Goffman, E. (1959). *The presentation of self in everyday life.* Garden City, NY: Doubleday.

———. (1967). *Interaction ritual: Essays on face-to-face interaction.* Garden City, NY: Doubleday.

———. (1971). *Relataions in public.* New York: Harper and Row.

Gudykunst, W., and Ting-Toomey, S. (1988). *Culture and interpersonal communication.* Newbury Park, CA: Sage.

Harre, R. (1984). *Personal being: A theory for individual psychology.* Cambridge, MA: Harvard University Press.

Harre, R. (Ed.) (1986). *The social construction of emotions.* Oxford: Basil Blackwell.

Hill, B., Ide, S., Ikuta, S., Kawasaki, A., and Ogino, T. (1986). Universals of linguistic politeness. *Journal of Pragmatics, 10,* 347–371.

Ho, D. (1976). On the concept of face. *American Journal of Sociology, 81,* 867–884.

Hofstede, G. (1980). *Culture's consequences: International differences in work-related values.* Beverly Hills, CA: Sage.

———. (1991). *Cultures and organizations: Software of the mind.* London: McGRaw-Hill.

Holtgraves, T. (1992). The linguistic realization of face management: Implications for language production and comprehension, person perception, and cross-cultural communication. *Social Psychological Bulletin, 55,* 141–159.

Holtgraves, T., and Yang, J. (1992). Interpersonal underpinnings of request strategies: General principles and differences due to culture and gender. *Journal of Personality and Social Psychology, 62,* 246–256.

Hu, H. C. (1944). The Chinese concept of "face." *American Anthropologist, 46*, 45–64.

Hui, C., and Triandis, H. (1986). Individualism-collectivism: A study of cross-cultural researchers. *Journal of Cross-Cultural Psychology, 17*, 225–248.

Hymes, D. (1986). Discourse: Scope without depth. *International Journal of the Sociology of the Language, 57*, 49–89.

Irvine, J. (1979). Formality and informality in communicative events. *American Anthropologist, 81*, 773–790.

Katriel, T. (1986). *Talking straight: Dugri speech in Israeli Sabra culture.* Cambridge: Cambridge University Press.

———. (1991). *Communal webs: Communication and culture in contemporary Israel.* Albany, NY: State University of New York Press.

Kim, M. (1992). Cross-cultural variations in implicit theories of requesting behavior. Paper presented at the International Communication Association convention, Miami, FL.

———. (1993). Culture-based interactive constraints in explaining intercultural strategic competence. In R. Wiseman and J. Koester (Eds.), *Intercultural communication competence.* Newbury Park, CA: Sage.

Lazarus, R. (1991). *Emotion and adaptation.* New York and Oxford: Oxford University Press.

Lebra, T. S. (1976). *Japanese patterns of behavior.* New York and Oxford: Oxford University Press.

LeVine, R. (1982). *Culture, behavior, and personality.* Chicago: Aldine.

Lim, T., and Bowers, J. (1991). Face-work: Solidarity, approbation, and tact. *Human Communication Research, 17*, 415–450.

Lonner, W. (1979). Issues in cross-cultural psychology. In A. Marsella, A. Tharp, and T. Cobrowski (Eds.), *Perspectives in cross-cultural psychology.* New York: Academic Press.

Luhtanen, R., and Crocker, B. (1992). A collective self-esteem scale: Self-evaluation of one's social identity. *Personality and Social Psychology Bulletin, 18*, 320–318.

Lutz, C. (1988). *Unnatural emotions.* Chicago: University of Chicago Press.

Markus, H., and Kitayama, S. (1991). Culture and the self: Implications for cognition, emotion, and motivation. *Psychological Review, 98*, 224–253.

Matsumoto, Y. (1988). Reexamination of the universality of face: Politeness phenomena in Japanese. *Journal of Pragmatics, 12*, 403–426.

Metts, S., Sprecher, S., Cupach, W. (1991). Retrospective self-reports. In B. Montgomery and S. Duck (Eds.), *Studying interpersonal interaction*. New York: Guilford.

Morisaki, S. (1992). Face in Japan and the United States: Interdependent and independent self. Unpublished master's thesis, California State University, Fullerton, CA.

O'Keefe, B. (1988). The logic of message design: Individual differences in reasoning about communication. *Communication Monographs, 55*, 80–103.

———. (1992). Developing and testing rational models of message design. *Human Communication Research, 18*, 637–649.

Penman, R. (1990). Facework and politeness: Multiple goals in courtroom discourse. *Journal of Language and Social Psychology, 9*, 15–38.

———. (1991). Goals, games and moral orders: A paradoxical case in court. In K. Tracy (Ed.), *Understanding face-to-face interaction: Issues linking goals and discourse*. Hillsdale, NJ: Lawrence Erlbaum.

Scheff, T. (1990). *Microsociology: Discourse, emotion, and social structure*. Chicago: University of Chicago Press.

Schlenker, B. (Ed.) (1985). *The self and social life*. New York: McGraw-Hill.

Schwartz, S., and Bilsky, W. (1990). Toward a theory of the universal content and structure of values. *Journal of Personality and Social Psychology, 58*, 878–891.

Shimanoff, S. (1985). Rules governing the verbal expression of emotions between married couples. *Western Journal of Speech Communication, 49*, 147–165.

———. (1987). Types of emotional disclosure and request compliance between spouses. *Communication Monographs, 54*, 85–100.

———. (1988). Degree of emotional expressiveness as a function of face-needs, gender and interpersonal relationship. *Communication Reports, 1*, 43–53.

Schwartz, S., and Bilsky, W. (1990). Toward a theory of the universal content and structure of values. *Journal of Personality and Social Psychology, 58*, 878–891.

Spradley, J. (1979). *The ethnographic interview*. New York: Holt, Rinehart and Winston.

Sillars, A. (1991). Behavioral observation. In B. Montgomery and S. Duck (Eds.), *Studying interpersonal interaction*. New York: Guilford.

Ting-Toomey, S. (1988). Intercultural conflict styles: A face-negotiation theory. In Y. Kim and W. Gudykunst (Eds.), *Theories in intercultural communication*. Newbury Park, CA: Sage.

————. (1991). Intimacy expressions in three cultures: France, Japan, and the United States. *International Journal of intercultural Relations, 15*, 29–46.

————. (1993). Communicative resourcefulness: An identity negotiation perspective. In R. Wiseman and J. Koester (Eds.), *Intercultural communication competence*. Newbury Park, CA: Sage.

Ting-Toomey, S., and Cole, M. (1990). Intergroup diplomatic communication: A face-negotiation perspective. In F. Korzenny and S. Ting-Toomey (Eds.), *Communicating for peace: Diplomacy and negotiation*. Newbury Park, CA: Sage.

Ting-Toomey, S., Gao, G., Trubisky, P., Yang, Z., Kim, H. S., Lin, S., and Nishida, T. (1991). Culture, face maintenance, and styles of handling interpersonal conflict: A study in five cultures. *The International Journal of Conflict Management, 2*, 275–296.

Tracy, K. (1990). The many faces of facework. In H. Giles and W. Robinson (Eds.), *Handbook of language and social psychology*. Chichester, UK: John Wiley and Sons.

————. (1991). Discourse. In B. Montgomery and S. Duck (Eds.), *Studying interpersonal interaction*. New York: Guilford.

Triandis, H. (1988). Collectivism vs. individualism. In G. Verma and C. Bagley (Eds.), *Cross-cultural studies of personality, attitudes and cognition*. London: Macmillan.

————. (1990). Cross-cultural studies of individualism and collectivism. In J. Berman (Ed.), *Nebraska symposium on motivation*. Lincoln: University of Nebraska Press.

Triandis, H., Brislin, R., and Hui, C. H. (1988). Cross-cultural training across the individualism-collectivism divide. *International Journal of Intercultural Relations, 12*, 269–289.

Waldron, V., and Cegala, D. (1992). Assessing conversational cognition: Levels of cognitive theory and associated theory and associated methodological requirements. *Human Communication Research, 18*, 599–622.

Wheeler, L., Reis, H., and Bond, M. (1989). Collectivism-individualism in everyday social life: The Middle Kingdom and the melting pot. *Journal of Personality and Social Psychology, 57*, 79–86.

Contributors

Sheryl Baratz, Department of Speech, Temple University, Philadelphia, PA 19122, USA.

Hui-Ching Chang, Department of Speech Communication, University of South Dakota, Vermillion, SD 57069, USA.

Beth-Ann Cocroft, Department of Speech Communication, California State University at Fullerton, Fullerton, CA 92634, USA.

Robert Edelmann, Department of Psychology, University of Surrey, Guildford, Surrey GU2 5XH, UNITED KINGDOM.

William B. Gudykunst, Department of Speech Communication, California State University at Fullerton, Fullerton, CA 92634, USA.

G. Richard Holt, Department of Speech Communication, University of South Dakota, Vermillion, SD 57069, USA.

David Yau-Fai Ho, Department of Counseling, California State University at Fullerton, Fullerton, CA 92634, USA.

Tae-Seop Lim, Department of Journalism and Communication Studies, Kwangwoon University, Wolgye-dong, Nowon-gu, Seoul 139 701, SOUTH KOREA.

Seiichi Morisaki, Department of Communication, University of Kentucky, Lexington, KY 40506, USA.

Robyn Penman, Communication Research Institute of Australia, Inc., GPO Box 655, Canberra ACT 2601, AUSTRALIA.

Ron Scollon, Department of English, City Polytechnic University of Hong Kong, Kowloon, HONG KONG.

Suzie Wong Scollon, Department of English, City Polytechnic University of Hong Kong, Kowloon, HONG KONG.

Susan B. Shimanoff, Department of Speech and Communication Studies, San Francisco State University, 1600 Holloway Ave., San Francisco, CA 94132, USA.

Karen Tracy, Department of Communication, Campus Box 270, University of Colorado, Boulder, CO 80309, USA.

Stella Ting-Toomey, Department of Speech Communication, California State University at Fullerton, Fullerton, CA 92634, USA.

Index